The Soup Mix Gourmet

THE Soup Mix

GOURMET

DIANE PHILLIPS

THE HARVARD COMMON PRESS

Boston, Massachusetts

The Harvard Common Press
535 Albany Street
Boston, Massachusetts 02118

Printed in the United States of America

Printed on acid-free paper

LIBRARY OF CONGRESS CATALOGING-IN-PUBLICATION DATA

Phillips, Diane.
  The soup mix gourmet : 375 short-cut recipes using dry and canned soups to cook up everything from delicious dips and sumptuous salads to hearty pot roasts and homey casseroles / Diane Phillips.
    p. cm.
  Includes index.
  ISBN 1-55832-208-6 (hc : alk. paper) — ISBN 1-55832-209-4 (pbk. : alk. paper)
  1. Cookery. 2. Brand name products. 3. Soups. 4. Quick and easy cookery. I. Title.

TX714 .P476 2001
641.5—dc21

2001014433

Special bulk-order discounts are available on this and other Harvard Common Press books. Companies and organizations may purchase books for premiums or resale, or may arrange a custom edition, by contacting the Marketing Director at the address above.

Cover design by Suzanne Heiser, Night & Day Design

Interior design by Richard Oriolo

10 9 8 7 6

To Bruce and Nonnie,

Fair winds and following seas,

May God bless you on this journey together

Acknowledgments

WRITING A COOKBOOK IS MUCH LIKE making a pot of soup. The author is assisted by individuals who contribute their individual talents to help build the flavor, and intensify the ingredients, until the book is published. During the writing of this book, I was blessed to work with so many talented people and to be supported by dear friends and colleagues. I would be remiss if I did not recognize and thank them publicly.

To my agent, Susan Ginsburg, the woman who makes my career sizzle, a ladle full of gratitude not only for her friendship, but also for being the best agent in the world. To her assistant, Annie Leuenberger, a sprinkle of thanks for all of her help keeping things straight during the marathon.

To my new family at The Harvard Common Press: Bowls of praise and gratitude to my editor, Pam Hoenig, who ate more chocolate than was necessary to keep the pages flowing, and for taking my words and recipes and making them bubble. To President Bruce Shaw, a serving of thanks for his generous support and commitment to this project, and for going the extra mile to get us to publication on time. To Valerie Cimino, Christine Alaimo, Skye Stewart, Sunshine Erickson, Abbey Phalen, Jodi Marchowsky, Georgina Duff, and Virginia Downes, spoons of appreciation for their help with managing the manuscript, marketing, design, and publicity. A special spoonful of thanks to Jed Lyons, Rich Freese, Spencer Gale, Keith Owens, James Penfield, and all the reps at NBN for their generous support and promotion of the book. Copy editor Maggie Carr deserves the silver spoon for taking my words and making them logical, organized, and, above all, coherent. Thanks to all who put so much time and effort into making this book a reality.

At home, I would like to make a toast to my husband, Chuck, who tasted, tested, and gave good advice with each trial and error. Above all, he is always there at the end of the day with a hug, and reassurance that it's okay to have five cases of soup in the dining room, and that we'll be having chicken for the tenth day in a row. Thanks, honey, I promise we won't eat any more soup for a while! To our children, Carrie and Ryan, a big hug for being there, and for cheering me on even when I forget to bake cookies and instead make another test recipe.

To my colleagues, cookbook authors extraordinaire Rick Rodgers and Lora Brody, bowls brimming with affection and respect—you are the most generous people I know and have been tremendous sources of inspiration and encouragement; thanks for that. A ladle of appreciation to Greg Smith at Lipton, Martha Reynolds at Knorr, Maureen Weiss at Unilever Corporate, and Lucinda Ayers at Campbell's for help with permissions and soup facts that have helped to sprinkle a little lightness into the text.

I would be inattentive if I did not thank my road families as well: the cooking schools and their students who welcome me into their kitchens and make my time on the road something special, giving me a home away from home. A stockpot filled to the brim with gratitude to the cooking school program managers, their staff, and students at: Draegger's, Sur La Table, Ramekins, Central Markets, Viking Culinary Centers, Kitchen Art, Cooks Wares, Kitchen Affairs, Dorothy Lane Markets, The Kitchen Shoppe, Loretta Paganini School of Cooking, Bama Cooking School, and Kitchen Conservatory.

Contents

Introduction

LOOK IN ANY PANTRY ACROSS the country and you will find dry and canned soups lining the shelves. With a glance into any group organization cookbook you will easily find that 75 percent of the recipes include soup as the main ingredient. Soup is a part of our culinary landscape, whether we know it or not. A lot of us may not know that our favorite meal growing up began with a can of soup.

Soups can be used to create any number of tasty dishes just by doctoring them up with a few additional ingredients. From appetizers to side dishes, soup (of course!) to main courses, soups can be gold in your pantry with just a little help from the *The Soup Mix Gourmet.*

Like many people today, my time is precious. If I can make my family a comforting, home-cooked meal by using something that will save time, I am all for it. Soups and soup mixes are a vital part of my pantry, and I've learned their strengths and limitations. Some soups just don't make the grade, while others help make my son's favorite chicken pot pie and my husband's favorite beef pot roast. Throughout this book you will find old favorites and new ideas for using soups to help you create memorable meals for your family. The best part is you don't have to stand over the stove for hours, there aren't a lot of labor-intensive steps or hard-to-find ingredients, and most of these dishes can be made ahead of time and either refrigerated or frozen.

I teach students all over the country, and my most popular classes are those we term "marathons," where I prepare eight to ten dishes in two and a half hours. Many of the recipes I teach in these classes use time-savers such as canned or dry soups to prepare dinners that you would be proud to serve to your family or the boss. These tricks also free home cooks from the bondage of thinking they have to make everything from scratch. Not all restaurants make their own stocks; they use a commercial soup base that comes in gallon drums. So why not take a cue from those chefs, and use the great resources available on the shelf in your supermarket to make some really good food?

Dry soups come in a variety of flavors and brands. Lipton and Knorr are the leading brands, and each makes a line of soup mixes that can be made into a soup or, by adding other ingredients to the mix, can serve as the basis for dips, salads, and dressings, main courses, sauces, and pastas. Another type of dry soup mix is ramen, a combination of dry noodles and a soup base that comes in a variety of flavors.

Reconstituted or condensed soups are available in almost every flavor imaginable. Campbell's, that old standby, is the largest brand available on the market and features the broadest variety of soups, including low-sodium and lowfat varieties of their most popular soup flavors. Swanson makes chicken, vegetable, beef, and seasoned chicken broths, which are available canned and in larger boxes for easy refrigerator storage.

Reconstituted soups can be used to make everything from a delicate shrimp mousse to hearty beef burgundy. They are just what the doctor ordered when you are looking for inspiration in your pantry.

How do we get away from the processed taste of some of these convenience products? The prescription is to add bold flavors and turn your dishes into something special. Cooking the soup with bold seasonings refocuses the taste, helps build the flavor layers, and makes a dinner that's simple yet delicious. Don't worry, old standbys like Mom's green bean casserole will be revisited, along with a new version for this millennium, and dishes like Cajun Shrimp Barbecue (page 53) will tickle your palate and make your tummy feel good. These recipes are what home cooking is all about: simple, homey dishes that are easy to prepare and that in most cases can be on the table in under 60 minutes.

Stocking the Pantry

THE PANTRY I DESCRIBE HERE ISN'T much different from the pantry that I recommend to my beginning cooking students. If you have limited space, look at the items called for and decide which ones you will actually use; these will be your basics. Once you get started, you may want to add a few things that you may not have tried before. After all, Mom always made you take one bite of everything, didn't she?

Spices are your secret weapon when it comes to making your meals interesting and flavorful. Check the spices you have in your pantry and use the three-month rule: if you haven't touched it, shaken it, or smelled it in three months, get rid of it. Some people still have the paprika that they got from their bridal shower spice rack—enough said. If there are things that you have thrown away using the three-month rule, think about whether you will ever use that spice, even if it is on my list. Better to be honest and not waste your money. Store your spices in airtight jars in a cool, dry pantry; that is, don't leave them on the counter in the sun, and don't store them under a damp sink. Airtight jars will keep your spices fresher. I recommend buying dehydrated herbs if you can find them at your grocer; they tend to have the closest flavor to that of the fresh herbs. If you cannot find dehydrated herbs, then use whole dried herbs rather than ground or rubbed herbs. Once the herb is ground, it loses a lot of the essential oils that make it potent. Fresh herbs are marvelous additions to any dish, but I don't recommend using them for dishes that will simmer for longer than thirty minutes—fresh herbs break down and they lose most of their flavor when cooked for long periods of time. Use dried herbs, and try stirring fresh herbs in at the end of the cooking time to refresh the flavor of a long-simmering sauce.

To store fresh herbs, I recommend washing them in cold water and thoroughly drying them in a salad spinner or dry towels. Store fresh herbs in resealable plastic bags with a dry paper towel to absorb the moisture. If you have lots of fresh parsley, chop it in the food processor and store it in plastic bags in the freezer. Use it right from the bag.

DRIED HERBS AND SPICES

- dried basil
- bay leaves
- black peppercorns
- ground cinnamon
- Creole Seasoning (page 458)
- ground cumin
- curry powder
- dillweed
- ground ginger
- dry mustard
- dried marjoram
- whole nutmeg

- **Old Bay seasoning**
- **dried oregano**
- **dried rosemary**
- **sea salt or kosher salt**
- **dried sage**
- **sesame seeds**
- **dried thyme**

The following list assumes that you have the essentials in your refrigerator already, those being: milk, butter (or margarine), eggs, juice, and frozen Snickers bars.

Breadcrumbs Fresh and dry breadcrumbs can be stored in the freezer indefinitely. They can be used to encrust fish and chicken as well as for topping casseroles. When that baguette gets too hard, place it in a resealable plastic bag and run a rolling pin over it to make breadcrumbs. Store the breadcrumbs in the freezer.

Capers Small in size, big on flavor, this cousin of the green peppercorn can make chicken and veal into deliciously different dinners. Add capers to a condensed cream soup along with fresh lemon juice and you have a terrific sauce for chicken or fish.

Cheddar cheese Everyone has a favorite type of cheddar. I love Cabot Farms white cheddar, and mild and extra sharp New York cheddar. Pick your favorite and have a block ready in the refrigerator for everything from quesadillas to cheddar cheese biscuits.

Chicken I buy boneless, skinless chicken breasts and freeze them in packages of four, but if you have a larger family, you may want to freeze more in each package. Boneless breasts can be used to make quick dinners anytime.

Frozen vegetables Corn, petite-size peas, and chopped spinach can always be found in my freezer. These vegetables can be used to make almost any dinner special.

REFRIGERATOR AND FREEZER

Fines Herbes

Many a French chef uses a combination of dried parsley, chives, tarragon, and chervil called fines herbes. This medley of seasonings can be purchased in the spice section of your grocery or gourmet store. (See Source Guide.) Sometimes basil, oregano, and sage are added to the mix, so check the ingredients on the label.

Frozen shrimp Quick and easy to use, peeled and deveined shrimp turn a weeknight dinner into a feast.

Granny Smith apples Tart and crunchy, these are great for eating, but they also make a delicious pie or can go into pork and chicken dishes as well.

Lemon juice Fresh lemon juice adds zip and zest to many dishes. Don't buy the little plastic lemon at the grocer; it's really awful. If you don't want fresh lemons hanging around in your vegetable drawer, Minute Maid sells a frozen lemon juice, available in your frozen juice section. Freeze the zest from lemons in resealable plastic bags; it'll keep for up to 6 months.

Packaged salad greens Always appropriate, a nice simple salad is like wearing pearls; it's never out of style.

Parmesan cheese There is nothing more sublime, in my humble opinion, than slivers of Parmigiano-Reggiano cheese. Since it is expensive, keep a small wedge in your fridge. To store the cheese, dampen a paper towel with some olive oil, then wrap the cheese in it and store it in a resealable plastic bag. I also keep a small container of grated imported Parmesan in the refrigerator to help perk up sauces and vegetables.

Pesto in a tube Prepared pesto can add pizzazz to sauces, salads, and pastas. The tube keeps for a long time in the fridge.

Puff pastry sheets Frozen, these sheets defrost in 20 minutes on the counter and roll out to become delicious crusts or appetizers.

Sour cream makes a rich addition to dips and spreads and keeps well in the refrigerator.

Tortillas Flour or corn, these wrappers can be used for quesadillas, southwestern wraps, and casseroles. Refrigerate or freeze them.

The following list assumes that your have the essentials in your dry pantry, such as flour, sugar, brown sugar, leavenings (yeast, baking powder, and baking soda), cornmeal, and chocolate.

Artichoke hearts Canned artichoke hearts are great to use in a pinch—they can be paired with other vegetables, and marinated artichokes help to make salads special.

Canned beans Keep an assortment of canned beans on hand to add protein to your meals and help stretch your food dollar. I'd suggest chickpeas, kidney beans, white beans, and black beans.

Canned chopped tomatoes When fresh tomatoes are looking sad at the grocers, feel free to use canned chopped tomatoes in any of your recipes. It is great to have a few cans in your pantry so you can put together a quick pasta sauce, soup, or stew.

Canned broth can make the difference when you want to prepare certain dishes and you don't have a lot of time. Try different brands and decide which one you like. There are also several soup bases on the market that reconstitute with water; these tend to be a bit more economical. Many gourmet grocers sell their own stock "concentrate" as well, but it tends to be a bit pricey.

Dijon mustard adds a creamy piquant flavor to dishes and can also be used to make a killer ham sandwich.

Dried pastas are great to keep in your pantry for those days when you need a quick fix for dinner. Try to keep several different shapes on hand.

Fresh garlic There is nothing better than the mellow flavor of garlic. Try not to substitute the granulated garlic for the fresh garlic called for in recipes; the flavor will not be nearly as good. I don't recommend buying the chopped garlic that is preserved in jars, as it tends to have an "off" taste.

Fresh ginger A peeled and sliced knob of ginger stored in some sherry, will keep in the refrigerator for months. To store fresh ginger, unpeeled, keep it in a cool, dry spot. I've had good luck using the minced fresh ginger sold in jars in the produce section. It tends to have a truer flavor than the processed garlic.

Herb-seasoned stuffing cubes or crumbs Not only are dried bread cubes good to use as an ingredient in casseroles, they are also delicious as a topping for some vegetable and main-dish casseroles instead of plain breadcrumbs.

Hoisin sauce A condiment used in China as often as ketchup is used here, hoisin has a sweet and smoky quality that perks up salad dressings, stir-fries, and tortilla-wrapped Asian sensations. You can find it in the Asian section of your grocery store. I recommend an imported brand like Lee Kum Kee.

Mirin A Japanese sweet rice wine, mirin can be found in the Asian section of your grocery store. It's great in marinades and stir-fry sauces.

Olive oil If you can afford the space, buy a small bottle of good extra virgin olive oil and one of a lighter variety. For everyday cooking, use the lighter-tasting pure olive oil (I like Bertolli), but for a robust taste, use extra virgin. I find the extra virgin can overpower a lot of things, so use it sparingly.

Onions I keep red onions in my basket all year, for salads and sometimes for cooking. I buy sweet yellow onions as well. In the winter, yellow onions tend to be very strong tasting, so spend the extra money and buy sweet Maui onions, Texas sweets, Walla Wallas, or Vidalias, when they are available.

Orzo pasta is shaped like rice and makes an interesting side dish or can be added to soup.

Potatoes Baking or russet potatoes and new potatoes (I prefer the red variety) can be used for boiling, sautéing, or roasting. Russets make great potato pancakes and mashed potatoes, whereas the red potatoes are a bit waxier and are wonderful roasted.

Rice can be stored for a long time in airtight containers. If you have space, try keeping some wild rice and basmati rice on hand along with long-grain rice. Arborio is a short-grain rice used in making risotto and paella.

Sesame oil Made from toasted sesame seeds, sesame oil adds an exotic flavor to many different dishes. After opening it, make sure you refrigerate it.

Shallots A member of the onion family, shallots pack a lot of flavor into a small bulb. Keep a few on hand.

Sherry adds a delightful flavor to any dish, so keep a small bottle in the pantry and refrigerate it once it is opened. My personal preference is for the nutty, slightly sweeter flavor of cream sherry, although I also use dry sherry.

Soy sauce An imported soy sauce will add an Asian flavor to your dishes.

Sun-dried tomatoes I like to buy sun-dried tomatoes packed in olive oil. You can use the oil to flavor dishes, and the tomatoes make a colorful addition to any dish.

Tabasco sauce Everyone needs a little heat in their dishes, and Tabasco is still the most reliable for flavor and heat. If you have a favorite hot sauce, feel free to use that instead. Once you open a bottle, you should refrigerate it, unless you use it regularly.

Tomato paste in a tube The tiny cans of tomato paste are hard to open, and you never use all of a can, so I bless the person who invented tomato paste in a tube. You can use as much as you want. Once it is opened it stores in the refrigerator and keeps for up to twelve months.

Vermouth Dry vermouth keeps well and can be used in place of white wine in cooking.

Worcestershire sauce A flavoring no kitchen should be without, Worcestershire enlivens seafood, chicken, and beef.

Vinegar Vinegar contributes a great deal to salad dressings and main dishes. I like to keep several varieties on hand in my pantry. *Balsamic vinegar* is a must for adding flavor to dishes. I recommend that you buy a good brand. The Williams-Sonoma catalogue sells a nice selection of balsamic vinegars. This vinegar is used only as an accent, so a little bottle will last you a while. *Rice vinegar* adds a light sparkly taste to salads and some main dishes. *Sherry vinegar* imported from Spain is great to use when you want to make a bold statement in a salad dressing. Mixing the bolder sherry vinegar with balsamic or rice vinegar gives a nice balance. *White wine vinegar* is an all-purpose vinegar and allows the flavors in a dressing to come through. Buy a plain one, not one flavored with herbs. *Red wine vinegar* gives a bold splash of color and flavor to salads and dressings. Keep a small bottle in the cupboard. *Apple cider vinegar* gives a crisp taste to salad dressings, and it can be used when you want just a little bit more punch. All vinegars should be stored in a cool, dry place, out of the sunlight.

Once you have your regular pantry in place, you will need to keep a supply of soups handy so you can whip up any number of gourmet meals at a moment's notice. Monosodium glutamate, or MSG, is used as a flavor enhancer in a variety of prepared foods. Some people may not be able to tolerate MSG, so you should check the labels of any prepared food if you have a problem with MSG.

Condensed Soups

Beginning with condensed soups during recipe testing, I thought the simplest were best. Although Campbell's makes soups with roasted garlic and additional flavorings, like Cream of Chicken and Mushroom, I tended to stick with the old standbys like Condensed Cream of Chicken, adding roasted garlic or fresh mushrooms to them if needed. My favorite condensed "cream of" soups that I'm never without are

- **Cream of Celery**
- **Cream of Chicken**
- **Cream of Potato**
- **Cream of Mushroom**
- **Cream of Shrimp**
- **New England Clam Chowder**

Other soups on my pantry shelf are Campbell's Condensed Cheddar Cheese, Tomato, Tomato Bisque (a little creamier, with bits of tomato), Fiesta Chili Beef, Fiesta Nacho Cheese, and French Onion (great for pot roast) Soups, and chicken and beef broths. Campbell's specialty soups such as Condensed Fiesta Chili Beef and Cream of Shrimp can sometimes be hard to find, so if you enjoy them, ask your grocer to begin carrying them. The manufacturer recommends that you dilute condensed soups with a can of water, but for the most part in my recipes I found that doing so weakened the flavor of the finished dish, so we did not dilute the canned soups. If you are just preparing a can of soup to eat, then by all means follow the recipe on the can and dilute it.

Here are some ideas for how to use these soups to create quick and tasty meals.

Campbell's Condensed Cream of Potato Soup relieves you of the time-consuming task of peeling and cooking potatoes and gives you an instant soup with potatoes.

- For an easy clam chowder, combine Cream of Potato Soup with 1 cup milk, a can of drained chopped clams, and 1 teaspoon Worcestershire sauce in a saucepan, heat to boiling, and stir in a few chopped fresh chives for color and flavor.

- For a quick corn chowder, combine Cream of Potato Soup with 1/2 cup chopped ham, 1/2 cup milk, and 1 cup corn kernels (fresh or frozen and defrosted) in a saucepan and heat to boiling.

This spicy cake has been around since the early part of the 1900s when Campbell's first developed this recipe. It was originally made with canned tomatoes, but they were replaced by condensed tomato soup in the 1920s. This recipe is mentioned in M. F. K. Fisher's *How to Cook a Wolf*, and has been called "Mystery Cake." Tomato Soup Cake has been made into a loaf, Bundt, and sheet cake, but the original was a layer cake frosted with cream cheese frosting.

Tomato Soup Cake

CAKE

2 cups all-purpose flour

1⅓ cups sugar

4 teaspoons baking powder

1 teaspoon baking soda

1½ teaspoons allspice

1 teaspoon ground cinnamon

½ teaspoon ground cloves

½ cup vegetable shortening

1 can Campbell's Condensed Tomato Soup

2 eggs

¼ cup water

FROSTING

6 ounces cream cheese, softened

1 tablespoon milk

One 1-pound box confectioners' sugar

½ teaspoons pure vanilla extract (optional)

■ For an instant vichyssoise, combine Cream of Potato Soup with 1 envelope Knorr Leek Soup Mix and 1 soup can of milk, blend in the blender, and garnish with chopped fresh chives.

■ For creamy vegetables, combine Cream of Potato Soup with 3/4 cup milk and 1½ cups mixed vegetables (fresh or frozen and defrosted) in a saucepan until heated through, and stir in 2 tablespoons chopped fresh chives. Jazz up this soup by baking it sprinkled with buttered breadcrumbs or grated cheese in a preheated 350-degree oven for 15 to 20 minutes.

Preheat oven to 350°F. Grease and flour two round layer pans, 8 or 9 x 1½" or an oblong pan, 13 x 9 x 2". Sift dry ingredients together into large bowl. Add shortening and soup. Beat at low to medium speed for 2 minutes (300 strokes with a spoon) scraping sides and bottom of bowl constantly. Add eggs and water. Beat 2 minutes more, scraping bowl frequently. Pour into pans. Bake 25 to 30 minutes. Let stand in pans 10 minutes; remove and cool on rack. Frost with Cream Cheese Frosting.

Blend 2 packages (3 ounces each) cream cheese (softened) with 1 tablespoon milk. Gradually add 1 package (1 pound) sifted confectioners' sugar; blend well. Mix in ½ teaspoon vanilla extract, if desired.

NUT OR RAISIN TOMATO SOUP CAKE: After mixing, fold in 1 cup chopped nuts or 1 cup raisins. Bake 35 to 40 minutes.

DATE AND WALNUT TOMATO SOUP CAKE: After mixing, fold in 1 cup chopped walnuts and 1 cup chopped dates. (Sprinkle 1 to 2 tablespoons of flour over the dates while chopping them.) Bake in 9-inch round cake pans for 40 to 45 minutes.

Campbell's Condensed Cream of Chicken Soup can be used as an all-purpose sauce when it's reconstituted with ½ to 1 soup can of milk. Add a few tablespoons of sherry or white wine and ½ teaspoon dried herbs and you have a little gourmet sauce to pour over chicken breasts, leftover turkey, rice, pasta, or vegetables. Add ½ to ¾ cup grated cheese along with the milk and you have a wonderfully rich sauce for covering and baking any of the items I've just listed. If you have leftover rotisserie chicken, stir it into cream of chicken soup diluted with 1 can of milk, add 2

As ships go out to sea,
I spoon my soup away
from me.
—A childhood rhyme

Stocking the Pantry

When I first saw this recipe, I thought, no way, but surprise, the Campbell's home economists knew what they were doing. These spicy oatmeal cookies are just perfect with a glass of cold milk.

Quick Tomato Spice Cake

1 package (2-layer) spice cake mix

1 teaspoon baking soda

1 can Campbell's Condensed Tomato Soup

1/2 cup water

2 large eggs

Combine only these ingredients. Beat and bake as directed on package.

Rosy Rocks

1 1/2 cups all-purpose flour

1 1/3 cups sugar

1 teaspoon baking powder

1/2 teaspoon baking soda

2 teaspoons cinnamon

1 teaspoon allspice

1 cup shortening

1 egg

1 can Campbell's Condensed Tomato Soup

2 cups uncooked rolled oats

1 cup seedless raisins

1 cup chopped walnuts

Preheat oven to 350°F. Sift dry ingredients except oats together into large bowl. Add shortening, egg, and soup. Beat at medium speed for 2 minutes (300 strokes with a spoon), scraping sides and bottom of bowl constantly. Stir in oats, raisins, and nuts. Drop rounded teaspoonfuls on ungreased cookie sheet. Bake about 15 minutes or until lightly browned. Makes about 7 dozen cookies.

cups frozen mixed vegetables, defrosted, pour it into a pie pan, cover it with a pastry crust, and you have a chicken pot pie.

Campbell's Condensed Cream of Celery Soup is also a great sauce when diluted with 1 soup can of milk. I use it in place of Cream of Mushroom Soup when I have the kid who doesn't like mushrooms eating at home. It makes a great sauce for chicken, fish, or pork with additions such as wine, herbs, or grated cheese.

Campbell's Condensed Cream of Mushroom Soup is the mother of all the soups. It was the first "cream of" soup on the market. Use this soup, diluted with 1/2 to 1 soup can of milk, to make a creamy mushroom sauce for vegetables or chicken. Adding an envelope of Lipton Onion or Golden Onion Soup Mix to the sauce gives it a richer, deeper flavor. Sauté a few mushrooms and add them to the sauce for a fresher flavor and added texture. White wine, sherry, and chopped fresh chives also improve the flavor.

Campbell's Condensed Tomato Soup is great to use when you need a sweeter tomato flavor, like a barbecue sauce, or Pretty-in-Pink Shrimp Mousse (page 48). Although the Campbell's folks use it for pasta sauces, I found it much too sweet for that. Instead I liked it when I added more robust flavors like a package of Lipton Beefy Onion Soup Mix for a barbecue sauce, or white cheddar cheese for a soothing winter soup.

Campbell's Condensed Cheddar Cheese Soup is the instant cheese sauce. I didn't like diluting this soup fully, so I used only 1/2 cup milk; otherwise, the cheesy flavor wasn't as pronounced. I also found that four to five drops of Tabasco sauce helped to bring out the cheesy flavor, and adding some grated cheese helped to liven things up. One of my favorite accidents was the day I heated undiluted cheddar cheese soup with a 14-ounce can of Ro-tel tomatoes, and served it with tortilla chips. I threw in a handful of freshly grated cheddar and garnished the dip with sour cream, making it souper bowl food!

Campbell's Condensed Black Bean Soup is delicious all by itself or as the basis for a southwestern bean dish. Sautéing a few onions and green chilies gives it texture and a little heat.

Campbell's Condensed Fiesta Nacho Cheese Soup is a can waiting to be opened. Pour it into a saucepan, dilute it with 1/2 cup milk, heat it, and serve it with tortilla chips. It has all the elements of the accidental dip I have already described, but with even less hassle, if that's possible. It is great served over sautéed chicken breasts, mixed into cooked rice or pasta, or served over cooked broccoli for a southwestern flavor. I like to add a bit more cheese, and a little chopped fresh cilantro helps as well.

Campbell's Condensed Cream of Shrimp Soup was one of my favorite surprises during my testing. If I wanted a creamy sauce for fish or shellfish, it was there, waiting on the shelf. If I wanted a creamy shrimp soup, it came to the rescue. Condensed Cream of Shrimp Soup is helped along with additions of Old Bay seasoning, white wine or sherry, and Worcestershire sauce.

Campbell's Condensed Golden Mushroom Soup is a hearty beef-based soup with large slices of mushrooms in the broth. This soup makes a delicious sauce for beef or pork and needs only the addition of 1 cup water and a little red wine and it's ready for dinner. It provides a flavor boost when used with Lipton Onion Mushroom, Beefy Onion, or Onion Soup Mix for a pot roast.

Campbell's Condensed French Onion Soup is a great addition to chicken and beef dishes, as well as pork. Sautéing 2 large onions in butter until golden and then adding them to the soup intensifies the flavor for a nice bowl of French onion soup. Added to stews along with a can of chopped tomatoes and some herbs, this soup will light up the beef or chicken in the dish. I did not dilute the soup, because I liked the intense beefy flavor the soup lent to the dishes I tested.

Campbell's Condensed Fiesta Chili Beef Soup is a can of chili, but it can be used as a topper for nachos or as the base for a more flavorful chili filled with beans and chile peppers. Just sautéing 1/2 cup chopped onion in 2 tablespoons olive oil along with 1 teaspoon ground cumin gives this soup a much bigger personality. I also didn't dilute this soup, because I liked it just the way it was.

Pepperidge Farm Condensed Lobster Bisque is delicious all by itself, or with the addition of a few tablespoons of brandy.

Chicken, beef, and vegetable broths are sold in condensed form and in reconstituted form at your grocer. They contain varying levels of sodium and fat, as well as MSG, so choose the one that is right for you, in both content and taste. I always have broths on my shelves to help make my dinners a little easier to prepare. To give a condensed soup a deeper flavor, I will sometimes use broth to reconstitute it instead of water.

Dry Soups

Dry soups pack a load of flavor into one small package. Dried herbs and spices are concentrated with broth, and the result is a bold flavor for your dish. All you need to add are a few other ingredients to get a great home-cooked meal. Lipton's soup mixes come in a package with two envelopes, and they are called *Lipton Recipe Secrets Soup Mix*. Knorr Soups come in a package with one envelope and are called *Knorr Recipe Classics*.

Of the dry soup mixes, these are ones I am never without

- **Lipton Onion Soup Mix**
- **Lipton Beefy Onion Soup Mix**
- **Lipton Savory Herb with Garlic Soup Mix**
- **Lipton Golden Onion Soup Mix**
- **Lipton Fiesta Herb with Red Pepper Soup Mix**
- **Lipton Garlic Mushroom Soup Mix**
- **Knorr Vegetable Soup Mix**
- **Knorr Cream of Spinach Soup Mix**
- **Knorr Leek Soup Mix**
- **Knorr Tomato Beef Soup Mix**
- **Knorr Tomato with Basil Soup Mix**

Instant Flavored Breadcrumbs

Mix an envelope of dry soup mix with 2 cups dry breadcrumbs for a crispy coating for chicken, pork, or seafood.

While testing the recipes for this book, I realized that these little packages can mean the difference between a ho-hum meal and a great meal. Adding them to a dish took as much as an hour off the cooking times, strengthened the flavors in an instant, and added balanced seasoning without the need to season and re-season the dish throughout the cooking process. Adding Lipton Beefy Onion Soup mix to a beef dish brought out the flavor of the beef and created a delectable sauce with the help of a few other ingredients. These packets of flavor save me time and effort, and in my life that is an added bonus. One thing that these soup mixes all seem to lack is enough pepper for my taste. If you would like to use onion soup mixes, Lipton, Knorr, and Campbell all make them, and they are fine to use interchangeably. Your grocer may even stock a store brand and these all seemed to work well in the recipes.

Dry soups do have their limitations when it comes to certain flavors. If they include dehydrated vegetables, you will need to add more fresh vegetables to the mix to get an authentic flavor. If we haven't included a brand or flavor of dry soup in this book, it was became we didn't like the test results. My friend Lora Brody calls this the "Thumper" principle: if you can't say anything nice, then don't say anything at all.

Ramen are dry noodles that come with a flavor packet. They are inexpensive and can make great meals in minutes. The seasoning packets flavor everything from salad dressings to vegetables, and the noodles and seasonings can also be put together for great one-dish meals. Keep several varieties on hand; I usually have the chicken and oriental flavors in my pantry.

Miso soup comes in a package with three envelopes of individual miso. I used all three packets for glazing and basting seafood and chicken. The miso makes a great soup all by itself, but I liked adding a little chopped green onion and, to be authentic, you should add a few tiny cubes of tofu as well.

I've included a listing of all the soups that we have used in the book, and some great quick ideas for using them.

LIPTON INVENTED THE "INSTANT" SOUP CATEGORY WITH THE INTRODUCTION OF CUP-A-SOUP IN 1970.

Lipton Onion Soup Mix is the big daddy of them all—Americans consume over 73,000,000 packages each year—and I'm sure half of that is used to make California dip. Onion soup mix can be stirred into any long-simmering stew to give it a deep, robust flavor. Stir a packet into rice and water and you will have a seasoned rice dish in 20 minutes.

Lipton Beefy Onion Soup Mix is great for beef dishes: stews, pot roasts, burgers, and meat loaves. Mix it with Campbell's Condensed Tomato Soup for a quick barbecue sauce.

Lipton Golden Onion Soup Mix is specifically formulated for chicken and pork. When stirred into reconstituted Campbell's Condensed Cream of Chicken Soup, it makes a sauce for chicken. It is also a great sauce when simply reconstituted with 1 1/2 cups water. It can also be used in place of Lipton Onion or Beefy Onion Soup Mix in meat loaves, rice dishes, and burgers.

Lipton Fiesta Herb with Red Pepper Soup Mix can provide the south of the border flavor for any dishes that you want to spice up.

Lipton Onion Mushroom Soup Mix can be used interchangeably with Lipton Onion or Beefy Onion Soup Mix.

Lipton Noodle Soup Mix with Chicken is a great chicken noodle soup all on its own, but adding a few cooked vegetables gives you a quick chicken vegetable soup, and you can flavor it with a little soy sauce and sesame oil to give it an Asian flavor. Add a little tomato juice, 1/4 teaspoon dried basil, and a garnish of grated Parmesan cheese and the flavor becomes Mediterranean.

Lipton Savory Herb with Garlic Soup Mix had to be the most versatile soup mix I tested. I could put it in literally anything and it was delicious. It turned ordinary canned chopped tomatoes into pasta sauces and bruschetta toppings, and it transformed canned white beans into a gourmet dip for vegetables. It was great in stews, and it perked up vegetables and pastas. Tossed with breadcrumbs it's the star of the Ten-Minute Baked Halibut (page 421). I would call this my "desert island" soup mix, meaning that I would pack it in my suitcase, on the off chance that I might be marooned!

Knorr Leek Soup Mix gave a mild onion flavor to everything I tested. It had a thickening agent in it, so that sauces were creamy when I added milk. Following the package directions, you could have a delicious creamy sauce in the time it took for the milk to come to a boil. The soup added a smooth texture to dips, sauces, salad dressings, vegetable dishes, and pasta sauces. It came alive when I sautéed onions or leeks in butter and then added them to the soup mix, deepening the flavor of the mix and giving it a fresher taste.

Knorr Tomato with Basil Soup Mix was the Italian flavoring I was looking for in sauces, stews, salad dressings, and breads. The soup also has a thickener in it, making adding other thickening agents to sauces or stews unnecessary.

Knorr Cream of Spinach Soup Mix added color and creaminess to everything from dips to vegetable dishes. I found that a grating of nutmeg and some freshly ground black pepper helped to give it additional character. Most of my recipes added more spinach, but this soup is fine by itself.

Knorr Vegetable Soup Mix is probably most famous for the dip made from it that is so popular. I found that once the soup was mixed with a liquid, the flavors became very pronounced, so I sautéed additional vegetables to give more texture to the dishes.

Knorr Spring Vegetable Soup Mix has a lighter flavor, so this soup is great for light soups, salad dressings, and vegetable dishes.

Knorr Tomato Beef Soup Mix is another soup with a deep flavor base and a thickener to help long-simmering beef dishes. It is great in meat loaf, can be used to make a barbecue sauce or rub, and turns sour cream into a beefy ranchero dip.

Knorr Cream of Broccoli Soup Mix gives color and flavor to sauces, vegetables, dips, and casseroles. Think of this soup when you don't have broccoli in the house but want the flavor in a dish.

Original California Dip

Blue California Dip

Crunchy California Dip

Santa Fe Onion Dip

California Shrimp Dip

Tuscan White Bean Dip

Tijuana Tilly Dip

Grecian Veggie Dip

Dilly Dip

Down East Clam Dip

Vegetable Florentine Dip

Cucumber Yogurt Dip

Confetti Guacamole

Roasted Eggplant Dip

Seven-Layer Nacho Dip

Madras Plaid Vegetable Curry Spread

White Cheddar Shrimp Dip

White Pizza Dip

Swiss Spinach Dip

Chili con Queso Dip

Hot Broccoli Mushroom Dip

Cinco de Mayo Corn Dip

Golden Gate Sourdough Shrimp Dip

Crabby Artichoke Dip

Beefy Cheese Fondue

Frito Pie Dip

Fire-Roasted Caponata

Garlic Herb Cheese Ball

Pretty-in-Pink Shrimp Mousse

Crazy Crackers

Asian Shrimp Bites

Marinated Shrimp

Cajun Shrimp Barbecue

Polynesian Chicken Wings

Buffalo-Style Chicken Wings

Smoked Salmon Cheesecake

Shrimply Delicious Cheesecake

Everyone's Favorite Party Mix

Irish Nachos

That's Italian Wraps

Sombrero Wraps

Peking Wraps

Basic Souped-Up Bruschetta

Wild Mushroom Bruschetta

Artichoke Bruschetta

Spinach Squares

Sausalito Sourdoughs

Souper Starters

WHEN I GOT MARRIED, I RELIED on Lipton Onion Soup Mix to help me make the one dip I had learned to make in college, California Dip. Sounding sunny and exotic to a Boston coed, it was cheap, reliable, tasted pretty good, and went well with beer. Some of my foodie friends will not ever admit to having eaten this dip, but if you serve it on a buffet table with some chips, they will be the first ones running to get a taste of childhood. Nowadays I jazz up this old standby by adding crumbled blue cheese, chopped clams, bay shrimp, or chopped crisp vegetables.

Your Souper Pantry can save you when unexpected company comes over and you are in need of a quick snack. A can of beef broth helps make a hearty cheese fondue, tomato soup can be made into a delectable shrimp mousse, and dry vegetable soup mixed with cream cheese and cilantro can transform flour tortillas into wrapped sensations. The great thing is that you can make the appetizers ahead of time or on the spur of the moment.

Any dry soup mix mixed with 2 cups of sour cream or yogurt becomes a dip for vegetables and chips. Each package of dry mix comes with a recipe for dip, but the dips that I've included are different from the ones on the packages, with the exception of California Dip, which has been on the Lipton Onion Soup Mix package since 1958. Condensed soups make excellent warm and cold dips, and there's no worry that the dip will separate when heated. With just a few additions, you can have a fondue, dip, or spread in no time.

CALIFORNIA DIP (FIVE WAYS)

Legend has it that California dip was the inspiration of a Los Angeles housewife who, in 1954, mixed Lipton Onion Soup Mix with sour cream, and word of this phenomenon spread back to the executives at the Lipton company. In 1958 the company began to print the recipe on every box of Lipton Onion Soup Mix, where it still appears today. I like to jazz up this old standby a bit to give it a new twist.

Original California Dip

SERVES 6 TO 8

2 cups sour cream

1 envelope Lipton Onion Soup Mix

1. In a small mixing bowl, combine the sour cream and soup mix. Stir until well blended.

2. Cover the bowl with plastic wrap and refrigerate the dip for at least 2 hours, or for up to 24 hours. Serve the dip with fresh vegetables and potato or tortilla chips.

VARIATION: **Yogurt or lower-fat sour cream can be substituted in these recipes; the result will be a little thinner dip. To avoid a thin dip, drain 1 cup plain yogurt or low-fat or nonfat sour cream in cheesecloth before combining it with the other ingredients.**

Blue California Dip

2 cups sour cream

1 envelope Lipton Onion Soup Mix

1/2 cup crumbled Maytag or other blue cheese

1/4 cup chopped green onions for garnish

1. In a small mixing bowl, combine the sour cream, soup mix, and blue cheese. Stir until well combined.

2. Cover the bowl with plastic wrap and refrigerate the dip for at least 2 hours and for up to 24 hours. Stir it before serving and garnish it with the green onions. Serve the dip with fresh vegetables or crackers.

SERVES 6 TO 8

Maytag blue cheese gives this dip a mellow flavor. If you can't find Maytag blue, try your favorite blue-veined cheese.

Crunchy California Dip

2 cups sour cream

1 envelope Lipton Onion Soup Mix

1/2 cup seeded and chopped red bell pepper

1/2 cup seeded and chopped green bell pepper

1/2 cup chopped red onion

6 strips bacon, cooked until crisp, drained on paper towels, and crumbled

1. In a small mixing bowl, combine the sour cream and soup mix. Stir until well blended. Add the bell peppers, onion, and bacon, stirring until combined.

2. Cover the bowl with plastic wrap and refrigerate the dip for at least 2 hours or for up to 24 hours before serving. Serve the dip with fresh vegetables.

SERVES 6 TO 8

Crunchy bits of vegetables and crispy bacon make this dip out of the ordinary.

EVERY DAY, AMERICANS USE OVER 220,000 ENVELOPES OF LIPTON RECIPE SECRETS ONION SOUP MIX.

Souper Starters

Santa Fe Onion Dip

SERVES 6 TO 8

Flavors of the Southwest liven up this version of California dip.

2 cups sour cream

1 envelope Lipton Onion Soup Mix

1/4 cup chopped fresh cilantro leaves

1/4 cup seeded and finely chopped Anaheim chiles

1/2 cup grated pepper Jack cheese

1/4 cup finely chopped red onion

1/2 cup peeled and finely chopped jícama

1/2 cup finely chopped fresh tomatoes for garnish

Tortilla chips

1. In a medium mixing bowl, combine the sour cream and soup mix, stirring until well blended. Add the cilantro, chiles, cheese, onion, and jícama, stirring to blend.

2. Cover the bowl with plastic wrap and refrigerate for at least 2 hours and for up to 24 hours. Garnish the dip with the tomatoes and serve with tortilla chips.

California Shrimp Dip

SERVES 6 TO 8

The addition of bay shrimp and Old Bay seasoning make this dip extra special. You may substitute a can of chopped clams, drained, for the shrimp if you'd like.

1 cup sour cream

1 cup mayonnaise

1 envelope Lipton Onion Soup Mix

1/4 pound cooked bay shrimp or chopped shrimp (about 1 cup)

1 tablespoon Old Bay seasoning

1 teaspoon Worcestershire sauce

Crackers

1. In a medium mixing bowl, combine the sour cream, mayonnaise, and soup mix, stirring until blended. Add the shrimp, Old Bay seasoning, and Worcestershire, stirring again until well combined.

2. Cover the bowl with plastic wrap and refrigerate for at least 2 hours and for up to 12 hours. Serve with crackers.

Tuscan White Bean Dip

One 19-ounce can cannellini beans or small white beans, drained and rinsed

1 tablespoon red wine vinegar

2 tablespoons extra virgin olive oil

1 teaspoon freshly ground black pepper

1 envelope Lipton Savory Herb with Garlic Soup Mix

1/4 cup chopped fresh Italian parsley leaves

Toasted bread rounds, fresh vegetables, and crackers

1. Combine the beans, vinegar, olive oil, pepper, soup mix, and parsley in a food processor and process until smooth.

2. Cover the bowl with plastic wrap and refrigerate until serving time, or for up to 2 days. Serve the dip with toasted bread rounds, vegetables, and crackers.

SERVES 6

We call this Italian hummus! Garlicky and smooth, this delicious dip comes together in the food processor and can be kept in the refrigerator for several days before serving.

Crudités are raw (or almost raw) cut-up vegetables served with a dip before dinner or as a snack. If you are in a hurry, your grocer may already have done some of the work for you by providing prepackaged baby carrots and cut-up vegetables in the produce section.

Arranging crudités in a basket or on a large ceramic platter can be like flower arranging if you want to get that creative, or you can simply fan out leaves of endive, or choose two vegetables to arrange for a simpler platter. Hollowing out a vegetable such as a purple cabbage, large bell pepper, or large artichoke and pouring the dip inside keeps the natural theme going. Using leaves from cabbage, decorative kale, or a bag of prepared field green salad for the base of the crudité arrangement adds to the presentation. Try garnishing the platter with bouquets of fresh herbs, chives, pea shoots, or broccoli sprouts. Edible flowers also add a designer touch. Try arranging all green vegetables with a white dip; or red, white, and green for an Italian-flavored dip. Remember, it's not the number of veggies in the basket, but their color, size, texture, and compatibility with the dip that is important.

The following vegetables work well in crudités arrangements. Remember to wash all vegetables in cold water before serving them.

Artichokes Cut the top 1 inch off globe artichokes and steam them. Place them on a platter with other vegetables and make sure you have a plate handy so guests can discard the leftover leaves. Or steam baby artichokes, quarter them lengthwise, and arrange them on a platter.

Asparagus Trim off the tough ends, plunge the spears into boiling salted water for 30 seconds, shock them in ice water, pat them dry, and refrigerate them until you are ready to use them. (I have some friends who use pencil-thin spring asparagus raw.)

Beans Tender green or yellow wax beans need to be trimmed of tough strings, blanched in boiling salted water for one minute, shocked in ice water, patted dry, and refrigerated until you are ready to use them. Stand the beans upright in the arrangement.

Belgian endive Trim the bottom and separate the leaves.

Broccoli and cauliflower Some people like their broccoli or cauliflower raw; others blanch it for 1 minute in boiling water. Either method is fine; I find blanched broccoli has a brighter green color.

Carrots Your grocer sells baby carrots in bags, and I recommend using these to save time. If they are looking a little sad or dry, place them in a bowl of water in the refrigerator for two hours or overnight. Drain and pat them dry before using. You can serve the carrots whole or cut them in half. They will add color and crunch to your arrangement, and, if you are serving children, you can count on these being their vegetable of choice.

Celery This is another item that your grocery store may sell already cut up, but celery doesn't do well once it's cut. You can soak the precut variety in cold water for a few hours to perk it up, or buy hearts of celery and trim the stalks into 2-inch lengths. Store the cut-up celery in water in the refrigerator until you are ready to serve it.

Cucumbers I buy only European cucumbers; they don't have seeds, and you get more usable cucumber for your dollar. You don't need to peel cucumber, but do scrub the outside and trim the ends. Then slice the cucumber into $1/2$-inch-thick rounds, or 2-inch lengths, and then cut the lengths into quarters.

Jícama Peel and cut it into 2-by-$1/2$-inch lengths.

Mushrooms Wipe button mushrooms with a paper towel to clean them and serve whole, halved, or quartered, depending on their size.

Peas Sugar snap and snow peas should be blanched for 30 seconds in boiling salted water then shocked in ice water. Pat them dry and refrigerate before serving. If the peas are especially tender (from your garden), serve them raw.

Peppers Green, yellow, orange, red, purple, and white bell peppers all add color and crunch to an arrangement. Seed the peppers and cut them into strips about $3/4$ inch in width.

Radishes Red and white radishes can be cut in half or served whole if they are small. Keep them fresh in a bowl of cold water in the fridge. Then pat them dry and arrange.

Tomatoes Tiny cherry tomatoes and pear-shaped orange and yellow tomatoes add color and taste to a crudités basket. You can leave the stems on or remove them; personally, I feel like the stem gives my guests something to hold onto when dipping.

Zucchini and yellow squash Baby vegetables have become quite common in our supermarkets. I love to include whole baby zucchini, yellow squash, and pattypan squashes in my vegetable arrangements. If they are too costly, use the larger varieties, cutting zucchini into 2-inch lengths and cutting the lengths into quarters for nice long dippers. Cut yellow squash into $1/2$-inch-thick slices.

Tijuana Tilly Dip

This festive south of the border dip serves an army of hungry hombres. Serve it with lots of cold beer and frosted margaritas.

4 cups shredded Monterey Jack cheese

1 cup seeded and chopped fresh tomatoes

6 green onions, chopped

1 Anaheim chile, seeded and minced ($\frac{1}{4}$ cup)

2 tablespoons chopped fresh cilantro leaves

One 4-ounce can sliced black olives, drained

1 large ripe Hass avocado, peeled, pitted, and diced

$\frac{2}{3}$ cup vegetable oil

$\frac{1}{4}$ cup rice vinegar

$\frac{1}{4}$ cup fresh lime juice

1 envelope Lipton Savory Herb with Garlic Soup Mix

1 teaspoon freshly ground black pepper

Tortilla chips

1. In a large mixing bowl, combine the cheese, tomatoes, green onions, chile, cilantro, olives, and avocado, stirring to blend.

2. In a small mixing bowl, whisk together the oil, vinegar, lime juice, soup mix, and pepper. Pour the dressing over the cheese mixture and stir until well combined.

3. Refrigerate for at least 2 hours and for up to 6 hours. Serve the dip with tortilla chips.

Grecian Veggie Dip

2 cups sour cream

4 ounces feta cheese, crumbled

1 envelope Lipton Savory Herb with Garlic Soup Mix

1/4 cup chopped red onion

1 teaspoon dried oregano

1/2 teaspoon dried basil

1. In a small mixing bowl, combine the sour cream, feta, soup mix, onion, oregano, and basil until blended.

2. Refrigerate the dip for at least 4 hours before serving.

SERVES 8

I love the salty taste of feta cheese, and, when it's available, I love to buy feta flavored with tomato and basil or garlic and pepper and use it in this spicy dip. This dip is great with crisp vegetables and pita chips. You can also serve it with grilled lamb.

Dilly Dip

1 cup sour cream

1 cup mayonnaise

1 envelope Knorr Leek Soup Mix

1 tablespoon dillweed

1 tablespoon dried parsley

1 teaspoon celery salt

1. In a small mixing bowl, combine the sour cream, mayonnaise, and soup mix, whisking to blend. Add the dillweed, parsley, and celery salt, stirring to combine.

2. Cover the bowl with plastic wrap and refrigerate the dip for at least 2 hours and for up to 24 hours. Serve it with raw vegetables.

SERVES 6

This dip has an exotic flavor, thanks to the leek soup mix. Using dried herbs intensifies the flavors in this versatile dish. I use this dip as a topping for baked potatoes, and I've also been known to stir it into mashed potatoes and potato salads. It's great as a dressing for pasta salads as well.

Down East Clam Dip

SERVES 6 TO 8

This simple dip using a can of New England clam chowder is delicious with chips or sliced raw vegetables. It's best made ahead of time and refrigerated for at least six hours, so that the flavors have a chance to get to know one another. It is also good warm. I like to pour it into a hollowed-out round of sourdough bread and heat the entire loaf in a preheated 350-degree oven for 30 minutes, until the dip is bubbly.

One 8-ounce package cream cheese, softened

1 can Campbell's Condensed New England Clam Chowder

One 4-ounce can chopped clams, drained, reserving 2 tablespoons of the clam juice

3 green onions, chopped

1 clove garlic, minced

1 tablespoon Worcestershire sauce

6 shakes Tabasco sauce

1 teaspoon anchovy paste

Salt and freshly ground black pepper

1. In a large bowl, using an electric mixer, cream together the cream cheese and clam chowder until smooth. Fold in the clams, green onions, garlic, Worcestershire, Tabasco, and anchovy paste, stirring to blend. If the dip is too stiff, add some of the reserved clam juice to thin it. Taste the dip for seasoning, and adjust the seasoning by adding salt, pepper, or additional Tabasco to taste.

2. Cover the bowl tightly with plastic wrap and refrigerate the dip for at least 6 hours before serving.

AMERICANS PURCHASE AN AVERAGE OF 100 CANS OF SOUP EVERY SECOND OF EVERY DAY IN JANUARY.

Vegetable Florentine Dip

One 10-ounce package frozen chopped spinach, defrosted and squeezed dry

2 cups sour cream or lowfat plain yogurt, drained

1 cup mayonnaise

1 envelope Knorr Vegetable or Cream of Spinach Soup Mix

1 cup peeled and chopped jícama

3 green onions, chopped

½ cup freshly grated Parmesan cheese

1. In a medium mixing bowl, stir all the ingredients together until blended.

2. Cover the bowl tightly with plastic wrap and refrigerate the dip for at least 2 hours before serving it with fresh vegetables.

SERVES 8

This old standby is a staple at many potluck dinners when someone is asked to bring a dip. My favorite way to serve this dip is in a hollowed-out round loaf of bread. I freeze the bread, then, when I am ready to serve the dip, I spoon it into the bread, and the dip stays cool for hours. I cut the inside of the bread into cubes to use as dippers along with fresh vegetables.

Jícama is a tuberous root vegetable with a papery brown skin. Once peeled, jícama has a crunchy texture and sweet flavor.

IN 1870, ALFRED AND CARL KNORR BEGAN EXPERIMENTING WITH DRIED VEGETABLES AND SEASONINGS THAT TURNED INTO SOUPS WHEN SIMMERED WITH WATER.

Souper Starters

Cucumber Yogurt Dip

SERVES 6 TO 8

Cool and creamy, this dip is great with pita chips or fresh vegetables. It is also delicious with falafel or drizzled over lamb shish kebabs. Try tossing it into leftover pasta for a quick pasta salad.

2 cups nonfat plain yogurt

1 envelope Knorr Leek Soup Mix

$3/4$ cup seeded, peeled, and chopped cucumber

$1/4$ cup chopped fresh Italian parsley leaves

2 tablespoons chopped fresh dill or 1 tablespoon dillweed

1. In a medium mixing bowl, combine the yogurt with the soup mix, stirring to blend. Add the cucumber, parsley, and dill and fold until well combined.

2. Cover the bowl with plastic wrap and refrigerate the dip for at least 2 hours and for up to 8 hours.

Confetti Guacamole

SERVES 8

This colorful dip is always the life of the party. You can let your imagination run wild with the design of the toppings on this work of art; best of all, the entire dish can be prepared up to eight hours ahead of time.

4 large, ripe Hass avocados, peeled and pitted

$1/2$ teaspoon salt

$1/4$ cup fresh lime juice

2 cups sour cream

1 envelope Knorr Vegetable Soup Mix or Lipton Fiesta Herb with Red Pepper Soup Mix

$1/4$ cup finely chopped pickled jalapeño chiles

$1/4$ cup finely chopped red onion

$1/2$ cup cooked small shrimp

$1/3$ cup grated mild cheddar cheese

$1/4$ cup sliced pitted black olives

$1/4$ cup finely seeded and chopped fresh tomato

$1/4$ cup finely chopped fresh cilantro leaves

Tortilla chips

1. Using a 12- to 14-inch round platter, mash the avocados in the center of the plate and spread them to within 1 inch of the edge of the platter, so that the mashed avocados are about 1/2 inch thick. Sprinkle them with salt and lime juice.

2. In a small mixing bowl, combine the sour cream and soup mix, stirring until they are well blended. Spread the sour cream mixture over the avocados, covering them entirely.

3. Working from the center, arrange the jalapeño, onion, shrimp, cheese, olives, tomatoes, and cilantro in concentric circles, using each ingredient to form a circle, and repeating as necessary. Or separate the items into seven spokes and use one ingredient to fill each spoke. Wrap the platter in plastic and refrigerate it until serving time.

4. When you are ready to serve the dip, tuck tortilla chips around the guacamole and serve.

Roasted Eggplant Dip

2 medium eggplants

2 tablespoons extra virgin olive oil

4 cloves garlic

6 green onions, chopped

1 can Campbell's Condensed Cream of Celery Soup

1 cup Bloody Mary mix or spiced tomato juice

1/2 cup chopped fresh Italian parsley leaves

1/2 teaspoon salt

1/2 teaspoon freshly ground black pepper

1 cup plain yogurt for garnish

1. Preheat the oven to 425 degrees. Line a baking sheet with aluminum foil.

2. Cut each eggplant in half lengthwise and brush the cut sides with some of the oil. Spread the garlic cloves on the baking sheet and drizzle them with the remaining oil. Roast the eggplant until tender, 20 to 30 minutes.

SERVES 8

This dip can be served as a side dish with grilled lamb or as a prelude to dinner with Savory Pita Chips (page 195). The dip can be prepared ahead of time and is actually better after a few hours in the refrigerator.

3. Remove the eggplants from the oven and, when they are cool enough to handle, scoop out the insides into a food processor. Squeeze the garlic cloves out of their skins into the food processor. Add the green onions, soup, Bloody Mary mix, parsley, salt, and pepper and pulse on and off until smooth. Remove from the work bowl and refrigerate until you are ready to serve.

4. Garnish the dip with plain yogurt and serve.

Seven-Layer Nacho Dip

SERVES 6 TO 8

Colorful layers of ingredients make this "walking taco" a hit with the crowd. You'll love the ease of preparation and the fact that you can make it ahead of time then pull it out of the refrigerator just before serving. Make sure to serve this dip with yellow and blue corn tortilla chips.

1 can Campbell's Condensed Fiesta Chili Beef Soup

One 14-ounce can refried beans

1 teaspoon chili powder

2 cups sour cream

2 cups shredded mild cheddar cheese

2 cups shredded cooked chicken or turkey

2 cups shredded lettuce

2 cups seeded and chopped fresh tomatoes

One 4-ounce can sliced black olives, drained

$\frac{1}{2}$ cup pickled jalapeño slices, drained and rinsed

2 medium ripe Hass avocados

1. In a medium mixing bowl, using an electric mixer, or in the work bowl of a food processor, combine the soup, beans, chili powder, and 1 cup of the sour cream until smooth.

2. Spread this mixture over the bottom of a 13-by-9-inch baking dish or a 12-by-2-inch-high round dish. Layer on top of this mixture, in order, the cheese, chicken, lettuce, tomatoes, olives, jalapeños, and the remaining 1 cup sour cream.

3. Just before serving, peel, pit, and dice the avocados and sprinkle them over the top.

Madras Plaid Vegetable Curry Spread

2 tablespoons butter

½ cup finely chopped onion

2 cloves garlic, minced

½ cup finely chopped carrot

½ cup seeded and finely chopped red bell pepper

½ cup finely chopped celery

½ cup finely chopped zucchini

½ cup finely chopped yellow squash

1½ teaspoons curry powder

1 envelope Lipton Golden Onion Soup Mix

½ cup Major Grey chutney

½ cup peeled, seeded, and finely chopped cucumber

1 cup plain yogurt

1. Melt the butter in a 10-inch sauté pan over medium heat. Add the onion and garlic and cook, stirring, until the onion begins to soften, 2 to 3 minutes. Add the carrot, bell pepper, celery, zucchini, squash, and curry powder and cook, stirring, until the vegetables are tender but still crisp, 5 to 7 minutes. Add the soup mix and ³/₄ cup water, stirring constantly. Bring the mixture to a boil and simmer it for 7 to 10 minutes.

2. Remove the pan from the heat and allow the mixture to cool for 15 minutes. Stir in the chutney and cucumber and serve the spread with yogurt on the side.

SERVES 6

Another great appetizer or side dish, this curry mixes finely chopped cooked vegetables with cooling cucumber and chutney at the end of the cooking time. I love this with pita and tortilla chips.

Souper Smart

Not all chutneys are sweet and cooling. Major Grey is a type of chutney that you will find readily at your grocer; it is a sweeter chutney. If you prefer to kick up the heat, buy a hot mango chutney.

White Cheddar Shrimp Dip

SERVE 6

Cold and tangy with sharp white cheddar cheese, this quick dip is served with crackers or pita chips. You can heat it in a hollowed-out round loaf of French bread.

HOT WHITE CHEDDAR SHRIMP DIP: Turn the dip into a 2-quart baking dish and bake it in a pre-heated 325-degree oven until bubbling, 20 to 30 minutes.

Two 8-ounce packages cream cheese, softened

1 can Campbell's Condensed Cream of Shrimp Soup

2 cups shredded sharp white cheddar cheese

2 green onions, chopped

1 teaspoon Worcestershire sauce

1 teaspoon prepared horseradish

1/2 cup cooked bay shrimp or chopped shrimp, plus more for garnish

Sprigs of fresh Italian parsley for garnish

1. In a large mixing bowl, using an electric mixer, cream together the cream cheese and soup. Fold in the cheese, green onions, Worcestershire, horseradish, and shrimp.

2. Turn the mixture into a fancy mold or a 9-inch quiche dish. Refrigerate the dip until you are ready to serve it. Garnish it with additional bay shrimp and parsley sprigs.

White Pizza Dip

SERVES 6 TO 8

This can be served with all kinds of dippers, from fresh veggies to bread sticks, string cheese, cooked chicken chunks, and small meatballs.

WHITE CON QUESO DIP: Substitute Lipton Fiesta Herb with Red Pepper Soup Mix and shredded mild cheddar cheese for the Parmesan. Serve with tortilla chips and veggies.

One 8-ounce package cream cheese, softened

1 cup ricotta cheese

1 cup shredded mozzarella cheese

1/2 cup freshly grated Parmesan cheese

1 envelope Knorr Tomato with Basil Soup Mix

1. Preheat the oven to 350 degrees.

2. In a medium mixing bowl, using an electric mixer, cream together the cream cheese and ricotta. Fold in the mozzarella, Parmesan, and soup mix.

3. Pour the mixture into a 1-quart casserole dish and bake it until bubbly, about 30 minutes. Serve it immediately.

Swiss Spinach Dip

1 cup mayonnaise

1 envelope Knorr Cream of Spinach Soup Mix

½ cup chopped onion

One 10-ounce package frozen chopped spinach, defrosted and squeezed dry

1 cup grated Swiss cheese

½ cup freshly grated Parmesan cheese

1. Preheat the oven to 350 degrees.

2. In a medium mixing bowl, combine the mayonnaise, soup mix, onion, spinach, and cheese until blended.

3. Pour the mixture into a 1-quart casserole dish. Bake it until it is golden brown and bubbling, 20 to 30 minutes.

This dip comes together in no time, and you probably have the ingredients in your pantry. Serve it with tortilla chips, crackers, or French bread rounds.

SOUTH OF THE BORDER SPINACH DIP: Add one 4-ounce can diced green chiles, drained and rinsed.

SPINACH ARTICHOKE DIP: Add one 14-ounce can artichoke hearts, drained and chopped.

SEAFARING SPINACH DIP: Add 1 cup flaked fresh lump or Dungeness crabmeat or cooked bay shrimp or chopped shrimp.

Souper Starters

Chili con Queso Dip

SERVES 6 TO 8

A bit like a south of the border fondue, this dip has just the right amount of heat and is great dipped with tortilla chips, as well as fresh vegetables. If you decide to make it a fondue, use cooked chicken, small cooked red potato wedges, bell pepper slices, zucchini rounds, and cooked shrimp as dippers.

3 tablespoons butter

1 cup chopped onion

2 cloves garlic, minced

One 4-ounce can chopped green chiles, drained and rinsed

One 14.5-ounce can diced tomatoes, drained

1 teaspoon chili powder

1 teaspoon ground cumin

1 can Campbell's Condensed Cheddar Cheese Soup

1 cup grated Monterey Jack cheese

1. In a 3-quart saucepan, melt the butter over medium heat, add the onion, and cook, stirring, until softened, about 3 minutes. Add the garlic and chiles and cook, stirring, for another 3 minutes. Add the tomatoes, chili powder, and cumin and cook for 5 minutes, stirring frequently. Add the soup, stirring to combine. Bring the mixture to a boil.

2. Remove the pan from the heat and add the cheese, stirring until it is melted. Serve the dip immediately or refrigerate it, tightly covered with plastic wrap, for up to 2 days. Reheat over low heat before serving.

Hot Broccoli Mushroom Dip

SERVES 6 TO 8

4 cups water

2 teaspoons salt, divided

1 pound broccoli, stalks peeled and cut into $1/2$-inch pieces and head cut into florets

2 tablespoons butter

1 cup chopped onion

2 cloves garlic, minced

3 stalks celery, chopped

½ pound mushrooms, sliced

½ teaspoon freshly ground black pepper

1 can Campbell's Condensed Cream of Celery Soup or Cream
    of Mushroom Soup

1 tablespoon fresh lemon juice

1 teaspoon Worcestershire sauce

4 shakes Tabasco sauce

2 tablespoons cream sherry

2 cups grated cheddar cheese

1. In a 5-quart saucepan, combine the water and 1 teaspoon of the salt and bring to a boil. Add the broccoli and cook it for 2 minutes. Drain it thoroughly and set aside.

2. Melt the butter in a 3-quart saucepan over medium heat. Add the onion, garlic, and celery and cook, stirring, until the vegetables begin to soften, about 3 minutes. Add the mushrooms, seasoning the mixture with the remaining 1 teaspoon salt and the pepper. Toss the vegetables and cook them over high heat until the mushrooms give off some of their moisture, 4 to 5 minutes. Set the mixture aside until you are ready to proceed.

3. Combine the vegetables with the broccoli in the 5-quart saucepan over medium heat and add the soup, lemon juice, Worcestershire, Tabasco, and sherry. Heat the mixture to boiling. Remove the pan from the heat and add the cheese, stirring until it is melted. Serve the dip immediately or refrigerate it until you are ready to serve it. Then reheat it over low heat.

This vegetarian dip is delicious with tortilla chips. Use it as "nacho" sauce for potato skins, or stir it into cooked rice for a delicious side dish. It can be made up to two days ahead of time and refrigerated, or freeze it for up to one month.

VARIATION: Substitute 1 envelope Knorr Cream of Broccoli Soup and 1 cup milk for the Campbell's "cream of" soup and proceed as directed in the recipe.

Cinco de Mayo Corn Dip

Spiked with chiles and cumin, this dip will be a big hit at your next Cinco de Mayo party. Serve it with yellow and blue corn tortilla chips. The dip benefits from being made ahead of time and can be refrigerated for up to three days before serving.

2 tablespoons butter

2 green onions, chopped

2 cloves garlic, minced

One 4-ounce can diced green chiles, drained and rinsed

$\frac{1}{2}$ cup seeded and finely chopped red bell pepper

$1\frac{1}{2}$ teaspoons ground cumin

$\frac{1}{2}$ teaspoon chili powder

1 can Campbell's Condensed Cream of Chicken Soup

2 cups corn kernels, either cut fresh from the cob or frozen (and defrosted)

1 cup grated mild cheddar cheese

1 cup grated Monterey Jack cheese (for more heat, try pepper Jack)

$\frac{1}{2}$ cup sour cream

1. Melt the butter in a 3-quart saucepan over medium heat, add the green onions and garlic, and cook, stirring, until they have softened, 3 to 4 minutes. Add the chiles, bell pepper, cumin, and chili powder and cook for 2 to 3 minutes, stirring constantly so that the spices do not burn. Add the soup and corn, stirring to blend the ingredients. Bring the mixture to a boil and remove the pan from the heat.

2. Add the cheeses and sour cream, stirring until they are melted. Serve warm.

Golden Gate Sourdough Shrimp Dip

1 round loaf sourdough or French bread

2 tablespoons butter

2 cloves garlic, minced

1 teaspoon Old Bay seasoning

1 can Campbell's Condensed Cream of Shrimp Soup

1 tablespoon dry sherry

4 cups shredded Swiss cheese

½ cup sour cream

1. Cut the top off the bread so that it can be used later as a lid. Then, leaving a ½-inch-thick shell, remove the inside of the bread. Set the shell aside. Cut the soft insides of the bread into cubes and toast them until they are dry but not browned.

2. In a 3-quart saucepan, melt the butter over medium heat, add the garlic and Old Bay seasoning, and cook, stirring, for 3 minutes. Add the soup and sherry, stirring to combine. Bring the mixture to a boil, remove it from the heat, add the cheese and sour cream, and stir until the cheese melts. (At this point, you may refrigerate the dip for up to 2 days.)

3. Preheat the oven to 350 degrees. Pour the dip into the bread shell, place the bread on a baking sheet lined with aluminum foil, and cover the top with the bread lid. Bake the dip until it is bubbling, 30 to 40 minutes. Remove the bread from the oven and serve the dip immediately.

(If you decide to serve the dip in a chafing dish or fondue pot, reheat the dip in a saucepan over medium-low heat until it comes to serving temperature. Pour it into the chafing dish and serve.)

This dip is baked in a hollowed-out loaf of sourdough bread. Use the inside of the bread for dippers, as well as crab claws, shrimp, and fresh vegetables. When the dip is gone, cut the bread into wedges and broil it to serve along with dinner another night.

CHEESY VARIATIONS: Substitute white cheddar or smoked gouda for the Swiss cheese.

Crabby Artichoke Dip

This dip is so popular that I often make a double batch to keep everyone happy. You can vary the ingredients to suit what you have in the pantry, and it's delicious dipped with tortilla chips, crackers, French bread rounds, and cucumber slices. You can bake this dip in a bread shell or ovenproof serving dish.

SHRIMPY ARTICHOKE DIP: Substitute cooked bay shrimp or chopped shrimp for the crabmeat.

CRABBY ARTICHOKE DIP WITH CHEDDAR: Substitute medium-sharp cheddar cheese for the Swiss and Parmesan.

CRABBY CHILE ARTICHOKE DIP: Add one 4-ounce can diced green chiles, drained and rinsed.

One 8-ounce package cream cheese, softened

1 can Campbell's Condensed Cream of Shrimp Soup

1 teaspoon garlic salt

One 14-ounce can artichoke hearts, drained and chopped

½ cup freshly grated Parmesan cheese

½ cup grated Swiss cheese

½ pound fresh lump or Dungeness crabmeat, picked over for cartilage and shells and flaked apart

1. Preheat the oven to 350 degrees. Coat a 2-quart baking dish with nonstick cooking spray.

2. In a medium mixing bowl, using an electric mixer, cream together the cream cheese and soup. Stir in the garlic salt, artichoke hearts, cheeses, and crabmeat. Turn the mixture into the prepared dish and bake the dip until it is golden brown and bubbling, about 30 minutes. Serve it hot.

Beefy Cheese Fondue

1 can Campbell's Condensed Beef Broth or French Onion Soup

½ cup milk

3 cloves garlic, minced

4 cups grated Swiss cheese

½ teaspoon freshly ground black pepper

1. Heat the soup and milk together in a 3-quart saucepan, bringing the liquid to a boil. Add the garlic and simmer for 10 minutes.

2. Remove the pan from the stove and add the cheese a few handfuls at time, stirring to melt. When the cheese has melted and the sauce is smooth, season with the pepper. Refrigerate the fondue, covered with plastic wrap, until you are ready to serve it.

3. When you are ready to serve the fondue, warm it in a saucepan over medium-low heat until it is hot. Transfer it to a fondue pot and keep it warm for dipping.

Serve this hearty fondue for an après-ski snack or as a warm-up before a winter dinner. The fondue can be prepared up to two days ahead of time and refrigerated until you are ready to serve it. We like to dip sourdough bread chunks, cooked shrimp and chicken, as well as fresh vegetables, in the fondue.

SOUP

Frito Pie Dip

Frito pie is a popular "hand food" in the South. A small bag of Fritos is opened, and then the baked chili filling is spooned right into the bag and topped with cheddar cheese. It's pure heaven to connoisseurs. The chili filing is good all by itself, but this dish is a great football "couch potato" dish as well.

2 tablespoons vegetable oil

1 large onion, chopped

2 cloves garlic, minced

2 teaspoons chili powder

1 teaspoon ground cumin

1 teaspoon dried oregano

1½ pounds ground beef

1 can Campbell's Condensed Fiesta Chili Beef Soup

One 4-ounce can tomato sauce

1 teaspoon salt

½ teaspoon freshly ground black pepper

3 tablespoons yellow cornmeal

⅓ cup water

2 cups grated mild cheddar cheese, divided

One 14-ounce bag Frito corn chips

½ cup chopped red onion for garnish

1 cup sour cream for garnish

½ cup pickled jalapeño slices, drained, for garnish

1. Preheat the oven to 350 degrees. Coat a 13-by-9-inch baking dish with nonstick cooking spray.

2. In a 5-quart saucepan, heat the oil over medium heat. Add the onion, garlic, chili powder, cumin, and oregano and cook for 3 minutes, stirring constantly so that the spices do not burn. Add the ground beef, stirring to break up the meat, and cook until the beef loses its pink color. Drain off any excess fat from the pan. Add the soup and tomato sauce and simmer for 20 minutes. Season with salt and pepper.

3. Place the cornmeal in a small cup, add the water, and stir until the mixture is smooth. Gradually add this mixture to the chili, stirring until it's thickened. (At this point, the chili can be refrigerated for up to 2 days or frozen for 2 months.)

4. Pour the chili into the prepared baking dish and cover it with 1 cup of the cheese. Bake the chili until the cheese is melted and the chili is bubbling, about 25 minutes.

5. Remove the baking dish from the oven and tuck Fritos in along the side of the dish. Garnish with the remaining 1 cup cheese, the onion, sour cream, and jalapeños. Serve immediately.

Fire-Roasted Caponata

This savory spread was such a hit when I tested it that I ate it hot, cold, and at room temperature! Roasting the eggplant and garlic gives the finished dish a mellow, nutty flavor. Serve caponata cold with pita chips, at room temperature as part of an antipasto tray, or warm over grilled chicken, fish, or beef.

1 medium eggplant

2 tablespoons extra virgin olive oil

3 cloves garlic

2 tablespoons olive oil

1/2 cup chopped red onion

3 stalks celery, chopped

One 14.5-ounce can diced tomatoes, with their juices

1 envelope Lipton Savory Herb with Garlic Soup Mix

3 tablespoons sugar

1/3 cup balsamic vinegar

1/2 cup capers, drained and chopped

1/2 cup pitted green olives, drained and coarsely chopped

1/2 cup chopped fresh Italian parsley leaves

1 teaspoon freshly ground black pepper

Salt

1. Preheat the oven to 400 degrees. Line a rimmed baking sheet with aluminum foil.

2. Cut the eggplant in half lengthwise and drizzle 1 tablespoon of the extra virgin olive oil over the cut surface. Place the eggplant cut side down on the foil. Scatter the garlic cloves around the eggplant and sprinkle the remaining 1 tablespoon extra virgin olive oil over the garlic. Roast the eggplant until it is tender, 20 to 25 minutes. When the eggplant is done, remove it from the oven and allow it to cool enough to handle. Scoop out the inside of the eggplant and coarsely chop it. Reserve the garlic cloves.

3. In a 10-inch skillet, heat the olive oil over medium heat, add the onion and celery, and cook, stirring, until the vegetables begin to soften, about 3 minutes. Squeeze the garlic out of its skin, and add it with the tomatoes to the skillet. Cook, stirring, until the tomatoes begin to give off some of their juices, about 5 minutes. Add the soup mix, sugar, and vinegar and cook an additional 3 minutes. Add the eggplant, capers, olives, parsley, and pepper, stirring to blend.

4. Remove the skillet from the heat, taste, and correct the seasoning with salt and more pepper if necessary. Let the caponata cool before serving.

Garlic Herb Cheese Ball

Two 8-ounce packages cream cheese, softened

½ cup (1 stick) butter, softened

1 envelope Knorr Leek Soup Mix

1 teaspoon dried fines herbes (see page 3)

1 teaspoon garlic powder

1 teaspoon fresh lemon juice

1 tablespoon chopped fresh chives

½ cup chopped fresh Italian parsley leaves

2 tablespoons coarsely ground black pepper

1. In a large mixing bowl, using an electric mixer, cream together the cream cheese and butter until smooth. Add the soup mix, fines herbes, garlic powder, lemon juice, and chives, mixing until well blended.

2. On a sheet of wax paper, combine the parsley and pepper. On another sheet of wax paper, shape the cream cheese mixture into a log or ball, and then roll it in the parsley mixture.

3. Cover the cheese log or ball tightly in plastic wrap and refrigerate it for at least 2 hours and for up to 1 week, or freeze it for up to 2 months, defrosting it before serving.

SERVES 8

This savory cream cheese spread will remind you of Boursin or other garlic herb cheeses, but at half the cost! It's great to spread on crackers, toasted bagels, or French bread slices. I've even used this in mashed potatoes and twice-baked potatoes. Make a double recipe and freeze one to have on hand for unexpected company.

VARIATION: Substitute Lipton Savory Herb with Garlic Soup Mix and add ¼ teaspoon each dried thyme and chervil to the cream cheese mixture.

Souper Starters

Pretty-in-Pink Shrimp Mousse

SERVES 8 TO 10

No one in his or her wildest imagination will guess that the secret to this dish is Campbell's tomato soup. When the soup is blended with cream cheese and a few other ingredients, the result is a delicately flavored and elegant presentation. You can substitute crab for the shrimp if you would like.

OF THE TOP-SELLING DRY GROCERY ITEMS IN SUPERMARKETS NATIONALLY, TOMATO SOUP RANKS NUMBER SIX.

2 envelopes Knox unflavored gelatin

1/2 cup cold water

1 can Campbell's Condensed Tomato Soup

One 8-ounce package cream cheese, cut into cubes and softened

1 cup mayonnaise

3/4 cup finely chopped celery

1/2 cup finely chopped red onion

1/2 teaspoon Old Bay seasoning

2 cups cooked bay shrimp or chopped shrimp

Sprigs of fresh Italian parsley, lemon wedges, and additional shrimp for garnish

1 European cucumber, cut into 1/2-inch-thick rounds

Ritz crackers

1. Coat a 4 1/2-cup fish mold or quiche dish with nonstick cooking spray. Sprinkle the gelatin over the water in a 2-cup measuring cup, stirring to blend.

2. In a small saucepan, heat the soup over medium heat and add the cream cheese, stirring with a whisk until it is melted. Remove the pan from the heat, pour the mixture into a large mixing bowl, and allow it to cool for 10 to 15 minutes. (To hasten the cooling, place the bowl in a larger bowl filled with ice.)

3. Add the gelatin mixture and mayonnaise, whisking until thoroughly blended. Add the celery, onion, Old Bay seasoning, and shrimp, stirring to blend. Pour the mousse into the prepared mold and refrigerate it for at least 4 hours, until firm.

4. When you are ready to serve the mousse, immerse the bottom of the mold in a tray of hot water, and then place a serving dish over the top of the mold. Holding on to both the serving dish and the mold, flip the dish over to unmold the mousse. If you are using a quiche dish, leave the mousse in the dish, place the dish on a tray, and surround the dish with crackers. Garnish the mousse with parsley, lemon wedges, and additional shrimp. Serve it with cucumber slices and crackers.

Crazy Crackers

2 boxes Sunshine Oyster Crackers

1 envelope Knorr Leek Soup Mix

1 teaspoon dried fines herbes (see page 3)

1 cup Orville Redenbacher's Buttery Flavor Popping Oil or Wesson oil

2 tablespoons dillweed

1 tablespoon lemon pepper

$\frac{1}{2}$ teaspoon chili powder

1. Pour the crackers into a large mixing bowl. Add the soup mix, fines herbes, oil, dill, lemon pepper, and chili powder. Stir the mixture with a wooden spoon or rubber spatula, tossing to coat the crackers with the oil and spices. Continue to toss the mixture until it appears dry, about 5 minutes.

2. Store the crackers in airtight jars or resealable plastic bags at room temperature for up to 5 days, or in the freezer for 2 months. Defrost the crackers at room temperature for 1 hour before serving.

SERVES 8 TO 10

Here's the perfect munchy food for watching football games. I'm not exactly sure why this works, but I do know that you will be making extra batches for impromptu gatherings. These crackers store beautifully in resealable plastic bags in the freezer.

VARIATION: If you prefer a less hot version of this recipe, omit the chili powder.

Souper Starters

Asian Shrimp Bites

These morsels are kissing cousins to Chinese shrimp toasts, except they are baked instead of fried. Asian Shrimp Bites can be made up ahead of time, baked, and then refrigerated until you are ready to serve them. They will require only a quick warming up in the oven before serving.

3 strips bacon

1 pound raw shrimp, peeled and deveined

½ cup sliced water chestnuts, drained

2 green onions, cut into 1-inch lengths

Flavor packet from 1 package oriental flavor ramen noodles (reserve noodles for another use)

2 tablespoons soy sauce

1 teaspoon dry sherry

Dipping sauces (recipes follow)

1. Preheat the oven to 400 degrees. Line a rimmed baking sheet with aluminum foil.

2. Place the bacon, shrimp, water chestnuts, green onions, soup mix flavor packet, soy sauce, and sherry in a food processor and pulse the machine on and off 4 to 5 times. Scrape the bowl and pulse another 3 to 4 times, until the mixture is a paste. Wet your hands and form the paste into 1-inch balls. Set them on the prepared baking sheet. (At this point, you can place the balls in an airtight container and refrigerate them overnight or freeze them for up to 1 month, defrosting them before you continue with the recipe.)

3. Bake the shrimp bites until they are golden brown, 15 to 20 minutes. Drain them on paper towels and serve them with dipping sauces.

SWEET AND PUNGENT DIPPING SAUCE

1 cup apricot preserves

½ cup Major Grey chutney

2 tablespoons fresh lemon juice

Combine all the ingredients in a food processor and process until smooth. Refrigerate the sauce until you are ready to serve it.

SOY DIPPING SAUCE

½ cup soy sauce

3 cloves garlic, minced

1 tablespoon red wine vinegar

1 tablespoon toasted sesame oil

1 teaspoon sesame seeds

In a small glass mixing bowl, stir together the soy sauce, garlic, vinegar, sesame oil, and sesame seeds. Refrigerate the sauce until you are ready to serve it.

Marinated Shrimp

I love this kind of appetizer. It looks so appealing your guests will think you slaved all afternoon in the kitchen to make it, when, in fact, it's been sitting in the refrigerator while you have been lying on the couch reading mystery novels. The marinade can be refrigerated for several days, and the shrimp should marinate for at least four hours.

½ cup olive oil

½ cup vegetable oil (canola is fine)

⅓ cup rice vinegar

¼ cup fresh lemon juice

1 envelope Knorr Leek Soup Mix

1 teaspoon dried fines herbes (see page 3)

½ cup chopped red onion

½ cup seeded and chopped green bell pepper

½ cup seeded and chopped red bell pepper

½ cup chopped fresh Italian parsley leaves

2 pounds large shrimp, cooked, peeled, and deveined

1. In a large glass bowl, whisk together the olive oil, vegetable oil, vinegar, lemon juice, soup mix, and fines herbes. Add the onion, bell peppers, and parsley, stirring to blend. At this point you can refrigerate the marinade for up to 2 days.

2. Add the shrimp to the bowl and toss to combine. Cover the bowl with plastic wrap, or transfer the shrimp to a large resealable plastic bag, and marinate the shrimp in the refrigerator for at least 4 hours.

3. To serve, drain the liquid from the shrimp and serve it mounded on a large platter accompanied by crusty French bread slices and toothpicks for spearing the shrimp.

THE LADIES OF THE FRENCH COURT OF LOUIS XI SUBSISTED MAINLY ON SOUP BECAUSE THEY BELIEVED THAT CHEWING WOULD CAUSE THEM TO DEVELOP FACIAL WRINKLES.

Cajun Shrimp Barbecue

SERVES 6

½ cup (1 stick) butter

¼ cup olive oil

4 cloves garlic, minced

1 envelope Lipton Savory Herb with Garlic Soup Mix

½ teaspoon freshly ground black pepper

½ teaspoon cayenne pepper

½ teaspoon sweet paprika

2 tablespoons Worcestershire sauce

¼ cup fresh lemon juice

2 pounds large shrimp, peeled and deveined (leave the tails on if you like)

French bread

When I visit New Orleans, I usually head to Mr. B's Bistro to have this dish. It has the essence of the city—juicy Gulf shrimp, spicy butter sauce, and crusty French bread to dip into the sauce. This is a dish your family and friends will enjoy often. If you would like to serve this as a family-style dinner, double the recipe.

1. In a large sauté pan, melt the butter with the oil over medium heat. Add the garlic and cook, stirring, until it has softened, about 2 minutes. Add the soup mix, black pepper, cayenne, and paprika and cook, stirring, for 3 to 4 minutes. Add the Worcestershire and lemon juice and cook, stirring, for another 3 to 4 minutes. At this point, the sauce may be refrigerated until you are ready to proceed.

2. When you are ready to serve this dish, heat the sauce to bubbling in a large skillet, add the shrimp, tossing them in the sauce, and cook the shrimp until they just turn pink. Remove the shrimp and sauce from the heat and serve them immediately with lots of French bread to dip in the sauce.

Polynesian Chicken Wings

Sweet and savory, these little bites are the perfect appetizer for an al fresco dinner on the patio. For a main course, marinate 1-inch cubes of chicken or pork, skewer them with vegetables and pineapple, and grill the ensemble over hot coals.

1 envelope Lipton Onion or Golden Onion Soup Mix

1/4 cup canola oil

1/2 cup water

1/2 cup firmly packed light brown sugar

1 cup soy sauce

1/4 cup ketchup

2 tablespoons toasted sesame oil

3 pounds chicken wing drumettes or 1 1/2 pounds chicken tenders

1 medium red bell pepper, seeded and cut into 1-inch squares

1 medium green bell pepper, seeded and cut into 1-inch squares

One 10.5-ounce can pineapple chunks, drained

1/2 cup sesame seeds for garnish

1. Combine the soup mix, canola oil, water, brown sugar, soy sauce, ketchup, and sesame oil in a small saucepan and simmer the mixture over medium heat for about 10 minutes. Let the marinade cool.

2. Wash the chicken in cold water, pat it dry, and place it in a large baking dish or resealable plastic bag. Pour the marinade over the chicken, making sure everything is coated evenly, and marinate the chicken overnight, refrigerated, turning the chicken in the marinade several times.

3. When you are ready to bake the chicken, preheat the oven to 350 degrees, and coat a 13-by-9-inch baking dish with nonstick cooking spray. Remove the chicken from the marinade, and place it in the prepared dish, stirring in the bell peppers and pineapple. Bake the chicken until it is golden brown, 30 to 40 minutes, turning it halfway through the cooking time.

4. Sprinkle the chicken with the sesame seeds to garnish. Serve hot or at room temperature.

A SPANISH PROVERB SAYS: "OF SOUP AND LOVE, THE FIRST IS BEST."

Buffalo-Style Chicken Wings

4 pounds chicken wing drumettes (the drumstick-like part of a chicken wing), washed and patted dry

³⁄₄ cup (1¹⁄₂ sticks) butter

1 envelope Lipton Golden Onion Soup Mix

2 tablespoons Tabasco sauce

1. Preheat the broiler for 10 minutes. Line a large baking dish with aluminum foil.

2. Place the chicken in a large resealable plastic bag or mixing bowl. Melt the butter in a small saucepan, add the soup mix and Tabasco, and stir until the mixture is well combined. Let the sauce cool, and then pour it over the chicken wings in the plastic bag. Stir or shake the chicken to make sure it is coated completely.

3. Place the chicken in the prepared dish and broil it for 6 minutes on each side. Reduce the oven temperature to 400 degrees. Brush the chicken with any sauce remaining in the bottom of the pan and bake the chicken until it is crispy and golden, 3 minutes more on each side. (If you would like to make the wings ahead of time, cook them to this stage, and then let them cool, cover them with plastic wrap, and refrigerate them. When you are ready to serve them, heat the wings in a preheated 400-degree oven until they are warmed through, about 10 minutes.) Serve immediately.

These wings may be baked, rather than deep-fried like the original, but you won't be able to get enough of these savory bites. Plan to make a double batch, so you can reheat them in the toaster oven for a quick snack. Traditionally these wings are served with Maytag Blue Cheese Dressing (page 117) and celery sticks.

Souper Starters

Smoked Salmon Cheesecake

2 tablespoons butter

1/2 cup finely chopped red onion

1/2 cup seeded and finely chopped yellow bell pepper

1/2 cup seeded and finely chopped red bell pepper

2 cloves garlic, minced

Three 8-ounce packages cream cheese, softened

2 cups sour cream

1 can Campbell's Condensed Cream of Celery Soup

2 large eggs

1/2 cup flaked smoked salmon

2 tablespoons finely chopped fresh dill or 1 tablespoon dillweed

1/2 teaspoon freshly ground black pepper

Chopped fresh dill and red onion for garnish

Crackers, French bread, and cucumber rounds

Savory cheesecake makes a dramatic statement before dinner. Your guests will want the recipe for this tall and stately cheesecake studded with smoky nuggets of salmon, herbs, sweet peppers, and onions. This dish is best made a day ahead and refrigerated; it can be frozen for up to one month.

1. Preheat the oven to 350 degrees. Coat the sides and bottom of a 9-inch springform pan with nonstick cooking spray.

2. In a small sauté pan, melt the butter over medium heat, add the onion, bell peppers, and garlic, and cook, stirring, until the vegetables begin to soften, about 4 minutes. Remove the pan from the heat and allow the vegetables to cool.

3. In a large mixing bowl, using an electric mixer, cream together the cream cheese, 1 cup of the sour cream, the soup, and eggs until smooth. Stir in the sautéed vegetables, salmon, dill, and black pepper until well combined. Pour the mixture into the prepared springform pan and bake for 1 hour. Turn off the oven and let the pan stand in the oven for 30 minutes. (This helps to prevent cracking.) Let the cheesecake cool completely in the pan and then refrigerate it until serving time.

THE MOCK TURTLE IN Alice's Adventures in Wonderland SAID, "SOUP OF THE EVENING, BEAUTIFUL SOUP."

4. When you are ready to serve the cheesecake, release the pan from the cheesecake and slide the cheesecake onto a serving platter. Spread the remaining 1 cup sour cream over the cheesecake like an icing, and garnish with additional chopped fresh dill and chopped red onion. Serve the cheesecake with crackers, French bread slices, and cucumber rounds.

Shrimply Delicious Cheesecake

2 tablespoons butter

1/2 cup finely chopped shallots

1/3 cup seeded and finely chopped yellow or red bell pepper

2 cloves garlic, minced

1 tablespoon Creole Seasoning (page 458)

2 cups finely chopped cooked shrimp

Three 8-ounce packages cream cheese, softened

1 can Campbell's Condensed Cream of Shrimp Soup

2 large eggs

1/2 cup mayonnaise

2 teaspoons fresh lemon juice

1 1/2 teaspoons Worcestershire sauce

6 shakes Tabasco sauce

Large cooked shrimp, sprigs fresh Italian parsley, and lemon slices for garnish

1. Preheat the oven to 325 degrees. Coat the sides and bottom of a 9-inch springform pan with nonstick cooking spray.

2. In a small sauté pan, melt the butter over medium heat, add the shallots, bell pepper, garlic, Cajun seasoning, and shrimp, and cook, stirring, until the vegetables begin to soften, 3 to 4 minutes. Remove the pan from the heat and let the mixture cool.

SERVES 10

Here is another savory cheesecake, but this time the stars of the show are Creole seasonings and shrimp. You could substitute crab for the shrimp if you'd like. This cheesecake is also delicious made in individual ramekins and served as a first course with Creamy Shrimp Sauce (recipe follows).

3. In a large mixing bowl, using an electric mixer, cream together the cream cheese and soup until smooth. Add the eggs, mayonnaise, lemon juice, Worcestershire, and Tabasco, blending until smooth. Fold in the shrimp and vegetable mixture and pour the batter into the prepared pan. Bake for 1 hour. Turn off the oven and let the cheesecake stand in the oven or 30 minutes. Remove from the oven and let the cheesecake cool completely in the pan and then refrigerate it until serving time.

4. When you are ready to serve the cheesecake, release the pan from the cheesecake and slide the cheesecake onto a serving platter. Garnish with shrimp, parsley sprigs, and lemon slices. Serve with crackers, French bread slices, and cucumber rounds.

CREAMY SHRIMP SAUCE

2 tablespoons butter

2 tablespoons chopped shallots

1 teaspoon Old Bay seasoning

1 can Campbell's Condensed Cream of Shrimp Soup

2 teaspoons cream sherry

1 cup milk

$1/8$ teaspoon freshly grated nutmeg

1. Melt the butter in a 2-quart saucepan over medium heat, add the shallots and Old Bay seasoning, and cook, stirring, until the shallots soften, 2 to 3 minutes. Stir in the soup, sherry, and milk and bring the mixture to a boil.

2. Reduce the heat to low, stir in the nutmeg, and serve. Refrigerate any leftover sauce for up to 3 days.

Everyone's Favorite Party Mix

One 14-ounce box Crispix cereal (or any of the Chex cereals)

2 cups mixed nuts

Two 10-ounce bags pretzel sticks (not pretzel rods)

Two 5-ounce bags plain Pepperidge Farm Goldfish crackers

1 cup (2 sticks) butter or margarine, melted

1 envelope Lipton Savory Herb with Garlic Soup Mix

2 tablespoons Worcestershire sauce

6 shakes Tabasco sauce

1. Preheat the oven to 300 degrees.

2. Empty the cereal, nuts, pretzels, and Goldfish crackers into a large ovenproof pan.

3. Combine the melted butter, soup mix, Worcestershire, and Tabasco in a small mixing bowl, stirring to blend. Pour the mixture evenly over the cereal mixture. Using a rubber spatula, carefully blend the butter mixture into the cereal, being careful not to break any of the cereal pieces or pretzels.

4. Place the pan in the oven and bake the mix for 30 to 45 minutes, stirring every 10 to 15 minutes. Remove the pan from the oven and allow the mix to cool. Store it in resealable plastic bags.

SERVES 8 TO 10

Every Thanksgiving I make up several batches of this delicious snack mix. Over the years, it's become as much of a tradition as the turkey itself. This snack keeps very well in the freezer, so make plenty to keep on hand. You will need a large roasting pan for this recipe.

VARIATION: Lipton Golden Onion Soup Mix and Onion Soup Mix also work well in this recipe. Add 1 teaspoon garlic salt to the melted butter mixture.

Souper Starters

Irish Nachos

Using potato skins instead of chips, these nachos are simple to make and can be prepared ahead of time, needing just a last-minute run under the broiler before serving. Make several batches and prepare the suggested variations.

BROCCOLI SKINS: Distribute 1½ cups cooked broccoli over the soup and continue with the recipe as directed.

SANTA FE SKINS: Distribute 1 cup minced cooked chicken and ¼ cup diced green chiles over the soup and continue with the recipe as directed. Garnish with chopped fresh cilantro leaves instead of green onions.

BLUE SKINS: Substitute Campbell's Condensed Cream of Celery Soup, top with ½ cup crumbed blue cheese instead of the cheddar cheese, and continue with the recipe as directed.

6 large russet potatoes, scrubbed and dried

1 tablespoon vegetable oil

1½ teaspoons salt

1 teaspoon freshly ground black pepper

1 teaspoon Tabasco sauce

1 can Campbell's Condensed Cheddar Cheese Soup

10 strips bacon, cooked until crisp, drained on paper towels, and crumbled

4 green onions, chopped

1 cup grated sharp cheddar cheese

1 cup sour cream for garnish

1. Preheat the oven to 425 degrees. Prick each potato several times with a small paring knife. Rub the potatoes with the oil and place them in the oven. Bake the potatoes until they are soft when squeezed with a potholder, 55 to 65 minutes. Remove them from the oven.

2. When the potatoes are cool enough to handle, using a serrated knife, cut them in half lengthwise. Scoop out the pulp, reserving it for another use, leaving a ¼- to ½-inch-thick potato skin shell. Sprinkle each shell with salt and pepper.

3. Preheat the broiler for 10 minutes. Coat a baking sheet with nonstick cooking spray.

4. In a small mixing bowl, stir the Tabasco into the soup. Place 1 tablespoon of the soup in each potato skin, top with the bacon, green onions, and cheddar cheese, and broil the potato skins until the cheese is melted and bubbling. Garnish with additional green onion and the sour cream.

These colorful appetizers are known as "wrappetizers" in our house. You can vary the seasonings mixed into the cream cheese and create totally different flavors. These are best if made several hours ahead of time so the tortillas have time to soften.

That's Italian Wraps

SERVES 6

Two 8-ounce packages cream cheese, softened

1 envelope Knorr Tomato with Basil Soup Mix

2 tablespoons milk

Six 12-inch flour tortillas

1 cup prepared pesto

¼ pound thinly sliced Genoa salami, cut into thin strips

2 cups grated provolone cheese

1 cup pine nuts, plus more for garnish, toasted (see sidebar)

½ cup oil-packed sun-dried tomatoes, drained and cut into strips

Chopped fresh basil leaves for garnish

1. In a large mixing bowl, with an electric mixer, beat the cream cheese, then add the soup mix and milk and cream until smooth.

2. Place a sheet of plastic wrap on the counter and center a tortilla on it. Spread a thin layer of the cream cheese mixture over the tortilla. Top it with some of the pesto, salami, cheese, pine nuts and tomatoes. Roll up the tortilla tightly, seal it in the plastic wrap, and repeat with the remaining ingredients. Refrigerate the wraps for at least 4 hours.

3. When ready to serve, slice the rolls into 1-inch-thick rounds. Serve the rounds garnished with additional pine nuts and sprigs of fresh basil.

Toasting Pine Nuts

To toast pine nuts, place them in a skillet over medium heat and shake the pan often, so that the pine nuts toast evenly. When they are golden brown and fragrant, remove them from the pan and allow them to cool.

Souper Starters

Sombrero Wraps

Two 8-ounce packages cream cheese, softened

1 envelope Knorr Vegetable Soup Mix or Lipton Fiesta Herb
    with Red Pepper Soup Mix

2 tablespoons milk

Six 12-inch flour or corn tortillas

One 4-ounce can diced green chiles, drained and rinsed

One 4-ounce can sliced black olives, drained

2 cups grated sharp cheddar cheese

4 green onions, chopped

1 cup chopped fresh plum tomatoes

1/2 cup chopped fresh cilantro leaves, plus more for garnish

1. In a large mixing bowl, using an electric mixer, cream together the cream cheese, soup mix, and milk.

2. Place a large sheet of plastic wrap on the counter and center a tortilla on it. Spread a thin layer of the cream cheese mixture over the tortilla. Sprinkle on some of the chiles, olives, cheese, green onions, tomatoes, and cilantro. Roll up the tortilla tightly, seal it in the plastic wrap, and repeat with the remaining ingredients. Refrigerate the wraps for at least 4 hours.

3. When ready to serve, slice the wraps into 1-inch-thick rounds. Garnish them with additional cilantro.

Taking the Cake

Make a cake out of these tortillas by layering them, instead of rolling them, after they are filled. Refrigerate the "cake" for several hours and then cut it into wedges and serve.

If your grocer carries flavored "wraps," try the southwestern, spinach, or tomato basil flavors. The colors will make your dish the hit of the party.

Peking Wraps

One 8-ounce package cream cheese, softened

Flavor packet from 1 package oriental flavor ramen noodles
(reserve noodles for another use)

2 tablespoons soy sauce

Four to six 12-inch flour tortillas

$1/4$ cup hoisin sauce

2 cups finely shredded cooked chicken

6 green onions, chopped

$1^1/_2$ cups fresh bean sprouts, rinsed and dried thoroughly

$1/4$ cup grated carrot for garnish

4 green onions, cut into fans (see sidebar), for garnish

1. In a medium mixing bowl, using an electric mixer, blend the cream cheese with the ramen flavor packet. Blend in the soy sauce.

2. Place a large sheet of plastic wrap on the counter and center a tortilla on it. Spread a thin layer of the cream cheese mixture over the tortilla. Spread a small amount of the hoisin sauce over the cream cheese mixture, and then sprinkle on some chicken, green onions, and bean sprouts. Roll up the tortilla tightly and seal it in the plastic wrap. Repeat with the remaining ingredients. Refrigerate the wraps for at least 4 hours.

3. When ready to serve, cut the wraps into 1-inch-thick rounds and serve them garnished with grated carrot and green onion fans.

Souper Smart

I love to make these wraps with leftover duck, sliced thinly, and I include some crispy skin for a knock-off of Peking Duck.

Green Onion Fans

To make green onion fans, remove the roots of the green onions and cut the white part of the onions into 3-inch-long sections. Slit both ends of the section with several $1/2$-inch-deep cuts and then soak the onions in cold water in the refrigerator for one to two hours. When the ends of the onions have opened up, drain off the water and pat the onions dry.

Souper Starters

Basic Souped-Up Bruschetta

SERVES 8

In Italy, bruschetta is prepared with everything from tomatoes to wild mushrooms. Here is a great way to use up those tomatoes that are taking over your summer garden. You can make the topping a day ahead of time, letting the flavors get to know each other. The wild mushroom variation is simple, and the topping makes a great accompaniment to grilled chicken, too.

½ cup olive oil

1 envelope Lipton Savory Herb with Garlic Soup Mix

¼ cup chopped fresh basil leaves

¼ cup chopped fresh Italian parsley leaves

4 cups seeded and diced fresh tomatoes

2 cloves garlic, minced

½ teaspoon freshly ground black pepper

Toasted French bread rounds

Sprigs fresh basil and parsley for garnish

1. In a medium glass mixing bowl, whisk together the oil, soup mix, basil, and parsley until combined. Add the tomatoes, garlic, and pepper, stirring until the mixture is blended. Refrigerate the topping until you are ready to serve it.

2. Place 1 tablespoon of the tomato topping on each slice of bread, garnish it with basil and parsley sprigs, and serve.

Wild Mushroom Bruschetta

SERVES 8

Earthy crimini mushrooms make this a delectable topper for French bread rounds or a side dish with grilled chicken.

2 tablespoons butter

1 pound crimini mushrooms, sliced ½ inch thick

1 envelope Lipton Savory Herb with Garlic Soup Mix

½ cup heavy cream

2 tablespoons dry sherry

Salt and freshly ground black pepper

2 tablespoons chopped fresh Italian parsley leaves

Toasted French bread rounds

1. Melt the butter in a 10-inch skillet over medium heat. Add the mushrooms and soup mix and cook, stirring, for 4 minutes, until the liquid evaporates. Add the cream and sherry and bring to a boil. Taste and correct the seasoning with salt and pepper.

2. Stir in the parsley and serve the topping warm on French bread rounds.

Artichoke Bruschetta

SERVES 8

1 envelope Lipton Savory Herb with Garlic Soup Mix

One 14-ounce can artichoke hearts, drained and chopped

¼ cup olive oil

2 teaspoons red wine vinegar

¼ cup pine nuts, toasted (page 61)

¼ cup chopped fresh Italian parsley leaves

Toasted French bread slices

1. In a small mixing bowl, sprinkle the soup mix over the artichoke hearts. Pour the oil and vinegar over the artichokes hearts and toss to combine. Add the pine nuts and parsley, stirring to blend. (At this point, you can refrigerate the topping for up to 24 hours.)

2. Spread 1 tablespoon of the topping over each bread slice and serve.

Souper Smart

Serve all three bruschetta toppings with toasted bread rounds and allow your guests to make their own bruschetta. It helps get conversations going when you let your guests play with their food.

Spinach Squares

SERVES 8

These colorful tidbits can be prepared ahead of time and then refrigerated or frozen, so you can have on hand a spur-of-the-moment appetizer that will rate rave reviews from everyone.

ARTICHOKE SQUARES: Substitute two 14-ounce cans artichoke hearts, drained and chopped, for the spinach and continue with the recipe as directed.

ARTICHOKE-SPINACH SQUARES: Use only 1 package spinach, add one 14-ounce can artichoke hearts, drained and coarsely chopped, and continue with the recipe as directed.

2 tablespoons butter

1 cup chopped onion

Two 10-ounce packages frozen chopped spinach, defrosted and squeezed dry

6 large eggs

1 envelope Knorr Cream of Spinach Soup Mix

2 cups dry breadcrumbs

1 cup freshly grated Parmesan cheese

1/4 teaspoon freshly grated nutmeg

1. Preheat the oven to 350 degrees. Coat a 13-by-9-inch baking dish with nonstick cooking spray.

2. In a 10-inch sauté pan, melt the butter over medium heat, add the onion, and cook, stirring, until softened, 4 to 5 minutes. Add the spinach and cook, stirring, for 2 minutes.

3. Transfer the mixture to a large mixing bowl. Add the eggs, soup mix, breadcrumbs, cheese, and nutmeg and stir until combined. Pour the mixture into the prepared dish and bake until a toothpick inserted into the center comes out clean, 20 to 25 minutes. Allow the dish to rest for 10 minutes before cutting into squares.

Sausalito Sourdoughs

1 cup mayonnaise

½ cup sour cream

1 envelope Knorr Leek Soup Mix

½ cup finely chopped celery

1 cup grated cheddar cheese

1 teaspoon Worcestershire sauce

1 cup fresh lump or Dungeness crabmeat, picked over for cartilage or shells and flaked

8 English muffins, toasted

1. Preheat the broiler for 10 minutes.

2. In a small mixing bowl, combine the mayonnaise, sour cream, soup mix, celery, cheese, Worcestershire, and crabmeat, stirring to blend.

3. Spread the mixture on the muffins. Broil until the tops are golden brown. Cut each English muffin into wedges and serve immediately.

I first had these savory snacks in a small bar looking out at the Golden Gate Bridge on a gorgeous fall afternoon. They also make a great brunch dish, with two English muffin halves per person. Or serve them with a nice white wine before dinner.

VARIATION: Have any leftover turkey or chicken? Substitute it for the crabmeat.

Gazpacho Salad

Crunchy Cabbage Salad with Cashews

Souper Slaw

Asian Slaw

Herb and Garlic Mushroom Salad

Marinated Mushroom Salad

Wilted Spinach Salad

Copper Penny Salad

Bistro Carrot Salad

Tuscan Green Bean Salad

Creamy Garlic Potato Salad

Black Bean Corn Salad

Mom's Picnic Potato Salad

Olive and Caper Salad

Tomato, Cucumber, and Feta Salad

Layered Vegetable Salad with Garlic Parmesan Dressing

Grilled Vegetable Salad with Yogurt Dijon Dressing

Vegetarian Basmati Rice Salad

Pickled Vegetables

Tomato, Basil, Brie, and Pasta Salad

Tortellini Artichoke Salad

Mediterranean Pasta Salad

Cold Sesame Noodles

Shrimp Dillyicious Pasta Salad

Chicken and Dill Pasta Salad

Turkey and Dried Cranberry Salad

White Bean, Sun-Dried Tomato, and Chicken Salad

Curried Chicken and Fruit Salad

Popcorn Chicken Salad with Creole Mustard Dressing

BLT Club Salad

California Chopped Chicken Salad

Chinese Chicken Salad

Cobb Salad

Hawaiian Chicken Velvet Salad

Herbed Garden Chicken Salad

Tuna Salad

Salade Niçoise

Raspberry Shrimp and Fruit Salad

Mediterranean Seafood and Rice Salad

Grilled Shrimp Caesar Salad

Antipasto Salad

Roast Beef and Stilton Salad

Thai Pork and Noodle Salad

Taco Salad

Maytag Blue Cheese Dressing

Sweet Tomato Dressing

Ranch House Dressing

Herbed Vinaigrette

Balsamic Vinaigrette

Red Wine Vinaigrette

Souped-Up Salads and Dressings

GONE ARE THE DAYS WHEN the word *salad* conjured up the image of a rabbit daintily munching away at lettuce leaves. Today's salads are made with heartier stuff, to be enjoyed as a main course for dinner or as a substantial side dish. Using soups to make these salads, you will be able to transform the ingredients into a meal that will satisfy even the meat and potato lovers in your house.

Classic salads such as Cobb, Caesar, spinach, and tuna can be made using soups, and soup mixes and condensed soups can be blended with oil, vinegar, mayonnaise, buttermilk, herbs, and spices to make spectacular dressings. Salads are great vehicles for transforming leftovers into a deliciously new entreé the next night. With your soup arsenal at the ready, you can create any number of tasty salads for your family and friends at a moment's notice.

Gazpacho Salad

SERVES 8

This delightful summer salad takes all my favorite vegetables from the cold soup and combines them into a beautiful salad. For the best flavor, make sure to use vine-ripened tomatoes, as well as European cucumbers (they are long and thin and are sold wrapped in plastic). The dressing can be made several days ahead of time, and the vegetables can be cut up the night before, but make sure to toss the salad just before serving. A glass bowl makes an elegant presentation.

SALAD

3 cups chopped romaine lettuce

1 European cucumber, cut into ½-inch dice

½ cup chopped red onion

1 medium yellow bell pepper, seeded and cut into ½-inch dice

2 medium ripe tomatoes, cut into ½-inch dice (about 2 cups)

¼ cup seeded and chopped green bell pepper

DRESSING

½ cup canola oil

½ cup olive oil

¼ cup sherry vinegar

2 tablespoons fresh lemon juice

1 envelope Knorr Vegetable Soup Mix

GARNISHES

1 medium ripe Hass avocado, peeled, pitted, and sliced ½ inch thick

2 cups Garlic Croutons (page 111)

1. Layer the romaine, cucumber, onion, yellow pepper, tomatoes, and green pepper in that order in a medium glass serving bowl. Refrigerate until ready to serve.

2. In a small glass mixing bowl, combine the oils. Whisk in the sherry vinegar, lemon juice, and soup mix. You can refrigerate the dressing, covered, for up to 1 week.

3. When you are ready to serve the salad, pour ¾ cup of the dressing over the salad and toss, adding more dressing if needed. Garnish each serving with several slices of avocado and garlic croutons.

Crunchy Cabbage Salad with Cashews

SALAD

4 cups cored and thinly sliced green cabbage

3 medium carrots, grated

3 green onions, chopped

One 4½-ounce can mandarin orange segments, drained

1 package chicken flavor ramen noodles

DRESSING

Ramen flavor packet

½ cup canola oil

¼ cup rice vinegar

2 tablespoons toasted sesame oil

3 tablespoons sugar

GARNISH

2 cups unsalted dry-roasted cashews or peanuts

1. In a large serving bowl, combine the cabbage, carrots, green onions, and orange segments. Refrigerate until ready to toss the salad.

2. Crush the ramen noodles into ½-inch pieces.

3. Empty the ramen flavor packet into a small mixing bowl. Whisk in the canola oil, vinegar, sesame oil, and sugar, stirring until the dressing is well blended. Refrigerate until ready to serve.

4. When you are ready to serve the salad, pour the dressing over the salad and toss to coat everything evenly. Add the cashews or peanuts and noodles, tossing again. Serve immediately.

The taste of the Orient in this salad comes from ramen noodles and the soup base, which is used to make a delicious dressing. Try using romaine and adding chicken or shrimp for an entrée salad. The dressing will keep for a week refrigerated.

Souper Slaw

SERVES 8

A great side dish with barbecued chicken or beef, this colorful salad can be made a day ahead of time. If you are in a hurry, buy the bags of already cut slaw in your grocer's produce section. Feel free to substitute lowfat or nonfat mayonnaise in this dish.

IN THE PINK SLAW:
For a colorful variation, try using raspberry vinegar instead of the white vinegar.

4 cups cored and shredded green cabbage

2 cups shredded carrots

2 green onions, chopped

1½ cups mayonnaise

¼ cup white vinegar

1 package Knorr Leek Soup Mix

2 tablespoons sugar

2 tablespoons milk

2 tablespoons poppy seeds (optional)

1. Combine the cabbage, carrots, and green onions in a large serving bowl.

2. In a small mixing bowl, combine the mayonnaise, vinegar, soup mix, sugar, and milk, whisking until blended. Toss the dressing with the cabbage mixture and blend in the poppy seeds, if you are using them. Refrigerate the slaw for up to 8 hours. Drain off any excess liquid before serving.

Asian Slaw

4 cups cored Napa cabbage cut into $\frac{1}{4}$-inch-wide strips

2 cups carrot matchsticks

4 green onions, chopped

1 package oriental flavor ramen noodles

$\frac{1}{2}$ cup vegetable oil

2 tablespoons toasted sesame oil

2 tablespoons rice vinegar

1 teaspoon red pepper flakes

1 teaspoon sugar

1. Combine the cabbage, carrots, and green onions in a large serving bowl.

2. Empty the flavor packet from the ramen noodles into a small mixing bowl. In another small mixing bowl, break up the noodles into small pieces and set aside.

3. Stir the oils, vinegar, red pepper flakes, and sugar into the bowl with the flavor packet until well blended. Pour the dressing over the cabbage mixture, tossing to coat the salad evenly. Add the noodles and toss again.

4. Refrigerate the slaw for at least 1 hour and for up to 4 hours.

SERVES 6

Reminiscent of kim chee, that spicy hot Korean side dish, this slaw will make your family sit up and take notice!

Herb and Garlic Mushroom Salad

Whether you serve this salad as part of an antipasto platter or toss some of it into romaine and top it with slivers of Parmigiano-Reggiano cheese, it will become a favorite. The salad benefits from being made ahead of time and keeps for two days refrigerated.

SALAD

1 pound button mushrooms, sliced ½ inch thick

1 large onion, thinly sliced

½ cup chopped fresh Italian parsley leaves

DRESSING

1 cup olive oil

½ cup sherry vinegar

1 envelope Lipton Garlic Mushroom Soup Mix

1 teaspoon freshly ground black pepper

1. Combine the mushrooms, onion, and parsley in a large serving bowl.

2. In a 2-cup glass measuring cup, combine the oil, vinegar, soup mix, and pepper, whisking until blended.

3. Pour the dressing over the salad, tossing to combine and coat evenly.

4. Cover the salad with plastic wrap and refrigerate it for at least 6 hours and for up to 2 days.

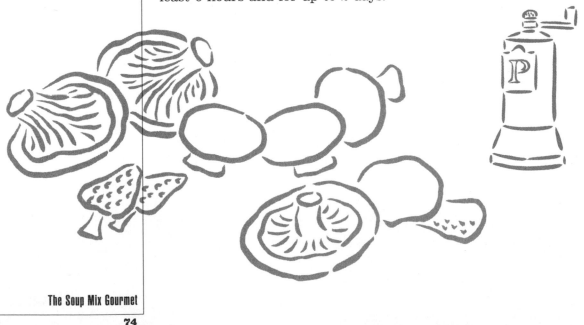

Marinated Mushroom Salad

SALAD

1 pound button mushrooms, stems trimmed

1 large onion, sliced ½ inch thick and separated into rings

DRESSING

⅔ cup red wine vinegar

½ cup vegetable oil

1 clove garlic, minced

2 teaspoons sugar

½ teaspoon freshly ground black pepper

2 teaspoons dried tarragon

4 teaspoons Tabasco sauce

1 bay leaf

1½ teaspoons dried marjoram

1 envelope Lipton Garlic Mushroom Soup Mix

1. Place the mushrooms and onion in a large serving bowl.

2. In a medium glass mixing bowl, whisk together the vinegar, oil, garlic, sugar, pepper, tarragon, Tabasco, bay leaf, marjoram, and soup mix until thoroughly combined. Pour the dressing over the mushrooms and onions and toss to coat evenly.

3. Cover the bowl with plastic wrap, refrigerate, and let the salad marinate for at least 2 hours and for up to 2 days. Remove the bay leaf before serving.

SERVES 6

These tasty morsels, fragrant with tarragon, are delicious as a side dish, served as an appetizer before dinner, or tossed into mixed field greens.

Souper Smart

If you are short on refrigerator space, store the mushrooms in a resealable plastic bag instead of in a serving bowl.

Wilted Spinach Salad

SERVES 6

The hot bacon dressing for this salad is the perfect complement for the fresh spinach leaves. You can make the dressing several hours ahead and then reheat it just before serving.

6 strips bacon, cut into 1-inch pieces

¼ cup chopped red onion

½ cup firmly packed light brown sugar

2 tablespoons Dijon mustard

¼ cup rice vinegar

1 envelope Lipton Golden Onion Soup Mix

Two 10-ounce bags baby spinach, washed well and spun dry

½ pound button mushrooms, sliced

4 hard-boiled eggs, peeled and chopped

1. Fry the bacon over medium-high heat in a 10-inch sauté pan until just crisp, add the onion, and cook, stirring, for another 2 minutes. Add the brown sugar, mustard, vinegar, and soup mix and stir until bubbling.

2. Place the spinach in a large serving bowl, pour the hot dressing over the spinach, add the mushrooms and eggs, and toss to combine well. Serve immediately.

Copper Penny Salad

SERVES 6

The carrots in this delicious salad look like copper coins.

6 cups ½-inch-thick carrot rounds

4 green onions, chopped

1 cup sugar snap peas, tough ends removed

2 cups Sweet Tomato Dressing (page 117)

1. Combine the carrots, green onions, and peas in a large serving bowl.

2. Pour the dressing over the vegetables and marinate them, covered, in the refrigerator for at least 4 hours and for up to 24 hours.

3. Pour off any extra dressing before serving the salad.

Bistro Carrot Salad

SALAD

6 cups shredded carrots

2 green onions, chopped

DRESSING

1 cup vegetable oil

½ cup red wine vinegar

¼ cup sugar

1 package Knorr Leek Soup Mix

1 teaspoon dried fines herbes (see page 3)

1. In a large serving bowl, toss together the carrots and green onions.

2. In a small mixing bowl, blend together the oil, vinegar, sugar, soup mix, and fines herbes. Pour the dressing over the carrot mixture and stir to combine.

3. Refrigerate the salad for at least 1 hour and for up to 8 hours.

SERVES 6

My favorite bistro serves this side dish with pork and chicken dishes. Colorful and simple to put together, it can be prepared a day ahead of time. The food processor makes quick work of shredding the carrots.

Tuscan Green Bean Salad

This is a delicious side dish that is best served with grilled chicken, steak, or seafood. The dressing is also good as a dipper for crusty French bread.

SALAD

2 pounds green beans, ends trimmed, cooked in boiling water to cover until crisp-tender, and drained

1 teaspoon salt

½ teaspoon freshly ground black pepper

½ cup pine nuts

½ cup smoked mozzarella cheese cut into matchsticks

DRESSING

1 cup olive oil

½ cup balsamic vinegar

1 envelope Lipton Savory Herb with Garlic Soup Mix

1 teaspoon sugar

½ teaspoon freshly ground black pepper

1. While the beans are still warm, toss them with the salt and the pepper and transfer them to a large serving bowl.

2. Place the pine nuts in a small nonstick pan over medium-high heat and toast them until golden brown, about 5 minutes. Remove the pan from the heat and allow the pine nuts to cool. Stir the pine nuts and mozzarella into the beans.

3. In a small glass mixing bowl, whisk together the oil, vinegar, soup mix, sugar, and pepper until well blended.

4. Drizzle ½ cup of the dressing over the salad, tossing until combined. Let the salad sit at room temperature for 2 hours; otherwise refrigerate it until 30 minutes before you are ready to serve it, then take it out and let it come to room temperature again. Serve the salad with the additional dressing on the side.

Creamy Garlic Potato Salad

8 medium red potatoes (about 3 pounds)

5 cloves garlic

1½ teaspoons salt

1 teaspoon freshly ground black pepper

½ cup chopped red onion

3 stalks celery, chopped

1½ cups mayonnaise

2 tablespoons Dijon mustard

¼ cup chopped fresh Italian parsley leaves

1 envelope Lipton Savory Herb with Garlic Soup Mix

1. Place the potatoes and garlic in a 5-quart saucepan with water to cover. Bring to a boil and let the potatoes cook until they are tender, 25 to 35 minutes. Drain the potatoes, saving the garlic cloves.

2. When the potatoes are cool, cut them into bite-size pieces and place in a large mixing bowl. Season them with the salt and pepper, add the onion and celery, and toss to combine.

3. In a medium mixing bowl, mash the boiled garlic cloves, add the mayonnaise, mustard, parsley, and soup mix, and whisk to blend. Pour the dressing over the potatoes and toss the salad until the potatoes are evenly coated.

4. Cover the bowl tightly and refrigerate the salad for at least 2 hours and for up to 24 hours.

Just like the title suggests, this creamy potato salad has a delicious garlic flavor. Great with grilled steak, chicken, or fish, it's best made early in the day if you are serving it for dinner.

Your Own Carry-Along "Refrigerator"

Mayonnaise-based salads should be kept refrigerated or cold at all times to prevent spoilage. You can make your own "cooler" by lining a cardboard soft drink case with aluminum foil and then filling it with ice cubes. Set your salad bowl on the ice and cover the entire box with a towel. This is a great portable cooler, and you can throw it away when you are done!

Black Bean Corn Salad

This colorful, nutritious salad is a great one-dish meal for summer patio dining. You can also serve it as a dip using yellow and blue corn tortilla chips. The dressing can be made three days ahead of time and refrigerated until you are ready to serve the salad. The salad should be put together the day you plan to serve it. Toss in some cooked chicken if you'd like.

SALAD

Two 15-ounce cans black beans, drained and rinsed

1 cup peeled and chopped jícama

$\frac{1}{4}$ cup chopped green onions

2 cups corn kernels, either cut fresh from the cob or frozen (and defrosted)

$\frac{1}{2}$ cup seeded and chopped red bell pepper

DRESSING

2 cups chopped fresh tomatoes

1 medium ripe Hass avocado, peeled, pitted, and cut into $\frac{1}{2}$-inch dice

$\frac{1}{4}$ cup chopped red onion

$\frac{1}{2}$ cup seeded and chopped Anaheim chile

$\frac{1}{4}$ cup chopped fresh cilantro leaves

$\frac{1}{3}$ cup fresh lime juice

1 cup vegetable oil

1 envelope Lipton Savory Herb with Garlic Soup Mix

$\frac{1}{2}$ teaspoon freshly ground black pepper

1. In a large salad bowl, combine the black beans, jícama, green onions, corn, and bell pepper. Stir to combine, cover with plastic wrap, and refrigerate.

2. In a medium glass mixing bowl, stir together the tomatoes, avocado, onion, chile, cilantro, lime juice, oil, soup mix, and black pepper. Refrigerate the dressing until you are ready to serve the salad.

3. To serve, toss the dressing with the salad until all the ingredients are well coated.

Mom's Picnic Potato Salad

2½ pounds red potatoes, scrubbed but not peeled

½ cup finely chopped celery

¼ cup finely chopped red onion

4 hard-boiled eggs, peeled and chopped

1 teaspoon salt

½ teaspoon freshly ground black pepper

1½ cups mayonnaise

1 envelope Knorr Leek Soup Mix

¼ cup Dijon mustard

¼ cup milk

2 tablespoons chopped fresh dill or 1 tablespoon dillweed

1. Place the potatoes in a 5-quart saucepan with water to cover. Bring the pot to a boil and simmer the potatoes, partially covered, until they are tender when pierced with a fork, 20 to 25 minutes. Drain the potatoes and refrigerate them until they are completely cool.

2. Peel the potatoes or leave the skins on (depending on your preference), and cut into bite-size pieces. Place the potatoes in a large serving bowl. Add the celery, onion, and eggs, tossing to combine. Sprinkle the potatoes with the salt and pepper, stirring to blend.

3. In a small mixing bowl, combine the mayonnaise, soup mix, mustard, milk, and dill with a whisk. When the mixture is smooth, spread it over the potatoes and stir until the dressing is incorporated.

4. Cover the bowl tightly and refrigerate the salad for at least 4 hours before serving.

SERVES 8

A quick survey of potato salad lovers will probably reveal that Mom did make the best potato salad, but since there are more versions of this salad than there are moms, I am including one that is pretty close to my mom's. Flavored with dill, and with the addition of hard-boiled eggs, this salad is great to serve alongside Mom's Barbecue Beef Brisket (page 397), Onion Burgers (page 372), or any picnic food that you enjoy.

The Best Potatoes for the Best Potato Salad

The best potatoes to use for potato salad are a waxy type, such as red or white "new" potatoes. Yukon Gold potatoes also make a wonderful golden salad.

Souped-Up Salads and Dressings

Olive and Caper Salad

SERVES 8

A salty and savory side dish, this salad is great served on mixed greens with rounds of smooth goat cheese, or as a filling for those great New Orleans treats, muffaletta sandwiches, which are layers of Italian meats and cheeses on crusty bread. You can prepare this salad up to one week ahead of time.

SALAD

2 cups pitted Kalamata olives, drained

1½ cups pimiento-stuffed green olives, drained

1 cup pitted black olives, drained

1½ cups capers, drained

½ cup chopped red onion

2 cloves garlic, minced

1 cup chopped celery

DRESSING

½ cup vegetable oil

¼ cup extra virgin olive oil

¼ cup red wine vinegar

1 envelope Lipton Savory Herb with Garlic Soup Mix

½ teaspoon freshly ground black pepper

2 tablespoons chopped fresh Italian parsley leaves

1. In a large glass mixing bowl, place the olives, capers, onion, garlic, and celery and stir to combine.

2. In a small mixing bowl, whisk together the oils, vinegar, soup mix, pepper, and parsley. Pour the dressing over the olive mixture and stir.

3. Cover the bowl tightly and refrigerate the salad for at least 6 hours before serving. If refrigerator space is an issue, you can store the salad in a large heavy-duty resealable plastic bag.

Tomato, Cucumber, and Feta Salad

SALAD

6 large ripe tomatoes, cut into $\frac{1}{2}$-inch dice

2 European cucumbers, cut into $\frac{1}{2}$-inch dice

$\frac{1}{2}$ cup chopped red onion

DRESSING

$1\frac{1}{4}$ cups olive oil

$\frac{1}{2}$ cup red wine vinegar

1 envelope Lipton Savory Herb with Garlic Soup Mix

$\frac{1}{4}$ cup chopped fresh dill

$\frac{1}{2}$ teaspoon freshly ground black pepper

1 cup crumbled feta cheese (try using a flavored feta for extra pizzazz)

GARNISH

$\frac{1}{2}$ cup chopped fresh Italian parsley leaves

1. Place the tomatoes, cucumbers, and onion in a large serving bowl.

2. In a small mixing bowl, whisk together the oil, vinegar, soup mix, dill, pepper, and feta. Pour the dressing over the vegetables and toss until combined. Refrigerate the salad for up to 6 hours before serving.

3. Garnish it with the parsley before serving.

SERVES 8

This cooling summer salad is a great way to use up those garden tomatoes and cucumbers that are taking over the yard. Serve this dish on the side with grilled meats or seafood, or use it as a salsa to give grilled sea bass a Mediterranean flavor.

Layered Vegetable Salad with Garlic Parmesan Dressing

Another throwback to potluck suppers, this layered salad is nothing like its older cousin, with layered vegetables covered with mayonnaise. The creamy garlic dressing accents all the colorful vegetables, and I like to serve this salad in a large glass serving bowl for a brilliant presentation. For barbecues or as part of a cold buffet, this salad will be a showstopper at your next party. The dressing is great on mixed greens, and you can also toss it with chicken and celery for a delicious chicken salad.

SALAD

4 cups thinly sliced iceberg or romaine lettuce

1 large red bell pepper, seeded and cut into $1/4$-inch-thick rings

1 medium green bell pepper, seeded and cut into $1/4$-inch-thick rings

$1^1/2$ cups thinly sliced or grated carrots

4 stalks celery, thinly sliced

1 European cucumber, thinly sliced

4 hard-boiled eggs, peeled and thinly sliced

1 medium red onion, cut into $1/2$-inch-thick slices

2 cups frozen petite peas, defrosted

GARLIC PARMESAN DRESSING

$1^1/2$ cups mayonnaise

$1/2$ cup milk

1 envelope Lipton Savory Herb with Garlic Soup Mix or Knorr Leek Soup Mix

$1/2$ cup freshly grated Parmesan cheese

$1/2$ teaspoon freshly ground black pepper

6 shakes Tabasco sauce

GARNISHES

2 cups grated sharp cheddar cheese

$1/2$ pound sliced bacon, cooked until crisp, drained on paper towels, and crumbled

1. In a large serving bowl, layer the lettuce, red and green peppers, carrots, celery, cucumber, hard-boiled eggs, onion, and peas.

2. In a small mixing bowl, whisk together the mayonnaise, milk, and soup mix. Gradually add the Parmesan, black pepper, and Tabasco, stirring until blended. Pour the dressing over the salad and cover with the cheddar cheese and bacon.

3. Cover the bowl tightly and refrigerate the salad for at least 12 hours before serving.

Grilled Vegetable Salad with Yogurt Dijon Dressing

DRESSING

1½ cups nonfat plain yogurt

¼ cup Dijon mustard

½ cup crumbled feta cheese

1 tablespoon fresh lemon juice

2 tablespoons chopped fresh dill or 1 tablespoon dillweed

1 teaspoon salt

½ teaspoon freshly ground black pepper

SALAD

1 cup olive oil

1 envelope Lipton Savory Herb with Garlic Soup Mix

1 teaspoon dried rosemary

1 teaspoon freshly ground black pepper

1 medium eggplant, ends trimmed and cut into ³/₄-inch-thick rounds

1 large onion, cut into ½-inch-thick rounds

2 medium red bell peppers, seeded and cut into 1-inch-thick rings

3 medium zucchini, ends trimmed and cut into ½-inch-thick rounds

2 portobello mushrooms, stems removed

SERVES 8

This colorful dish can be made a day ahead and arranged on a serving platter. All you need to do is drizzle the tangy yogurt dressing over the vegetables before serving. The grilled vegetables are also great in a sandwich. Spread dressing on each slice of bread and then layer the veggies on top.

1. In a medium mixing bowl, whisk together the dressing ingredients until blended. Refrigerate the dressing until you are ready to use it.

2. In a 2-cup measuring cup, whisk together the oil, soup mix, rosemary, and black pepper.

3. Preheat the broiler for 20 minutes and line baking sheets with aluminum foil.

4. Place the eggplant rounds on the prepared baking sheet, brush the eggplant with the flavored oil, and broil the eggplant until it is golden, turning and brushing the rounds with additional oil, and broiling them until the other side is golden. Remove the eggplant from the baking sheets and repeat with the rest of the vegetables, brushing them with the flavored oil and broiling them until they are softened and browned.

5. If you are grilling the vegetables, use a grill basket to prevent the vegetables from falling through the grates. Brush each side with the flavored oil and grill the vegetables until they are softened and cooked through. Each vegetable will take a different amount of time, so watch each batch carefully and remove the vegetables from the grill when they are done.

6. Remove the vegetables to a serving platter and refrigerate them or leave them out at room temperature until you are ready to serve them.

7. To serve, drizzle the vegetables with the dressing.

Vegetarian Basmati Rice Salad

SALAD

4 cups cooked basmati rice, cooled

1 medium red bell pepper, seeded and chopped

1 medium yellow bell pepper, seeded and chopped

1/2 cup chopped celery

4 green onions, chopped

1 cup chopped fresh spinach, well washed

1 cup grated carrots

1 cup fresh or frozen (and defrosted) petite peas

DRESSING

1 1/2 cups vegetable oil

1/3 cup rice vinegar

1 envelope Knorr Cream of Spinach Soup Mix

1. Place the cooled rice in a large serving bowl. Add the bell peppers, celery, green onions, spinach, carrots, and peas.

2. In a medium mixing bowl, whisk together the oil, vinegar, and soup mix until blended. Pour half of the dressing over the rice and vegetables, stirring until the ingredients are coated.

3. Cover the bowl tightly and refrigerate the salad and remaining dressing for at least 2 hours. When you are ready to serve the salad, add more dressing as needed.

Basmati rice is an aromatic rice, and this colorful salad studded with chopped veggies is a welcome addition to any dinner table. Make sure to cool the rice completely before assembling the salad. Then it can be refrigerated for up to 24 hours.

Pickled Vegetables

This simple recipe makes hearty broccoli, cauliflower, and carrots into a delicious side dish. The marinade can be made several days ahead of time, and the vegetables get better if they marinate for a day or two before serving.

2 cups broccoli florets

2 cups ¼-inch-thick carrot slices

2 cups cauliflower florets

1 small red onion, thinly sliced

1 medium red bell pepper, seeded and cut into ½-inch-wide strips

1½ cups vegetable oil

⅔ cup red wine vinegar

¼ cup sugar

1 envelope Lipton Savory Herb with Garlic Soup Mix

1 teaspoon dried oregano

1. Place the vegetables in a large resealable plastic bag or glass bowl.

2. In a medium mixing bowl, whisk together the oil, vinegar, sugar, soup mix, and oregano. Pour the dressing over the vegetables and stir to blend.

3. Cover the bowl tightly or zip up the plastic bag and refrigerate the vegetables for at least 24 hours and for up to 4 days, stirring or rotating the bag often.

4. Pour off the marinade and serve the vegetables as part of an antipasto platter or alongside grilled meats or poultry.

Tomato, Basil, Brie, and Pasta Salad

8 quarts water

12 ounces fresh fettuccine

1½ cups olive oil

1 envelope Lipton Savory Herb with Garlic Soup Mix

2 large ripe tomatoes, seeded and coarsely chopped

1 cup packed fresh basil leaves, roughly chopped

1 teaspoon freshly ground black pepper

½ pound Brie cheese, cut into ½-inch-thick slices

1. In a large pot, heat the water to boiling and add the fettuccine. Bring the water back to a boil and then turn off the heat and drain the pasta. Toss it with 2 tablespoons of the oil.

2. In a large serving bowl, combine the remaining oil with the soup mix, whisking until combined. Add the tomatoes, basil, pepper, and all but 6 slices of the Brie to the fettuccine and toss with ³/4 cup of the dressing, stirring to combine.

3. Refrigerate the salad for at least 2 hours. One hour before serving, remove the salad from the refrigerator and let it come to room temperature. If the salad needs more dressing, add some and toss the salad just before serving. Garnish with the remaining slices of Brie.

This colorful and tasty salad is a favorite with my students. Easily put together in the morning, it just needs a nice white wine and some grilled seafood to make the perfect al fresco dinner.

BRIE

Tortellini Artichoke Salad

This colorful side dish of spinach and egg tortellini gets its punch from a delightful balsamic vinaigrette.

VARIATION: For a whole-meal salad, try adding 2 cups of shredded cooked chicken or turkey.

SALAD

24 ounces fresh cheese tortellini (I like to use ½ spinach and ½ egg pasta), cooked al dente, drained, and tossed with 3 tablespoons olive oil

½ cup chopped red onion

½ cup chopped celery

1 medium yellow bell pepper, seeded and cut into matchsticks

1 medium red bell pepper, seeded and cut into matchsticks

Two 14-ounce cans artichoke hearts, drained and quartered

DRESSING

1½ cups olive oil

⅓ cup balsamic vinegar

1 envelope Knorr Leek Soup Mix

1 teaspoon dried fines herbes (see page 3)

1 teaspoon freshly ground black pepper

¼ cup chopped fresh chives

1. In a large serving bowl, combine the tortellini, onion, celery, bell peppers, and artichoke hearts.

2. In a medium mixing bowl, whisk together the oil, vinegar, soup mix, fines herbes, black pepper, and chives. Pour the dressing over the pasta and vegetables, tossing until combined.

3. Refrigerate the salad for at least 2 hours before serving.

Mediterranean Pasta Salad

SALAD

1 pound shell-shaped pasta, cooked al dente, drained well, and tossed with 2 tablespoons olive oil

½ cup chopped red onion

1 cup chopped European cucumber

1 medium yellow bell pepper, seeded and chopped

1 medium red bell pepper, seeded and chopped

½ cup chopped celery

1 cup pitted Kalamata olives, chopped

One 4-ounce jar marinated artichoke hearts, drained and cut into quarters

DRESSING

½ cup vegetable oil

½ cup olive oil

⅓ cup red wine vinegar

1 envelope Knorr Tomato Basil Soup Mix

1 teaspoon freshly ground black pepper

2 tablespoons chopped fresh basil leaves

2 tablespoons chopped fresh Italian parsley leaves

1 cup crumbled feta cheese

1. In a large serving bowl, toss together the pasta, onion, cucumber, bell peppers, celery, olives, and artichoke hearts. Refrigerate the salad for up to 24 hours.

2. In a medium glass mixing bowl, whisk together the oils, vinegar, soup mix, black pepper, basil, parsley, and feta until well blended. Pour 1 cup of the dressing over the salad and toss.

3. Refrigerate the salad for at least 6 hours. When ready to serve, toss the salad with the remaining dressing.

SERVES 8

A great addition to any picnic basket, potluck dinner, or barbecue, this salad comes together in minutes, and the results are delicious. Make the dressing up to three days ahead of time, and put the salad together the day before you intend to serve it. Vary the vegetables and pasta shapes to suit your own tastes; try adding a flavored feta cheese to the dressing, or, for a whole-meal salad, add cooked chicken, steak, lamb, or seafood.

Souper Smart

Olive oil has a tendency to solidify when refrigerated. A quick zap in the microwave will help it to liquefy. Otherwise, use half vegetable oil and half olive oil for a dressing that is ready to go anytime.

Cold Sesame Noodles

On a hot summer day in New York City, a friend took me to a hole-in-the-wall Chinese restaurant for lunch. The last thing I expected to eat was this cool, soothing salad. An old Chinese proverb says that long noodles are the metaphor for a long life, so don't crush the noodles; leave them long!

VARIATION: To make this a whole-meal salad, add grilled shrimp, scallops, or thinly sliced chicken or beef.

4 packages chicken flavor ramen noodles

½ cup vegetable oil

3 tablespoons toasted sesame oil

½ cup sesame seeds

2 medium shallots, chopped

1 clove garlic, minced

1 teaspoon peeled and minced fresh ginger

2 tablespoons soy sauce

3 tablespoons rice vinegar

3 tablespoons sugar

6 shakes Tabasco sauce

½ cup snow peas, blanched in boiling water for 1 minute, drained, and sliced in half on the diagonal

1 cup thinly sliced green onions

½ cup thin 1-inch-long carrot strips

½ cup chopped unsalted dry-roasted peanuts for garnish

¼ cup chopped fresh cilantro leaves for garnish

1. Fill a 5-quart saucepan with water, bring to a boil, add the ramen noodles (reserving the flavor packets), bring to a boil again, and then remove it from the heat. Drain the noodles and place them in a large mixing bowl. Toss them with 2 tablespoons of the vegetable oil.

2. In a 10-inch skillet, heat the remaining 6 tablespoons vegetable oil with the sesame oil over medium heat. Add the sesame seeds and toast them for about 2 minutes. Add the shallots, garlic, and ginger and cook, stirring, for another 2 minutes. Remove the skillet from the heat and let the mixture cool.

3. Transfer the mixture to a blender or food processor and add the soy sauce, rice vinegar, sugar, Tabasco, and flavor packets from the ramen noodles. Process the dressing until it is smooth. Toss the noodles with half the dressing. Then add the snow peas, green onions, and carrots, tossing until blended. Add more dressing if needed.

4. Mound the noodles in a large serving bowl and garnish with peanuts and cilantro.

Shrimp Dillyicious Pasta Salad

SALAD
1 pound rotelle pasta, cooked al dente, drained, and tossed with 2 tablespoons vegetable oil

½ cup chopped celery

½ cup peeled, seeded, and chopped cucumber

½ cup chopped red onion

1 pound medium shrimp, peeled, deveined, and cooked

DRESSING
1 cup mayonnaise

½ cup milk

1 envelope Knorr Leek Soup Mix

¼ cup chopped fresh dill or 2 tablespoons dillweed

1. Place the drained pasta in a large serving bowl. Add the celery, cucumber, onion, and shrimp.

2. In a small mixing bowl, whisk together the mayonnaise, milk, soup mix, and dill, stirring until they are blended. Pour the dressing over the pasta mixture and stir to combine. Refrigerate the salad until you are ready to serve it.

SERVES 8

This is an old favorite at our house. The pink shrimp and bright green dill make this colorful and tasty salad one that your family will love. If you would like to use tuna, it works well, as does chicken or leftover cooked salmon. Make the salad at least four hours before serving.

Chicken and Dill Pasta Salad

SERVES 8

This creamy salad is a wonderful summer supper for the patio. Serve it with a cool fruit soup and some garlic bread for a special after-noon or evening. This salad benefits from being made ahead of time so that the flavors can get to know each other.

To Dress or Not to Dress

Some of us prefer our salads "dry," or without a lot of dressing; others love the dressing and want lots of it. I suggest that you toss your salads with about half of the dressing and then taste and decide if you want to add more. Sometimes, as is the case with pasta salads, the ingredients will absorb a lot of dress-ing, and you will need to add more right before serving.

DILL DRESSING

1 cup mayonnaise

$1/2$ cup sour cream

$1/4$ cup milk

1 package Knorr Leek Soup Mix

$1/4$ cup chopped fresh dill or 2 tablespoons dillweed

2 tablespoons fresh lemon juice

$1/4$ cup freshly grated Parmesan cheese

$1/4$ teaspoon freshly ground black pepper

SALAD

Two 9-ounce packages fresh cheese tortellini, cooked according to the package directions, drained, and cooled

2 tablespoons olive oil

$1/2$ cup finely chopped red onion

1 cup finely chopped celery

1 cup golden raisins

Two 4-ounce jars marinated artichoke hearts, drained and chopped

$1^1/2$ cups seedless red grapes

2 cups $1/2$-inch chunks cooked chicken or turkey

1. In a medium glass mixing bowl, whisk together all the dressing ingredients until they are thoroughly combined. The dressing can be refrigerated, covered, for up to 1 week.

2. In a large serving bowl, toss the cooked pasta with the olive oil until evenly coated. Add the onion, celery, raisins, arti-choke hearts, grapes, and chicken or turkey and toss. Pour on the dressing and stir to combine and coat the ingredients even-ly. Taste the salad for seasoning, adding more salt, pepper, or dill to suit your taste. The salad can be refrigerated, covered, for up to 24 hours before serving.

Turkey and Dried Cranberry Salad

SALAD

4 cups 1/2-inch cubes cooked turkey

1 cup chopped celery

1 cup dried cranberries

1/2 cup chopped pecans

DRESSING

1 1/2 cups mayonnaise

1/4 cup milk

1 teaspoon fresh lemon juice

1 envelope Knorr Leek Soup Mix

1. In a large serving bowl, combine the turkey, celery, cranberries, and pecans. Stir to blend.

2. In a medium mixing bowl, whisk together the mayonnaise, milk, lemon juice, and soup mix. Pour 1/2 cup of the dressing over the turkey mixture, stirring to combine. Add more as necessary and serve remaining dressing on the side.

SERVES 6

A great way to recycle that Thanksgiving turkey, this salad benefits from being made ahead of time. Serve it on field greens, or as a sandwich filling using rye or seven-grain bread.

IN 1928, CLASSIC KNORR SOUP MIXES WERE EXPORTED TO THE UNITED STATES.

Souped-Up Salads and Dressings

White Bean, Sun-Dried Tomato, and Chicken Salad

When I'm asked to bring something for a picnic or barbecue, this unusual salad is always a winner. The beans soak up the tangy dressing, and the sun-dried tomatoes provide color and a great flavor for the dish. If you would like to substitute cooked shrimp for the chicken, you will need about a pound of medium shrimp.

DRESSING

1 cup olive oil

1/2 cup oil-packed sun-dried tomatoes, drained, reserving the oil, and chopped

1/3 cup red wine vinegar

1 envelope Lipton Savory Herb with Garlic Soup Mix

1/4 cup chopped fresh chives

1 teaspoon freshly ground black pepper

SALAD

One 15-ounce can small white beans, drained and rinsed

4 cups shredded cooked chicken

1/2 cup chopped red onion

1/4 cup packed fresh basil leaves, chopped

6 cups field greens

1. In a small mixing bowl, whisk together the olive oil, reserved sun-dried tomato oil, tomatoes, vinegar, soup mix, chives, and pepper until blended. Refrigerate the dressing until you are ready to use it.

2. In a large serving bowl, gently toss together the beans, chicken, onion, and basil. Toss these ingredients with 3/4 cup of the dressing, tasting for seasoning. Mound the salad on field greens and serve additional dressing on the side.

Curried Chicken and Fruit Salad

SALAD

4 cups $\frac{1}{2}$-inch cubes cooked chicken or turkey

$\frac{1}{2}$ cup chopped celery

2 green onions, chopped

1 cup peeled, cored, and chopped apple

2 cups $\frac{1}{2}$-inch cubes cantaloupe

1 cup $\frac{1}{2}$-inch cubes fresh pineapple

1 cup dry-roasted salted peanuts or cashews

DRESSING

$1\frac{1}{2}$ cups mayonnaise

$\frac{1}{4}$ cup milk

Flavor packet from 1 package chicken flavor ramen noodles (reserve the noodles for another use)

1 teaspoon curry powder

$\frac{1}{4}$ cup Major Grey chutney

GARNISH

$\frac{1}{2}$ cup sweetened shredded coconut (optional)

1. Combine the chicken, celery, green onions, apple, cantaloupe, pineapple, and peanuts in a large serving bowl.

2. In a medium mixing bowl, mix together the mayonnaise, milk, ramen flavor packet, curry powder, and chutney. Pour the dressing over the salad, tossing to combine.

3. Cover the bowl tightly and refrigerate the salad for at least 1 hour and for up to 6 hours. Toss the salad again before serving. Garnish with the coconut, if desired.

This salad has something different in every bite, a little chicken, some fruit, crunchy peanuts, and a dynamite curry and chutney dressing.

Souper Smart

Not all chutneys are sweet and cooling. Major Grey is a type of chutney that you will find readily at your grocer; it is a sweeter chutney. If you prefer to kick up the heat, buy a hot mango chutney.

Souped-Up Salads and Dressings

Popcorn Chicken Salad with Creole Mustard Dressing

Spicy warm chicken morsels crackling with a delectable coating make this simple Southern dish irresistible. The honey mustard dressing cools down the heat of the chicken. Leftover chicken and dressing make a great sandwich with vine-ripened tomatoes and fresh lettuce. The Creole Mustard Dressing keeps in the refrigerator for one week.

CHICKEN

1 package Knorr Tomato with Basil Soup Mix

2 teaspoons cayenne pepper

1½ cups all-purpose flour

4 boneless, skinless chicken breast halves, cut into 1-inch chunks

4 cups vegetable oil

CREOLE MUSTARD DRESSING

1 cup mayonnaise

⅓ cup Creole mustard

3 tablespoons honey

2 teaspoons fresh lemon juice

¼ cup chopped onion

2 tablespoons poppy seeds

SALAD

Mixed greens

Sliced red onion

3 medium ripe tomatoes, cut into wedges

1. In a medium mixing bowl or resealable plastic bag, combine the soup mix, cayenne, and flour. Add the chicken and toss to coat.

2. Heat the oil to 350 degrees in a deep skillet, Dutch oven, or deep fryer. Add the chicken a few pieces at a time and fry it until it is golden brown. With a slotted spoon, remove the chicken to paper towels to drain. (The chicken can be kept warm, covered so it won't dry out, in a preheated 300-degree oven for about 20 minutes.)

Creole Mustard

Creole mustard is a whole-grain mustard that's a little spicy. Zatarain's is a brand that seems to be widely available. You can find it in the mustard section of your grocery store.

3. In a small mixing bowl, combine the dressing ingredients, whisking until blended. Toss some of the dressing with the mixed greens on a large serving plate, arrange the onion and tomatoes around the outside of the plate, mound the chicken on the center of the greens, and pass the remaining dressing.

BLT Club Salad

SERVES 6

SALAD

4 cups ½-inch cubes cooked chicken or turkey

3 cups chopped iceberg lettuce

12 strips bacon, cooked until crisp, drained on paper towels, and crumbled

DRESSING

2 cups mayonnaise

1 envelope Knorr Leek Soup Mix

2 tablespoons fresh lemon juice

¼ cup milk

½ cup oil-packed sun-dried tomatoes, drained and cut into matchsticks

2 tablespoons chopped fresh Italian parsley leaves

GARNISH

2 cups Garlic Croutons (page 111)

My husband, Chuck, loves a club sandwich, and when I came up with this salad, he gave it two thumbs up. It has all his favorites in one salad, with a bit of a twist— using sun-dried tomatoes in place of fresh tomatoes.

1. Combine the chicken or turkey, lettuce, and bacon in a large serving bowl. Refrigerate the ingredients until you are ready to serve the salad.

2. In a medium mixing bowl, combine the mayonnaise, soup mix, lemon juice, milk, tomatoes, and parsley, stirring to blend. Pour half of the dressing over the salad and stir to blend. Add the croutons and toss the salad with more of the dressing if needed. Serve the remaining dressing on the side.

California Chopped Chicken Salad

I'm positive that this salad originated with an angry chef at a Los Angeles restaurant who took out his frustrations on the salad ingredients. You can vary the ingredients to suit your own preferences, using your favorite cheese (try Maytag blue) and vegetables.

SALAD

4 cups chopped lettuce (iceberg and romaine work best, but use your favorites)

1½ cups shredded mozzarella or provolone cheese

1 cup chopped ripe tomatoes

1 cup thin strips Genoa salami

½ cup seeded and chopped green bell pepper

3 green onions, chopped

½ cup pitted black olives, halved

1 cup ½-inch cubes or thin strips cooked chicken

DRESSING

1 cup canola oil

⅓ cup red wine vinegar

1 envelope Lipton Savory Herb with Garlic Soup Mix

¼ cup chopped fresh Italian parsley leaves

½ teaspoon sugar

½ teaspoon freshly ground black pepper

1. In a large serving bowl, combine the lettuce, cheese, tomatoes, salami, bell pepper, green onions, olives, and chicken.

2. In a medium mixing bowl, whisk together the oil, vinegar, soup mix, parsley, sugar, and black pepper until well blended. Pour the dressing over the salad, tossing to combine. Serve immediately. The chopped salad ingredients can be prepared 1 day ahead of time. The dressing will keep in the refrigerator, covered, for up to 1 week.

Chinese Chicken Salad

SALAD

4 cups chopped romaine lettuce

2 cups cored and thinly sliced Savoy or other cabbage

4 green onions, chopped

1 medium red bell pepper, seeded and cut into thin strips

2 cups mandarin orange segments, drained

2 cups bite-size pieces cooked chicken

1 package chicken flavor ramen noodles

DRESSING

Ramen flavor packet

$3/4$ cup vegetable oil

$1/2$ cup rice vinegar

1 teaspoon peeled and grated fresh ginger

$1/4$ cup soy sauce

2 tablespoons toasted sesame oil

1. Combine the lettuce, cabbage, green onions, bell pepper, orange segments, and chicken in a large serving bowl. Crush the ramen noodles and set them aside.

2. In a medium glass mixing bowl, whisk together the flavor packet, the vegetable oil, vinegar, ginger, soy sauce, and sesame oil until well blended. Refrigerate the dressing until you are ready to use it.

3. To serve the salad, pour about $1/2$ cup of the dressing over the salad and toss to coat the ingredients evenly. Add the reserved noodles and toss again. Add more dressing if needed. (I found that one recipe of dressing makes enough for two salads.)

SERVES 6

There are more recipes for this salad than I can count. This one is simple and uses ramen soup, but I have included a few ideas for variations on the theme. All the ingredients can be chopped and refrigerated, along with the dressing, up to 24 hours ahead of serving time.

VARIATIONS:

■ Add 1 cup cashew pieces to the salad just before tossing the ingredients with the dressing.

■ Substitute peeled and deveined shrimp for the chicken.

■ Add $1/2$ cup snow peas that have been cut into thin slices on the diagonal.

■ Add 1 tablespoon sesame seeds to the dressing.

■ For a thicker dressing with a darker color, add 1 tablespoon hoisin sauce to the dressing.

Cobb Salad

A classic dish from the famed Brown Derby Restaurant in Beverly Hills, this salad can make you feel like a star right in your own kitchen. The classic salad must include all the finely diced vegetables, blue cheese, hard-boiled egg, and bacon. If you decide to vary from the classic, I recommend poached salmon instead of chicken, slivers of Parmigiano-Reggiano instead of blue cheese, and finely chopped Granny Smith apples for extra crunch.

SALAD

2 cups finely chopped iceberg lettuce

2 cups finely chopped romaine lettuce

1 cup finely chopped watercress

1/4 cup finely chopped red onion

1 cup diced ripe tomatoes

2 cups finely diced cooked chicken

8 strips bacon, cooked until crisp, drained on paper towels, and crumbled

1 medium ripe Hass avocado, peeled, pitted, diced, and tossed with 1 tablespoon fresh lemon or lime juice to retain color

3 hard-boiled eggs, peeled and diced

1/2 cup crumbled blue cheese

DRESSING

1/4 cup red wine vinegar

2 tablespoons water

1 tablespoon fresh lemon juice

1 teaspoon Worcestershire sauce

1/2 teaspoon Dijon mustard

1/4 cup olive oil

1/2 cup vegetable oil

1 envelope Lipton Savory Herb with Garlic Soup Mix

1. Toss the lettuce, romaine, and watercress in a wide, shallow serving bowl. Arrange the onion, tomatoes, chicken, bacon, avocado, and eggs in narrow strips or wedges across the greens. Sprinkle the blue cheese on top. The salad can be refrigerated, covered, for up to 8 hours before serving.

2. In a small glass mixing bowl, whisk together the vinegar, water, lemon juice, Worcestershire, mustard, oils, and soup mix.

The dressing can be stored in the refrigerator, covered, for up to 7 days.

3. To serve, toss the salad at the table with half of the dressing, and pass the remaining dressing.

Hawaiian Chicken Velvet Salad

¼ cup cold water

1 envelope unflavored gelatin

1 can Campbell's Condensed Cream of Chicken Soup

One 3-ounce package cream cheese, softened

2 tablespoons fresh lemon juice

Dash of ground ginger

1 cup diced cooked chicken

½ cup drained pineapple tidbits

¼ cup chopped celery

¼ cup seeded and chopped green bell pepper

Salad greens

Toasted slivered almonds (page 125) for garnish

1. Sprinkle the gelatin over the water in a small saucepan. Place the pan over low heat and stir the gelatin until it is dissolved. Remove the pan from the heat.

2. In a large mixing bowl, blend the soup into the cream cheese. Stir in the gelatin, lemon juice, and ginger. Add the chicken, pineapple, celery, and bell pepper. Pour the salad into a greased 1-quart mold and chill for 4 hours or until firm.

3. Unmold the salad on a serving platter lined with crisp salad greens, garnish with toasted almonds, and serve.

SERVES 6

This luncheon staple from the 1950s is a smooth and creamy gelatin salad. If you would just like to make a plain chicken velvet salad, omit the fruit and proceed as directed.

Herbed Garden Chicken Salad

A simple supper or luncheon dish, this colorful salad is delicious served over mixed greens or in a sandwich on challah or rye bread. You can also stuff this salad into cooked zucchini boats, sprinkle grated cheddar cheese on top, and broil the stuffed zucchini for an unusual dinner entrée.

SALAD

4 cups cubed cooked chicken

1 cup chopped celery

¼ cup chopped yellow onion

¼ cup finely chopped carrot

¼ cup seeded and finely chopped red bell pepper

½ cup peeled and chopped jícama or peeled, cored, and chopped Granny Smith apple

DRESSING

1 cup mayonnaise

1 cup sour cream

½ cup milk

1 envelope Knorr Leek Soup Mix

1 teaspoon dried fines herbes (see page 3)

1 teaspoon fresh thyme leaves or ½ teaspoon dried

½ teaspoon freshly ground black pepper

2 teaspoons chopped fresh Italian parsley leaves

Mixed greens

1. In a large mixing bowl, combine the chicken, celery, onion, carrot, bell pepper, and jícama, tossing to combine. Refrigerate the salad, covered tightly, for up to 24 hours.

2. In a small mixing bowl, blend together the mayonnaise, sour cream, milk, soup mix, fines herbes, thyme, black pepper, and parsley with a wire whisk.

3. Toss the salad with 1 cup of the dressing. Refrigerate the salad for up to 6 hours.

4. To serve, toss the salad with more dressing and serve it cold on the mixed greens.

Tuna Salad

1½ cups mayonnaise

½ cup milk

1 envelope Knorr Leek Soup Mix

1 tablespoon chopped fresh dill or 1½ teaspoons dried dillweed

1 cup chopped celery

¼ cup chopped red onion

2 tablespoons capers, drained

Two 6-ounce cans albacore tuna packed in oil, drained

1. In a medium mixing bowl, whisk together the mayonnaise, milk, soup mix, and dill. Chill the dressing until you are ready to serve the salad.

2. In large mixing bowl, stir together the celery, onion, capers, and tuna, flaking the tuna. Add the dressing to taste (about ¾ cup), stirring to blend. Refrigerate the salad until you are ready to serve it, with remaining dressing on the side.

Yes, tuna salad made with soup! When I was testing recipes, I had some dressing left over that was made from Knorr Cream of Leek Soup, so I tossed it together with a few other things and came up with this salad, which can be served on a bed of lettuce or as a sandwich filling. The dressing also works well with cooked chicken or salmon.

Salade Niçoise

Until Julia Child brought this salad into American homes via her *French Chef* television show in the 1960s, most of us had no idea what it was. This is one of my favorite summer suppers, and it comes together so easily. The dressing can be made several days ahead of time, and the vegetables can be prepared the day before serving.

DRESSING

1 cup olive oil

½ cup red wine vinegar

1 envelope Knorr Leek Soup Mix

1 teaspoon dried fines herbes (see page 3)

¼ cup chopped shallots

2 tablespoons Dijon mustard

1 teaspoon freshly ground black pepper

2 tablespoons chopped capers

SALAD

6 cups salad greens

Two 6-ounce cans tuna, packed in olive oil, drained

5 medium red potatoes, cooked in boiling water to cover until tender and drained

¼ cup finely chopped red onion

1 pound green beans, ends trimmed, cooked in boiling water to cover until crisp-tender, and drained

5 hard-boiled eggs, peeled

2 medium ripe tomatoes, cut into wedges

1 European cucumber, cut into ½-inch-thick rounds

1. In a small mixing bowl, whisk together the oil, vinegar, soup mix, fines herbes, shallots, mustard, pepper, and capers until blended. Refrigerate until ready to use.

2. At serving time, toss the salad greens in a large mixing bowl with 2 to 4 tablespoons of the dressing. Spread the lettuce over a large serving platter or shallow bowl. Place a mound of tuna on opposite sides of the serving platter and drizzle it with a few tablespoons of the dressing.

3. Place the potatoes in the mixing bowl and toss them with 2 to 4 tablespoons of the dressing and 1 tablespoon of the onion. Taste for seasoning, adding more salt and pepper if necessary. Arrange the potatoes on the platter.

4. In the mixing bowl, toss the green beans with 2 to 3 tablespoons of the dressing, and arrange them on the platter.

5. Slice or quarter the hard-boiled eggs and place them on the platter. Arrange the tomato wedges on the platter and drizzle them with some of the dressing.

6. In the mixing bowl, combine the cucumber with the remaining onion, tossing them with 2 to 4 tablespoons of the dressing. Arrange them on the salad platter. Serve the remaining dressing on the side or drizzle it evenly over the salad. Serve immediately.

Raspberry Shrimp and Fruit Salad

This gorgeous salad is great to serve to the ladies who lunch. Vary the fruits with the seasons. Melons are usually available all year round, and if strawberries aren't available, substitute kiwis.

SALAD

2 pounds medium shrimp, peeled, deveined, cooked, and chilled

1 cup chopped celery

1/2 cup chopped green onions

1 cup peeled, cored, and chopped Granny Smith apple

2 cups 1/2-inch cubes cantaloupe

2 cups hulled and quartered ripe strawberries

6 cups mixed field greens

DRESSING

1 cup vegetable oil

1/2 cup raspberry vinegar

1 envelope Lipton Savory Herb with Garlic Soup Mix

1 tablespoon sugar

1. In a large mixing bowl, combine the shrimp, celery, green onions, apple, cantaloupe, and strawberries, tossing gently to blend. Arrange the field greens evenly on each of 6 plates.

2. In a small mixing bowl, combine the oil, vinegar, soup mix, and sugar, whisking until the ingredients are well combined. At this point, the dressing may be refrigerated until you are ready to proceed.

3. Toss the shrimp mixture with 1/2 cup of the dressing. Drizzle 2 tablespoons of the dressing over the field greens on each plate. Mound the salad on top of the greens and pass the remaining dressing.

Mediterranean Seafood and Rice Salad

5 tablespoons extra virgin olive oil

½ cup chopped onion

Two 10.5-ounce cans Swanson's Italian-Flavored Chicken Broth

1 cup long-grain rice

1 pound large shrimp, peeled and deveined

3 tablespoons fresh lemon juice

1 cup crumbled feta cheese

2 tablespoons chopped fresh basil leaves

1. Heat 1 tablespoon of the oil in a 3-quart saucepan over medium heat, add the onion, and cook, stirring, until softened. Add the broth and rice. Bring the mixture to a boil and simmer it for 15 minutes. Stir in the shrimp and continue cooking for another 3 minutes. Remove the pan from the stove and stir. Transfer the mixture to a serving bowl and allow it to come to room temperature.

2. In a small mixing bowl, combine the remaining ¼ cup oil, the lemon juice, feta, and basil. Stir the mixture into the warm shrimp and rice and refrigerate the salad until you are ready to serve it. Toss the ingredients again before serving.

Put together only a few ingredients, and you can have a show-stopping entrée salad for your family. Make this salad early in the day and refrigerate it until you are ready to serve it. Feel free to substitute cooked sea bass, calamari, clams, or scallops for the shrimp in this dish.

Grilled Shrimp Caesar Salad

GRILLED SHRIMP

2 pounds large shrimp, peeled and deveined

1 cup olive oil

2 tablespoons fresh lemon juice

1 envelope Lipton Savory Herb with Garlic Soup Mix

CAESAR DRESSING

2 cloves garlic, mashed

1 tablespoon Worcestershire sauce

1 tablespoon anchovy paste (optional)

$\frac{1}{3}$ cup fresh lemon juice

1 envelope Knorr Leek Soup Mix

1 teaspoon dried fines herbes (see page 3)

$1\frac{1}{4}$ cups olive oil

SALAD

8 cups torn romaine hearts

$1\frac{1}{2}$ cups shredded Parmesan cheese

2 cups Garlic Croutons (see page 111)

1 teaspoon coarsely ground black pepper

Everyone has his or her favorite Caesar dressing, and for this salad I am sticking close to the original from Caesar's Hotel in Tijuana, just a few miles from my home. As a child, I was fascinated by the maitre d's performance as he made this salad for me, and my love for this classic has not faded. The grilled shrimp are easy to prepare ahead of time, and they can be refrigerated for up to six hours before serving.

1. Preheat the broiler or grill for 10 minutes. Thread the shrimp onto skewers. In a small mixing bowl, combine the oil, lemon juice, soup mix, and fines herbes, whisking until blended. (Save $\frac{1}{2}$ cup of this mixture for making the croutons.) Brush the shrimp with the flavored oil and grill them over hot coals or 4 inches below the broiler. Turn the shrimp after 3 minutes, brush them with the oil again, and grill or broil them until they are barely pink; they will continue to cook for several minutes after you remove them from the heat. Brush them again with the oil.

2. In a blender, combine the garlic, Worcestershire, anchovy paste if you are using it, lemon juice, and soup mix. Blend the mixture for 30 seconds, and then, with the motor running, slowly add the oil. The dressing can be refrigerated for up to 4 days.

3. Place the lettuce in a large serving bowl and toss it with $1/2$ cup of the dressing. Add the Parmesan and croutons and toss again. Sprinkle the pepper over the salad and add more dressing as needed. Serve the salad on dinner plates and garnish each plate with 4 large shrimp.

Making Garlic Croutons

To make your own garlic croutons, brush sliced French, Italian, or sourdough bread heavily with the reserved garlic herb oil. Broil the bread, and then turn it over and brush it again with more oil. When the bread is evenly toasted, remove it from the broiler and let it cool. Cut the bread into $1/2$- to $3/4$-inch cubes. Store croutons in resealable plastic bags at room temperature for up to three days.

Antipasto Salad

Not only is this salad beautiful to look at, it's like peanuts—you cannot stop eating it! It keeps for a week in the refrigerator, and you can substitute your own favorites for some of the ingredients called for in the recipe.

VARIATION: Toss 1 cup of the salad with 1 pound cooked rotelle pasta for a great pasta salad.

SALAD

Two 8-ounce jars pickled Italian vegetables (sometimes called "Giardiniera"), drained

Two 6-ounce jars marinated artichoke hearts, drained

1/2 pound button mushrooms, halved

One 4-ounce can pitted black olives, drained

One 6-ounce jar stuffed green olives, drained

One 4-ounce jar peperoncini, drained

One 4-ounce jar roasted peppers, drained and cut into 1-inch squares

1/2 pound Italian salami, cut into 1/2-inch chunks

1/2 pound provolone cheese, cut into 1/2-inch chunks

DRESSING

1 cup olive oil

1/4 cup red wine vinegar

1 teaspoon freshly ground black pepper

1 envelope Lipton Savory Herb with Garlic Soup Mix or Knorr Leek Soup Mix

1. In a large serving bowl, combine the pickled vegetables, artichoke hearts, mushrooms, olives, peperoncini, roasted peppers, salami, and provolone.

2. In a small mixing bowl, whisk together the oil, vinegar, pepper, and soup mix. Pour the dressing over the vegetables and stir until they are well combined.

3. Cover the bowl tightly and refrigerate the salad for at least 2 hours before serving.

Roast Beef and Stilton Salad

SERVES 8

8 cups mixed field greens or your favorite lettuces

½ cup olive oil

1 cup vegetable oil

½ cup red wine vinegar

1 envelope Knorr Leek Soup Mix

1 teaspoon dried fines herbes (see page 3)

¼ cup chopped fresh chives

½ teaspoon freshly ground black pepper

1 cup crumbled Stilton cheese

4 cups leftover roast beef cut into ½-inch-wide strips

2 pounds small new potatoes, cut into quarters and steamed until tender

1. Arrange the greens on a large serving platter.

2. In a small mixing bowl, whisk together the oils, vinegar, soup mix, fines herbes, chives, pepper, and Stilton until blended. Drizzle some of the dressing over the greens.

3. Arrange the roast beef on one side of the platter in an attractive pattern, and then arrange the potatoes on the other side. Drizzle the beef and potatoes with some of the dressing and pass the remaining dressing.

Leftover roast beef just isn't the same when it's reheated, so, when I was looking for a way to use up some leftover prime rib, this salad was the perfect solution. With tiny red potatoes and crisp greens it's a whole-meal salad; you'll need only a bottle of red wine and candles to make your bistro dinner complete.

Thai Pork and Noodle Salad

SERVES 6

Acolorful addition to your dinner table, this salad is filled with contrasting textures, colors, and flavors. The crunchy peanuts and vegetables complement the noodles, and the smooth peanut butter in the dressing lends an exotic flavor to the mix.

SALAD

6 cups water

2 packages oriental flavor ramen noodles

1 tablespoon plus ½ teaspoon toasted sesame oil

1 tablespoon vegetable oil

1 clove garlic, mashed

1 pound boneless pork loin, trimmed of fat and cut into ½-inch-wide strips

1 medium red bell pepper, seeded and cut into ½-inch-wide strips

6 green onions, chopped

½ cup dry-roasted peanuts

GINGER-PEANUT DRESSING

1 ramen flavor packet

¼ cup vegetable oil

3 tablespoons smooth peanut butter

1 teaspoon peeled and grated fresh ginger

5 shakes Tabasco sauce

3 tablespoons rice vinegar

1. In a medium saucepan, bring the water to a boil and cook the ramen noodles for 1 minute. Drain the noodles and toss them with 1 tablespoon of the sesame oil in a large serving bowl.

2. In a wok or large sauté pan, heat the vegetable oil and the remaining ½ teaspoon sesame oil over medium-high heat. Add the garlic, and cook, stirring, for 1 minute. Add the pork and cook, stirring, until it is cooked through, about 5 to 7 minutes.

3. Remove the mixture from the wok and toss it with the noodles. Add the bell pepper, green onions, and peanuts.

4. In a blender or food processor, blend together one of the ramen flavor packets (reserve the other packet for another use), the vegetable oil, peanut butter, ginger, Tabasco, and vinegar until smooth. Pour the dressing over the noodles and pork, stirring to blend.

5. Refrigerate the salad for at least 1 hour and for up to 8 hours.

Taco Salad

MEAT

2 pounds lean ground beef

1 cup chopped onion

1 envelope Knorr Tomato Beef Soup Mix

½ teaspoon chili powder

1 teaspoon ground cumin

1 cup water

1 can Campbell's Condensed Black Bean Soup

DRESSING

1 cup vegetable oil

¼ cup fresh lime juice

2 tablespoons white vinegar

¼ cup chopped fresh cilantro leaves

4 shakes Tabasco sauce

SALAD

8 cups torn lettuce (I like to use romaine and red leaf)

2 medium ripe tomatoes, cut into wedges

2 medium ripe avocados, peeled, pitted, cut into wedges, and tossed with 2 tablespoons fresh lemon or lime juice

2 cups grated cheddar cheese

½ cup sliced black olives, drained

½ cup pickled jalapeños, drained

2 cups sour cream

8 cups tortilla chips (I like to mix white, yellow, and blue corn for variety and color)

SERVES 8

This old standby is a staple at our house on nights when everyone has a different activity. The meat-and-bean mixture can be kept warm in a slow cooker or microwaved, and the rest of the ingredients can be cut up and served buffet-style.

Brown the ground beef and onion and drain off any fat that may have accumulated in the bottom of the pan. Transfer the mixture to the slow cooker, adding 2 tablespoons of the soup mix, the chili powder, cumin, water, and black bean soup. Cook on high for three hours.

1. In a 5-quart Dutch oven over high heat, brown the ground beef and onion. Drain off any fat or water that accumulates in the bottom of the pan. Add 2 tablespoons of the soup mix, reserving the rest for the dressing. Stir in the chili powder, cumin, water, and black bean soup, bringing the mixture to a boil. Reduce the heat to medium-low and simmer for 30 minutes. Taste for seasoning and add more salt and pepper if needed. (At this point, the meat-and-bean mixture can be refrigerated until serving time, and then reheated, or you can transfer it to a slow cooker set on low.)

2. In a small glass mixing bowl, whisk together the oil, lime juice, vinegar, remaining soup mix, cilantro, and Tabasco until blended. Refrigerate the dressing until serving time or for up to 3 days.

3. In a large serving bowl, toss the lettuce with 1/2 cup of the dressing. Arrange the meat-and-bean mixture in the center of the lettuce. Surround the meat with the tomatoes and avocados. Top the meat with the cheddar cheese, olives, jalapeños, and sour cream. Tuck the tortilla chips around the edges of the platter and serve. Pass the remaining dressing.

Maytag Blue Cheese Dressing

2 cups mayonnaise

$1/2$ cup sour cream

$1/4$ cup red wine vinegar

2 teaspoons Worcestershire sauce

1 envelope Lipton Savory Herb with Garlic Soup Mix

$1/2$ teaspoon freshly ground black pepper

1 cup crumbled Maytag blue cheese

In a medium mixing bowl, whisk together the mayonnaise, sour cream, vinegar, Worcestershire, soup mix, and pepper until well combined. Stir in the blue cheese and refrigerate the dressing for at least 4 hours before serving. The dressing will keep, covered, in the refrigerator for up to 5 days.

Sweet Tomato Dressing

1 can Campbell's Condensed Tomato Soup

$1/4$ cup sugar

$1/2$ cup rice vinegar

$1/4$ cup vegetable oil

1 teaspoon Worcestershire sauce

In a medium mixing bowl or glass jar, whisk or shake together the soup, sugar, vinegar, oil, and Worcestershire. The dressing will keep, covered, in the refrigerator for up to 1 week.

MAKES 2 CUPS

Mellow Maytag blue cheese blends with dry soup mix to create a creamy blue cheese dressing that is delicious over wedges of iceberg lettuce, tossed with mixed greens, drizzled over vine-ripened tomatoes, or stirred into mashed potatoes.

MAKES 2 CUPS

This sweet and pungent dressing is reminiscent of the Catalina dressing that is sold in the grocery store. Try this dressing on the Copper Penny Salad (page 76) or toss it with mixed greens.

Souped-Up Salads and Dressings

Ranch House Dressing

MAKES 2½ CUPS

An envelope of soup mix can help make a delicious dressing for your next dinner salad. Try this dressing, and then try some of the variations.

CHEESY SPINACH RANCH DRESSING: Substitute Knorr Cream of Spinach Soup Mix, omit the herbs, and add ¼ cup freshly grated Parmesan cheese.

DILLY RANCH DRESSING: Omit the herbs and add 2 tablespoons dillweed.

1 cup buttermilk, or 1 cup milk mixed with 2 teaspoons fresh lemon juice

1½ cups mayonnaise

1 envelope Knorr Leek Soup Mix

1 teaspoon dried thyme

1 teaspoon dried marjoram

1 teaspoon dried chervil

1 teaspoon lemon pepper

In a medium mixing bowl or glass jar, whisk or shake together the buttermilk, mayonnaise, soup mix, thyme, marjoram, chervil, and lemon pepper. The dressing will keep, covered, in the refrigerator for up to 4 days.

Herbed Vinaigrette

MAKES 2 CUPS

1 cup vegetable oil

½ cup olive oil

½ cup white wine vinegar

1 envelope Knorr Leek Soup Mix

1 teaspoon dried fines herbes (see page 3)

½ teaspoon freshly ground black pepper

1. In a medium mixing bowl or glass jar, whisk or shake together the oils, vinegar, soup mix, fines herbes, and pepper until well combined. The dressing will keep, covered, in the refrigerator for up to 1 week.

2. Remove the dressing from the refrigerator 1 hour before serving to allow the oil to liquefy.

Balsamic Vinaigrette

1 cup vegetable oil

¼ cup extra virgin olive oil

⅓ cup balsamic vinegar

1 envelope Lipton Savory Herb with Garlic Soup Mix

½ teaspoon freshly ground black pepper

1. In a medium bowl or glass jar, whisk or shake together the oils, vinegar, soup mix, and pepper. The dressing will keep, covered, in the refrigerator, for up to 1 week.

2. Remove the dressing from the refrigerator 1 hour before serving to allow the oil to liquefy.

MAKES 1½ CUPS

Instant Vinaigrette

All the Knorr soup mixes can be blended with 1 cup vegetable oil and ⅓ cup vinegar to make a flavored vinaigrette. However, some Lipton dry mixes will not work.

Red Wine Vinaigrette

1½ cups vegetable oil

½ cup olive oil

½ cup red wine vinegar

2 tablespoons chopped shallot

1 tablespoon Dijon mustard

1 envelope Lipton Savory Herb with Garlic Soup Mix

½ teaspoon freshly ground black pepper

1. In a medium mixing bowl or glass jar, whisk or shake together the oils, vinegar, shallot, mustard, soup mix, and pepper. The dressing will keep, covered, in the refrigerator for up to 1 week.

2. Remove the dressing from the refrigerator 1 hour before serving to allow the oil to liquefy.

MAKES 2½ CUPS

Souped-Up Salads and Dressings

Sailor Man Cream of Spinach Soup

Stracciatella alla Pasquini

Tomato Florentine Soup

White Cheddar Tomato Bisque

White Gazpacho

Broccoli Cheese Soup

Zucchini Marinara Soup with Peas and Shell Pasta

Creamy Yellow Squash Soup

Curried Cream of Pumpkin Soup

French Onion Soup Gratinée

Monterey Bay Bean Soup

Tuscan White Bean and Chard Soup

Quick Vegetable Soup with Alphabet Noodles

Potato Leek Soup

Triple Mushroom Soup with Brie

Stir-Fry Chicken Noodle Soup

Chicken Enchilada Soup

Tortilla Soup

Mom's Prescription Chicken Soup

Cream of Chicken and Wild Rice Soup

Foot-Stomping Chicken Chili

Thanksgiving Minestrone

Wedding Soup

Turkey White Bean Chili

Sicilian Minestrone

Black Bean Sirloin Chili

Cousin Vinny's Pasta Fagioli

Kansas City Steak and Vegetable Soup

Old-Fashioned Beef Barley Soup

Creamy Corn Chowder

Potato, Bacon, and Gruyère Soup

Baked Potato Soup

Stormy Weather BLT Soup

Old-Fashioned Navy Bean Soup

Bob's Spicy Lentil Soup

Cuban Black Bean Soup

Narragansett Bay Shrimp Bisque

Cajun Corn and Shrimp Chowder

Creole Shrimp and Rice Soup

Down East Clam Chowder

Fisherman's Wharf Cioppino

Souper Bowls

REMEMBER THE CAMPBELL'S SOUP COMMERCIAL where the announcer would tell us that the soup was M'm! M'm! Good!® The smell of soup in the kitchen can cure a bad day, take care of that fight with the boss, and put a smile on your face. Soup can warm your tummy and your heart. There is something about the aroma of soup, even Campbell's Chicken Noodle, that make most of us nostalgic for days that were less complicated and stressed. Sitting down to a bowl of soup can soothe you, and, because it's hot, you have to take your time to eat it, and that can mean the difference between an enjoyable meal and a track meet.

Many people shy away from making soup because they envision long hours standing over a pot making homemade stock. No more! With just a few additions, a flavor-packed bowl of comfort can be ready in just minutes. When choosing the recipes for this chapter, I left the recipes on the boxes and cans and did not duplicate any of them here. What I tried to do was use the soups in interesting ways to get more flavor and taste from their usual preparation. Using soups to make soup sounds like a given, but these soups take soup out of the box (or can) and have you creating comfort food with style. The problem with this chapter was limiting the number of soups to include in it. Lots of different tastes, textures, and culinary influences from around the world are represented here. Quick and easy, as well as having the advantage of being on the table in under 60 minutes, any of these soups can be a lifesaver on a night when you want something soothing and satisfying to eat.

Sailor Man Cream of Spinach Soup

Remember Popeye? He loved to eat spinach, and you will too, once you try this easy soup filled with crunchy chopped vegetables. It's comforting on a fall night, and you probably have most of the ingredients in your pantry. Try serving this soup with the BLT Club Salad (page 99).

2 tablespoons butter

1/2 cup chopped onion

1/2 cup grated carrot

2 cups chopped fresh spinach

1 envelope Knorr Cream of Spinach Soup Mix

2 1/2 cups milk

1/8 teaspoon freshly grated nutmeg

1/4 teaspoon freshly ground black pepper

1. In a 3-quart saucepan, melt the butter over medium heat, add the onion, carrot, and spinach, and cook, stirring, until softened, 3 to 4 minutes.

2. Add the soup mix and whisk in the milk until the mixture is smooth. Bring the soup to a boil, season with the nutmeg and black pepper, reduce the heat to medium-low, and simmer for 5 minutes before serving.

Stracciatella alla Pasquini

7 cups water

2 envelopes Lipton Noodle Soup with Real Chicken Broth Soup Mix

2 cups chopped escarole, spinach, or Swiss chard (stems removed from Swiss chard)

4 large eggs, beaten

⅔ cup freshly grated Parmesan cheese, plus more for serving

6 drops Tabasco sauce

1. In a medium saucepan, bring the water to a boil. Add the soup mix, reduce the heat to medium-low, and simmer for 5 minutes. Add the escarole and cook until tender, about 5 minutes.

2. In a small mixing bowl, beat the eggs with the Parmesan cheese and Tabasco. Gradually pour the cheese and egg mixture into the boiling soup, stirring with a fork to scramble the eggs. Serve the soup immediately with additional grated cheese.

SERVES 6

Serving me this soup was my Italian grandmother's way to make me feel better when I was sick. It was also a good way to get me to eat my greens! She would make this with her own homemade chicken stock, and, as the recipe got passed down, I turned to Lipton's for an easy way to make my favorite prescription soup! The name *stracciatella* translated literally means "torn to rags," which is how the eggs look when they are cooked this way.

IN ONE YEAR, CAMPBELL'S USES ALMOST ONE MILLION MILES OF NOODLES IN CHICKEN SOUP, ENOUGH TO CIRCLE THE EQUATOR APPROXIMATELY 40 TIMES.

Souper Bowls

Tomato Florentine Soup

SERVES 8

This simple soup is fre-
quently on the menu at
Nordstom's café. You can
make it in less than 30
minutes. The rich tomato
broth is filled with
chopped vegetables and
cheese tortellini.

2 tablespoons extra virgin olive oil

1 medium onion, chopped

2 stalks celery, chopped

2 medium carrots, chopped

1 envelope Knorr Tomato with Basil Soup Mix

3 cups water

2 cups chopped fresh spinach

1 cup fresh cheese tortellini

4 fresh basil leaves, finely chopped, or $\frac{1}{2}$ teaspoon dried

1. In a stockpot, heat the oil over medium heat and cook the
onion, celery, and carrots, stirring, until they begin to soften, 3
to 4 minutes. Add the soup mix and water and bring the soup to
a boil.

2. Add the spinach, tortellini, and basil and simmer until the
tortellini are tender, 3 to 4 minutes. Serve the soup immediately, refrigerate it for up to 2 days, or freeze it for up to 1 month.

White Cheddar Tomato Bisque

SERVES 6

White cheddar cheese
added to tomato
bisque brings back
memories of lunch at
mom's when she would
serve tomato soup and
grilled cheese sand-
wiches. This is a terrific
après-ski snack.

2 cans Campbell's Condensed Tomato Bisque

2 soup cans half-and-half or light cream

2 cups grated sharp white cheddar cheese

2 cups herbed croutons

1. In a 3-quart saucepan, whisk together the soup and half-
and-half. Heat the soup over medium heat until it reaches serving temperature.

2. Divide the cheese among 6 soup bowls and pour the soup
over the cheese in the bowls. Garnish the soup with the croutons. Serve immediately.

White Gazpacho

2½ cups boiling water

1 package Knorr Leek Soup Mix

2 European cucumbers, diced

3 tablespoons white wine vinegar

1 clove garlic, minced

2 medium-size firm, ripe tomatoes, cut into ½-inch dice
(about 1 cup)

½ cup ½-inch dice red or orange bell pepper

2 green onions, chopped

3 cups sour cream

Salt and freshly ground black pepper

½ cup slivered almonds, toasted

¼ cup chopped fresh parsley leaves

1 medium ripe Hass avocado, peeled, pitted, and cut into
½-inch dice

1. Pour the boiling water into a 6-cup glass measuring cup
and add the soup mix. Stir the soup until it is dissolved and
allow the soup to come to room temperature.

2. Place 1 cucumber, 1 cup of the soup, the vinegar, and garlic in a food processor and process until smooth. Pour the
cucumber mixture into the remaining soup, adding the remaining diced cucumber, the tomatoes, bell pepper, and green onions,
stirring to blend. Whisk in the sour cream. Adjust the seasoning with salt and black pepper.

3. Refrigerate the soup until you are ready to serve it. Just
before serving, stir in the almonds, parsley, and avocado.

Cool and seductive,
this beautiful soup is
studded with colorful,
crunchy vegetables and
can be made the day
before serving. If you
aren't making this during
tomato season, try using
Roma tomatoes; they are
pretty reliable year-round
and are not as watery as
the other varieties.

Toasting Almonds

To toast almonds, pre-
heat the oven to 400
degrees and place the
almonds on a baking
sheet. Bake the almonds,
stirring frequently, until
they are golden, five to
ten minutes. Remove the
almonds from the baking
sheet to cool and prevent
further browning.

Souper Bowls

Broccoli Cheese Soup

Broccoli is one of my favorite vegetables, and this soup is a great warm-up on a cold winter afternoon or evening.

WORRIES GO DOWN BETTER WITH SOUP THAN WITHOUT.
—JEWISH PROVERB

2 tablespoons butter

1/2 cup chopped onion

2 cups broccoli florets

1 teaspoon salt

1/2 teaspoon freshly ground black pepper

2 cans Campbell's Condensed Cream of Celery Soup

4 shakes Tabasco sauce

1/2 cup milk

2 cups grated mild cheddar cheese

1/2 cup freshly grated Parmesan cheese

1. In a 3-quart saucepan, melt the butter over medium heat, add the onion, and cook, stirring, until it is softened, about 3 minutes. Add the broccoli, season the vegetables with the salt and pepper, and cook for 3 to 4 minutes. Add the soup, Tabasco, and milk and bring the soup to a boil.

2. Remove the pan from the heat. Add the cheeses and stir until they are melted. Serve immediately.

The Soup Mix Gourmet

Zucchini Marinara Soup with Peas and Shell Pasta

2 tablespoons olive oil

½ cup chopped onion

1 clove garlic, minced

4 cups ½-inch-thick slices zucchini

One 14.5-ounce can diced tomatoes, with their juices

1 envelope Knorr Tomato with Basil Soup Mix

2 cups chicken broth

1 cup petite peas, either fresh or frozen (and defrosted)

½ cup small shell pasta

Freshly grated Parmesan cheese for garnish

1. In a 5-quart saucepan, heat the olive oil over medium heat, add the onion, and cook, stirring, until softened, about 3 minutes. Add the garlic and cook, stirring, for another minute. Add the zucchini and cook, stirring, until it begins to soften, about 3 minutes. Add the tomatoes and soup mix, stirring to blend. Bring the soup to a boil and add the chicken broth, stirring up any browned bits from the bottom of the pan. Reduce the heat to medium-low and simmer the soup for 15 minutes.

2. Add the peas and pasta and simmer until the pasta is tender, about another 10 minutes. Serve the soup garnished with grated Parmesan cheese.

SERVES 8

This soup came about when the zucchini were overtaking the garden, and we needed to use them up. Simple peasant food, this dish is best made just before serving.

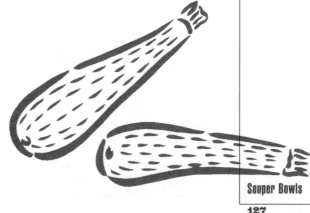

Souper Bowls

Creamy Yellow Squash Soup

This elegant but easy soup can be made in a flash with condensed soup and a food processor or blender. Velvety, with an exquisite taste, this soup is best served the day you make it.

1/2 cup (1 stick) butter

2 medium leeks, white parts only, washed well and cut into 1-inch pieces

6 medium yellow crookneck squash, cut into 1-inch chunks

1 teaspoon salt

1/2 teaspoon freshly ground black pepper

1 tablespoon chopped fresh dill, plus more for garnish

1 can Campbell's Condensed Cream of Chicken Soup

1 cup heavy cream

1. In a 3-quart saucepan, melt the butter over medium heat, add the leeks, squash, salt, pepper, and dill, cover, and let the vegetables soften for about 5 minutes, stirring a few times to make sure they do not brown. Add the soup and heavy cream, stir until blended, and heat through.

2. In several batches, carefully transfer the hot soup to a food processor or blender and process until smooth. Serve the soup hot garnished with additional chopped fresh dill. Or refrigerate it until you are ready to serve it. Reheat the soup over low heat before serving.

Curried Cream of Pumpkin Soup

2 tablespoons butter

¼ cup finely chopped onion

½ cup cored, peeled, and finely chopped apple

¼ cup finely chopped carrot

¾ teaspoon curry powder

1 can Campbell's Condensed Cream of Chicken Soup

1 cup canned pumpkin purée

1½ cups half-and-half or light cream

½ cup chopped mango chutney for garnish

½ cup chopped unsalted roasted peanuts for garnish

½ cup sweetened flaked coconut, toasted (page 324),
    for garnish

1. In a 3-quart saucepan, melt the butter over medium heat, add the onion, apple, carrot, and curry powder, and cook, stirring, until they are softened, about 3 minutes. Stir in the soup, pumpkin purée, and half-and-half and bring to a simmer.

2. Serve the soup warm, garnished with the chutney, peanuts, and coconut.

This soup is the perfect prelude to a fall dinner, or even to Thanksgiving dinner. Serve it in hollowed-out squash or tiny pumpkins, and garnish each serving with a dollop of chutney and a sprinkling of toasted coconut.

French Onion Soup Gratinée

SERVES 8

When I first saw Julia Child make this rich soup on *The French Chef* television show, I was hooked, and when she said I could use a "tinned broth," making this soup became an obsession. Crusted with Gruyère cheese and French bread croutons, and full of caramelized onions, this soup has a deep, rich flavor. A hot bowl of this is all I need to make me feel better on a cold night.

½ cup (1 stick) butter

4 large onions, thinly sliced

1 teaspoon salt

½ teaspoon freshly ground black pepper

1 teaspoon sugar

½ cup red wine

2 envelopes Lipton Beefy Onion Soup Mix

4 cups beef broth

1½ teaspoons dried thyme

1 bay leaf

1½ cups shredded Gruyère cheese

½ cup freshly grated Parmesan cheese

Eight ¾-inch-thick slices French bread, toasted on both sides

1. Melt the butter over medium heat in a 5-quart stock pot. Add the onion and season with the salt, pepper, and sugar. Toss the onions in the butter, cover and cook, stirring occasionally, for 5 minutes. Uncover the onions and cook them, stirring, until they begin to caramelize and turn golden brown, another 15 minutes. Add the wine, soup mix, beef broth, thyme, and bay leaf, bring the soup to a simmer, and let it simmer, uncovered, for 45 minutes to 1 hour. Taste the soup and correct the seasoning as necessary.

2. Preheat the broiler for 10 minutes. Combine the cheeses in a small mixing bowl. For each serving, ladle some of the soup into a heat-proof bowl, float toasted bread on top, and sprinkle on some of the cheese mixture. Place the bowls on a baking sheet and run them under the broiler until the cheese melts.

Monterey Bay Bean Soup

3 tablespoons vegetable oil

1 cup chopped onion

1 clove garlic, mashed

4 jalapeño chiles, seeded and chopped

1 teaspoon chili powder

One 14.5-ounce can peeled tomatoes, with their juices

2 envelopes Lipton Golden Onion Soup Mix

4 cups water

Two 15-ounce cans pinto beans, drained and rinsed

2 cups broken tortilla chips

1 cup grated mild cheddar cheese

Sour cream, chopped green onions, and chopped fresh cilantro leaves for garnish

1. In a 5-quart stockpot, heat the oil over medium heat, add the onion, garlic, and jalapeños, and cook them, stirring, until they are softened, about 4 minutes. Add the chili powder and cook, stirring constantly, for 2 minutes. Add the tomatoes and soup mix and bring to a boil. Add the water and pinto beans, bring the soup to a boil again, reduce the heat to medium-low, and simmer for 10 minutes.

2. Divide the tortillas and cheddar cheese evenly among 8 soup bowls. Pour the hot soup into the bowls and garnish each serving with sour cream, green onions, and cilantro.

SERVES 8

This warming soup gets plenty of fire from the jalapeños and can be on the table in less than 30 minutes. Add some corn-bread and a salad, and you've got a great week-night supper.

Souper Bowls

Tuscan White Bean and Chard Soup

SERVES 8

In this hearty soup from Tuscany, the dried soup mix packs a punch and helps to give the otherwise bland beans a lot of personality. I like to serve this soup with a drizzle of really good extra virgin olive oil.

2 tablespoons extra virgin olive oil

1 thin slice pancetta or 1 strip bacon, cut into ½-inch pieces

2 cloves garlic, minced

2 bunches Swiss chard, tough stems removed and leaves cut into 1-inch pieces

1 envelope Lipton Golden Onion Soup Mix

1½ cups water

One 14.5-ounce can diced tomatoes, drained

Two 16-ounce cans small white beans, drained and rinsed

1 teaspoon dried rosemary

½ teaspoon freshly ground black pepper

Grated Pecorino Romano cheese and extra virgin olive oil for garnish

1. In a 5-quart saucepan, heat the oil over medium-high heat, add the pancetta, and cook, stirring, until it is crisp. Reduce the heat to medium, add the garlic, and cook, stirring, until it softens, about 3 minutes, taking care not to let the garlic brown. Add the chard and toss it in the oil mixture. Cover the pan and cook the chard for 2 minutes. Add the soup mix, water, and tomatoes. Bring the soup to a boil, reduce the heat to medium-low, and simmer until the chard is tender, about 10 minutes.

2. Add the beans, rosemary, and pepper and simmer the soup for another 10 minutes.

3. Serve the soup garnished with some cheese and a drizzle of oil.

Quick Vegetable Soup with Alphabet Noodles

2 tablespoons butter

¼ cup chopped onion

1 teaspoon dried thyme

¼ cup Knorr Tomato Base Chicken Bouillon

3½ cups water

One 16-ounce bag mixed baby vegetables or mixed vegetables
(peas, corn, carrots, and green beans)

½ teaspoon freshly ground black pepper

¼ cup alphabet noodles

1. In a 5-quart stockpot, melt the butter over medium heat, add the onion and thyme, and cook, stirring, until the onion is softened, about 3 minutes. Add the bouillon, water, vegetables, and pepper, bring to a boil, reduce the heat to medium-low, and simmer the soup for 10 minutes.

2. Add the noodles and simmer until they are tender, another 7 minutes, and serve.

A good warm-up after Saturday afternoon soccer games, this soup is ready quick as a wink, and it's great with grilled cheese sandwiches.

EACH YEAR CAMPBELL PRODUCES ALMOST 11 BILLION LETTERS FOR ITS ALPHABET SOUPS.

Potato Leek Soup

Two soups combine to make this old favorite. The leek is a member of the onion family with a very mellow flavor. If you would like to serve this soup cold, process it in the food processor until it is smooth, and chill.

2 tablespoons butter

2 leeks, white parts only, washed well and cut into
    $1/2$-inch pieces

1 envelope Knorr Leek Soup Mix

1 can Campbell's Condensed Cream of Potato Soup

2 cups milk

$1/2$ teaspoon freshly ground black pepper

$1/2$ cup chopped fresh chives for garnish

1. Melt the butter in a 3-quart saucepan over medium heat. Add the leeks and cook, stirring, until softened, about 3 minutes.

2. Add the soup mix and canned soup, whisk in the milk and pepper, and bring the soup to a simmer. Simmer the soup for 5 minutes, garnish it with the chives, and serve.

Triple Mushroom Soup with Brie

SERVES 8

¼ cup (½ stick) butter

¼ chopped shallots

½ pound button mushrooms, sliced

½ pound crimini mushrooms, sliced

½ pound shiitake mushrooms, stems removed and caps sliced

¼ cup all-purpose flour

1 envelope Lipton Golden Onion Soup Mix

2 cups water

2 tablespoons cream sherry

1 cup heavy cream

½ cup chopped fresh chives for garnish

⅓ pound Brie cheese, cut into strips, for garnish

1. Melt the butter in a 5-quart stock pot over medium heat, add the shallots, and cook, stirring, until they have softened, about 3 minutes. Add the mushrooms and cook, stirring, until they begin to soften. Add the flour and stir until it is absorbed into the mushrooms. Blend in the soup mix and water, stirring until the mixture comes to a boil and thickens. Add the sherry and cream and bring the soup to a simmer.

2. Ladle the soup into bowls and garnish each serving with some chives and a slice of Brie.

This soup is a favorite with students who take my Do-Ahead Thanksgiving class. It's rich but light enough to serve before a meal, and the Brie melts right into the soup.

Souper Bowls

135

Stir-Fry Chicken Noodle Soup

SERVES 8

Here's another quick soup with terrific flavor from ramen noodles and vegetables. It is fun to serve this one from a wok at the table with chopsticks, letting everyone serve themselves from the main dish. Remember that in Japan it is polite to slurp your soup!

1 tablespoon vegetable oil

1 tablespoon plus 1 teaspoon toasted sesame oil

2 clove garlic, minced

1 teaspoon peeled and grated ginger

1 whole boneless, skinless chicken breast, cut into ½-inch-wide strips

4 green onions, cut on the diagonal into 1-inch pieces

2 medium carrots, cut into thin strips

One 15-ounce can baby corn, drained and cut in half lengthwise

½ cup snow peas, cut in half diagonally

1 cup sliced mushrooms

4 packages chicken flavor ramen noodles

6 cups water

¼ cup soy sauce

1 tablespoon sesame seeds

1. In a wok or large stockpot, heat the vegetable oil and 1 tablespoon of the sesame oil together over high heat. Add the garlic and ginger and stir-fry them for 1 minute. Add the chicken and stir-fry it until it turns white on all sides. The chicken will not be cooked through.

2. Remove the chicken from the wok, add the green onions, carrots, baby corn, snow peas, and mushrooms, and stir-fry until the mushrooms begin to soften. Add the ramen flavor packets and water and bring to a boil. Add the chicken and the noodles from the ramen packages, bring the soup to a boil again, reduce the heat to medium-low, and simmer for 2 minutes.

3. Remove the pot from the heat, stir in the remaining 1 teaspoon sesame oil and the soy sauce, sprinkle the soup with the sesame seeds, and serve.

Chicken Enchilada Soup

2 tablespoons butter

½ cup chopped onion

½ cup seeded and chopped red bell pepper

One 4-ounce can chopped green chiles, drained and rinsed

1 teaspoon chili powder

½ teaspoon ground cumin

1 can Campbell's Condensed Cream of Chicken Soup

1 cup chicken broth

2 cups diced cooked chicken

6 corn tortillas, cut into ½-inch pieces

1 cup sour cream

1 cup shredded Monterey Jack cheese

1. Melt the butter in a 3-quart saucepan over medium heat. Add the onion and bell pepper and cook, stirring, until they are softened, about 3 minutes. Add the chiles, chili powder, and cumin and stir constantly for 2 minutes. Add the chicken soup and broth, whisking until smooth.

2. Over medium-low heat, stir in the chicken, tortillas, sour cream, and cheese, stirring until the cheese is melted and the soup reaches serving temperature. At this point, the soup may be refrigerated until you are ready to serve it. Reheat over medium to low heat and serve.

Soups can be great vehicles for transforming leftovers into a totally different meal to serve the next night. This soup uses up leftover cooked chicken or turkey, along with tortillas and some vegetables in a southwestern treat. We like to serve guacamole, cheddar cheese, chopped fresh cilantro, and sour cream on the side so that everyone can select his or her own garnishes.

Each year, 99 percent of American households purchase soup.

Souper Bowls

Tortilla Soup

Hot and spicy with a cool avocado and corn salsa to serve on top, this soup is a great party dish when you allow your guests to garnish it themselves.

2 tablespoons vegetable oil

1 large red bell pepper, seeded and cut into $\frac{1}{2}$-inch-wide strips

1 large green bell pepper, seeded and cut into $\frac{1}{2}$-inch-wide strips

1 large yellow bell pepper, seeded and cut into $\frac{1}{2}$-inch-wide strips

2 cups thinly sliced yellow onion

6 cloves garlic, minced

$\frac{1}{4}$ cup chili powder

2 tablespoons ground cumin

Two 14.5-ounce cans diced tomatoes, drained

2 envelopes Lipton Golden Onion Soup Mix

7 cups water

4 cups coarsely chopped cooked chicken

2 cups fried corn tortilla strips

$1\frac{1}{2}$ cups grated Monterey Jack cheese for garnish

Leaves from 1 bunch fresh cilantro, chopped, for garnish

Avocado Corn Salsa (recipe follows) for garnish

1. In an 8-quart stockpot, heat the oil over medium heat, add the peppers and onion, and cook until they have softened, about 5 minutes, stirring frequently. Add the garlic, chili powder, and cumin and cook, stirring constantly, until the garlic is softened, about 3 minutes. Add the tomatoes and soup mix and bring the liquid to a boil. Add the water and chicken, bring to a boil again, reduce the heat to medium-low, and simmer the soup for 15 minutes.

2. To serve, place some tortillas strips in each bowl and ladle the soup into the bowls. Garnish each serving with some cheese, chopped cilantro, and Avocado Corn Salsa.

AVOCADO CORN SALSA

1 medium ripe Hass avocado, peeled, pitted, and chopped

½ cup corn kernels, either cut fresh from the cob or frozen (and defrosted)

½ cup chopped green onion

2 tablespoons fresh lime juice

1 teaspoon salt

4 shakes Tabasco sauce

Combine the avocado, corn, and green onion together in a small glass mixing bowl. Sprinkle in the lime juice, salt, and Tabasco and stir to blend. Refrigerate the salsa, covered with plastic wrap, until you are ready to serve it.

Mom's Prescription Chicken Soup

4 cups water

2 envelopes Lipton Chicken Noodle Soup Mix

½ cup finely chopped carrot

½ cup finely chopped celery

1 cup finely diced cooked chicken

1. Bring the water to a boil in a 3-quart saucepan. Add the soup mix, carrot, and celery and bring the soup back to a boil. Reduce the heat to medium-low and simmer until the noodles are tender, about 10 minutes.

2. Add the chicken and simmer the soup for another 5 minutes before serving.

MY GREATEST STRENGTH IS COMMON SENSE. I'M REALLY A STANDARD BRAND, LIKE CAMPBELL'S TOMATO SOUP.
—KATHARINE HEPBURN

SERVES 8

This prescription for whatever ails you is sure to bring a smile to your face, and your stomach. My mom made me this soup when I was home from school with the sniffles. She served it to me on a tray in my bed, with ginger ale and saltine crackers. Somehow I knew I'd get better!

Souper Bowls

Cream of Chicken and Wild Rice Soup

I love the creamy flavor of this soup and the nutty crunch of the wild rice. It tastes great with fresh focaccia. Making this soup is a great way to use up leftover chicken.

2 tablespoons butter

½ cup chopped shallots

½ cup chopped celery

½ cup chopped carrot

1 teaspoon chopped fresh thyme leaves or ½ teaspoon dried

1 can Campbell's Condensed Cream of Chicken Soup

1 cup chicken broth

½ cup heavy cream

1 cup cooked wild rice

1 cup finely diced cooked chicken or turkey

½ teaspoon freshly ground black pepper

1. In a 3-quart saucepan, melt the butter over medium heat, add the shallots, celery, carrot, and thyme, and cook, stirring, until the vegetables begin to soften, 3 to 4 minutes.

2. Stir in the soup, broth, and heavy cream, whisking until smooth. Stir in the rice, chicken, and pepper and bring the soup to serving temperature. At this point, the soup may be refrigerated until you are ready to serve it. Reheat over medium to low heat and serve.

Foot-Stomping Chicken Chili

¼ cup vegetable oil

1½ cups chopped onion

3 cloves garlic, mashed

2 teaspoons ground cumin

2 teaspoons chili powder

1 teaspoon dried oregano

2 envelopes Lipton Golden Onion Soup Mix

3 tablespoons masa harina (this is a corn flour, found in the
    baking section of the supermarket)

2 cups water

One 15-ounce can tomato sauce

One 12-ounce can beer

3 cups diced or shredded cooked chicken

One 16-ounce can pinto beans, rinsed and drained

Grated cheddar cheese, sour cream, and chopped fresh cilantro
    for garnish

1. In a 5-quart stockpot, heat the oil over medium heat, add the onion, garlic, cumin, chili powder, oregano, soup mix, and masa harina, and cook, stirring constantly so that the spices don't burn, for 4 minutes. Add the water, tomato sauce, and beer and bring the liquid to a boil. Reduce the heat to medium-low and add the chicken and pinto beans. Cook the chili until it is thick, 45 minutes to an hour.

2. Serve the chili garnished with cheddar cheese, sour cream, and chopped cilantro.

SERVES 8

When I tried this recipe out on some Texans, they initially turned up their noses at the thought of chicken in chili, but once they tried it, they became believers. It may have been the addition of Lone Star beer to the broth! This chili is best made a day or two ahead of time. It can be frozen for up to one month.

Thanksgiving Minestrone

This soup will help you use up the leftover turkey at Thanksgiving. You'll love the rich broth studded with vegetables, chunks of turkey, and tender cheese tortellini. Try floating little Sage Parmesan Crostini (recipe follows) on top of each serving. The rind from the Parmigiano-Reggiano softens as it cooks, and flavors the soup.

2 tablespoons extra virgin olive oil

1 cup chopped onion

2 cloves garlic, minced

1 teaspoon chopped fresh sage leaves or ½ teaspoon dried

½ teaspoon chopped fresh thyme leaves or ¼ teaspoon dried

1 medium leek, white part only, washed well and sliced ½ inch thick

1 cup chopped carrots

1 cup chopped celery

One 14.5-ounce can diced tomatoes, with their juices

2 envelopes Lipton Golden Onion Soup Mix

6 cups water

½ cup white wine

2 cups cored and chopped Savoy cabbage

2 medium zucchini, ends trimmed and sliced ½ inch thick

One 16-ounce can garbanzo beans, drained and rinsed

Rind from Parmigiano-Reggiano cheese (optional)

6 cups coarsely chopped cooked turkey or chicken

1 cup fresh cheese tortellini

1 teaspoon freshly ground black pepper

1. In an 8-quart stockpot, heat the olive oil over medium heat, add the onion, garlic, sage, thyme, leek, carrots, and celery, cover the pot, and let the vegetables soften for 4 minutes, stirring occasionally.

2. Uncover the pot, add the tomatoes, and bring the liquid to a boil. Add the soup mix, water, and wine, bring to a boil again, and add the cabbage, zucchini, garbanzos, Parmigiano-Reggiano rind, and chicken. Reduce the heat to medium-low and simmer the soup for 30 minutes.

3. Add the tortellini and pepper and simmer the soup for another 5 minutes to heat the tortellini through before serving.

SAGE PARMESAN CROSTINI

½ cup (1 stick) butter, softened

3 tablespoons chopped fresh sage leaves

¾ cup freshly grated Parmesan cheese

1 loaf French bread, cut into 1-inch-thick slices and toasted on both sides

1. In a small mixing bowl, cream together the butter, sage, and cheese.

2. Spread the mixture on the toasted bread and float the bread in the soup, or serve it on the side.

Wedding Soup

I have no clue where this Italian soup got its name, but it shouldn't be reserved just for weddings. Filled with tiny meatballs floating in a chicken-based broth, this soup will make your family members of the clean plate club!

Souper Smart

Some grocers sell tiny meatballs already made up in the frozen food section. When you want to make this soup in a hurry, pull out the frozen meatballs and proceed as directed. You don't even have to defrost them; just increase the simmering time a bit.

³/₄ pound ground turkey

1 large egg

2 tablespoons dry breadcrumbs

2 tablespoons freshly grated Parmesan cheese

¹/₂ teaspoon dried basil

2 tablespoons finely chopped onion

¹/₂ teaspoon salt

¹/₄ teaspoon freshly ground black pepper

¹/₄ cup olive oil

5 cups water

2 envelopes Lipton Chicken Noodle Soup Mix

2 cups chopped fresh spinach

¹/₄ cup grated carrot

Freshly grated Parmesan cheese for garnish

1. In a medium mixing bowl, combine the turkey, egg, breadcrumbs, cheese, basil, onion, salt, and pepper. Shape the mixture into ³/₄-inch meatballs.

2. In a medium sauté pan, heat the olive oil over medium-high heat, add the meatballs a few at a time, and brown them on all sides. Remove the meatballs from the pan and drain them on paper towels.

3. In a 5-quart saucepan, bring the water to a boil, add the soup mix, reduce the heat to medium-low, and simmer the soup for 5 minutes. Add the meatballs, spinach, and carrot and simmer for 10 minutes. Serve the soup immediately, garnished with grated Parmesan cheese.

Turkey White Bean Chili

SERVES 8

¼ cup (½ stick) butter

1 cup chopped onion

3 cloves garlic, minced

2 jalapeño chiles, seeded and cut into ½-inch dice

1½ teaspoons chili powder

1 teaspoon ground cumin

One 14.5-ounce can diced tomatoes, with their juices

One 12-ounce can beer

1 envelope Lipton Golden Onion Soup Mix

2 cups water

2 cups corn kernels, either cut fresh from the cob or frozen (and defrosted)

One 16-ounce can small white beans, drained and rinsed

3 cups ½-inch pieces cooked turkey

Another way to recycle turkey or chicken leftovers, this hearty chili is studded with green chiles, corn, tomatoes, and tiny white beans. Served with corn bread and a salad, this chili makes a great meal to accompany a Sunday afternoon of watching football.

1. In an 8-quart stockpot, melt the butter over medium heat, add the onion, garlic, and jalapeños, and cook the vegetables, stirring, until they have softened, about 3 minutes. Add the chili powder and cumin and cook for 3 minutes, stirring constantly so the spices don't burn.

2. Add the tomatoes, bring the mixture to a boil, and add the beer, soup mix, and water, stirring to loosen any browned bits that may be stuck to the bottom of the pot. Add the corn, beans, and turkey, reduce the heat to medium-low, and simmer the chili, uncovered, until it has thickened, about 30 minutes. Leftover chili freezes well for up to about 6 weeks.

Souper Bowls

Sicilian Minestrone

This hearty soup is a favorite in my "soup marathon" classes, where we do eight soups in two and a half hours! Thick with vegetables and meat, it is topped with a delicious lemon zest mixture that gives the soup added pizzazz. The soup is great if it is made a few days ahead of time, and it freezes well for about two months.

2 tablespoons extra virgin olive oil

1 cup chopped onion

1 cup chopped celery

1 cup chopped carrots

2 cloves garlic, minced

4 ounces prosciutto, finely chopped

1 teaspoon dried rosemary

1 pound extra-lean ground beef

One 14.5-ounce can diced tomatoes, with their juices

1 cup red wine

1 teaspoon freshly ground black pepper

1 envelope Knorr Tomato with Basil Soup Mix

4 cups beef broth

One 20-ounce can beans (garbanzos, kidney, or small white beans)

⅓ cup orzo

Lemon-Parsley Garnish (recipe follows)

1. In an 8-quart stockpot, heat the oil over medium heat, add the onion, celery, carrots, garlic, prosciutto, and rosemary and cook, stirring, until the vegetables have softened, 5 to 7 minutes. Add the ground beef and cook it until it loses its pink color. Drain off any excess fat that has accumulated in the pan. Add the tomatoes, wine, and pepper and cook the mixture for about 5 minutes. Add the soup mix, beef broth, and beans, bring the soup to a boil, reduce the heat to medium-low, and simmer for 45 minutes.

2. Sprinkle the orzo over the top of the soup and simmer the soup for an additional 15 minutes.

3. Garnish each serving with 1 tablespoon of the Lemon-Parsley Garnish.

LEMON-PARSLEY GARNISH

⅓ cup freshly grated Parmesan cheese

½ cup minced fresh Italian parsley leaves

1 large clove garlic, minced

Grated zest of 1 lemon

In a small mixing bowl, stir together the Parmesan cheese, parsley, garlic, and lemon zest.

Black Bean Sirloin Chili

2 tablespoons vegetable oil

2½ pounds boneless sirloin, trimmed of fat and cut into
  ½-inch pieces

1½ teaspoons salt

½ teaspoon freshly ground black pepper

1½ cups chopped onion

5 cloves garlic, chopped

1 cup seeded and chopped jalapeño chiles (about 4)

¼ cup chili powder

¼ teaspoon cayenne pepper

1 teaspoon ground cumin

2 envelopes Knorr Tomato Beef Soup Mix

5 cups water

Two 15-ounce cans black beans, drained and rinsed

Sour cream, shredded cheddar cheese, chopped red onion,
  pickled jalapeños, guacamole, and chopped fresh cilantro
  leaves for garnish

> MEMORIES ARE LIKE MULLIGATAWNY SOUP IN A CHEAP RESTAURANT. IT IS BEST NOT TO STIR THEM.
> —P. G. WODEHOUSE

SERVES 8

This hearty chili will cure what ails you. Loaded with sirloin, jalapeños for some heat, and black beans for extra protein, this whole meal will warm your heart and your tummy. This dish is best made the day before serving, and it can be frozen for up to two months.

Souper Bowls

1. Heat the oil in an 8-quart stockpot over medium-high heat. Dry the sirloin with paper towels and sprinkle it evenly with the salt and pepper. Add the beef to the pot a few pieces at a time, browning the meat evenly and removing pieces to a bowl when they are brown.

2. Add the onion, garlic, and jalapeños and cook them, stirring, until they begin to soften, about 3 minutes. Add the chili powder, cayenne, and cumin and cook, stirring so that the spices do not burn, for 2 to 3 minutes.

3. Return the beef to the pot along with any meat juices that may have accumulated in the bowl. Add the soup mix and water, stirring to loosen any browned bits that may have stuck to the bottom of the pot. Bring the chili to a boil, reduce the heat to medium-low, and simmer, uncovered, stirring occasionally, until the beef is tender, about an hour.

4. Taste the chili and correct the seasoning with salt and pepper. Stir in the beans and simmer for an additional 15 minutes. Serve the chili with garnishes and let each diner garnish his or her own chili.

Cousin Vinny's Pasta Fagioli

2 tablespoons extra virgin olive oil

2 strips bacon, cut into ½-inch dice

¾ pound lean ground beef

½ cup chopped onion

½ cup chopped celery

½ cup chopped carrot

One 14.5-ounce can diced tomatoes, with their juices

1 teaspoon dried rosemary

1 envelope Knorr Tomato Beef Soup Mix

3 cups water

½ teaspoon freshly ground black pepper

1 teaspoon chopped fresh rosemary or ¼ teaspoon dried

One 16-ounce can small white beans, drained and rinsed (or substitute your favorite; garbanzos work well, as do kidney beans)

2 cups cooked pasta (short, fat pasta such as tubetti or elbow macaroni are best)

Grated Pecorino Romano cheese for garnish

1. In a 5-quart stockpot, heat the oil over medium-high heat, add the bacon, and cook, stirring, until it is crisp. Add the ground beef and cook it until it loses its pink color. Drain off some of the fat in the bottom of the pot.

2. Add the onion, celery, and carrot and cook the vegetables, stirring, until they have softened, 3 to 4 minutes. Add the tomatoes, rosemary, and soup mix and bring the soup to a boil. Add the water, pepper, rosemary, and beans, bring to a boil again, reduce the heat to medium-low, and simmer the meat and vegetables for 20 minutes.

3. Add the pasta and simmer for 10 minutes. Serve the dish garnished with Pecorino Romano cheese.

Literally, "pasta beans," this one-dish dinner is spicy, and filled with meat, vegetables, and pasta. In Italy, no two bowls of pasta fagioli are alike, because each cook adds his or her own special touch to it.

Kansas City Steak and Vegetable Soup

This soup was inspired by the steak soup at Plaza III Steak House in Kansas City, Missouri. The original relied too much on a beef-flavored base and ground beef, whereas in this version chunks of sirloin simmer in a beef and tomato broth, creating a delicious hearty beef soup.

Slow Cooker Savvy

Brown the meat first and then place it in a slow cooker along with all the other ingredients. Cook the soup on high for four hours.

2 tablespoons olive oil

1½ pounds boneless sirloin, trimmed of fat and cut into ½-inch pieces

1 teaspoon salt

½ teaspoon freshly ground black pepper

1 cup chopped onion

2 cloves garlic, mashed

1 cup chopped celery

1 cup chopped carrots

1 envelope Knorr Tomato Beef Soup Mix

1 envelope Lipton Beefy Onion Soup Mix

4 cups water

1 cup peeled potatoes cut into ½-inch dice

1½ cups corn kernels, either cut fresh from the cob or frozen (and defrosted)

2 cups green beans cut into 1-inch pieces

1. Heat the oil in a 5-quart stockpot over medium-high heat. Dry the beef with paper towels and sprinkle it with the salt and pepper. Brown the beef in batches in the hot oil, turning it frequently. When all of the beef is browned, return it to the stockpot, add the onion, garlic, celery, and carrots, and cook, stirring, until the vegetables begin to soften, about 4 minutes. Add the soup mixes, water, and potatoes and bring the soup to a boil. Reduce the heat to medium-low and simmer until the beef is tender, 45 minutes to 1 hour.

2. Add the corn and green beans and cook the soup until the beans are tender, another 6 minutes. Correct the seasoning with salt and pepper if needed.

Old-Fashioned Beef Barley Soup

2 tablespoons vegetable oil

1½ pounds boneless sirloin, trimmed of fat and cut into
     ½-inch pieces

1 cup chopped onion

1 cup chopped celery

1 cup chopped carrots

1 cup chopped fresh or canned tomatoes

1 teaspoon dried thyme

2 envelopes Lipton Beefy Onion Soup Mix

6 cups water

1½ cups diced squash (zucchini or yellow crookneck)

½ cup pearl barley

1. In an 8-quart stockpot, heat the oil over medium-high heat, pat the beef dry with paper towels, and then add the beef to the pot and brown it on all sides.

2. Add the onion, celery, and carrots and cook, stirring, until softened, about 5 minutes. Add the tomatoes and thyme and bring the soup to a simmer. Add the soup mix and water and bring to a boil again. Reduce the heat to medium-low and simmer the soup for 45 minutes.

3. Add the squash and barley and cook until tender, an additional 30 minutes.

SERVES 8

Thick and hearty, this soup is awesome served with crusty sourdough bread.

Souper Smart

If you are using leftover roast beef, quickly sauté it in the oil with the vegetables and proceed with the recipe as directed.

Souper Bowls

Creamy Corn Chowder

Corn chowder is a staple in the Midwest, and there are as many recipes for it as there are cooks! I like the smoky flavor that the ham lends this creamy soup. If you prefer yours plain, omit the ham.

VARIATION: Try substituting diced chicken or turkey for the ham.

2 tablespoons butter

$1/2$ cup chopped onion

$1/2$ cup chopped celery

$1/2$ cup chopped carrot

1 cup finely diced ham

1 teaspoon chopped fresh thyme leaves or $1/2$ teaspoon dried

2 cans Campbell's Condensed Cream of Potato Soup

1 cup milk

2 cups corn kernels, either cut fresh from the cob or frozen (and defrosted)

$1/2$ teaspoon freshly ground black pepper

1. In a 3-quart saucepan, melt the butter over medium heat, add the onion, celery, carrot, ham, and thyme, and cook, stirring, until the vegetables are softened, about 3 minutes.

2. Whisk in the soup and milk until blended. Add the corn and pepper and bring to a boil. Remove the pot from the heat and serve immediately.

Potato, Bacon, and Gruyère Soup

This hearty soup reminds me of a smoky cheese fondue. It is a great warm-up for après ski, or on a cold fall day after raking leaves. The soup can be made several days ahead, and it's great served in a hollowed-out bread loaf.

6 strips bacon, cut into $1/2$-inch dice

$1/2$ cup finely chopped onion

2 cans Campbell's Condensed Cream of Potato Soup

$1/2$ cup white wine

$1/2$ cup milk

$2 1/2$ cups grated Gruyère cheese

1. In a 4-quart saucepan over medium-high heat, cook the bacon, stirring, until it is crisp. Add the onion and cook, stirring, until it is softened, about 3 minutes. Whisk in the soup, wine, and milk and bring the soup to a boil.

2. Remove the soup from the heat and add the cheese, stirring until it is melted. Serve immediately.

Baked Potato Soup

2 tablespoons butter

¼ cup chopped onion

¼ cup chopped celery

2 cans Campbell's Condensed Cream of Potato Soup

1 cup heavy cream

2½ cups grated mild cheddar cheese

6 shakes Tabasco sauce

6 green onions, chopped, for garnish

12 strips bacon, cooked until crisp, drained on paper towels,
     and crumbled, for garnish

½ cup sour cream (optional) for garnish

1. In a 3-quart saucepan, melt the butter over medium heat, add the onion and celery, and cook, stirring, until they are softened, about 2 to 3 minutes. Stir in the soup and heavy cream and bring to a boil. Reduce the heat to medium-low and simmer the soup for 4 minutes.

2. Remove the pan from the heat and add 1½ cups of the cheese and the Tabasco, stirring until the cheese is melted.

3. Serve the soup garnished with the green onions, bacon, sour cream, and the remaining 1 cup cheese.

SERVES 6

My son, Ryan, loves this soup because it has all the elements of a "loaded" baked potato, but it can be on the table in under 15 minutes.

Stormy Weather BLT Soup

SERVES 4

Although we hardly ever have what I call real weather here in San Diego, during a recent storm when my cupboard was bare, I wanted something comforting and warm. This soup was what I came up with. My husband, Chuck, is a connoisseur of BLTs, and he thinks this version is terrific.

2 strips bacon, cut into ¼-inch pieces

2 cups romaine lettuce, cut into 1-inch pieces (or 2 cups from a bag of prepared romaine)

1 can Campbell's Condensed Tomato Soup

1 cup herb croutons for garnish

1. In a 2-quart saucepan, fry the bacon until it is crisp. Drain off all but 1 teaspoon of the fat, and add the romaine. Cook the romaine, stirring, until it is softened.

2. Add the soup and 1 soup can water and stir until the mixture is smooth. Bring the soup to a simmer, and serve it garnished with croutons.

Old-Fashioned Navy Bean Soup

SERVES 6

Traditional Navy bean soup like that served in congressional dining rooms is pretty bland. I've taken a few liberties with the original, and I think that this version will stand the test of time.

2 tablespoons olive oil

6 strips bacon, cut into ½-inch pieces

1 cup chopped onion

1 envelope Knorr Tomato Beef Soup Mix

3 cups water

One 16-ounce can small white beans, drained and rinsed

1 teaspoon dried thyme

½ teaspoon freshly ground black pepper

1 bay leaf

1. In a 3-quart saucepan, heat the olive oil over medium-high heat, add the bacon, and cook, stirring, until it is crisp. Add the onion and soup mix and cook, stirring, until the onions are softened, about 3 minutes. Add the water, stirring to loosen any browned bits that may have formed on the bottom of the pot.

2. Add the beans, thyme, pepper, and bay leaf, bring the soup to a boil, reduce the heat to medium-low, and simmer the soup for 20 minutes. Remove the bay leaf and serve the soup in heated bowls.

Bob's Spicy Lentil Soup

2 tablespoons vegetable oil

1 pound kielbasa, andouille, or Polish sausage, cut into 1-inch-thick rounds

1 cup chopped onion

2 cloves garlic, crushed

1 cup chopped carrots

1 cup chopped celery

1 teaspoon cumin seeds

$1/8$ teaspoon cayenne pepper

1 bay leaf

2 envelopes Lipton Golden Onion Soup Mix

6 cups water

2 cups dried lentils, rinsed and picked over for stones

$1/2$ teaspoon freshly ground black pepper

1. In an 8-quart stockpot, heat the oil over medium-high heat, add the sausage slices, and brown them. Add the onion, garlic, carrots, and celery and cook, stirring, until they are softened, 3 to 4 minutes. Add the cumin seeds, cayenne, bay leaf, and soup mix and cook for 2 minutes, being careful to stir the mixture so that the spices don't burn. Add the water, lentils, and pepper and bring the soup to a boil.

2. Reduce the heat to medium-low, cover the pot, and simmer the soup until the lentils are soft and creamy, $1^{1}/2$ to 2 hours. Remove the bay leaf before serving. The soup can be stored in the refrigerator for 2 days or frozen for up to 6 weeks.

SERVES 8

My friend Bob knows his soups, as evidenced by this hearty lentil soup flavored with cumin and filled with spicy sausage. Serve this with some really hearty black bread and unsalted butter.

Cuban Black Bean Soup

This easy soup uses condensed black bean soup and a few other ingredients to create a spicy and flavorful bowl. Make sure to use spicy chorizo sausage for an authentic taste. If you can't find chorizo, substitute andouille or a Polish sausage.

2 tablespoons vegetable oil

½ pound chorizo sausage, sliced into ½-inch-thick rounds

½ cup chopped onion

1 teaspoon ground cumin

1 teaspoon dried thyme

1 bay leaf

2 cans Campbell's Condensed Black Bean Soup

2½ cups water

1. In a 5-quart saucepan, heat the oil over medium-high heat and brown the sausage.

2. Add the onion, cumin, and thyme and cook, stirring, until the onions are softened, 3 to 4 minutes. Add the bay leaf, soup, and water and bring the soup to a boil. Reduce the heat to medium-low and simmer the soup, uncovered, for 15 minutes. Remove the bay leaf before serving. The soup can be refrigerated for up to 2 days. Reheat over low heat before serving.

Narragansett Bay Shrimp Bisque

SERVES 8

¼ cup (½ stick) butter

¼ cup chopped shallots

½ pound medium shrimp, peeled and deveined

2 cans Campbell's Condensed Cream of Shrimp Soup

1½ cups half-and-half or light cream

2 tablespoons Harvey's Bristol Cream Sherry

1. In a 3-quart saucepan, melt the butter over medium heat, add the shallots, and cook, stirring, until they are softened, about 3 minutes.

2. Add the shrimp and toss it in the butter mixture for 2 minutes. Stir in the soup, half-and-half, and sherry and bring the soup to a simmer. Serve it immediately. The soup can be refrigerated overnight.

This elegant and velvety soup takes me back to my childhood when I went to a restaurant with my parents and ordered shrimp bisque, not knowing what it was, but loving the way the words rolled off my tongue. When the soup arrived, I was smitten; smooth and filled with flavor, it became my favorite thing to order. Years later I can have my favorite soup with the help of a can of Campbell's and some pantry ingredients.

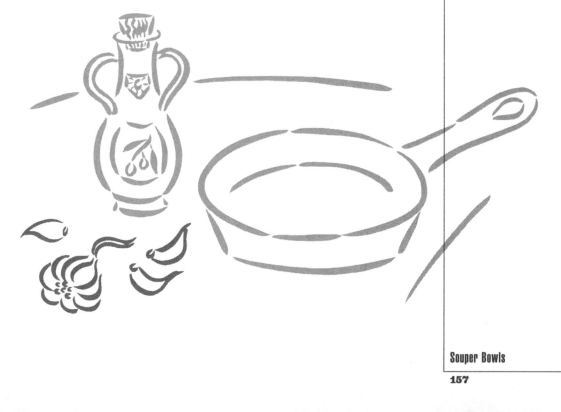

Souper Bowls

Cajun Corn and Shrimp Chowder

SERVES 8

Deceptively easy, this soup is velvety smooth, a little spicy, and filled with sweet corn and shrimp—life doesn't get much better than this. Make sure to sauté the spices to let them release their oils and give the soup a full-bodied flavor. You can make this soup in the morning, let it cool, and then refrigerate it. At serving time, bring the chowder to room temperature, heat it, and serve. A crusty baguette and a crisp white wine are all you need.

$\frac{1}{2}$ cup (1 stick) butter

1 medium onion, chopped

$\frac{1}{8}$ teaspoon cayenne pepper

$\frac{1}{4}$ teaspoon sweet paprika

$\frac{1}{2}$ teaspoon garlic salt

$\frac{1}{2}$ teaspoon ground black pepper

$\frac{1}{4}$ teaspoon dried oregano

$\frac{1}{4}$ teaspoon dried thyme

$\frac{1}{4}$ cup all-purpose flour

1 envelope Lipton Golden Onion Soup Mix

3 cups boiling water

3 cups corn kernels, either cut fresh from the cob or frozen (and defrosted)

$\frac{3}{4}$ pound medium shrimp, peeled and deveined

$\frac{1}{2}$ cup heavy cream

1. In a large saucepan, melt the butter over medium heat, add the onion, and cook, stirring, until it is softened, about 3 minutes. Add the cayenne, paprika, garlic salt, black pepper, oregano, thyme, and flour and cook the mixture, stirring, for 1 to 2 minutes. Add the soup mix and boiling water, whisking until the mixture is smooth. Bring the soup to a boil while whisking.

2. Reduce the heat to medium and add the corn and shrimp. Cook the chowder until the shrimp turn pink, 2 to 3 minutes, and then add the heavy cream. Taste for seasoning, adding salt as necessary. Cook the chowder over low heat until it reaches serving temperature, about 5 minutes.

Creole Shrimp and Rice Soup

2 tablespoons vegetable oil

½ cup chopped onion

½ cup seeded and chopped green bell pepper

½ cup chopped celery

1 cup finely chopped andouille or Polish sausage

2 tablespoons Creole Seasoning (page 458)

One 14.5-ounce can diced tomatoes, drained

2 cans Campbell's Condensed Cream of Shrimp Soup

1 cup water

1 cup cooked rice

2 cups peeled and deveined cooked shrimp or frozen crawfish tails (defrosted)

Chopped green onions for garnish

1. Heat the oil in a 4-quart saucepan over medium-high heat. Add the onion, bell pepper, celery, and sausage and cook, stirring, until the vegetables are softened, about 4 minutes. Add the Creole Seasoning and cook the vegetables and sausage, stirring so the spices don't burn, for another 2 minutes.

2. Add the tomatoes and cook them until they give off some of their juices, about 4 minutes. Add the soup, water, rice, and shrimp, stirring to blend. Bring the soup to serving temperature and serve it garnished with chopped green onions.

Spicy, creamy, and smoky, this bit of Louisiana will become a favorite at your dinner table. It is best made ahead of time so that the flavors can get to know each other. You can make the soup spicier by adding more Creole Seasoning.

Souper Bowls

Down East Clam Chowder

Although there is a pre-pared clam chowder on the market, this one is far superior in taste. Starting out like most New England clam chowders with pork and onions, it has a down-home flavor your family will love. Make dinner special by hollowing out small loaves of sourdough bread and serving the chowder in bread bowls.

6 strips bacon, cut into 1-inch pieces

1 cup chopped onion

2 cans Campbell's Condensed Cream of Potato Soup

2 cups fresh shucked clams with their juice or 2 cans chopped clams, drained with their juice reserved (the clam juice should come to 1/2 cup)

1/2 cup heavy cream

2 teaspoons chopped fresh thyme leaves or 1 teaspoon dried

1. In a 3-quart saucepan, cook the bacon over medium-high heat, stirring, until it is crisp. Add the onion and cook, stirring, until softened, about 3 minutes.

2. Stir in the soup, clams, and 1/2 cup of clam juice. Add the heavy cream and thyme, heat to serving temperature, and serve.

Fisherman's Wharf Cioppino

Cioppino is a fish stew that San Francisco fishermen traditionally made with leftovers from the catch. The soup base can be made and frozen up to one month ahead of time; add the seafood before serving. The stew is best made with firm-fleshed white fish such as sea bass, orange roughy, or halibut.

1/4 cup extra virgin olive oil

1 cup chopped onion

4 cloves garlic, chopped

1 medium green bell pepper, seeded and coarsely chopped

2 cups white wine

Three 14.5-ounce cans diced tomatoes, drained

6 tablespoons tomato paste

1 envelope Knorr Tomato with Basil Soup Mix

1 teaspoon dried oregano

1/2 teaspoon dried basil

2 whole cooked crabs or lobsters, cracked, cut into serving pieces

2 pounds halibut, sea bass, or rock cod (any firm white-fleshed fish) fillets, cut into 1-inch chunks

24 clams, discarding any with broken or opened shells, scrubbed

½ pound sea scallops

1 pound large shrimp, peeled and deveined

1 teaspoon freshly ground black pepper

½ cup chopped fresh Italian parsley leaves

1. In an 8-quart stockpot, heat the oil over medium heat, add the onion, garlic, and bell pepper, and cook, stirring, until the vegetables are softened, about 3 minutes. Add the wine and then the tomatoes, tomato paste, soup mix, oregano, and basil. Bring the mixture to a boil, reduce the heat to medium-low, and simmer the soup base for 30 minutes. (At this point, you may refrigerate the soup base for up to 2 days or freeze it for up to 1 month, until you are ready to serve the soup.)

2. Thirty minutes before serving, bring the soup base back to a boil and add the crabs or lobsters. Cover the pot, and steam the crabs or lobsters for 10 minutes. Add the fish, clams, scallops, shrimp, and black pepper and simmer the stew until the clams are open, another 5 to 10 minutes. Discard any unopened clams and stir in the chopped parsley. Serve the stew in bowls with plenty of sourdough bread for dipping.

> ONLY A PURE HEART CAN MAKE A GOOD SOUP.
> —BEETHOVEN

Parmesan Garlic Bread

Onion Cheese Bread

Overstuffed Artichoke Bread

Broccoli Cheese Bread

Herbed Parmesan Batter Bread

Taco Loco Bread

Cheesy Jalapeño Corn Bread

Tomato Basil Bread

Parmesan Spinach Bread

Dilly Bread

My Hero Bread

Swiss Garden Vegetable Loaf

Bacon, Onion, and Potato Bread

Tomato Herb Focaccia

Onion Herbed Focaccia

Pizza 101

It Isn't Easy Bein' Green Pizza

Buttery Onion Pizza Dough

Garlic Parmesan Pizza Dough

Garlic Sesame Bread Sticks

Chicken Herb Biscuits

Potato Chive Biscuits

Onion Burger Buns

Blue Cheese Bites

Onion Cheddar Crescents

Spicy Popovers

Savory Pita Chips

Bread 'n' Soup

WE ALL KNOW HOW DELICIOUS SOUP tastes with fresh bread, but how about putting the soup *in* the bread? Delectable combinations such as Tomato Herb Focaccia, biscuits lighter than air made with condensed soup, and even store-bought loaves slathered with a souper spread will be the highlight of your meals. With soup added, ordinary rolls and breads become an extraordinary accompaniment to dinner. We'll take focaccia and pizza dough to new levels and mix up fillings for refrigerated biscuits so those of you in a hurry can have a quick bread or snack to go with your meal.

Ground Rules for Baking Yeast Dough Breads

1. Always start with fresh yeast; check the expiration date on the package to make sure it's not from the last millennium.

2. Store your yeast in the refrigerator or freezer.

3. Always proof the yeast before you continue. To proof it, just stir the yeast into warm (105–110 degrees F) liquid with a small amount of sugar. If the yeast begins to bubble after ten minutes, then it is active. If it doesn't, you need to begin again with new yeast—better to begin anew than to have flat bread that doesn't rise. Some reasons for the yeast not bubbling can be that the liquid was too hot and killed the yeast, or the yeast was not active—even though you might have used it before its expiration date. If you are worried about how warm your water is, use an instant-read thermometer. Or you can start with colder water; it will just take longer for the yeast to proof.

4. After a yeast dough has risen the first time, punch it down, and then you can place the dough in an oiled resealable plastic bag and refrigerate it for up to two days or freeze it for up to one month. Defrost the dough and proceed as directed in the recipe. I sometimes use a Sharpie pen to write on the plastic bag the name of the recipe and the date I put the dough in the freezer, along with directions so that I don't forget what I'm doing.

5. Most yeast breads can be frozen after they are baked. Let the bread cool to room temperature and then store it in an airtight bag in the freezer for up to a month.

Ground Rules for Baking Batter Breads

1. Make sure that your leavening, baking soda, or baking powder is fresh. If it's rusting in the can, replace it.

2. I store my baking soda and baking powder in the refrigerator in labeled plastic airtight containers.

3. Batter breads don't freeze as well as yeast breads do, but if you want to freeze leftovers, they may be frozen for up to two weeks.

Parmesan Garlic Bread

One 8-ounce loaf unsliced French bread

³/₄ cup (1¹/₂ sticks) butter, softened

1 envelope Lipton Savory Herb with Garlic Soup Mix

1 teaspoon sweet paprika

1 cup freshly grated Parmesan cheese

1. Preheat the broiler for 10 minutes.

2. Slice the bread in half lengthwise and place it on a baking sheet.

3. In a medium mixing bowl, cream the butter together with the soup mix, paprika, and ¹/₂ cup of the cheese.

4. Spread the mixture over each half of the bread. Sprinkle on the remaining ¹/₂ cup cheese. Broil the bread until it is golden brown, and serve it hot.

SERVES 8

For as long as I can remember, this has been my son Ryan's favorite version of garlic bread. He calls it "cheese toast." It's simple and great with just about anything.

AMERICANS CONSUME MORE THAN **10** BILLION BOWLS OF SOUP EACH YEAR.

Onion Cheese Bread

SERVES 8

The uses for Lipton Onion Soup Mix are infinite, and this easy spread for bread will become one of your favorites. Also try using a dollop of this butter on grilled steak or chicken. The flavored butter keeps for two weeks in the refrigerator or for two months in the freezer.

BACON ONION CHEESE BREAD: Omit the grated cheese from the flavored butter and substitute thin slices of pepper Jack cheese between the slices. Cover the top of the re-assembled bread with 4 to 5 strips of bacon, bring the foil to within 1 inch of the top of the bread, so that the bacon is exposed, and bake the bread as directed.

1 long loaf of Italian or French bread, cut into ½-inch-thick slices

1 envelope Lipton Onion Soup Mix

1 cup (2 sticks) butter or margarine, softened

2 tablespoons Dijon mustard

6 shakes Tabasco sauce

1 cup grated cheese (cheddar, Swiss, or Parmesan—all work well)

1. Prepare a grill or preheat the oven to 375 degrees.

2. Place the bread in the center of a sheet of aluminum foil three times as long as the bread.

3. In a medium mixing bowl, cream together the soup mix, butter, mustard, Tabasco, and cheese.

4. Spread the mixture on the bread slices, reassemble the bread, and push the slices together.

5. Wrap the bread in the foil and place it over the hot grill or in the oven until the butter is melted, 15 to 20 minutes. Serve the bread at once.

Overstuffed Artichoke Bread

1 loaf French bread, cut in half lengthwise and hollowed out, saving the insides

½ cup (1 stick) butter

4 cloves garlic, crushed

1 envelope Lipton Golden Onion Soup Mix

2 cups sour cream

Two 4-ounce jars marinated artichoke hearts, drained and chopped

1 teaspoon lemon pepper

1 cup grated mozzarella cheese

1 medium ripe tomato, thinly sliced

½ cup freshly grated Parmesan cheese

1. Preheat the oven to 350 degrees. Cut the bread you removed from the loaf into ½-inch cubes.

2. Melt the butter in a 10-inch skillet over medium heat and add the garlic cloves. Cook the garlic until it begins to soften, 2 to 3 minutes. Add the bread cubes and toss them to coat them with the butter.

3. Scrape the bread cubes into a large mixing bowl. Add the soup mix, sour cream, artichoke hearts, lemon pepper, and mozzarella. Stir to blend. At this point, the mixture may be refrigerated until you are ready to bake the loaf, for up to 24 hours.

4. Stuff each half of the hollowed-out bread with the artichoke mixture and place the stuffed bread on a baking sheet lined with aluminum foil. Overlap the slices of tomato on top of the stuffing and sprinkle with the Parmesan. Bake the bread until the cheese is golden brown, 20 to 25 minutes.

5. Let the bread rest for 5 minutes. Cut each half with a serrated knife into 1-inch-thick slices and serve.

SERVES 8

This recipe turns a store-bought loaf into an amazing side dish that is great served with grilled steak or fish. You can make the filling the day before serving the bread, and then simply stuff the bread just before baking. Leftovers, if you have any, are great for breakfast!

Soup in the City

In the mid-1980s, Al's Soup Kitchen International opened for business in midtown Manhattan, selling delicious fresh soups to long lines of hungry office workers. Al quickly became a living tourist attraction because of his nasty approach to his customers. He also made delicious soup. Eventually he reached the attention of the producers of the *Seinfeld* TV show, who parodied him in an episode called "The Soup Nazi." Suddenly soup outlets started springing up everywhere—fresh gourmet soup seemed to have captured us all.

Broccoli Cheese Bread

This savory loaf is studded with bright green broccoli and savory cheddar cheese. It's great served with soup or toasted for sandwiches.

3 cups self-rising flour

¼ cup sugar

1½ cups grated medium-sharp cheddar cheese

1 envelope Knorr Cream of Broccoli Soup Mix

1 large egg

1½ cups milk

¼ cup (½ stick) butter, melted

1. Preheat the oven to 350 degrees. Coat a 9-by-5-by-3-inch loaf pan with nonstick cooking spray.

2. In a large mixing bowl, stir together the flour, sugar, cheese, and soup mix. Blend in the egg, milk, and 2 tablespoons of the melted butter. Stir until the ingredients are well combined.

3. Pour the batter into the prepared pan, drizzling the remaining 2 tablespoons of melted butter over the top. Bake the loaf until it is golden brown and a cake tester inserted in the center comes out clean, about 1 hour. Remove the bread from the oven and let it cool for 10 minutes. Remove it from the pan, and let it cool completely on a wire rack before slicing.

THE FIRST ARCHAEOLOGICAL EVIDENCE OF SOMEONE STIRRING UP SOUP FOR DINNER DATES BACK TO **6000** B.C. THE MAIN INGREDIENT OF THIS FIRST KNOWN SOUP: HIPPOPOTAMUS BONES!

The Soup Mix Gourmet

Herbed Parmesan Batter Bread

3 cups Bisquick baking mix

1 cup freshly grated Parmesan cheese

³/₄ cup milk

¹/₂ cup sour cream

1 envelope Lipton Savory Herb with Garlic Soup Mix

1 large egg

¹/₄ cup (¹/₂ stick) butter, melted

1. Preheat the oven to 350 degrees. Coat a 9-by-5-by-3-inch loaf pan with nonstick cooking spray.

2. Combine the Bisquick and cheese in a large mixing bowl. Stir in the milk, sour cream, soup mix, and egg, stirring until the ingredients are blended.

3. Pour the batter into the prepared pan, pour the melted butter over the top, and bake the loaf until it is golden brown and a cake tester inserted in the center of the bread comes out clean, 40 to 45 minutes. Remove the bread from the oven and let it cool for 10 minutes. Remove it from the pan, and let it cool for 30 minutes before slicing.

This simple bread is stellar when served alongside a hearty stew or soup. It seems to get better the next day as the flavors get to know one another. Make sure you wrap it tightly when storing it.

Taco Loco Bread

This striking bread is baked in a Bundt pan and has all the flavors of a taco. It's terrific served alongside chili or with an entrée salad. You'll get lots of requests for this bread.

$^{1}/_{2}$ cup yellow cornmeal

$2^{3}/_{4}$ cups unbleached all-purpose flour

1 tablespoon baking powder

1 teaspoon baking soda

1 envelope Lipton Fiesta Herb with Red Pepper Soup Mix

$^{2}/_{3}$ cup buttermilk

3 large eggs

$^{1}/_{3}$ cup chopped pitted black olives

4 green onions (whites and part of green tops), chopped

1 cup shredded mild cheddar cheese

1 cup shredded Monterey Jack cheese

$^{1}/_{2}$ cup (1 stick) butter, melted

1. Preheat the oven to 350 degrees. Coat a 10-inch tube pan or a 12-cup Bundt pan with nonstick cooking spray.

2. In a large mixing bowl, combine the cornmeal, flour, baking powder, baking soda, and soup mix. Stir in the buttermilk, eggs, olives, green onions, and cheeses.

3. Pour the batter into the prepared pan and then drizzle the melted butter evenly over the top. Bake the bread until a toothpick inserted in the center comes out clean, 45 to 50 minutes. Remove the loaf from the oven, let it cool for 15 minutes, and remove it from the pan. Let the bread cool completely before slicing.

WHAT'S DRACULA'S FAVORITE SOUP? SCREAM OF TOMATO!

Cheesy Jalapeño Corn Bread

1 can Campbell's Condensed Cream of Chicken Soup

2 large eggs

¼ cup milk

One 4-ounce can chopped green chiles, drained and rinsed

2 cups frozen corn kernels, defrosted

1½ cups grated mild cheddar cheese

1½ cups yellow cornmeal

1½ cups unbleached all-purpose flour

1 teaspoon salt

1 teaspoon sugar

1 tablespoon baking powder

1. Preheat the oven to 400 degrees. Coat a 13-by-9-inch baking pan with nonstick cooking spray.

2. In a medium mixing bowl, whisk together the soup, eggs, and milk until smooth. Fold in the chiles, corn, and cheese.

3. In a large mixing bowl, stir together the cornmeal, flour, salt, sugar, and baking powder. Gradually add the soup mixture to the cornmeal mixture and stir until blended.

4. Pour the batter into the prepared pan and bake the bread until it is nicely browned and a toothpick inserted in the center comes out clean and dry, 20 to 25 minutes. Serve the bread warm.

This colorful corn bread is loaded with green jalapeños and golden corn. The creamy soup gives the bread a finer texture than more rustic versions of this classic. If you would like to add a bit more heat, try substituting pepper Jack cheese for the cheddar.

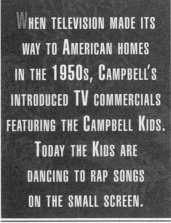

WHEN TELEVISION MADE ITS WAY TO AMERICAN HOMES IN THE 1950s, CAMPBELL'S INTRODUCED TV COMMERCIALS FEATURING THE CAMPBELL KIDS. TODAY THE KIDS ARE DANCING TO RAP SONGS ON THE SMALL SCREEN.

Bread 'n' Soup

Tomato Basil Bread

This recipe was so easy and the results so spectacular, I was astounded. A large, dense loaf with the flavors of tomato and basil will literally sing from your oven. I like to cut this bread into slices and make sandwiches with it.

Revolutionary Soup

George Washington had pepperpot soup prepared to feed his Valley Forge troops. Pepperpot soup was originally sold by women cooks who dispensed it from pushcarts on the streets in Philadelphia. Made with veal bones and tripe, the soup called for red pepper pods, potatoes, beef suet, and flour.

2½ teaspoons active dry yeast

1⅓ cups lukewarm water (105–110 degrees)

¼ teaspoon sugar

3½ cups bread or unbleached all-purpose flour

2 teaspoons salt

1 envelope Knorr Tomato with Basil Soup Mix

1 teaspoon extra virgin olive oil

1. In a small bowl, sprinkle the yeast over the water and stir in the sugar. Set the bowl aside until the yeast is bubbling, about 10 minutes. If the yeast doesn't begin to bubble, discard the mixture and begin again with new yeast.

2. Combine the flour, salt, and soup mix in a large mixing bowl or food processor fitted with the steel blade. Pour the proofed yeast mixture over the flour and process or stir the mixture with a wooden spoon until the dough begins to form a ball.

3. If you are mixing by hand, knead the dough on a floured work surface for about 5 minutes.

4. Oil a medium mixing bowl. Turn the dough into the bowl, flipping the dough over a couple of times to coat it with oil. Cover the bowl with plastic wrap and allow the dough to rise in a warm spot until it is doubled in bulk, about 1 hour.

5. Coat two 9-by-5-by-3-inch loaf pans with nonstick cooking spray. Punch the dough down, form it into loaves, and place it in the prepared pans. Cover the pans and let the dough rise in a warm spot for another 45 minutes.

6. Meanwhile, preheat the oven to 400 degrees.

7. Bake the loaves for 15 minutes, reduce the oven temperature to 375 degrees, and continue baking until the loaves sound hollow when tapped, an additional 20 to 25 minutes. Remove the bread from the oven and allow the loaves to cool in the pans for 15 minutes. Remove them from the pans and slice the bread while it is warm, if you like.

Parmesan Spinach Bread

2 tablespoons active dry yeast

3 cups lukewarm water (105–110 degrees)

2 teaspoons sugar

4$\frac{1}{2}$ cups bread flour, plus more for kneading

1 envelope Knorr Cream of Spinach Soup Mix

$\frac{1}{2}$ cup freshly grated Parmesan cheese

2 tablespoons olive oil, plus 1 teaspoon for the bowl

1. In a small bowl, sprinkle the yeast over the water and stir in the sugar. Allow the mixture to sit until it begins to bubble, about 10 minutes. If the yeast doesn't begin to bubble, discard the mixture and begin again with new yeast.

2. Place the flour, soup mix, and cheese in a large mixing bowl or in a food processor. Gradually stir in the proofed yeast mixture and oil, stirring until the dough begins to form a ball.

3. If mixing by hand, turn the dough out onto a floured board and knead it until it is elastic, about 5 minutes.

4. Oil a medium mixing bowl, transfer the dough to the bowl, and turn it a few times to coat it with oil. Cover the bowl with plastic wrap and let the dough rise in a warm, dry spot until it is doubled in bulk, about 1 hour.

5. Punch down the dough. Coat a 9-by-5-by-3-inch loaf pan with nonstick cooking spray. Form the dough into a loaf and

CHEESY TOMATO BASIL BREAD: If you would like a cheese bread, toss in $\frac{1}{2}$ to 1 cup of your favorite grated cheese when you add the liquid.

MAKES 1 LOAF

This simple yeast bread comes alive with the addition of soup mix and Parmesan cheese. It is great served at dinner and even better toasted for BLTs or club sandwiches the next day.

place it in the prepared pan. Cover the dough and let it rise again in a warm, dry spot for 45 minutes.

6. Meanwhile, preheat the oven to 375 degrees.

7. Bake the loaf until it is golden brown and it sounds hollow when tapped, 45 to 55 minutes. Let the bread cool in the pan for 20 minutes before removing and slicing.

Dilly Bread

MAKES 2 LOAVES OR 36 ROLLS

Moist and fragrant with dill, this versatile dough makes great rolls, or it can be braided into one dramatic large loaf to serve with a fancy dinner.

1½ tablespoons active dry yeast

½ cup lukewarm water (105–110 degrees)

3 tablespoons sugar

2 cups creamed cottage cheese

1 envelope Knorr Leek Soup Mix

1 large egg

4 teaspoons dillweed

4½ cups unbleached all-purpose flour, plus more for kneading

½ teaspoon baking soda

½ cup (1 stick) butter, melted

1. In a small bowl, sprinkle the yeast over the water and stir in the sugar. Let the mixture stand until it bubbles, about 10 minutes. If the yeast doesn't begin to bubble, discard the mixture and begin again with new yeast.

2. While the yeast is proofing, in a large mixing bowl or food processor fitted with a steel blade, stir or process together the cottage cheese, soup mix, egg, and dillweed. Add the proofed yeast mixture to the cottage cheese mixture and combine. Stir in the flour and baking soda, blending until the contents begin to form a sticky ball.

3. If mixing by hand, turn the dough out onto a floured board and knead it until it is smooth and elastic, about 5 minutes.

4. Place the dough in a bowl that has been brushed with some of the melted butter, turning the dough to coat it. Let the dough rise, covered, in a warm, dry spot until it is doubled in bulk, about 1 hour.

5. Coat two 9-by-5-by-3-inch loaf pans with nonstick cooking spray. Punch down the dough, shape it into 2 loaves, and place the loves in the prepared pans. Let the dough rise again, covered, in a warm, dry place for 30 to 40 minutes.

6. Meanwhile, preheat the oven to 350 degrees.

7. Brush the top of the loaves with the remaining melted butter and bake them until they are browned and sound hollow when tapped, 40 to 50 minutes. Let the bread cool in the pans for 20 minutes before removing and slicing.

DILLY ROLLS: For rolls, follow the same recipe, but after the first rise, form the dough into 2-inch balls, place them ½ inch apart on a baking sheet coated with nonstick cooking spray, and let the rolls rise again for 45 minutes. Brush the top of each roll with butter, and bake the rolls until they are browned and they sound hollow when tapped, about 20 minutes.

DILLY MONKEY BREAD: After the first rise, shape the dough into 1-inch balls and place the balls in the prepared loaf pans. Let the dough rise again for 45 minutes, brush it with the melted butter, and bake as directed.

My Hero Bread

MAKES 1 LOAF

Whether you call them grinders, hoagies, submarines, or po' boys, these savory sandwiches filled with meats, cheese, salad, and condiments are a classic. This bread takes the elements of the hero and stirs them into the bread, creating a sandwich bread that is flavored with tomato, basil, nuggets of cheese, and pepperoni.

2½ teaspoons active dry yeast

½ cup lukewarm water

½ teaspoon sugar

3 cups unbleached all-purpose flour, plus more for kneading

1 envelope Knorr Tomato with Basil Soup Mix

½ cup freshly grated Parmesan cheese

½ cup ½-inch dice pepperoni

3 tablespoons extra virgin olive oil plus 1 teaspoon for the bowl

1. In a small bowl sprinkle the yeast over the water and stir in the sugar. Let the mixture stand until it bubbles, about 10 minutes. If the yeast doesn't begin to bubble, discard the mixture and begin again with new yeast.

2. Place the flour, soup mix, Parmesan, pepperoni, and 2 tablespoons of the oil in a large mixing bowl or food processor. Stir in the proofed yeast mixture and mix until the dough begins to form a ball.

3. If mixing by hand, turn the dough out onto a floured board and knead it until it is smooth and elastic, about 5 minutes.

4. Brush a medium mixing bowl with olive oil and turn the dough into the bowl, coating it with the oil. Cover the bowl with plastic wrap and let the dough rise in a warm, dry spot until it is doubled in bulk, about 1 hour.

5. Coat a 9-by-5-by-3-inch loaf pan with nonstick cooking spray. Punch the dough down and shape it into a loaf. Brush the top of the loaf with the remaining 1 tablespoon olive oil and let the dough rise again, covered, in a warm, dry spot for 45 minutes.

6. Meanwhile, preheat the oven to 375 degrees.

7. Bake the bread until it is browned and sounds hollow when tapped, about 30 minutes. Let it cool in the pan for 15 minutes before removing. Let cool completely before slicing.

Swiss Garden Vegetable Loaf

2 1/2 teaspoons rapid-rise yeast

1 1/4 cups lukewarm milk (105–110 degrees)

2 teaspoons sugar

2 1/2 cups unbleached all-purpose flour

1 envelope Knorr Vegetable Soup Mix

1/2 pound Swiss cheese, cut into 1/2-inch cubes

1 large egg

1/4 cup (1/2 stick) butter, melted

1 teaspoon canola oil for the bowl

1. In a small bowl, sprinkle the yeast over the milk and stir in the sugar. Let the mixture stand until it bubbles, about 10 minutes. If the yeast doesn't begin to bubble, discard the mixture and begin again with new yeast.

2. In a large mixing bowl, combine the flour, soup mix, and cheese. Stir in the proofed yeast mixture and the egg. Knead the dough for 5 minutes.

3. Oil a medium mixing bowl and turn the dough into it, coating it with the oil. Cover the bowl with plastic wrap and let the dough rise in a warm, dry spot until it is doubled in bulk, about 1 hour.

4. Meanwhile, preheat the oven to 350 degrees. Coat a 2-quart round casserole dish with nonstick cooking spray.

5. Transfer the dough to the prepared casserole dish, brush the dough with the melted butter, and bake the loaf until it is golden brown and it sounds hollow when tapped, 35 to 45 minutes. Remove the bread from the oven, let it cool for 15 minutes, remove it from the dish, and let it cool completely on a wire rack before slicing.

This delectable yeast bread is filled with vegetables and melted nuggets of Swiss cheese.

CITY LAW IN OCEAN CITY, NEW JERSEY: "IT IS ILLEGAL TO SLURP YOUR SOUP."

Bacon, Onion, and Potato Bread

MAKES 2 LOAVES

In this recipe bacon and sautéed onions pair with cream of potato soup to make a bread reminiscent of a smothered baked potato. This is great toasting bread for sandwiches or poached eggs.

½ pound sliced bacon, cut into ½-inch dice

1 cup finely chopped onion

5 teaspoons active dry yeast

1 cup lukewarm milk (105–110 degrees)

2 tablespoons sugar

5½ cups unbleached all-purpose flour, plus more for kneading

1 can Campbell's Condensed Cream of Potato Soup

½ cup sour cream

½ cup chopped fresh chives

¼ cup (½ stick) butter, melted

1. In a large skillet over medium-high heat, fry the bacon until crisp. Drain off all but 2 tablespoons of the fat, add the onion, and cook, stirring, until it is softened, 3 to 4 minutes. Set the mixture aside to cool.

2. In a small bowl, sprinkle the yeast over the milk and stir in the sugar. Let the yeast mixture stand until it bubbles, about 10 minutes. If the yeast doesn't begin to bubble, discard the mixture and begin again with new yeast.

3. In a large mixing bowl, combine the flour, soup, sour cream, chives, and the onion and bacon mixture. Pour in the proofed yeast mixture and stir until the dough begins to form a ball. Add more flour if the dough is too sticky.

4. Turn the dough out onto a floured surface and knead it until it is smooth and elastic, about 5 minutes.

5. Place the dough in a bowl that has been brushed with some of the melted butter, turning the dough to coat it. Cover the bowl with plastic wrap and let the dough rise in a warm, dry spot until it is doubled in bulk, about 1 hour.

6. Brush two 9-by-5-by-3-inch loaf pans with some of the melted butter. Punch down the dough and divide it in half. Shape the dough into 2 loaves and place them in the prepared pans. Let them rise, covered, for 30 minutes.

7. Meanwhile, preheat the oven to 400 degrees.

8. Brush the loaves with the remaining melted butter and bake them until they are golden brown and sound hollow when tapped, 30 to 40 minutes. Remove the loaves from the oven, let them cool for 15 minutes, and remove them from the pans. Let the bread cool completely before slicing.

Tomato Herb Focaccia

Olive oil for oiling the baking sheet and the bowl

2 teaspoons active dry yeast

1¼ cups warm water (105–110 degrees)

1 teaspoon sugar

3½ cups unbleached all-purpose flour, plus more for kneading

1 package Knorr Tomato with Basil Soup Mix

3 tablespoons extra virgin olive oil

½ cup oil-packed sun-dried tomatoes, drained and chopped

½ cup freshly grated Parmesan cheese (optional)

1. Preheat the oven to 400 degrees. Line a baking sheet with aluminum foil and brush it with olive oil.

2. In a small bowl, sprinkle the yeast over the water and stir in the sugar. Let the mixture stand until it bubbles, about 10 minutes. If it doesn't bubble after 10 minutes, start over again with new yeast.

3. Place the flour, soup mix, and 1 tablespoon of the extra virgin olive oil in a large mixing bowl or food processor. Add the

SERVES 8

Focaccia is a rustic flat Italian bread that can be made plain or in different flavor combinations. The addition of Tomato with Basil Soup Mix and sun-dried tomatoes to this bread makes it extra special. You can make the dough one day ahead and refrigerate it, or you can bake the focaccia and freeze it for up to one month.

proofed yeast mixture and blend until the dough forms a ball. This dough will be a bit sticky.

4. If mixing by hand, turn the dough out onto a floured board and knead it 4 times.

5. Oil a medium mixing bowl and turn the dough into it, coating the dough with the oil. Cover the bowl with a clean kitchen towel and set the dough aside to rise in a warm, dry spot until it is doubled in bulk, about 1 hour. (At this point, the dough can be placed in an oiled resealable plastic bag and stored in the refrigerator for 24 hours or in the freezer for up to 1 month.)

6. Roll out the dough about 1/2 inch thick on a floured board. Transfer the dough to the prepared baking sheet, brush it with the remaining 2 tablespoons olive oil, and sprinkle it evenly with sun-dried tomatoes and cheese. Bake the bread until it is golden brown and the bottom crust is crisp, 20 to 30 minutes. Remove the focaccia from the oven, let it rest for 5 minutes, and then cut it with a pizza wheel.

MAKES TWO 8-INCH ROUNDS

This delectable flatbread is flavored with herbs and then covered with caramelized onions and enhanced by dry soup mix. The combination is a heavenly treat. You can serve this bread as is or split it to use for a great turkey, ham, or roast beef sandwich.

The Soup Mix Gourmet

Onion Herbed Focaccia

2 teaspoons active dry yeast

1¼ cups warm water (105–110 degrees)

3 teaspoons sugar

3¼ cups unbleached all-purpose flour

1 teaspoon salt

1 teaspoon dried oregano

½ teaspoon dried basil

½ teaspoon dried marjoram

2 tablespoons extra virgin olive oil, plus 1 teaspoon oil for bowl

¾ cup (1½ sticks) butter

4 large onions, thinly sliced

1 envelope Lipton Golden Onion Soup Mix

1. In a small bowl sprinkle the yeast over the water and stir in 1 teaspoon sugar. Let the mixture stand until it bubbles, about 10 minutes. If it doesn't bubble after 10 minutes, start over again with new yeast.

2. In a large mixing bowl or food processor fitted with the steel blade, combine the flour, salt, oregano, basil, and marjoram. Pour in the proofed yeast mixture and oil and process or stir to mix.

3. If mixing by hand, turn the dough out onto a floured board and knead it until it is smooth and elastic, about 5 minutes.

4. Oil a medium mixing bowl and turn the dough in the bowl, coating it with the oil. Cover the bowl and let the dough rise until it is doubled in bulk, about 1 hour.

5. Meanwhile, preheat the oven to 400 degrees. Coat two 8-inch round cake pans with nonstick cooking spray.

6. Melt the butter in a large sauté pan over medium heat. Add the onions and remaining sugar and cook, stirring, until they are softened, 4 to 5 minutes. Add the soup mix and continue to cook the onions over medium heat, stirring often, until they begin to turn golden brown, 15 to 20 minutes. Remove the pan from the heat.

7. Punch the dough down, cut it in half, and roll each piece out into an 8-inch circle. Place each piece of dough in a prepared pan and spread the onion mixture over the dough. Bake the loaves until they are golden brown, 35 to 45 minutes. Let the bread rest for 10 minutes before slicing.

Souper Smart

This focaccia does not require any cheese, but I did try it sprinkled with blue cheese, and it was fantastic. Parmesan, smoked Gouda, and Swiss are also good additions.

Pizza 101

This will be the master recipe for pizza dough. For flavored dough, simply add one envelope of dry soup mix. See "Quick Flavored Pizza Doughs" (next page) for suggestions of soup mixes you can add to the dough. In this recipe, we found that bread flour worked best, but you can substitute all-purpose flour if you like. I love to use the food processor to make dough; it's fast and there is no need to knead. You can use your bread machine to mix and knead the dough; just follow the manufacturer's directions. Remember that pizza dough freezes well, so you may want to make the basic recipe and freeze half of the dough for another time; it'll keep for up to two months.

2½ teaspoons active dry yeast

1⅔ cups warm water (105–110 degrees)

1 teaspoon sugar

4 cups bread flour, plus more for kneading

3 tablespoons extra virgin olive oil, plus more for the pan

1. In a small bowl, sprinkle the yeast over the water and stir in the sugar. Let the mixture stand until it bubbles, about 10 minutes. If the yeast doesn't begin to bubble, discard the mixture and begin again with new yeast.

2. Place the flour in a large mixing bowl or a food processor fitted with a steel blade. Add the proofed yeast mixture and oil and stir with a wooden spoon or process until the mixture forms a ball.

3. If mixing by hand, turn the dough out onto a floured board and knead it until it is smooth and elastic, about 5 minutes.

4. Oil the inside of a medium mixing bowl and turn the dough into the bowl, coating it with oil. Cover the bowl with plastic wrap and let the dough rise in a warm, dry spot until it is doubled in bulk, 60 to 90 minutes.

5. Preheat the oven to 425 degrees. Oil 2 pizza pans or baking sheets with olive oil.

6. Cut the dough in half, form each half into a ball, and, working on a floured counter, flatten the dough with a rolling pin, rolling out the dough into a 12-inch circle. Place each dough circle in a prepared pan or on a baking sheet. (If you would like a thick-crust pizza, allow the dough to rise another 30 minutes, top it, and bake.)

7. Top the dough with your favorite toppings and bake the pizza until the crust is crisp and golden and the toppings are cooked through, 15 to 20 minutes.

Quick Flavored Pizza Doughs

The Pizza 101 dough doesn't contain any soup mix, but you can add one envelope of any of these:

- **Lipton Golden Onion Soup Mix**
- **Lipton Onion Soup Mix**
- **Lipton Fiesta Herb with Red Pepper Soup Mix**
- **Knorr Leek Soup Mix**
- **Knorr Cream of Spinach Soup Mix**
- **Knorr Tomato with Basil Soup Mix**
- **Knorr Vegetable Soup Mix**

It Isn't Easy Bein' Green Pizza

MAKES TWO 12-INCH PIZZAS

My friend Lora Brody makes an amazing pizza with a pesto crust that is topped with more pesto and sun-dried tomatoes. With hers as my inspiration, this pizza has a spinach crust, a creamy cheese center, and a little pesto and garlic shrimp to top it off. All your friends will want the recipe, and I guarantee this will make you a convert to using soup mix to give your meals that extra flavor punch.

SPINACH PIZZA DOUGH

2 ½ teaspoons active dry yeast

1 ⅔ cups warm water (105–110 degrees)

1 teaspoon sugar

3 tablespoons extra virgin olive oil, plus more for the pan

4 cups bread flour, plus more for kneading

1 envelope Knorr Cream of Spinach Soup Mix

TOPPING

Two 4-ounce containers cream cheese with chives

1 cup prepared pesto

¼ cup olive oil

¼ cup (½ stick) butter, melted

6 cloves garlic, minced

Pinch of cayenne pepper

½ pound medium shrimp, peeled and deveined

½ cup freshly grated Parmesan cheese

1. In a small bowl, sprinkle the yeast over the water and stir in the sugar. Let the mixture stand until it bubbles, about 10 minutes. If the yeast doesn't begin to bubble, discard the mixture and begin again with new yeast.

2. Place the flour and soup mix in a large mixing bowl or a food processor fitted with a steel blade. Add the yeast mixture and oil and stir with a wooden spoon or process until the mixture forms a ball.

3. If mixing by hand, turn the dough out onto a floured board and knead it until it is smooth and elastic, about 5 minutes.

4. Oil the inside of a medium mixing bowl and turn the dough into the bowl, coating it with the oil. Cover the bowl with plastic wrap and let the dough rise in a warm, dry spot until it is doubled in bulk, 60 to 90 minutes.

5. Preheat the oven to 400 degrees. Oil 2 pizza pans.

6. Punch down the dough and cut it in half, forming 2 balls. Working on a floured counter, flatten each dough piece with a rolling pin, rolling out the dough into a 12-inch circle. Place each piece of dough into a prepared pizza pan.

7. Spread one container of the cream cheese over each dough round. Cover the cream cheese with a thin layer of pesto.

8. Combine the oil, melted butter, garlic, and cayenne in a medium mixing bowl and toss this mixture with the shrimp. Divide the shrimp evenly between the pizzas and pour the remaining garlic butter over the pizzas. Sprinkle on the cheese and bake the pizza until the crust is crisp and the cheese is bubbling, 20 to 30 minutes.

VARIATIONS: Don't like shrimp? Use the same technique but substitute cooked chicken, or omit the garlic butter and top the pizza with drained oil-packed sun-dried tomatoes. Two 4-ounce cans of clams also work well in place of the shrimp.

CAMPBELL'S SOUP SELLS MORE THAN **700,000** TONS OF SOUP EACH YEAR, ENOUGH TO FILL THE OCEAN LINER Queen Elizabeth II MORE THAN **10** TIMES.

Bread 'n' Soup

Buttery Onion Pizza Dough

Not only is this versatile dough great in a pizza, but it also makes great bread sticks. Top this pizza with traditional sauce and cheese, or try making it a four-cheese pizza.

2½ teaspoons active dry yeast

1⅔ cups warm water (105–110 degrees)

1 teaspoon sugar

4 cups bread flour, plus more for kneading

1 envelope Lipton Golden Onion Soup Mix

½ cup (1 stick) butter, melted

Olive oil for pizza pan

1. In a small bowl, sprinkle the yeast over the water and stir in the sugar. Let the mixture stand until it bubbles, about 10 minutes. If the yeast doesn't begin to bubble, discard the mixture and begin again with new yeast.

2. Place the flour and soup mix in a large mixing bowl or a food processor fitted with a steel blade. Add the yeast mixture and melted butter and stir with a wooden spoon or process until the mixture forms a ball.

3. If mixing by hand, turn the dough out onto a floured board and knead it until it is smooth and elastic, about 5 minutes.

4. Oil the inside of a medium mixing bowl and turn the dough into the bowl, coating it with oil. Cover the bowl with plastic wrap and let the dough rise in a warm, dry spot until doubled in bulk, 60 to 90 minutes.

BUTTERY ONION BREAD STICKS: After the first rise, pull the dough into 1-inch balls, then roll each one into a 5-by-½-inch log. Place the dough on baking sheets coated with nonstick cooking spray and brush the bread sticks with melted butter. Let the dough rise for 25 to 30 minutes and then bake the bread sticks until they are golden, 10 to 15 minutes.

5. Preheat the oven to 400 degrees. Coat 2 pizza pans with olive oil.

6. Punch the dough down and cut it in half. Form the dough into 2 balls, and, working on a floured counter, flatten each ball of dough with a rolling pin. Roll the dough into a 12-inch circle. Place the dough in the prepared pizza pans.

7. Top the dough with your favorite toppings and bake the pizza until the crust is crispy, 20 to 25 minutes.

The Soup Mix Gourmet

Garlic Parmesan Pizza Dough

2 1/2 teaspoons active dry yeast

1 2/3 cups warm water (105–110 degrees F)

1 teaspoon sugar

4 cups bread flour, plus more for kneading

1 envelope Lipton Savory Herb with Garlic Soup Mix

1 cup freshly grated Parmesan cheese

3 tablespoons extra virgin olive oil, plus more for the bowl and the pans

1. In a small bowl, sprinkle the yeast over the water and stir in the sugar. Let the mixture stand until it bubbles, about 10 minutes. If the yeast doesn't begin to bubble, discard the mixture and begin again with new yeast.

2. Place the flour, soup mix, and cheese in a large mixing bowl or food processor fitted with a steel blade. Add the yeast mixture and oil and stir with a wooden spoon or process until the mixture forms a ball.

3. If mixing by hand, turn the dough out onto a floured board and knead it until it is smooth and elastic, about 5 minutes.

4. Oil the inside of a medium mixing bowl and turn the dough into the bowl, coating it with the oil. Cover the bowl with plastic wrap and let the dough rise in a warm, dry spot until it is doubled in bulk, 60 to 90 minutes.

5. Preheat the oven to 400 degrees. Coat 2 pizza pans with olive oil.

6. Punch the dough down, cut it in half, and form it into two balls. Working on a floured counter, flatten each piece of dough with a rolling pin, rolling it out into a 12-inch circle. Place each dough round on a prepared pizza pan.

This is my personal favorite, because it's savory with garlic and Parmesan. Brush the dough with a little olive oil and bake it. Top the crust with a mixed green salad tossed with a simple oil and vinegar dressing and then sprinkle on diced ripe tomatoes and cubes of fresh mozzarella.

FOUR-CHEESE PIZZA: Dividing these ingredients between the two crusts, sprinkle 1 cup shredded mozzarella cheese, 1/2 cup freshly grated Parmesan cheese, 1 cup crumbled Gorgonzola cheese, and 1/2 cup shredded imported provolone cheese over each crust. Combine 1/4 cup olive oil with 4 crushed garlic cloves and 1 teaspoon dried oregano and drizzle evenly over the top of each pizza. Bake until the cheese is golden and the crust is crispy, 20 to 25 minutes.

Bread 'n' Soup

7. Top the dough with your favorite toppings and bake the pizza until the crust is crispy, 20 to 25 minutes.

Garlic Sesame Bread Sticks

2 1/2 teaspoons rapid-rise dry yeast

1/2 cups warm water (105-110 degrees)

2 teaspoons sugar

4 cups bread flour or unbleached all-purpose flour

1 envelope Lipton Savory Herb with Garlic Soup Mix

1/4 cup olive oil, plus more for the bowl

1/3 cup sesame seeds

1. In a small bowl, sprinkle the yeast over the water and stir in the sugar. Let the mixture stand until it bubbles, about 5 minutes. If it doesn't bubble, discard it and begin again with new yeast.

2. Place the flour and soup mix in a large mixing bowl or a food processor fitted with a steel blade. Add the proofed yeast mixture and 3 tablespoons of the oil and stir with a wooden spoon or process until the mixture forms a ball.

3. If mixing by hand, turn the dough out onto a floured board and knead it until it is smooth and elastic, about 5 minutes.

4. Oil the inside of a medium mixing bowl and turn the dough into the bowl, coating it with the oil. Cover the bowl with plastic wrap and let the dough rise in a warm, dry spot until it is doubled in bulk, 60 to 90 minutes.

5. Preheat the oven to 400 degrees. Coat a baking sheet with nonstick cooking spray.

This recipe is quicker than most yeast breads. You can have delicious garlicky bread sticks that are crispy on the outside and moist on the inside in about 90 minutes. Using rapid-rise dry yeast helps to move the process along. I sometimes mix the dough in the morning, refrigerate it, and then bake the sticks at dinnertime.

WHEN ARTIST ANDY WARHOL WAS ONCE ASKED WHY HE PAINTED SOUP CANS, HE REPLIED, "BECAUSE I USED TO DRINK SOUP. I USED TO HAVE THE SAME LUNCH EVERY DAY FOR 20 YEARS."

6. Pull off 1-inch balls from the dough and roll each dough ball into a 4- to 5-inch length. Place the bread sticks on the prepared baking sheet, brush them with the remaining 1 tablespoon olive oil, and sprinkle on the sesame seeds. Bake the bread sticks until they are golden brown, 12 to 16 minutes. Let them cool for 10 minutes before eating.

Chicken Herb Biscuits

2½ cups unbleached all-purpose flour

1 tablespoon baking powder

1 teaspoon salt

1 can Campbell's Condensed Cream of Chicken with Herbs Soup

2 tablespoons butter, melted

1. Preheat the oven to 375 degrees. Coat a baking sheet with nonstick cooking spray.

2. Place the flour, baking powder, and salt in a large mixing bowl. Gradually stir the soup into the flour mixture until the dough begins to come together.

3. Turn the dough out onto a floured board and roll out the dough ³/4 inch thick. Cut out 1-inch biscuits and place them on the prepared baking sheet. Brush the top of each biscuit with the melted butter.

4. Bake the biscuits until they are golden brown, 16 to 18

MAKES 10 TO 12 BISCUITS

The first time I made these biscuits, I was amazed at how light and fluffy they were, all with the help of a can of Campbell's Condensed Cream of Chicken with Herbs Soup. These biscuits are great as an accompaniment at dinner, or you can roll them out as a top crust for a chicken pot pie. If you like cheesy biscuits, add ¹/2 to 1 cup grated cheddar cheese to the dough.

CHICKEN BISCUITS: Substitute Campbell's Condensed Cream of Chicken Soup.

CHEDDAR CHEESE BISCUITS: Substitute Campbell's Condensed Cheddar Cheese Soup.

Bread 'n' Soup

Potato Chive Biscuits

Another easy recipe, this one uses cream of potato soup and chopped chives to produce a moist and flavorful biscuit.

2½ cups unbleached all-purpose flour

1 tablespoon baking powder

1 teaspoon salt

1 can Campbell's Condensed Cream of Potato Soup

¼ cup chopped fresh chives

2 tablespoons butter, melted

1. Preheat the oven to 375 degrees. Coat a baking sheet with nonstick cooking spray.

2. Place the flour, baking powder, and salt in a large mixing bowl. Gradually stir the soup and chives into the flour mixture until the dough begins to come together.

3. Turn the dough out onto a floured board and roll the dough out ¾ inch thick. Cut out 1-inch biscuits and place them on the prepared baking sheet. Brush the top of each biscuit with the melted butter.

4. Bake the biscuits until they are golden brown, 16 to 18 minutes.

Onion Burger Buns

These rolls will be the hit of your backyard barbecue. You can make the dough the day before and refrigerate it until you are ready to bake the rolls. I recommend serving them the day you bake them.

2½ teaspoons dry active yeast

1 cup lukewarm water (105–110 degrees)

1 tablespoon sugar

4 cups unbleached all-purpose flour, plus more for kneading

1 envelope Lipton Beefy Onion, Onion, or Golden Onion Soup Mix

3 tablespoons butter, melted

1 large egg, beaten

1. In a small bowl, sprinkle the yeast over the water and stir in the sugar. Let the mixture stand until it bubbles, about 10 minutes. If the yeast doesn't begin to bubble, discard the mixture and begin again with new yeast.

2. Place the flour, soup mix, and 2 tablespoons of the melted butter into a large mixing bowl or food processor fitted with a steel blade. Add the yeast mixture and stir or process until the mixture comes together in a ball.

3. If mixing by hand, turn the dough out onto a floured board and knead it until it is smooth and elastic, about 5 minutes.

4. Brush the remaining 1 tablespoon butter over the bottom of a medium mixing bowl and turn the dough in the bowl, coating it with the butter. Cover the bowl with plastic wrap and let the dough rise in a warm, dry spot place until it is doubled in bulk, about 1 hour.

5. Punch down the dough and shape it into 2-inch rolls. Place the rolls on a greased baking sheet, cover them, and let them rise, covered, in a warm, dry spot for 30 minutes.

6. Meanwhile, preheat the oven to 400 degrees.

7. Brush the rolls with the beaten eggs, and bake them for 15 minutes. Reduce the oven temperature to 375 degrees, and bake the rolls until they are golden brown, an additional 10 minutes. Cool the rolls for 30 minutes.

Red, White, and Soup

The familiar red-and-white label on the Campbell's soup can came about when company executive Herberton Williams attended a football game between archrivals Cornell University and the University of Pennsylvania. Williams found the new red-and-white uniforms for Cornell so striking that he convinced the company to adopt the colors as its own, changing the labels on the cans of Campbell's soups.

Bread 'n' Soup

Blue Cheese Bites

SERVES 6

This recipe takes refrigerated biscuits and turns them into a pull-apart bread that is a blue cheese–lover's dream. You can use the same technique and substitute grated Parmesan, Swiss, or smoked mozzarella cheese.

Two 10-ounce cans refrigerated biscuits

¾ cup (1½ sticks) butter or margarine

1 envelope Lipton Savory Garlic with Herb Soup Mix

1½ cups crumbled blue cheese

1. Preheat the oven to 375 degrees. Coat a 9-by-5-by-3-inch loaf pan with nonstick cooking spray.

2. Cut each biscuit into quarters and set the pieces aside.

3. Melt the butter and stir in the soup mix. Dip each biscuit quarter into the butter mixture and place it in the loaf pan, sprinkling some of the blue cheese between the layers of biscuit quarters.

4. When all the biscuits are used up, pour the remaining butter over the top of the loaf and sprinkle on any remaining cheese.

5. Bake the loaf until it is golden brown, 25 to 30 minutes. Remove the pan from the oven and let the loaf rest for 10 minutes. Remove the loaf from the pan. I find it's easier to serve the loaf whole and let everyone pick it apart, but the bread can be sliced with a serrated knife.

Onion Cheddar Crescents

Two 8-ounce cans refrigerated crescent rolls

½ cup (1 stick) butter or margarine, softened

1 envelope Lipton Golden Onion Soup Mix

1½ cups grated mild cheddar cheese

1. Preheat the oven to 400 degrees and coat a baking sheet with nonstick cooking spray.

2. On a flat surface, separate the dough into triangles.

3. In a medium mixing bowl, beat together the butter, soup mix, and cheese. Spread some of the mixture over each triangle and roll it up starting from the wide end to form a crescent.

4. Place the rolls on the prepared baking sheet and bake them until they are golden brown, 14 to 18 minutes. Let the rolls rest on the baking sheet for 5 minutes before removing them with a metal spatula.

These rolls are so good you may want to make a double batch! Fragrant with onion and filled with cheddar cheese, Poppin' Fresh never had it so good.

Souper Smart

For a fast appetizer, lay the dough flat and pinch the seams together. Roll the dough out to form a rectangle, cover with the filling, and roll the dough like a jelly roll. Cut the roll into ¾-inch-thick rounds, place them on a greased baking sheet, and bake until they are golden, eight to ten minutes.

Spicy Popovers

Popovers are a little bit of batter filled with a lot of air, but when they come hot out of the oven, they are ethereal. This version, made using Lipton Golden Onion Soup Mix, makes the perfect bread to serve with soup and a salad.

VARIATIONS:
Try using any of the following soup mixes instead of Golden Onion:

- Knorr Cream of Spinach Soup Mix
- Knorr Leek Soup Soup Mix
- Knorr Tomato with Basil Soup Mix
- Lipton Savory Herb with Garlic Soup Mix
- Lipton Beefy Onion Soup Mix
- Lipton Fiesta Herb with Red Pepper Soup Mix

¼ cup (½ stick) butter, melted

2 cups milk

4 large eggs

2 cups unbleached all-purpose flour

1 envelope Lipton Golden Onion Soup Mix

1. Preheat the oven to 425 degrees. Place 1 teaspoon of melted butter into each of 12 muffin cups and place the muffin tin in the oven while the oven is preheating.

2. In a large mixing bowl or blender, blend the milk and eggs together. Stir in the flour and soup mix until they are well blended. (The batter can be refrigerated for up to 2 days at this point. Bring the batter to room temperature and whisk the batter well before proceeding with the recipe.)

3. Fill each muffin cup half full with batter and bake the popovers for 20 minutes. Reduce the oven temperature to 350 degrees and bake the popovers until they are golden brown, an additional 15 to 20 minutes. Serve the popovers hot from the oven.

Savory Pita Chips

1 bag 6-inch round pita breads (there should be 6 or 8 in the bag)

½ cup (1 stick) butter

½ cup olive oil

1 envelope Lipton Savory Herb with Garlic Soup Mix

1. Preheat the oven to 350 degrees and line 2 baking sheets with aluminum foil.

2. With a large knife, cut each pita into quarters. Carefully separate the top from the bottom of the bread and lay the slices on the prepared baking sheets.

3. Melt the butter with the olive oil in a small saucepan over medium heat and stir in the soup mix.

4. Brush the garlic butter mixture over the pitas and bake them until they are hard like crackers and golden brown, 15 to 20 minutes. Let them cool and then store them in airtight containers.

Those tiny bags of pita chips in the grocery store cannot hold a candle to these savory little bites. You can bake these a few weeks ahead of time and then store them in the freezer; just defrost the chips and serve.

VARIATIONS:
Substitute any of these soup mixes for the Savory Herb and Garlic:

■ **Lipton Onion Soup Mix**

■ **Lipton Golden Onion Soup Mix**

■ **Lipton Fiesta Herb with Red Pepper Soup Mix**

■ **Knorr Vegetable Soup Mix**

■ **Knorr Spring Vegetable Soup Mix**

Artichoke Delight

Curly's Golden Cowboy Baked Beans

Southwestern Black Beans

Hill o' Beans Vegetarian Chili

Classic Green Bean Bake

Green Beans with Sherried Onion and Mushroom Sauce

Broccoli Frittata

Broccoli White Cheddar Pie

Glazed Baby Carrots

Oniony Grilled Corn on the Cob

Mexicorn

Corn Mediterranean Style

Corn Pancakes

Gulliver's Corn

Scalloped Corn Casserole

Corn, Zucchini, and Tomato Bake

Eggplant Rollatini

Eggplant Napoleons

Szechuan Eggplant

Wild Blue Mushroom Bread Pudding

Broiled or Grilled Portobello Mushrooms

Cheesy Sausage Portobello Pizzas

Portobello Pizza Caprese

Portobello Margherita

Caramelized Onions in Red Wine Sauce

Red, White, and Blue Cheese Onions

Glazed Sugar Snap Peas and Carrots

Roasted Garlic Red Potatoes

Country-Fried All-American Potatoes

Oven-Fried Potato Wedges

Potato Pizza

Herbed Goat Cheese Potato Pie

Easy Scalloped Potatoes

Savory Onion Mashed Potatoes

Garlic Herb Mashed Potatoes

Shrimply Delicious Mashed Potatoes

Popeye's Spinach and Mashed Potatoes

Skinny Leeky Potatoes

Bacon and Onion Mashed Potatoes

Red, White, and Blue Smashed Potatoes

Broccoli Cheddar Mashed Potatoes

Santa Fe Potatoes

Mashed Potatoes El Greco

Fiesta Nacho Mashed Potatoes

Make-Ahead Mashed Potatoes

Twice-Baked Stuffed Spuds

Stuffed Spuds Florentine

Hash Brown Casserole

Ten-Minute Creamed Spinach

Sweet Potatoes Stuffed with Asian Stir-Fried Vegetables

Braised Swiss Chard

Parmesan Herbed Tomatoes

Grandma's Stuffed Tomatoes

Old-Fashioned Stewed Tomatoes

Gruyère Zucchini Boats

Zucchini Florentine

Zucchini Corn Pancakes

Zucchini Stuffing Casserole

Summer Squash Bake

Peperonata

Vegetable Custards

Ratatouille

Roasted Garlic Vegetables

Vegetable Feta Bake

Vegetables

MOTHERS EVERYWHERE EXHORT THEIR CHILDREN TO "eat your vegetables." Unfortunately, that plate of limp gray broccoli is not nearly as appetizing as it could be. This chapter is for cooks everywhere who want their family to eat tasty vegetables at every meal. We all grew up with some version of the famous green bean bake using canned French green beans and cream of mushroom soup, topped with canned fried onion rings. Today soups pair with a myriad of fresh or frozen vegetables to make great side dishes such as Zucchini Stuffing Casserole (page 256), grilled vegetables, and a dozen different types of mashed potatoes. Using a little creativity and the soups in your pantry, you'll be able to perk up any weekday meal. Each recipe will be one that your family will ask for again and again, and they can take down the NO GRAY BROCCOLI sign!

Artichoke Delight

The delight in this recipe is its simplicity—just a few ingredients and you have a delectable side dish in less than 30 minutes. Artichokes are most affordable during their season, usually late January through April, but you can buy them all year round in most areas.

MORE THAN 100 MILLION ONIONS GO INTO THE MAKING OF LIPTON RECIPE SECRETS EVERY YEAR.

4 cups water

1 envelope Lipton Savory Herb with Garlic Soup Mix

1 lemon, cut into quarters

6 globe artichokes

1. In a 6-quart Dutch oven, combine the water, the soup mix, and lemon, squeezing the lemon quarters to release the juice as you place them into the pan.

2. Slice off the top third of each artichoke and trim the stem end. Remove any tough leaves near the stem, and rinse the artichoke in cold water. Dip each artichoke top into the soup mixture, and then place it stem side down in the pan. Repeat with the remaining artichokes.

3. Bring the soup mixture to a boil, reduce the heat to low, and simmer the artichokes, covered, until a leaf will come out fairly easily or until the tip of a small knife goes into the artichokes easily, 30 to 40 minutes.

4. Drain the artichokes and serve. If you would like to serve the artichokes cold, plunge them into ice water to stop the cooking process, and then refrigerate them for up to 12 hours.

The Soup Mix Gourmet

Curly's Golden Cowboy Baked Beans

6 strips bacon, cut into 1-inch pieces

1 pound lean ground beef

1 cup chopped onion

1 teaspoon chili powder (optional)

1 can Campbell's Condensed Tomato Soup

1 envelope Lipton Golden Onion Soup Mix

1/3 cup firmly packed light brown sugar

1 tablespoon rice vinegar or cider vinegar

1 tablespoon Dijon mustard

2 tablespoons Worcestershire sauce

Two 16-ounce cans baked beans

1. In a 5-quart Dutch oven, fry the bacon over medium-high heat until it is crisp. Using a slotted spoon, remove the bacon to paper towels to drain. Remove all the fat from the pan.

2. Add the ground beef and cook it over high heat until it loses its pink color, draining off any fat or water that accumulates in the bottom of the pan.

3. Add the onion and chili powder, if you are using it, and cook, stirring, until the onion is softened, 3 to 4 minutes. Add the tomato soup, soup mix, brown sugar, vinegar, mustard, Worcestershire, reserved bacon, and beans. Simmer the mixture over low heat until the sauce is thickened, about 45 minutes. The dish can be refrigerated for up to 48 hours or frozen for up to 1 month.

SERVES 8

This dish was a tradition at cookouts when I was a kid. The beans were cooked in a tangy barbecue sauce loaded with beef and bacon. This is a great way to get your kids to eat beans; just tell them it's like the food on the trail, only they get to sleep in their own beds!

Slow Cooker Savvy

Brown the bacon and beef and start the sauce. Transfer the meat to the slow cooker along with the remaining ingredients. Cook the beans on low for four to six hours.

CAMPBELL'S CONDENSED TOMATO SOUP WAS INTRODUCED IN 1897.

Vegetables

A great side dish to serve with fajitas or tacos, these black beans are great prepared in a slow cooker. Serve over rice for a whole meal.

Slow Cooker Savvy

Sauté the onion and spices, transfer them to the slow cooker along with the rest of the ingredients, and cook the beans on low for four hours.

Southwestern Black Beans

2 tablespoons vegetable oil

1 cup chopped onion

2 Anaheim chiles, seeded and finely chopped

2 teaspoons ground cumin

1 envelope Lipton Fiesta Herb with Red Pepper Soup Mix

One 14.5-ounce can chopped tomatoes, with their juices

1 cup water

2 tablespoons fresh lime juice

Three 15-ounce cans black beans, drained and rinsed

¼ cup chopped fresh cilantro leaves for garnish

1. In a 4-quart saucepan, heat the oil and cook the onion, chiles, cumin, and soup mix over medium heat, stirring, for 5 minutes. Add the tomatoes, water, and lime juice and let the ingredients simmer for 5 minutes.

2. Add the black beans, bring the pot to a boil, reduce the heat to medium-low, and simmer the beans, covered, for 30 minutes. Serve the beans garnished with the cilantro.

M y complaint with some vegetarian chili is that it doesn't have enough flavor, but this thick, hearty chili, filled with chunky vegetables and lots of beans, fills the bill. The dry soup mix intensifies the flavors and helps to make this a meal your

Hill o' Beans Vegetarian Chili

2 tablespoons olive oil

2 cups chopped onion

4 cloves garlic, coarsely chopped

2 Anaheim chiles, seeded and chopped

2 teaspoons chili powder

1 teaspoon ground cumin

1 envelope Lipton Fiesta Herb with Red Pepper Soup Mix

One 28-ounce can chopped tomatoes, with their juices

1 cup water or vegetable broth

2 tablespoons fresh lime juice

One 15-ounce can black beans, drained and rinsed

One 15-ounce can garbanzo beans, drained and rinsed

One 15-ounce can kidney beans, drained and rinsed

One 15-ounce can pinto beans, drained and rinsed

2 cups corn kernels, either cut fresh from the cob or frozen (and defrosted)

½ cup chopped fresh cilantro leaves

Sour cream, grated mild cheddar or Monterey Jack cheese, chopped red onion, and chopped jalapeños for garnish

1. In a 5-quart Dutch oven, heat the oil over medium heat, add the onion, garlic, and chiles, and cook, stirring, until the vegetables have softened a bit, 3 to 4 minutes. Add the chili powder, cumin, and soup mix and cook, stirring, for 2 to 3 minutes to allow the oils in the spices to cook. Add the tomatoes, bring the mixture to a boil, and add the water or vegetable broth and lime juice. Add the beans and corn and bring the chili to a simmer. Reduce the heat to medium-low and simmer the chili, partially covered, for 30 minutes.

2. Stir in the cilantro and serve the chili garnished with sour cream, cheese, red onion, and jalapeños. Leftover chili can be frozen for up to 6 weeks.

family will look forward to. This chili is best made a day or two ahead of time so that the flavors can meld, but you can also put it together in less than an hour.

Souper Smart

If you prefer dried beans to canned, soak the beans overnight in water to cover, drain the water, and then gently simmer the beans in water to cover until the beans are tender, about one hour, watching the water and adding more as necessary. Add the beans to the chili per the recipe. My personal opinion is that since there are so many other flavors in the chili, you may not notice having taken the extra time and steps to start with dried beans rather than canned.

Slow Cooker Savvy

Sauté the vegetables and spices and then transfer them to the slow cooker along with the remaining ingredients. Cook the chili on low for six hours.

Vegetables

Classic Green Bean Bake

After World War II, Campbell's home economists cooked up recipes like this one that fed scores of baby boomers. Lots of variations have evolved from it.

ASIAN GREEN BEAN BAKE: Omit the onions. Add one 4-ounce can sliced water chestnuts, drained, along with the beans, and top the casserole with crunchy chow mein noodles.

SOUTHWESTERN GREEN BEAN BAKE: Substitute 1/4 cup salsa for the soy sauce and milk. Top the casserole with 1/2 cup shredded mild cheddar cheese and 1 cup crushed tortilla chips along with the onions.

ITALIAN GREEN BEAN BAKE: Omit the soy sauce and onions, and add 1/2 teaspoon each dried basil and oregano to the soup. Top the casserole with sliced tomatoes and 1 cup grated mozzarella cheese.

1 can Campbell's Condensed Cream of Mushroom or Cream of Celery Soup

1/2 cup milk

1 teaspoon soy sauce

One 3.5-ounce can French fried onions

4 cups cooked green beans

Dash of freshly ground black pepper

1. Preheat the oven to 350 degrees.

2. In a 1 1/2-quart casserole dish, mix together the soup, milk, soy sauce, half of the onions, the beans, and pepper. Bake the casserole until it is hot, about 25 minutes.

3. Stir the casserole and sprinkle the remaining onions over the top. Bake the casserole for an additional 5 minutes, until the onions are golden.

Green Beans with Sherried Onion and Mushroom Sauce

2 pounds green beans, ends trimmed and cut into 1-inch lengths

1 teaspoon salt

$\frac{1}{2}$ teaspoon freshly ground black pepper

2 tablespoons butter

6 ounces pearl onions (about 12), peeled (page 387) and cut in half

1 pound mushrooms, cut into $\frac{1}{2}$-inch-thick slices

1 can Campbell's Condensed Cream of Mushroom Soup

$\frac{1}{2}$ cup half-and-half

3 tablespoons cream sherry

$\frac{1}{8}$ teaspoon freshly grated nutmeg

Chopped fresh chives for garnish

1. Place the green beans in water to cover in a large saucepan, bring to a boil, reduce the heat to medium, cover, and simmer the beans until they are just tender, 10 to 15 minutes. Drain the beans thoroughly and season them with salt and pepper. Keep the beans warm in the pan.

2. Melt the butter in a 10-inch sauté pan over medium heat and cook the onions, stirring, until they are softened, 3 to 4 minutes. Add the mushrooms and cook, stirring, until they begin to give off some of their liquid, 4 to 5 minutes. Add the soup and half-and-half and stir until the sauce comes to a boil. Stir in the sherry and nutmeg and remove the pan from the heat.

3. Place the green beans in a serving bowl and pour the sauce over them. Garnish with chopped chives and serve immediately.

SERVES 6 TO 8

A twist on the classic green bean bake, this recipe uses tiny pearl onions and mushrooms. The sauce can be prepared two days ahead of time.

GREEN BEANS WITH SHERRIED ONION AND CELERY SAUCE: Substitute Campbell's Condensed Cream of Celery Soup.

GREEN BEANS WITH SHERRIED ONION AND CHICKEN SAUCE: Substitute Campbell's Condensed Cream of Chicken Soup.

Souper Smart

For a do-ahead trick, blanch the green beans in boiling water for five minutes, shock them in cold water, drain them, and refrigerate them. When ready to serve, bring 5 cups water to a boil, plunge the beans into the water for one minute, drain, season with the salt and pepper, and pick up with step 2.

Vegetables

Broccoli Frittata

Broccoli is one of my favorite vegetables, and this classic is a great way to use up leftovers. Try this recipe with spinach, mushrooms, zucchini, or artichoke hearts for a luncheon or light supper.

3 tablespoons butter

1 tablespoon olive oil

¼ cup chopped shallots

3 cups cooked broccoli florets

6 large eggs

1 envelope Knorr Cream of Broccoli Soup Mix

½ cup freshly grated Parmesan cheese

½ teaspoon freshly ground black pepper

1. Preheat the oven to 350 degrees.

2. Melt the butter with the oil in a 10-inch ovenproof skillet over medium heat. Add the shallots and cook, stirring occasionally, until they are softened, about 2 minutes. Add the broccoli and cook the vegetables, stirring occasionally, for another 3 minutes.

3. While the shallots and broccoli are cooking, whisk together the eggs, soup mix, cheese, and pepper in a medium mixing bowl. Pour the eggs and soup mixture into the skillet, stirring the broccoli into the eggs.

4. Bake the frittata in the oven until it is set, 18 to 20 minutes. Let the frittata rest for 5 minutes before cutting it into wedges and serving.

Broccoli White Cheddar Pie

2 tablespoons butter

1 cup chopped onion

4 cups broccoli florets

½ cup mayonnaise

1 can Campbell's Condensed Cream of Celery Soup

2 cups grated sharp white cheddar cheese

½ cup dry breadcrumbs

2 tablespoons butter, melted

1. Preheat the oven to 350 degrees. Coat a 1½-quart casserole dish with nonstick cooking spray.

2. Melt the butter in a 10-inch sauté pan over medium heat and cook the onion, stirring, until softened, 3 to 4 minutes. Add the broccoli, cover the sauté pan, and cook the broccoli until it is crisp-tender, about 4 minutes. Let cool.

3. In a large mixing bowl, combine the mayonnaise, soup, and cheese. Stir in the broccoli mixture. Pour the contents of the bowl into the prepared casserole dish.

4. In a small mixing bowl, combine the breadcrumbs and melted butter and sprinkle the breadcrumbs on top of the casserole. Bake the casserole until it is bubbling and the breadcrumbs are golden brown, about 35 minutes.

SERVES 8

This casserole is a take-off on an old potluck dinner dish. I love the way broccoli pairs with cheddar cheese, and the sharp, smooth white cheddar makes this a dish your family members will put on their top ten list.

Vegetables

Glazed Baby Carrots

This side dish is simple yet elegant to serve with poultry, beef, or pork. Since baby carrots are so widely available, you can make this dish any night of the week.

ORANGE GLAZED CARROTS: These carrots were popular in the 1940s and 1950s served alongside roasted chicken. Combine 2 tablespoons orange marmalade with the soup mix and water, omitting the brown sugar, butter, and thyme, for this delicious variation. Proceed as directed in the recipe.

1 envelope Lipton Golden Onion Soup Mix

1½ cups water

½ cup firmly packed light brown sugar

¼ cup (½ stick) butter

1 teaspoon fresh thyme leaves or ½ teaspoon dried

4 cups baby carrots

1. Combine the soup mix, water, brown sugar, butter, and thyme in a 3-quart saucepan and bring the pot to a boil.

2. Add the carrots and simmer them, uncovered, over medium-low heat until they are tender but still crisp, stirring frequently, about 10 minutes. Serve immediately.

Oniony Grilled Corn on the Cob

8 ears fresh corn

4 cups water

1 tablespoon sugar

½ teaspoon salt

1 cup (2 sticks) butter, softened

1 envelope Lipton Golden Onion Soup Mix

1. Trimming the stem from the corn, but leaving it attached, carefully peel the husks from the corn straight down, but do not remove the husks. Remove all the corn silk and pull the husks back up around the corn.

2. Combine the water, sugar, and salt in a 5-quart stockpot. Soak the corn in the water for 20 minutes, turning it a few times.

3. In a medium mixing bowl, beat together the butter and soup mix until smooth; refrigerate the flavored butter until you are ready to use it, but let it soften again before using it.

4. Preheat a gas grill for 10 minutes.

5. Remove the corn from the water, draining it well. Peel back the husk and spread the inside with 2 to 3 tablespoons of the softened butter. Pull the husks back up around the corn, twisting the ends of the husks to secure them.

6. Grill the corn for 20 to 30 minutes, turning it frequently. Serve the corn with the remaining butter.

What could be better than sweet corn on the cob, smoky and drenched in onion- or herb-flavored butter? I'm not sure I can think of anything! The corn is simple to prepare, and the flavored butter can be made up and refrigerated for up to five days or frozen for up to two months.

VARIATIONS:
Substitute these soup mixes for a new twist on this delicious side dish:

- Lipton Fiesta Herb with Red Pepper Soup Mix
- Lipton Savory Herb with Garlic Soup Mix
- Lipton or Knorr Vegetable Soup Mix
- Knorr Leek Soup Mix
- Lipton Onion Soup Mix
- Knorr Tomato with Basil Soup Mix

Vegetables

Mexicorn

SERVES 6

Filled with sweet corn and salsa, flavored with cumin, and topped with melted cheese, this spicy corn dish is a great accompaniment to grilled meats, poultry, and fish.

QUICK MEXICORN: You can make a quicker version of this recipe by combining 1 can Campbell's Condensed Fiesta Nacho Cheese Soup with 1 cup milk and 3 cups corn kernels. Bake the casserole for 20 minutes.

2 tablespoons butter

1/2 cup chopped onion

1 clove garlic, minced

1 teaspoon ground cumin

1/2 cup medium-hot salsa

1 can Campbell's Condensed Cream of Celery or Cream of Chicken Soup

1 cup milk

3 cups corn kernels, either cut fresh from the cob or frozen (and defrosted)

1 1/2 cups grated mild cheddar cheese

1/2 cup sour cream for garnish

1/4 cup chopped fresh cilantro leaves for garnish

1. Preheat the oven to 350 degrees. Coat a 1 1/2-quart casserole dish with nonstick cooking spray.

2. In a large saucepan, melt the butter over medium heat, add the onion, garlic, and cumin, and cook, stirring, until the onion and garlic are softened, 3 to 4 minutes. Add the salsa, stirring to blend. Whisk in the soup and milk and then add the corn. Bring the mixture to a boil and then transfer it to the prepared casserole dish. (At this point, the casserole can be refrigerated for up to 2 days.)

3. Sprinkle the cheese evenly over the top of the corn and bake the casserole until it is bubbling and the cheese is melted, 20 to 25 minutes.

4. Garnish each serving with a dollop of sour cream and some cilantro.

Corn Mediterranean Style

SERVES 6

¼ cup (½ stick) butter

¼ cup chopped red onion

1 envelope Lipton Savory Herb with Garlic Soup Mix

¼ cup white wine

2 medium zucchini, ends trimmed, and cut into ½-inch-thick rounds

3 medium ripe tomatoes, cut into ¾-inch wedges

3 cups corn kernels, either cut fresh from the cob or frozen (and defrosted)

1 tablespoon chopped fresh basil leaves

2 tablespoons chopped fresh Italian parsley leaves

This quick dish takes corn, zucchini, and tomatoes and quickly cooks them with flavors of the Mediterranean to create a side dish that will help to get rid of some of the overflow from a summer garden. During the winter when tomatoes aren't at their best, use one 14.5-ounce can chopped tomatoes, drained of their juices.

1. Melt the butter in a 12-inch sauté pan over medium heat, add the onion, and cook, stirring, until it is softened, about 2 minutes. Add the soup mix and cook, stirring, for another 2 minutes.

2. Add the wine and then add the zucchini, tomatoes, and corn. Cover the pan and steam the vegetables for 2 minutes. Remove the cover and continue to cook the vegetables, stirring, until they are tender, about 5 minutes.

3. Stir in the basil and parsley and serve.

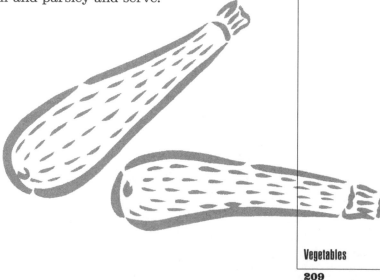

Vegetables

Corn Pancakes

SERVES 6

This is a great way to get breakfast for dinner. I love to serve these pancakes with maple syrup on the side, but they are delicious all by themselves. When I was having trouble coaxing my children to eat vegetables, I went through a pancake phase, making pancakes with almost every vegetable I could think of. They drew the line at beets—for some reason red pancakes were not appetizing. The basic recipe works well with grated zucchini, spinach, yellow squash, and chopped artichoke hearts.

2 cups buttermilk

1 envelope Knorr Leek Soup Mix

2 large eggs

3 tablespoons vegetable oil

1¼ cups yellow cornmeal

¼ cup all-purpose flour

½ teaspoon baking soda

1½ cups corn kernels, either cut fresh from the cob or frozen (and defrosted)

Vegetable oil or butter for frying

1. In a large mixing bowl, combine the buttermilk, soup mix, eggs, and oil. Stir in the cornmeal, flour, baking soda, and corn just until combined.

2. Heat a large nonstick griddle or skillet over medium-high heat. Pour 2 tablespoons of the batter onto the griddle or skillet for each pancake. Fry the pancakes until they are golden, about 2 minutes on each side. Serve them immediately or keep warm in a 300-degree oven.

Gulliver's Corn

¹/₂ cup freshly grated Parmesan cheese

1¹/₂ cups milk

1 envelope Knorr Leek Soup Mix

4 cups frozen corn kernels, defrosted

1 tablespoon sugar

2 tablespoons butter, cut into small pieces

1. Preheat the oven to 350 degrees. Grease a 1¹/₂-quart casserole dish with butter. Sprinkle 3 tablespoons of the cheese into the casserole, tilting the dish so that the cheese covers the butter evenly.

2. In a 2-quart saucepan, heat the milk and soup mix together, stirring, until it comes to a boil. Add the corn and sugar and bring the mixture back to a boil.

3. Transfer the corn to the prepared casserole dish. Sprinkle on the remaining 5 tablespoons cheese and dot the top of the casserole with the butter.

4. Bake the casserole until the sauce is bubbling and the cheese is golden, 20 to 30 minutes.

This is my son Ryan's favorite dish at Thanksgiving or Christmas dinner. Creamy corn baked with a Parmesan crust is the perfect side dish for meat, poultry, or fish. This dish is a takeoff on one served at Gulliver's restaurant in Orange County, California, a place that is famous for its prime rib dinners and delicious sides.

Scalloped Corn Casserole

This recipe for scalloped corn, updated from the 1950s, will have your family giving you a standing ovation.

SCALLOPED CHICKEN CORN CASSEROLE: Substitute Campbell's Condensed Cream of Chicken Soup and top the casserole with grated smoked Gouda cheese.

SCALLOPED SHRIMP CORN CASSEROLE: Substitute Campbell's Condensed Cream of Shrimp Soup, add 1 teaspoon Old Bay seasoning to the soup and milk, and top the casserole with grated white cheddar cheese.

SCALLOPED CHILE CORN CASSEROLE: Substitute Campbell's Condensed Cream of Celery Soup, stir in 1/4 cup canned diced green chiles, drained and rinsed, and top the casserole with grated mild cheddar cheese.

3 tablespoons butter

1/2 cup grated sharp white cheddar cheese

1 can Campbell's Condensed Cream of Celery Soup

1 1/2 cups milk

2 cups corn kernels, either cut fresh from the cob or frozen (and defrosted)

1 teaspoon sugar

1/4 cup fresh breadcrumbs

1. Preheat the oven to 350 degrees.

2. Grease a 1 1/2-quart casserole dish with 1 tablespoon of the butter. Sprinkle the inside of the dish with 2 tablespoons of the cheese, tilting the dish so that the cheese covers the butter on the bottom and sides.

3. In a 3-quart saucepan, whisk together the soup and milk, bringing the liquid to a boil. Add the corn and sugar and cook the mixture over medium-high heat until it comes back to a boil, about 3 minutes.

4. Spoon the mixture into the prepared casserole dish. (At this point, you can refrigerate the casserole for up to 2 days before proceeding.)

5. Melt the remaining butter and toss it with the remaining 6 tablespoons cheese and the breadcrumbs in a small mixing bowl. Sprinkle the breadcrumb and cheese mixture over the casserole and bake the casserole until it is bubbling and the cheese is golden, about 20 minutes.

Corn, Zucchini, and Tomato Bake

3 cups corn kernels, either cut fresh from the cob or frozen (and defrosted)

4 cups zucchini cut into matchsticks (about 5 medium)

¼ cup extra virgin olive oil

2 tablespoons all-purpose flour

One 14.5-ounce can Swanson Italian Herbs Seasoned Chicken Broth

5 fresh basil leaves, finely chopped, or about ½ teaspoon dried

2 teaspoons chopped fresh oregano leaves or about 1 teaspoon dried

1 teaspoon freshly ground black pepper

3 to 4 medium ripe tomatoes, sliced ½ inch thick

½ cup freshly grated Parmesan cheese

¼ cup dry breadcrumbs

1. Preheat the oven to 375 degrees.

2. Coat a 13-by-9-inch baking dish with nonstick cooking spray.

3. Layer the corn then the zucchini in the prepared dish.

4. Heat 3 tablespoons of the oil in a medium saucepan over medium heat, add the flour, and whisk until smooth, cooking the mixture until the flour begins to form white bubbles, about 3 minutes. Gradually add the broth, basil, oregano, and pepper. Whisk the sauce until it is smooth and the mixture comes to a boil.

5. Remove the pan from the heat, taste the sauce for seasoning, and pour the sauce over the corn and zucchini. (At this point, the casserole may be refrigerated for up to 8 hours.)

6. Lay the tomato slices over the sauce, overlapping them a bit.

SERVES 8

This colorful side dish for summer barbecue dinners will help you use up some of the overflow from your backyard garden, if you have one. An eye-appealing casserole, it can be made up the day before and then popped into the oven just before serving. I've chosen to use Italian herbs and cheese, but you can vary these ingredients to suit your own taste.

CAMPBELL'S PRODUCES ONE MILLION CANS OF SOUP PER DAY.

Vegetables

7. Combine the cheese, breadcrumbs, and remaining 1 tablespoon oil in a small mixing bowl. Sprinkle this mixture over the tomatoes.

8. Bake the casserole until the top is golden brown and the sauce is bubbling, 20 to 25 minutes. Let the dish rest for 5 minutes before serving.

Eggplant Rollatini

SERVES 6

In this easy recipe the eggplant is grilled and then rolled around a delectable ricotta filling, which firms up when baked. The eggplant is then topped off with marinara and grated Parmesan. Although this dish has a few steps, it can be made in advance, or you can complete it in about an hour and a half.

2 large eggplants

1 cup olive oil

1 envelope Lipton Savory Herb with Garlic Soup Mix

1 cup ricotta cheese

1 large egg

1 cup freshly grated Parmesan cheese

2 tablespoons chopped fresh Italian parsley leaves

¼ cup dry breadcrumbs

2 cups Basic Marinara (page 470)

1. Preheat the broiler for 10 minutes. Line 2 baking sheets with aluminum foil.

2. Cut the green stems off the eggplants and cut each eggplant lengthwise into ½-inch-thick slices. Lay the slices on the prepared baking sheets.

3. In a small mixing bowl, whisk together the oil and soup mix. Brush both sides of the eggplant slices with the flavored oil and broil the eggplant until softened, about 3 to 5 minutes on each side. Remove the pan from the oven and set the eggplant slices aside.

4. Reduce the oven temperature to 350 degrees.

5. In a medium mixing bowl, beat together the ricotta, egg, ½ cup of the Parmesan, the parsley, and breadcrumbs.

6. Spoon some of the marinara over the bottom of a 13-by-9-inch baking dish.

7. Lay an eggplant slice on a flat surface and place 1 to 2 tablespoons of the ricotta mixture at the wide end. Roll up the eggplant and place it seam side down on the marinara in the baking dish. Continue to fill the eggplant slices in the same way and transfer them to the dish.

8. Cover the eggplant rolls with the remaining marinara sauce and sprinkle the remaining ½ cup Parmesan over the casserole.

9. Bake the casserole until golden, 30 to 40 minutes.

To Peel or Not to Peel

When I am using eggplant slices, I generally do not peel the eggplant since the skin helps to keep the slices intact, especially if they are sliced thin. I actually like the contrast of the skin and the flesh of the eggplant in the finished dishes. If you don't like the skin, broil or sauté the eggplant with the skin on and then remove it once the eggplant is cooked.

Eggplant Napoleons

These gorgeous napoleons are made with grilled eggplant, fresh tomato, mozzarella, and basil leaves, drizzled with garlic-herb oil. Served at room temperature, they are a great do-ahead side dish.

1 cup olive oil

1 envelope Lipton Savory Herb with Garlic Soup Mix

1 large purple eggplant, ends trimmed and cut into ½-inch-thick rounds

4 large ripe plum tomatoes, cut into ½-inch-thick slices

One 8-ounce ball fresh mozzarella cheese, cut into ½-inch-thick slices

10 fresh basil leaves, finely chopped

1. Preheat the broiler and line 2 baking sheets with aluminum foil.

2. In a small mixing bowl, combine the oil and soup mix.

3. Lay the eggplant slices on the prepared baking sheets and brush them liberally with the oil mixture. Broil the eggplant slices until they begin to turn golden, 3 to 5 minutes on each side. Remove the eggplant slices from the oven and let them cool.

4. For each napoleon, place a slice of eggplant on a serving plate, top it with a tomato slice, drizzle on some of the remaining flavored oil, and top with a slice of mozzarella and some of the basil. Repeat with the remaining ingredients.

5. Drizzle the finished napoleons with additional oil and serve.

Szechuan Eggplant

3 tablespoons canola oil

1 teaspoon peeled and chopped fresh ginger

2 teaspoons garlic chili sauce

4 cups ¾-inch dice peeled eggplant

Flavor packet from 1 package oriental flavor ramen noodles
(reserve the noodles for another use)

2 tablespoons soy sauce

1 tablespoon toasted sesame oil

2 tablespoons sesame seeds

4 green onions, chopped

1. In a wok, heat the canola oil over high heat until it is almost smoking. Add the ginger and garlic chili sauce and stir-fry them for 2 minutes. Add the eggplant and stir-fry it until it begins to soften, 3 to 4 minutes. Add the ramen flavor packet and the soy sauce and stir-fry the mixture for 3 more minutes.

2. Stir in the sesame oil, sesame seeds, and green onions until they are well combined and heated through. Serve the eggplant over rice or as a side dish with beef or poultry.

SERVES 6

Hot and spicy, this simple side dish goes well with grilled steak or chicken. Garlic chili sauce is found in the Asian food section of your grocer, or, if you cannot find it, check the Source Guide for one of my favorite vendors.

To Salt or Not to Salt?

Some cookbooks will instruct you to cut the eggplant, place it in a colander, and salt it, leaving it to drain for 30 minutes. For the most part, I don't do this because I don't find much difference in the taste of the eggplant—and I don't want to waste 30 minutes.

CHINESE RECIPE FOR TIGER SOUP:
"FIRST CATCH THE TIGER."

Vegetables

Wild Blue Mushroom Bread Pudding

Loaded with mushrooms and crumbled blue cheese, this is a great do-ahead side dish to serve at your next buffet dinner. It can be made ahead, baked, and then reheated, covered with foil, in a 300-degree oven.

The Soup Mix Gourmet

2 tablespoons butter

1 tablespoon olive oil

3 cloves garlic, minced

½ pound shiitake mushrooms, stems removed and caps sliced ½ inch thick

½ pound crimini mushrooms, sliced ½ inch thick

½ pound white mushrooms, sliced ½ inch thick

2 portobello mushrooms, stems trimmed and coarsely chopped

6 large eggs

2 cups heavy cream

1 cup milk

1 envelope Lipton Golden Onion Soup Mix

1 cup crumbled blue cheese

½ teaspoon freshly ground black pepper

8 cups 1-inch cubes French bread

1. Preheat the oven to 350 degrees. Coat a 13-by-9-inch baking dish with nonstick cooking spray.

2. Heat the butter and oil together in a 12-inch sauté pan over medium-high heat. Add the garlic and cook, stirring, until it has softened, about 2 minutes. Add the mushrooms and cook, stirring, until they are tender. Remove the pan from the heat and drain off any excess liquid.

3. In a large mixing bowl, whisk together the eggs, heavy cream, milk, soup mix, blue cheese, and pepper. Add the bread cubes and toss them to coat. Let the mixture stand for 15 minutes.

4. Stir the mushrooms into the bread mixture and pour the contents into the prepared baking dish.

5. Bake the bread pudding until it is golden brown and set in the center, 50 to 60 minutes. Let it stand for 5 minutes before serving.

PORTOBELLO PIZZAS

These easy pizzas start with meaty grilled portobello mushrooms, which then become an artist's palette for creating wonderful taste treats. Try all the variations, as these pizzas make delicious side dishes with grilled meats, chicken, or fish.

Broiled or Grilled Portobello Mushrooms

SERVES 8

8 portobello mushrooms

1 cup olive oil

1 envelope Lipton Savory Herb with Garlic Soup Mix

$1/2$ teaspoon freshly ground black pepper

1. Preheat the broiler or grill for 10 minutes.

2. Remove the stems from mushrooms, saving them for another use, and wipe the caps clean with a moist paper towel.

3. Place the caps on a baking sheet lined with aluminum foil.

4. In a 2-cup measure combine the oil, soup mix, and pepper until blended.

5. Brush the mushrooms with some of the flavored oil and broil or grill them for 3 to 4 minutes on each side, brushing them with additional oil when you turn them.

6. Remove the mushroom caps from the oven or grill and set them aside. (At this point, the mushrooms can be refrigerated for up to 8 hours.) Reheat the mushrooms before serving. Save the remaining flavored oil for use in the fillings.

Cheesy Sausage Portobello Pizzas

SERVES 8

2 tablespoons flavored olive oil from Broiled or Grilled
    Portobello Mushrooms (page 219)

2 links sweet Italian sausage, removed from the casing

1/4 cup chopped oil-packed sun-dried tomatoes, drained

2 tablespoons heavy cream

1/2 cup grated Jarlsberg or Gruyère cheese

2 tablespoons freshly grated Parmesan cheese

8 Broiled or Grilled Portobello Mushrooms (page 219)

1. Preheat the broiler for 10 minutes.

2. In a small sauté pan, heat the flavored oil over medium-high heat, add the sausage, and cook, breaking the meat up with a fork, until it is no longer pink.

3. Drain off the fat from the pan, add the tomatoes and cream, and bring the mixture to a boil. Remove the pan from the heat and let the mixture cool slightly.

4. In a small mixing bowl, combine the cheeses.

5. Place the broiled mushrooms on a baking sheet lined with aluminum foil, spoon about 2 tablespoons of the sausage and cream mixture over each mushroom, and sprinkle it with the cheese.

6. Broil the mushrooms until the cheese is melted and golden brown, 3 to 5 minutes, and serve immediately.

The Story of Stone Soup

Once upon a time, there was a great famine. People jealously hoarded whatever food they could find, hiding it from friends and neighbors. One day a peddler came into a village, sold a few of his wares, and said he planned to stay the night.

"There's not a bite to eat in the whole province," he was told. "Better keep moving on."

"I have everything I need," he said. "In fact, I was thinking of making some stone soup to share with all of you." He pulled an iron cauldron from his wagon, filled it with water, and built a fire under it. Then, with great ceremony, he drew an ordinary stone from a velvet bag and dropped it in.

By now, hearing the rumor of food, most of the villagers had come to the square. As the peddler sniffed the broth and licked his lips, hunger began to overcome their skepticism.

Portobello Pizza Caprese

8 Broiled or Grilled Portobello Mushrooms (page 219)

1 large ripe tomato, cut into 1/2-inch-thick slices (you will need 8 slices)

¼ cup flavored olive oil from Broiled or Grilled Portobello Mushrooms (page 219)

One 8-ounce ball fresh mozzarella cheese, cut into 8 slices

16 fresh basil leaves

Freshly ground black pepper

1. Place the mushrooms stem side up on a serving platter.

2. Place one slice of tomato on each mushroom, drizzle on a bit of the flavored oil, then top with a slice of mozzarella and 2 basil leaves.

3. Drizzle on the remaining oil, garnish with a few grinds of pepper, and serve.

"Ahhh," the peddler said to himself rather loudly. "I do like a tasty stone soup. Of course, stone soup with cabbage—that's hard to beat."

A villager approached, looked around, and pulled a small cabbage from his coat. When he added it to the pot, the peddler beamed. "Excellent," he cried. "You know, I once had stone soup with cabbage and salt pork, and it was fit for a king." Then the village butcher approached. He had a little piece of salt pork under his apron.

And so it went—potatoes, onions, carrots, mushrooms. There finally was a delicious meal for all. The villagers offered the peddler a great deal of money for the stone, but he refused to sell and traveled on the next day. From that time on, long after the famine ended, the villagers reminisced about the finest soup they'd ever had.

Portobello Margherita

SERVES 8

Legend has it that Queen Margherita of Italy was a pizza lover and that her favorite pizza was topped with tomatoes, mozzarella, olive oil, and Parmesan cheese.

8 Broiled or Grilled Portobello Mushrooms (page 219)

1/2 cup Basic Marinara (page 470)

1/2 cup freshly grated Parmesan cheese

1 teaspoon dried oregano

1/4 cup flavored olive oil from Broiled or Grilled Portobello Mushrooms (page 219)

1. Preheat the broiler for 10 minutes.

2. Place the mushrooms stem side up on a baking sheet lined with aluminum foil.

3. Spread a thin layer of marinara sauce over each mushroom, then top with some of the cheese, a crumble of oregano, and a drizzle of the flavored oil.

4. Broil the mushrooms until the cheese is melted, 4 to 6 minutes, and serve immediately.

Caramelized Onions in Red Wine Sauce

SERVES 6

When onions are cooked slowly in butter, they mellow and turn into sweet morsels that melt into the sauce. These onions are caramelized and then finished with a red wine reduction sauce and are spectacular served with steak or over grilled fish fillets.

8 large sweet yellow onions, such as Vidalia, Maui, or Walla Walla

1/2 cup (1 stick) butter

2 teaspoons sugar

1 teaspoon salt

1/2 teaspoon freshly ground black pepper

1 1/2 cups red wine (Merlot, Burgundy, or Cabernet)

1 can Campbell's Condensed French Onion Soup

2 teaspoons fresh thyme leaves or 1 teaspoon dried

1. Cut the onions into quarters and then cut the quarters in half. Melt the butter in a 12-inch sauté pan, add the onions, and cook them over medium heat for 5 minutes, stirring frequently. Sprinkle the onions with the sugar, salt, and pepper and continue to cook the onions, stirring, until they begin to turn a caramel color; this may take 30 minutes.

2. While the onions are cooking, place the wine in a 2-quart saucepan, bring to a boil, and let the mixture continue to boil for 5 minutes. Add the soup and thyme and simmer the sauce over medium heat until it has reduced by one quarter, about 30 minutes.

3. When the onions have caramelized, pour the wine mixture into the pan and bring the liquid to a boil. Reduce the heat to medium and let the sauce simmer for 10 minutes. Serve the onions immediately or refrigerate them for up to 2 days before serving.

Red, White, and Blue Cheese Onions

4 large red onions, cut into 1/2-inch-thick slices

1 cup olive oil

2 tablespoons red wine vinegar

2 tablespoons fresh lemon juice

1 envelope Lipton Savory Herb with Garlic Soup Mix

1 cup crumbled blue cheese

1. Preheat the oven to 400 degrees.

2. Place the onions in a 13-by-9-inch baking dish. In a small bowl, whisk together the oil, vinegar, lemon juice, and soup mix. Pour the mixture over the onions.

3. Sprinkle the blue cheese over the onions and bake them until they are tender, about 30 minutes. Remove the baking dish from the oven and serve the onions immediately or refrigerate them for up to 12 hours.

Souper Smart

Use a stainless steel, rather than a non-stick, pan to caramelize onions. Non-stick pans tend to steam rather than brown onions.

SERVES 6

Don't wait till the Fourth of July to serve this savory side dish. Roasted red onions and blue cheese are a dynamite combination to serve with meats and chicken. The whole dish can be prepared ahead of time and then baked just before serving.

Vegetables

Golden glazed sugar snap peas and carrots make a stunning presentation on any dinner table, and this recipe takes less than 20 minutes to prepare.

Glazed Sugar Snap Peas and Carrots

$1/4$ cup ($1/2$ stick) butter

1 envelope Lipton Golden Onion Soup Mix

2 tablespoons firmly packed light brown sugar

$3/4$ cup water

2 cups baby carrots

$1/2$ pound sugar snap peas, tips removed and tough strings pulled

1. Melt the butter in a 4-quart saucepan over medium heat, add the soup mix, brown sugar, and water, and stir to combine. Add the carrots and simmer them in the broth for 5 minutes.

2. Add the snap peas and cook them, stirring occasionally, until they are tender, another 2 to 3 minutes.

3. Remove the peas and carrots from the pan with a slotted spoon, spoon some of the sauce over them, and serve immediately.

Roasted Garlic Red Potatoes

Tiny new red potatoes become sweet as candy when roasted in a hot oven. The garlicky olive oil makes these melt-in-your-mouth potatoes irresistible. Any leftovers are delicious scrambled with some eggs and cheese in a hungry-man frittata.

$2 1/2$ pounds red potatoes (if they are small, leave them whole; if they are larger, cut them into quarters)

8 cloves garlic, peeled

$1/2$ cup olive oil

1 envelope Lipton Savory Herb with Garlic Soup Mix

1 teaspoon salt

$1/2$ teaspoon freshly ground black pepper

1. Preheat the oven to 425 degrees.

2. Scrub the potatoes, pat them dry, and place them in a 13-by-9-inch baking dish with the garlic.

3. In a small mixing bowl, combine the oil and soup mix. Pour the mixture over the potatoes and toss them to coat them evenly.

4. Bake the potatoes for 30 minutes, stirring them halfway through the cooking time. Sprinkle them with the salt and pepper, stirring well. Bake the potatoes until they are cooked through and are crispy on the outside, an additional 15 minutes. Serve immediately.

BISTRO ROASTED POTATOES: Add 2 tablespoons Dijon mustard to the oil mixture. Bake as directed.

TUSCAN POTATOES: Add 1 tablespoon dried rosemary to the oil mixture. Bake as directed.

FLORENTINE POTATOES: Substitute Knorr Cream of Spinach Soup Mix and increase the oil to ³/₄ cup. Bake as directed.

FIESTA POTATOES: Substitute Lipton Fiesta Herb with Red Pepper Soup Mix and bake as directed, spreading ¹/₂ to 1 cup grated mild cheddar cheese over the tops of the potatoes during the last 20 minutes of baking. Garnish with chopped fresh cilantro leaves and sour cream.

ROASTED ONION POTATOES: Substitute Lipton Onion or Golden Onion Soup Mix, stir in a few quartered onions or shallots, and bake as directed.

Country-Fried All-American Potatoes

SERVES 6 TO 8

My son Ryan's favorite breakfast hangout is a place called the Potato Shack, where the specialty is "American fries," home fries that are served with all the restaurant's entrées, even the manhole-cover-sized pancakes! I've taken a little liberty with their recipe and added a few spicy touches of my own to give a crispier and spicier version of this true San Diego classic. Ryan likes these potatoes smothered with cheese, bacon bits, and a side of ranch-style dressing, even at 8 A.M.

2 tablespoons butter

3 tablespoons vegetable oil

6 cups ¾-inch dice cooked red potatoes, cooled

1 envelope Lipton Savory Herb with Garlic Soup Mix

1 teaspoon freshly ground black pepper

1. In a 12-inch nonstick skillet, melt the butter with the oil over medium-high heat. Add the potatoes and toss them in the hot butter and oil mixture.

2. Sprinkle the potatoes with the soup mix and pepper and cook them, turning often, until they are golden brown on each side; this should take about 20 minutes.

3. Remove the pan from the heat and serve the potatoes immediately. If you need to "hold" the potatoes, they will keep in a preheated 300-degree oven for about 20 minutes.

Oven-Fried Potato Wedges

¼ cup olive oil

1 package Lipton Golden Onion Soup Mix

¼ teaspoon sweet paprika

Pinch of cayenne pepper

4 medium russet potatoes, cut into ½-inch-thick wedges

1. Preheat the oven to 400 degrees.

2. In a large mixing bowl, combine the oil, soup mix, paprika, and cayenne. Add the potatoes and toss them to coat them evenly with the mixture.

3. Arrange the potatoes in a single layer on a jelly roll pan lined with aluminum foil and bake them until they are crisp, 45 minutes to 1 hour.

SERVES 6

Several years ago, Oprah Winfrey's chef told how she made Oprah "fried" potatoes in the oven. When I tried the recipe, I found the potatoes to be lacking a certain punch, so I fiddled around with the recipe, and this is my version of spicy oven fries.

To Peel or Not to Peel

The potato, that is. At my house, I have one child who wants his peeled and another who wants the skins on, so we compromise; whoever comes home first and puts in the order gets the spuds "their way."

Vegetables

Potato Pizza

SERVES 6

In this recipe a crust of garlicky potatoes is topped with traditional pizza sauce and then smothered in cheese; I don't know about you, but this kind of food could make me a vegetarian for life!

4 medium red potatoes, left unpeeled and sliced ¼ inch thick
½ cup olive oil
1 envelope Lipton Savory Herb with Garlic Soup Mix
1½ cups Basic Marinara (page 470)
2 cups grated mozzarella cheese
½ cup freshly grated Parmesan cheese
2 teaspoons chopped fresh oregano leaves

1. Preheat the oven to 425 degrees.

2. Place the potatoes in a large mixing bowl. In a small mixing bowl, whisk together the oil and soup mix. Pour ¼ cup of the flavored oil over the potatoes and toss to coat them evenly.

3. Spread the potatoes evenly in one layer in a 10-inch round baking dish and bake them for 15 minutes. Remove the pan from the oven and reduce the oven temperature to 375 degrees. Spread the marinara over the potatoes, cover them with the cheeses, and sprinkle on the oregano and 2 to 3 tablespoons of the remaining flavored oil.

4. Bake the pizza until the potatoes are tender and the cheese has melted, an additional 25 minutes. Let the pizza rest for 5 minutes before serving.

ACCORDING TO THE **American Heritage Dictionary of the English Language,** "SOUP UP" MEANS "TO MODIFY (SOMETHING) SO AS TO INCREASE ITS CAPACITY TO PERFORM OR SATISFY, ESPECIALLY TO ADD HORSEPOWER OR GREATER SPEED POTENTIAL TO (AN ENGINE OR VEHICLE)."

The Soup Mix Gourmet

Herbed Goat Cheese Potato Pie

SERVES 6 TO 8

1 envelope Knorr Leek Soup Mix

1 teaspoon dried fines herbes (see page 3)

1½ cups half-and-half

½ teaspoon freshly ground black pepper

6 medium red potatoes, sliced ¼ inch thick

8 ounces goat cheese, broken into small pieces

1. Preheat the oven to 400 degrees. Coat a 10-inch round pie plate that is at least 2½ inches deep with nonstick cooking spray.

2. In a medium mixing bowl, whisk together the soup mix, half-and-half, and pepper.

3. Arrange the potatoes evenly in layers in the prepared pie plate. Pour the soup mixture over the potatoes and dot the top of the potatoes with the goat cheese.

4. Bake until the potatoes are cooked through and the cheese is melted, 50 to 60 minutes. Let the pie rest for 10 minutes before cutting it into wedges.

Creamy goat cheese is a perfect partner for these herb-crusted potatoes. Great with a green salad for a luncheon or light supper, this potato pie can also be served as a side dish alongside grilled fish or chicken.

DON QUIXOTE, THE MAN OF LA MANCHA, ATE LENTIL SOUP EVERY FRIDAY.

Vegetables

Easy Scalloped Potatoes

"Cream of" soups make for an extraordinary way to serve potatoes. I tested this recipe with cream of potato, cream of celery, and cream of shrimp soup, and they were all stellar, each with its own personality.

SCALLOPED CELERY POTATOES: Substitute 2 stalks celery, sliced ½ inch thick on the diagonal, for one of the potatoes. Substitute Campbell's Condensed Cream of Celery Soup and top the potatoes with 1 cup grated Swiss cheese and ½ cup freshly grated Parmesan cheese.

SCALLOPED SHRIMP POTATOES: Substitute Campbell's Condensed Cream of Shrimp Soup, add 1½ teaspoons Old Bay seasoning and 1 teaspoon Worcestershire sauce to the soup mixture, and substitute white cheddar cheese for the Swiss cheese.

4 medium russet potatoes (about 2½ pounds), sliced ¼ inch thick

1 teaspoon salt

½ teaspoon freshly ground black pepper

1 can Campbell's Condensed Cream of Potato Soup

2 cups milk (do not substitute lowfat or nonfat)

2 cloves garlic, minced

2 cups grated Swiss cheese

1. Preheat the oven to 375 degrees. Coat a 13-by-9-inch baking dish with nonstick cooking spray.

2. Layer the potato slices in the baking dish, sprinkling each layer with some of the salt and pepper.

3. In a medium mixing bowl or 8-cup measure, whisk together the soup, milk, and garlic. Pour the soup mixture over the potatoes and sprinkle the cheese over the top.

4. Cover the dish with aluminum foil, bake the potatoes for 30 minutes, remove the foil, and bake them until they are cooked through and the cheese is golden brown, an additional 20 to 30 minutes.

A DOZEN MASHED POTATOES

Potatoes are one of my favorite foods; I could eat them for breakfast, lunch, and dinner, so coming up with a dozen mashed potato recipes was my idea of fun! Each of these recipes follows the same basic format, but each has a unique flavor. Once again, we come to that age-old question, to peel or not to peel, and my final answer is: do what your family prefers!

A few tips about potatoes and these recipes: mealy potatoes make the best mashed potatoes, so try to use russet Idaho potatoes for these recipes. But, that said, I love mashed red skin potatoes and Yukon Golds, so you should use the type of potato that you like best and adapt the recipe for that type of potato. All potatoes cook differently, even those of the same type, depending on how long they have been stored. Some potatoes may require more liquid when mashed than others, so the measurements in these recipes are as accurate as possible given the different water and starch content of each potato.

Never process potatoes in a food processor, or you will get something akin to wallpaper paste. You may mix potatoes with a hand mixer or in a stand mixer like a KitchenAid with a paddle attachment. Ricers are nice but time-consuming, and I think a mixer does a nicer job with easier cleanup. If you like your potatoes "smashed" rather than mashed, leave a few lumps.

I've instructed you to cut your potatoes into 1-inch chunks, but if you are in a hurry, cut the potatoes into smaller dice, and they will cook faster.

Savory Onion Mashed Potatoes

Tangy with a last-minute addition of sour cream, these golden potatoes are a winner with any dinner entrée.

3 pounds russet potatoes, cut into 1-inch chunks

1 teaspoon salt

4 to 6 tablespoons (^{1}/$_2$ to ^{3}/$_4$ stick) butter, to your taste

^{1}/$_2$ to ^{3}/$_4$ cup milk or heavy cream, to your taste

1 envelope Lipton Onion or Golden Onion Soup Mix

^{1}/$_4$ cup sour cream

1. Place the potatoes and salt in a 4-quart saucepan with water to cover. Bring the water to a boil and let it continue to boil until the potatoes are tender when pierced with a sharp knife, about 20 minutes.

2. While the potatoes are boiling, heat 4 tablespoons (^{1}/$_2$ stick) of the butter, ^{1}/$_2$ cup of the milk or heavy cream, and the soup mix together over low heat in a small saucepan, stirring until the soup mix is dissolved.

3. Drain the potatoes in a colander, return them to the pan over low heat, and shake them to dry them.

4. Add a little of the soup mixture to the potatoes and mash them. Gradually stir in more of the soup mixture and the sour cream and stir until the potatoes are light and fluffy. Add more butter, milk, or heavy cream if the potatoes are stiff or dry.

Garlic Herb Mashed Potatoes

3 pounds russet potatoes, cut into 1-inch chunks

3 cloves garlic, peeled

1 teaspoon salt

4 to 6 tablespoons (1/2 to 3/4 stick) butter, to your taste

1/2 to 3/4 cup milk or heavy cream, to your taste

1 envelope Lipton Savory Herb with Garlic Soup Mix

1. Place the potatoes, garlic, and salt in a 4-quart saucepan with water to cover. Bring the water to a boil and let it continue to boil until the potatoes are tender when pierced with a sharp knife, about 20 minutes.

2. While the potatoes are boiling, heat 4 tablespoons (1/2 stick) of the butter, 1/2 cup of the milk or heavy cream, and the soup mix together over low heat in a small saucepan, stirring until the soup mix is dissolved.

3. Drain the potatoes in a colander, return them to the pan over low heat, and shake them to dry them.

4. Add a little of the soup mixture to the potatoes and mash them. Gradually stir in more of the soup mixture until the potatoes are light and fluffy. Add more milk, heavy cream, or butter if the potatoes are too stiff or dry.

Savory and smooth, these spuds are great with roast beef and chicken.

Shrimply Delicious Mashed Potatoes

Smooth, spicy, and studded with tiny shrimp, these potatoes are great served with fish or used as a "crust" for a seafood pie.

3 pounds russet potatoes, cut into 1-inch chunks

1 teaspoon salt

4 to 6 tablespoons ($1/2$ to $3/4$ stick) butter, to your taste

1 can Campbell's Condensed Cream of Shrimp Soup

2 tablespoons milk

1 teaspoon Old Bay seasoning

1 teaspoon Worcestershire sauce

1. Place the potatoes and salt in a 4-quart saucepan with water to cover. Bring the water to a boil and let it continue to boil until the potatoes are tender when pierced with a sharp knife, about 20 minutes.

2. While the potatoes are boiling, heat 4 tablespoons of the butter, the soup, milk, Old Bay seasoning, and Worcestershire together over low heat in a small saucepan, stirring until the mixture is smooth.

3. Drain the potatoes in a colander, return them to the pan over low heat, and shake them to dry them.

4. Add a little of the soup mixture to the potatoes and mash them. Gradually stir in more of the soup mixture until the potatoes are light and fluffy. Add more butter if it is needed to improve the texture or flavor. Any leftover soup mixture can be refrigerated for up to 3 days or frozen for up to 6 weeks.

Popeye's Spinach and Mashed Potatoes

3 pounds russet potatoes, cut into 1-inch chunks

1 teaspoon salt

¼ cup (½ stick) butter

¾ cup milk

1 envelope Knorr Cream of Spinach Soup Mix

1 teaspoon freshly ground black pepper

¼ teaspoon freshly grated nutmeg

1. Place the potatoes and salt in a 4-quart saucepan with water to cover. Bring the water to a boil and let it continue to boil until the potatoes are tender when pierced with a knife, about 20 minutes.

2. While the potatoes are boiling, heat the butter, milk, soup mix, pepper, and nutmeg together in a small saucepan over low heat, stirring until the ingredients are well combined and the soup mix is dissolved.

3. Drain the potatoes in a colander, return them to the pan over low heat, and shake them to dry them.

4. Add the soup mixture to the potatoes and mash the potatoes until they are light and fluffy.

I'm not sure whether Popeye ever mixed his spinach with potatoes, but I think he'd approve of these great spuds.

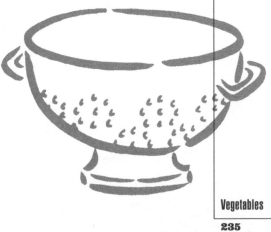

Skinny Leeky Potatoes

SERVES 6 TO 8

We have a saying in my house: "lowfat, no taste." Now, I know that isn't always true, but when certain chicken broth companies came out with their "skinny" mashed potatoes using broth instead of butter and milk or cream, I knew there had to a be a better way, and there is! Try these skinny potatoes and you'll know what I mean.

3 pounds russet potatoes, cut into 1-inch chunks

1 teaspoon salt

1 cup chicken broth

1 envelope Knorr Leek Soup Mix

3/4 teaspoon freshly ground black pepper

1. Place the potatoes and salt in a 4-quart saucepan with water to cover. Bring the water to a boil and let it continue to boil until the potatoes are tender when pierced with a knife, about 20 minutes.

2. While the potatoes are boiling, heat the broth with the soup mix and pepper in a small saucepan over low heat, stirring until the soup mix is dissolved.

3. Drain the potatoes in a colander, return them to the pan over low heat, and shake them to dry them.

4. Add 1/2 cup of the broth mixture to the potatoes and mash them. Gradually add more of the broth mixture, mashing the potatoes until they are light and fluffy.

Bacon and Onion Mashed Potatoes

3 pounds russet potatoes, cut into 1-inch chunks

1 teaspoon salt

¼ cup (½ stick) butter

½ cup milk or heavy cream

1 envelope Lipton Golden Onion Soup Mix

½ teaspoon freshly ground black pepper

6 strips bacon, cooked until crisp, drained on paper towels,
and crumbled

1. Place the potatoes and salt in a 4-quart saucepan and cover them with water. Bring the water to a boil and let it continue to boil until the potatoes are tender when pierced with a knife, about 20 minutes.

2. While the potatoes are boiling, in a small saucepan, heat the butter, milk or heavy cream, soup mix, and pepper together over low heat, stirring until the ingredients are well blended and the soup mix is dissolved.

3. Drain the potatoes in a colander, return them to the pan over low heat, and shake them to dry them.

4. Add the soup mixture to the potatoes and mash them. When the potatoes are light and fluffy, stir in the bacon and serve.

S tudded with crispy bacon and onions, these potatoes will become your favorites.

And Just a Few More Ideas for Super Mashed Potatoes

Try substituting these soup mixes in any of the mashed potato recipes:

- Lipton Golden Onion Soup Mix
- Lipton Savory Herb with Garlic Soup Mix
- Lipton Fiesta Herb with Red Pepper Soup Mix
- Knorr Vegetable Soup Mix
- Knorr Cream of Broccoli Soup Mix
- Knorr Cream of Spinach Soup Mix
- Lipton's Leek Soup Mix and 1 teaspoon dried fines herbes

Vegetables

Red, White, and Blue Smashed Potatoes

Unpeeled red potatoes, a little garlic, and blue cheese make a dynamite side dish for the Fourth of July or any other day! Feel free to make these potatoes lumpy or smooth—they are great either way.

2½ pounds red potatoes, cut into 1-inch chunks

¾ teaspoon salt

4 to 6 tablespoons (½ to ¾ stick) butter, to your taste

½ to ¾ cup milk, to your taste

1 envelope Lipton Savory Herb with Garlic Soup Mix

½ cup crumbled blue cheese

½ teaspoon freshly ground black pepper

1. Place the potatoes and salt in a 4-quart saucepan with water to cover. Bring the pot to a boil and let it continue to boil until the potatoes are tender when pierced with a knife, about 20 minutes.

2. While the potatoes are boiling, heat 4 tablespoons (½ stick) of the butter, ½ cup of the milk, and the soup mix together in a small saucepan over low heat, stirring until the ingredients are well combined and the soup mix is dissolved.

3. Drain the potatoes in a colander, return them to the pan over low heat, and shake them to dry them.

4. Add the soup mixture to the potatoes and mash the potatoes. Add more butter or milk if the potatoes are too stiff or dry. When the potatoes are light and fluffy, add the cheese and pepper, stirring until the cheese melts into the potatoes, and serve.

Broccoli Cheddar Mashed Potatoes

3 pounds russet potatoes, cut into 1-inch chunks

1 teaspoon salt

2 tablespoons butter

1 cup Campbell's Condensed Cheddar Cheese Soup

4 shakes Tabasco sauce

1 cup broccoli florets, steamed for 2 minutes

½ teaspoon freshly ground black pepper

Studded with broccoli and swirled with cheddar cheese, these potatoes are not only gorgeous, they taste great, too.

1. Place the potatoes and salt in a 4-quart saucepan with water to cover. Bring the water to a boil and let it continue to boil until the potatoes are tender when pierced with a knife, about 20 minutes.

2. While the potatoes are boiling, melt the butter in a small saucepan, whisk in the soup and Tabasco, and keep the mixture warm over low heat.

3. Drain the potatoes, return them to the pan over low heat, and shake them to dry them.

4. Add the soup mixture to the potatoes and mash them until they are light and fluffy. Stir in the steamed broccoli and pepper and serve.

Vegetables

A little bit of the Southwest, these potatoes are great with grilled meats and poultry.

Santa Fe Potatoes

3 pounds russet potatoes, cut into 1-inch chunks

1 teaspoon salt

4 to 6 tablespoons ($\frac{1}{2}$ to $\frac{3}{4}$ stick) butter, to your taste

$\frac{1}{2}$ to $\frac{3}{4}$ cup milk, to your taste

1 envelope Lipton Fiesta Herb with Red Pepper Soup Mix

$\frac{1}{4}$ cup canned roasted green chiles, drained, seeded, and chopped

$\frac{1}{4}$ cup chopped fresh cilantro leaves

1. Place the potatoes and salt in a 4-quart saucepan with water to cover. Bring the water to a boil and let it continue to boil until the potatoes are tender when pierced with a knife, about 20 minutes.

2. While the potatoes are boiling, heat 4 tablespoons ($\frac{1}{2}$ stick) of the butter, $\frac{1}{2}$ cup of the milk, and the soup mix together in a small saucepan over low heat, stirring until the soup mix is dissolved. Add the chiles. Keep the mixture warm over low heat.

3. Drain the potatoes in a colander, return them to a pan over low heat, and shake them to dry them.

4. Add the soup mixture to the potatoes and mash them. Add more butter or milk if the potatoes are too stiff or dry. When the potatoes are light and fluffy, sprinkle them with the cilantro and serve.

Mashed Potatoes El Greco

3 pounds red potatoes, cut into 1-inch chunks

1 teaspoon salt

3 cloves garlic, peeled

¼ cup (½ stick) butter

1 cup milk

1 envelope Knorr Leek Soup Mix

1 teaspoon dried fines herbes (see page 3)

4 ounces feta cheese, crumbled

½ teaspoon freshly ground black pepper

1 tablespoon chopped fresh dill or 1½ teaspoons dillweed

1. Place the potatoes, salt, and garlic in a 4-quart saucepan with water to cover. Bring the water to a boil and let it continue to boil until the potatoes are tender when pierced with a knife, about 20 minutes.

2. While the potatoes are boiling, in a small saucepan heat the butter, milk, soup mix, dried fines herbes, feta, pepper, and dill together over low heat, stirring until the soup mix dissolves and the cheese melts.

3. Drain the potatoes in a colander, return them to the pan over low heat, and shake them to dry them.

4. Add the soup mixture and mash the potatoes until they are light and fluffy.

With a little feta, some garlic, and dill, these potatoes will transport you to sunny Greece. Serve them with gyros, grilled meats, or poultry.

Fiesta Nacho Mashed Potatoes

Simplicity and ease define this crowd pleaser.

3 pounds Yukon Gold potatoes, peeled and cut into 1-inch chunks

1 teaspoon salt

1 can Campbell's Condensed Fiesta Nacho Cheese Soup

1/4 cup milk

1/2 teaspoon freshly ground black pepper

1. Place the potatoes and salt in a 4-quart saucepan with water to cover. Bring the water to a boil and let it continue to boil until the potatoes are tender when pierced with a knife, about 20 minutes.

2. While the potatoes are boiling, in a small saucepan whisk together the soup, milk, and pepper and bring the mixture to a boil. Set it aside.

3. Drain the potatoes in a colander, return them to the pan over low heat, and shake them to dry them.

4. Pour half the soup mixture into the potatoes and mash them, adding more soup until the potatoes are creamy and smooth.

Make-Ahead Mashed Potatoes

My Do-Ahead Thanksgiving dinner students love this recipe, and so will you! You can make these potatoes two days ahead of time and just pop them into a hot oven close to serving time.

1/2 cup freshly grated Parmesan cheese

8 to 10 large russet potatoes, cut into 1-inch chunks

One 8-ounce package cream cheese, softened

1 cup sour cream

1/2 cup (1 stick) plus 1 tablespoon butter

1 envelope Knorr Leek Soup Mix

1 teaspoon freshly ground black pepper

1. Preheat the oven to 350 degrees. Thoroughly grease a 13-by-9-inch baking dish with butter. Sprinkle ¼ cup of the cheese over the butter and tilt the pan so that the cheese adheres to the bottom and sides of the pan. Set the pan aside.

2. Place the potatoes in a 4-quart saucepan with water to cover. Bring the water to a boil, and let it continue to boil until the potatoes are tender when pierced with a knife, about 20 minutes.

3. Place the cream cheese, sour cream, ½ cup of the butter, and the soup mix in a medium mixing bowl.

4. Drain the potatoes in a colander and place them in the mixing bowl with the soup mixture.

5. Mash the potatoes until they are smooth. Mix in the pepper and transfer the mixture to the prepared baking dish.

6. Dot the top of the potatoes with the remaining tablespoon butter, cut into bits, and sprinkle the remaining ¼ cup cheese on top. (At this point, the potatoes can be covered with plastic wrap and refrigerated for up to 2 days. Remove the potatoes from the refrigerator 30 minutes before baking.)

7. Bake the potatoes until they are golden, 35 to 45 minutes.

You'll have no worrying about last-minute mashing, and the flavor is superb, almost like a soufflé, but less work.

Vegetables

Twice-Baked Stuffed Spuds

SERVES 6 TO 8

With your stocked soup pantry you can make delectable stuffed baked potatoes with hardly any fuss at all. These potatoes can be made a day ahead and then reheated just before serving.

8 large russet potatoes

2 tablespoons vegetable or olive oil

1 envelope Knorr Leek Soup Mix

1 cup milk

1/4 cup (1/2 stick) butter

1/2 cup sour cream

1 cup grated cheddar cheese

1 teaspoon freshly ground black pepper

1. Preheat the oven to 425 degrees.

2. Scrub the potatoes, prick them several times with a sharp knife, and rub them all over with the oil.

3. Bake the potatoes until they are soft when squeezed gently with a pot holder, 50 to 60 minutes. Reduce the oven temperature to 375 degrees.

4. Cut the potatoes in half and scoop out the pulp, leaving a 1/2-inch-thick shell all the way around inside the skin.

5. Place the potato pulp in a large mixing bowl and add the soup mix, milk, butter, sour cream, cheese, and pepper. Mash the potatoes until they are light and fluffy. Add more milk if the potatoes are stiff or dry.

6. Stuff the potato and cheese mixture back into the potato skins, place the skins on a baking sheet, and bake until they are heated through, about 12 to 15 minutes.

Cheddar

Jarlsberg

PARMESAN

NORWEGIAN EXPLORER AND NOBEL PEACE PRIZE RECIPIENT FRIDTJOF NANSEN WAS SAID TO HAVE TAKEN KNORR SOUPS TO THE NORTH POLE IN 1896.

The Soup Mix Gourmet

Stuffed Spuds Florentine

8 large russet potatoes

2 tablespoons vegetable or olive oil

1 envelope Knorr Spinach Soup Mix

1 cup milk

1/4 cup (1/2 stick) butter

1/2 cup sour cream

1 1/2 cups grated white cheddar cheese

1 teaspoon freshly ground black pepper

8 strips bacon, cooked until crisp, drained on paper towels, and crumbled

1. Preheat the oven to 425 degrees.

2. Scrub the potatoes, prick them several times with a sharp knife, and rub them all over with the oil.

3. Bake the potatoes until they are soft when squeezed gently with a pot holder, 50 to 60 minutes. Reduce the oven temperature to 375 degrees.

4. Cut the potatoes in half and scoop out the pulp, leaving a 1/2-inch-thick shell all the way around inside the skin.

5. Place the potato pulp in a large mixing bowl and add the soup mix, milk, butter, sour cream, cheese, pepper, and bacon. Mash the potatoes until they are light and fluffy. Add more milk if the potatoes are stiff or dry.

6. Stuff the potato and cheese mixture back into the potato skins, place the skins on a baking sheet, and bake until they are heated through, about 12 to 15 minutes.

SERVES 6 TO 8

This combination was one of my favorites when I was testing recipes. The crispy bacon, white cheddar, and spinach soup all combine to make this a colorful addition to any dinner.

Hash Brown Casserole

I am not sure where this recipe originated, but a version of it is a staple at Cracker Barrel restaurants. This casserole is easy to put together, and you can add 2 cups of ham cubes, crumbled fried bacon, or shredded cooked chicken to make it into a main dish to serve for brunch or dinner.

HASH BROWN BAKE OLÉ: Sauté ¼ cup canned roasted green chiles, drained, seeded, and chopped, with the onion, substitute Campbell's Condensed Fiesta Nacho Cheese Soup, and proceed as directed in the recipe. Garnish the casserole with sour cream and chopped fresh cilantro leaves.

2 tablespoons butter

½ cup chopped onion

1 can Campbell's Condensed Cheddar Cheese Soup

½ cup milk

4 shakes Tabasco sauce

1 package frozen shredded hash brown potatoes

2 cups shredded mild cheddar cheese

1. Preheat the oven to 350 degrees. Coat a 13-by-9-inch baking dish with nonstick cooking spray.

2. In a 2-quart saucepan, melt the butter over medium heat and cook the onion, stirring, until it is softened, 3 to 4 minutes. Add the soup, milk, and Tabasco, stir to blend, and heat through.

3. Place the potatoes in a large mixing bowl. Add the soup mixture and 1½ cups of the cheese, stirring to blend. Transfer the mixture to the prepared dish.

4. Sprinkle on the remaining ½ cup cheese and bake the casserole until the cheese is bubbling and golden, 30 minutes.

Ten-Minute Creamed Spinach

1 envelope Knorr Cream of Spinach Soup Mix

1½ cups milk

Two 16-ounce bags frozen chopped spinach, defrosted and
  squeezed dry

⅛ teaspoon freshly grated nutmeg

¼ teaspoon freshly ground black pepper

1. Place the soup mix and milk in a 3-quart saucepan and
bring the mixture to a boil.

2. Add the spinach, nutmeg, and pepper and bring the mixture to a boil again. Remove the pan from the heat and serve the
spinach immediately.

SERVES 6

Sometimes when people ask me for a recipe I'm reluctant to tell them how easy some things are to make. After all, if it's a spectacular recipe, they must think it takes me days to make it! This creamed spinach is a case in point: frozen spinach, milk, Knorr Cream of Spinach Soup Mix, a little nutmeg, freshly ground black pepper, and you're in business. I like to serve this dish with standing rib roast at Christmastime, or with beef, chicken, or fish at other times of the year. Try using it in an à la Florentine presentation—as a bed to which you add chicken or fish, topped with a Mornay sauce and sprinkled with cheese.

Most of us overlook sweet potatoes until holiday time—when we mash them with brown sugar and butter and then cover them with marshmallows, of all things! In this dish the colorful spuds are baked and then stuffed with a ginger-flavored vegetable medley.

VARIATION: Substitute your favorite vegetables for the ones suggested here—if you don't have baby corn, use 1 cup frozen (and defrosted) corn kernels instead. Broccoli florets, snow peas, and matchstick zucchini also work well.

The Soup Mix Gourmet

Sweet Potatoes Stuffed with Asian Stir-Fried Vegetables

6 large sweet potatoes

¼ cup vegetable oil

1 tablespoon toasted sesame oil

1 tablespoon peeled and grated fresh ginger

2 cloves garlic, minced

2 medium carrots, cut into matchsticks

One 16-ounce can baby corn, drained and cut in half lengthwise

1 cup sliced mushrooms

5 green onions, cut on the diagonal into 1-inch pieces

One 10-ounce bag fresh baby spinach

2 tablespoons soy sauce

Flavor packet from 1 package chicken flavor ramen noodles (reserve the noodles for another use)

1 teaspoon sugar

3 tablespoons sesame seeds

1. Preheat the oven to 425 degrees.

2. Rub the potatoes with 2 tablespoons of the vegetable oil and prick each one 3 to 4 times with a sharp knife. Place the potatoes in the oven and bake them until they are soft when squeezed gently with a pot holder, 50 to 60 minutes.

3. Heat the remaining 2 tablespoons vegetable oil and the sesame oil together in a wok or 10-inch skillet over high heat until the oils are almost smoking. Add the ginger and garlic and stir-fry them for 2 to 3 minutes. Add the carrots and stir-fry them for 1 minute, and then add the corn and mushrooms and stir-fry them for 3 to 4 minutes. Add the green onions and spinach, tossing the ingredients together.

4. Combine the soy sauce, ramen flavor packet, sugar, and sesame seeds in a small mixing bowl. Add this mixture to the wok and stir the vegetables until they are coated with the sauce.

5. To serve, split the sweet potatoes and push them together from either long end, so that you loosen some of the flesh. Spoon some of the stir-fry into each potato and serve immediately.

Braised Swiss Chard

4 strips bacon, cut crosswise into $\frac{1}{2}$-inch-wide strips

2 tablespoons olive oil

1 envelope Lipton Savory Herb with Garlic Soup Mix

3 bunches fresh Swiss chard, stems removed and leaves cut crosswise into 1-inch-wide strips

1 cup water

$\frac{1}{2}$ teaspoon freshly ground black pepper

1. In a 12-inch sauté pan, fry the bacon over medium-high heat, stirring, until it is crisp. Add the oil and soup mix, stirring to blend. Add the Swiss chard, turning it in the mixture.

2. Reduce the heat to medium-low, add the water, cover the pan, and cook the Swiss chard for 15 minutes, stirring every 5 minutes to make sure that the chard cooks evenly.

3. Stir in the pepper, remove the cover from the pan, and cook the chard for another 5 minutes before serving.

SERVES 6

Gorgeous greens, glistening with olive oil and studded with bacon, make a crowd-pleasing side dish to serve with grilled meats. I love both the red and green Swiss chard. For this recipe, I have omitted the stems, which tend to be tough, but if you would like to use them, chop them into $\frac{1}{2}$-inch pieces and boil them for ten minutes, drain them, and then stir them into the braise.

Vegetables

Parmesan Herbed Tomatoes

These colorful tomatoes make a delicious accompaniment to an otherwise plain plate of grilled meat or seafood. The crumb topping for the tomatoes can be made two days ahead of time; just top the tomatoes and bake them when you are ready.

Souper Smart

If you absolutely have to have this dish in the dead of winter, use one 28-ounce can chopped tomatoes, drain them, and toss with the salt and pepper. Sprinkle the tomatoes with the crumb topping and bake as directed.

¼ cup olive oil, divided

6 large ripe tomatoes, cut into ½-inch-thick slices

1 teaspoon salt

½ teaspoon freshly ground black pepper

2 cups freshly grated Parmesan cheese

½ cup fresh fine breadcrumbs

1 envelope Lipton Savory Herb with Garlic Soup Mix

1. Preheat the oven to 375 degrees. Spread 1 to 2 tablespoons of the oil over the bottom of a 13-by-9-inch baking dish.

2. Lay the tomatoes in the prepared baking dish, overlapping them if necessary. Sprinkle them with the salt and pepper.

3. In a medium mixing bowl, combine the cheese, breadcrumbs, and soup mix. Sprinkle the remaining 2 to 3 tablespoons oil over the breadcrumb mixture and toss the breadcrumbs until they begin to come together in clumps.

4. Spread the crumb topping over the tomatoes and bake the tomatoes until they are tender and the topping begins to turn golden, 20 to 30 minutes.

Grandma's Stuffed Tomatoes

¼ cup olive oil

4 large ripe tomatoes (about 3 inches in diameter)

1 envelope Lipton Savory Herb with Garlic Soup Mix

2 cups fresh French or Italian breadcrumbs

½ cup freshly grated Parmesan cheese

6 fresh basil leaves, finely chopped

¼ cup chopped fresh Italian parsley leaves

1. Pour 2 tablespoons of the oil into a 12-inch sauté pan.

2. Cut the tomatoes in half, place them in the sauté pan cut side up, and season them with a bit of the soup mix.

3. In a small mixing bowl, combine the rest of the soup mix, the breadcrumbs, cheese, basil, and parsley, tossing the mixture together.

4. Mound some of the breadcrumb mixture onto each tomato, sprinkle the remaining 2 tablespoons oil over the tomatoes, and set the pan over medium-high heat.

5. When the tomatoes begin to sizzle, shake the pan a bit to loosen the tomatoes, cover the pan, and cook the tomatoes until they begin to soften, about 20 minutes.

6. Remove the cover from the pan, spoon some pan juices over each tomato, and continue to cook the tomatoes, uncovered, until they are softened, another 10 to 15 minutes. Serve immediately.

SERVES 6

My daughter Carrie's favorite summer dinner is grilled steak or sea bass, fresh corn on the cob, and these delicious tomatoes. This recipe can only be made with vine-ripened tomatoes, so wait for the peak of the season to make this dish.

Souper Smart

You can make these tomatoes two to three hours ahead of time and just reheat them when you are ready to serve them.

By 1873 Carl Knorr and his sons were testing packaged soup mixes made of flour, dried vegetables, and some seasonings.

Vegetables

Old-Fashioned Stewed Tomatoes

An old favorite with a new twist, these tomatoes are pure comfort food, studded with onion and green pepper and covered with a crumbled breadcrumb topping. Your family will love this dish.

2 tablespoons butter

½ cup chopped onion

½ cup seeded and chopped green bell pepper (about ½ of a large pepper)

1 envelope Knorr Vegetable Soup Mix

Two 14.5-ounce cans whole plum tomatoes, drained

1 cup dry breadcrumbs

3 tablespoons olive oil

¾ cup freshly grated Parmesan cheese

1. Preheat the broiler for 10 minutes.

2. Melt the butter in a 4-quart saucepan over medium heat. Add the onion and green pepper and cook, stirring, until they are softened, 3 to 4 minutes. Add the soup mix and cook, stirring, for another 3 minutes.

3. Cut the tomatoes into halves, add them to the saucepan, and cook for 5 minutes. (At this point you may let mixture cool to room temperature, cover with plastic wrap, and refrigerate for up to 2 days. When ready to serve, reheat and proceed as directed.)

4. Pour the mixture into a 1½-quart casserole dish.

5. In a medium mixing bowl, combine the breadcrumbs, oil, and cheese, stirring to combine. Sprinkle the breadcrumb mixture over the tomatoes and broil them until the cheese is golden.

Gruyère Zucchini Boats

4 medium zucchini, ends trimmed, and halved lengthwise

2 tablespoons butter

$\frac{1}{2}$ cup chopped onion

$\frac{1}{2}$ cup finely chopped ham

1 envelope Knorr Leek Soup Mix

$1\frac{1}{2}$ cups milk

$\frac{1}{8}$ teaspoon freshly grated nutmeg

$\frac{1}{2}$ teaspoon freshly ground black pepper

$1\frac{1}{2}$ cups grated Gruyère cheese

1. Preheat the oven to 400 degrees. Grease a 13-by-9-inch baking dish.

2. Put the zucchini in a large saucepan with water to cover and bring to a boil. Remove the zucchini from the water, drain, and, when they are cool enough to handle, scoop the pulp from the center of the zucchini, leaving a $\frac{1}{2}$-inch-thick shell. Coarsely chop the pulp. Place the zucchini shells, skin side down, in the prepared dish.

3. To make the stuffing, melt the butter in a 10-inch skillet over medium heat. Add the onion and cook it, stirring, until it is softened, 3 to 4 minutes. Add the zucchini pulp and ham and cook, the mixture, stirring, for another 3 to 4 minutes. Add the soup mix and milk and bring the pot to a boil. Stir in the nutmeg and pepper and remove the pot from the stove.

4. Stuff each zucchini with some of the stuffing mixture and then sprinkle the cheese on top. (At this point you may refrigerate the zucchini for up to 1 day.) Bake the zucchini until the cheese is golden brown, about 15 minutes.

Zucchini is the chameleon of vegetables; it takes on whatever flavor you decide to give it, and it does so with style and grace. This elegant side dish is a great example of using soup mix to make a savory sauce that enhances the flavor of the dish.

Zucchini Florentine

3 tablespoons butter

$\frac{1}{2}$ cup chopped shallots

2 cups shredded zucchini

1 envelope Knorr Cream of Spinach Soup Mix

$1\frac{1}{2}$ cups milk

$\frac{1}{8}$ teaspoon freshly grated nutmeg

$\frac{1}{4}$ cup grated Parmesan cheese

Feathery shreds of zucchini and nuggets of spinach pair in this beat-the-clock side dish. Other additions to the basic recipe are crispy bits of bacon, white cheddar cheese, or smoked mozzarella.

1. Melt the butter in a 10-inch skillet over medium heat. Add the shallot and cook, stirring, until softened, about 2 minutes. Add the zucchini and cook, stirring, for 3 to 4 minutes.

2. Stir in the soup mix, milk, nutmeg, and cheese until the ingredients are well combined. Bring the mixture to a boil and keep it warm over low heat until you are ready to serve it.

Zucchini Corn Pancakes

These pancakes are a favorite around my house, even though I have a child who doesn't like green in his food. The zucchini provides moisture and texture for the pancakes, and the Parmesan and sweet corn add flavor. Leftover pancakes can be reheated in a preheated 350-degree oven, although you probably won't have any leftovers!

2 cups grated zucchini

1 teaspoon salt

3 large eggs

1 cup milk

$\frac{1}{2}$ cup all-purpose flour

$\frac{1}{2}$ cup yellow cornmeal

1 envelope Knorr Leek Soup Mix

2 cups corn kernels, either cut fresh from the cob or frozen (and defrosted)

1 teaspoon baking powder

$\frac{1}{4}$ teaspoon baking soda

$\frac{1}{2}$ cup freshly grated Parmesan cheese

¼ cup (½ stick) butter

2 tablespoons vegetable oil

1. Place the grated zucchini in a colander, sprinkle them with the salt, and toss. Let the zucchini drain in the sink or over a bowl for 30 minutes. Squeeze the zucchini dry.

2. In a large mixing bowl, whisk together the eggs, milk, flour, cornmeal, soup mix, corn, baking powder, baking soda, zucchini, and Parmesan.

3. Heat the butter and oil together in a 12-inch skillet over medium-high heat. When the foam subsides, drop 2 tablespoons of batter into the hot fat. Cook the pancakes until the edges begin to set and the undersides are golden brown. Flip the pancakes and cook them until they are golden brown and cooked through, another 2 minutes.

4. Drain the pancakes on paper towels, adding more butter or oil to the skillet as necessary to cook the rest of the pancakes. Serve immediately or keep them warm in a low oven.

FRANK SINATRA STIPULATED IN HIS CONCERT CONTRACTS THAT HE BE SERVED CAMPBELL'S CHICKEN WITH RICE SOUP.

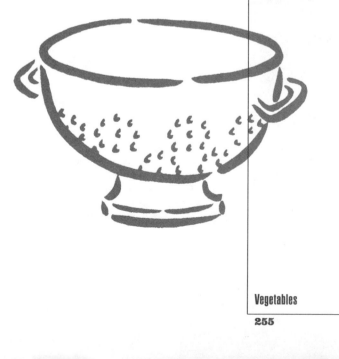

Zucchini Stuffing Casserole

SERVES 8

A favorite side dish from covered-dish dinners, this casserole can be made the day before and baked just before serving. This recipe is a great way to use up those baseball bat–size zucchini in the garden, and the food processor will make quick work of grating them. Freeze grated zucchini in resealable plastic bags so you can make this dish in the dead of winter.

2 tablespoons butter

1 medium onion, chopped

3 cups grated zucchini

2 medium carrots, grated

1 can Campbell's Condensed Cream of Celery or Cream of Mushroom Soup

1 cup sour cream

4 cups herb-seasoned stuffing cubes

1. Preheat the oven to 350 degrees. Coat a 3-quart casserole dish with nonstick cooking spray.

2. Melt the butter in a 10-inch sauté pan over medium-high heat. Add the onion, zucchini, and carrots and cook, stirring, until they are softened, 3 to 4 minutes.

3. In a large mixing bowl, whisk together the soup and sour cream. Add the sautéed vegetables and stuffing cubes, stirring until they are blended.

4. Transfer the mixture to the prepared casserole dish and bake until the top is browned, 35 to 40 minutes. Serve immediately.

In 1897 a can of Campbell's condensed soup sold for a dime.

Summer Squash Bake

½ cup (1 stick) butter

¼ cup chopped shallots

5 cups ½-inch dice yellow squash

One 16-ounce package frozen chopped spinach, defrosted and squeezed dry

1 envelope Knorr Cream of Spinach Soup Mix

1⅓ to 1½ cups milk (see Souper Smart)

½ teaspoon freshly ground black pepper

⅛ teaspoon freshly grated nutmeg

2 cups grated Jarlsberg cheese

1. Preheat the oven to 375 degrees. Coat a 10-inch round baking dish that is at least 2 inches deep with nonstick cooking spray.

2. In a 10- or 12-inch sauté pan, melt the butter over medium-high heat. Add the shallots and cook, stirring, until softened, about 2 minutes. Add the squash and cook it, stirring, until it begins to soften, 5 to 7 minutes. Add the spinach and stir until it is well combined, about 2 minutes. Add the soup mix, milk, pepper, and nutmeg and bring the mixture to a boil.

3. Remove the pan from the heat, stir in 1 cup of the cheese, and transfer the mixture to the prepared baking dish. Sprinkle the casserole with the remaining 1 cup cheese. (At this point, the casserole can be refrigerated for up to 12 hours.)

4. Bake the casserole until it is golden brown on top, 25 to 35 minutes. Let it rest for 5 minutes before serving.

SERVES 8

This golden vegetable dish is studded with brilliant green spinach and flavored with creamy Jarlsberg cheese. It comes together in no time and pairs beautifully with beef, chicken, and fish. For a different twist on dinner, try substituting smoked Gouda, cheddar, or pepper Jack cheese.

Souper Smart

Some squash and spinach will give off more liquid than others. When making this dish, start with 1⅓ cups milk; if the sauce seems too thick, thin it with additional milk. The sauce should be the consistency of a medium white sauce and should coat the back of a spoon. You can choose yellow crookneck, pattypan, or yellow zucchini for this recipe.

Peperonata

This colorful side dish of peppers, onions, and tomatoes is a staple from my childhood. My mother and grandmother seemed to have this on the table at a lot of meals; they'd stir it into eggs, serve it atop steak or chicken, spread it on pizza dough and cover it with cheese, or serve it on the side with crusty bread. It's simple to prepare, and the addition of soup mix punches up the flavor.

THE KNORR BRAND OF SOUPS BEGAN WITH CARL HEINRICH KNORR, WHO BUILT A FACTORY IN HEILBRONN, GERMANY, IN 1838 IN ORDER TO DRY CHICORY AND MAKE VARIOUS TYPES OF FLOURS.

3 tablespoons olive oil

2 large onions, cut into 1/2-inch-thick slices

2 medium red bell peppers, seeded and cut into 1/2-inch-thick rings

1 medium green bell pepper, seeded and cut into 1/2-inch-thick rings

1 medium yellow bell pepper, seeded and cut into 1/2-inch-thick rings

1 envelope Knorr Tomato with Basil Soup Mix

2 tablespoons balsamic vinegar

One 14.5-ounce can chopped tomatoes, with their juices

1 tablespoon chopped fresh oregano leaves or 1 1/2 teaspoons dried

2 tablespoons chopped fresh Italian parsley leaves

1 teaspoon freshly ground black pepper

1. Heat the oil in a 12-inch sauté pan over medium-high heat. Add the onions and cook, stirring, until softened, 3 to 4 minutes. Add all the peppers and cook, stirring, until they begin to soften, 5 to 7 minutes, stirring so that they don't stick. Add the soup mix and vinegar and continue to cook the vegetables for another 2 to 3 minutes, stirring.

2. Add the tomatoes, along with the oregano, parsley, and black pepper. Continue to cook the vegetables until most of the juices from the tomatoes have evaporated and the peppers are soft.

Vegetable Custards

SERVES 6 TO 8

1 can Campbell's Condensed Cream of Chicken Soup

2 large eggs

Pinch of freshly grated nutmeg

$1/2$ teaspoon freshly ground black pepper

2 cups chopped cooked vegetables (grated zucchini, corn, broccoli, spinach or chard, mushrooms, or leftover Peperonata, page 258, or Ratatouille, page 260)

$1\frac{1}{2}$ cups grated cheese (Swiss, cheddar, smoked Gouda, or blue cheese)

2 tablespoons freshly grated Parmesan cheese

1. Preheat the oven to 350 degrees. Coat 8 individual ramekins or a $1\frac{1}{2}$-quart soufflé dish with nonstick cooking spray.

2. In a large mixing bowl, whisk together the soup, eggs, nutmeg, and pepper. Fold in the vegetables and cheeses.

3. Pour the mixture into the prepared ramekins or dish and set the ramekins or dish in a larger pan filled with boiling water that comes halfway up the sides.

4. Bake the custard(s) until a knife inserted into the center comes out clean, about 45 minutes for the large custard and 20 to 25 minutes for the smaller ones. Let the custard cool for 5 minutes before serving it.

Comforting and homey, these custards can be a first course, light luncheon, or supper entrée. Savory, studded with your choice of vegetable and cheese, these are a favorite at our house.

Vegetables

259

Ratatouille

Ratatouille is another taste of the Mediterranean. I think that ratatouille is best made a day ahead to let the flavors get to know one another. This dish is great served with eggs for brunch or alongside grilled meats or poultry.

3 tablespoons olive oil

1 large onion, cut into ½-inch-thick slices

3 cloves garlic, minced

1 medium green bell pepper, seeded and cut into ½-inch-thick rings

3 medium Japanese eggplants, ends trimmed, peeled, and cut into ½-inch-thick slices

1 medium zucchini, ends trimmed, and cut into ½-inch-thick rounds

One 14.5-ounce can chopped tomatoes, with their juices

1 envelope Knorr Tomato with Basil Soup Mix

½ teaspoon dried oregano

½ teaspoon dried marjoram

½ teaspoon dried basil

½ cup freshly grated Parmesan cheese

½ cup grated Swiss cheese

1. Preheat the broiler for 10 minutes.

2. Heat the oil in an ovenproof 12-inch sauté pan over medium-high heat. Add the onion and cook it, stirring, until it is softened, 3 to 4 minutes. Add the garlic and cook it, stirring, for 2 minutes. Add the bell pepper, eggplant, and zucchini and cook them, stirring, until they begin to soften, 6 to 8 minutes. Add the tomatoes, soup mix, and herbs, reduce the heat to medium-low, and simmer the vegetables until the juices have evaporated, 6 to 8 minutes.

3. Sprinkle the cheeses over the top of the ratatouille and run the pan under the broiler until the cheeses have melted and turned golden brown.

Roasted Garlic Vegetables

½ cup olive oil

1 envelope Lipton Savory Herb with Garlic Soup Mix

2 tablespoons fresh rosemary leaves

1 teaspoon freshly ground black pepper

1 teaspoon salt

3 pounds mixed root vegetables (potatoes, carrots, sweet potatoes, parsnips, shallots, small onions), peeled if necessary and cut into 1-inch chunks

2 heads garlic, separated into cloves

1. Preheat the oven to 425 degrees.

2. In a small mixing bowl, combine the oil, soup mix, rosemary, pepper, and salt.

3. Place the vegetables and garlic in a large roasting pan and pour the flavored oil over them, tossing to coat them evenly.

4. Roast the vegetables for 20 minutes and then reduce the oven temperature to 375 degrees and bake the vegetables until they are tender, an additional 30 minutes.

Roasted vegetables glistening with olive oil and flavored with roasted garlic are the stars of this dish. Make sure that your roasting pan can handle them in one layer; that way they will brown and cook evenly.

Vegetable Feta Bake

SERVES 6

With the salty flavor of feta cheese, colorful zucchini, and tomato and basil sauce, this dish is sure to be a crowd pleaser at your next dinner.

6 tablespoons olive oil

12 ounces feta cheese, crumbled

1 envelope Knorr Tomato with Basil Soup Mix

4 medium zucchini, ends trimmed, and cut lengthwise into ½-inch-thick slices

2 leeks, washed well and cut into ½-inch-thick rounds, discarding the tough green parts

Two 14-ounce cans artichoke hearts, drained and cut into quarters

1. Preheat the oven to 350 degrees. Coat a 2-quart soufflé dish with nonstick cooking spray.

2. In a small mixing bowl, combine the oil, feta, and soup mix.

3. Place a layer of zucchini, a layer of leeks, and then a layer of artichokes in the prepared soufflé dish. Spread some of the feta mixture over the vegetables. Continue layering, finishing with the feta mixture. Cover the casserole with plastic wrap until you are ready to bake it, for up to 12 hours.

4. Bake the vegetables until they are cooked through, about 40 minutes. Let the casserole rest for 5 minutes before serving.

Penne Pasta with Pork Rib Ragu

Pasta with Chicken and Sun-Dried Tomatoes

Linguine with Shellfish

Seafood Lasagne

Vegetarian Lasagne

Red, White, and Green Cannelloni

Pasta Primavera

Pasta with Roasted Vegetables

Pasta with Tomato Basil Salsa

Quickie Farfalle with Mushroom Ragout

Souper Baked Four-Cheese Pasta

Lemon Garlic Orzo

Blue Plate Macaroni and Cheese

Baked Macaroni and Cheese

Old-Fashioned Macaroni and Cheese

Yaki Soba

Vegetable Couscous

Basic Souped-Up Risotto

Feta Florentine Rice

Kaleidoscope Garden Vegetable Rice

Company Rice

Santa Fe Rice

Another Santa Fe Rice

Side Dish Paella

Herbed Wild Cranberry Rice

Fruited Rice

Triple Mushroom Oven-Baked Rice

Quick Rice Pilaf

Wild Rice Casserole

Creamy Seafood Rice

Kitchen Sink Fried Rice

Cajun Crawfish Rice Stuffing

Kiss My Grits Casserole

Huevos Rancheros Casserole

Country Hash Browns and Egg Casserole

Del Mar Soufflé

Chile Relleno Soufflé

Spinach and Artichoke Quiche

Chicken and Broccoli Quiche

Green Chile Frittata

Asparagus Frittata

Mushroom and Onion Bread Pudding

Bacon and Leek Bread Pudding

Spinach and Canadian Bacon Bread Pudding

Zucchini Strata

Absolutely the Best Corn Bread Stuffing

Old-Fashioned Bread Stuffing

Pasta, Rice, Eggs, and Stuffings

AS A CHILD, I REMEMBER MY grandmother making what she called "macaroni,"

and what we today call "pasta." She would make a marinara sauce and lightly

toss the noodles in it, and then serve them with a sprinkling of freshly grated

Parmigiano-Reggiano or Pecorino Romano—this was *my* macaroni and cheese.

When I would ask my mother to buy the blue box of Kraft macaroni and cheese,

she would look at me and shake her head, realizing that she was losing another

child to the fast-food revolution. I've come a long way since those days in my

grandma's kitchen, and, fortunately for me and my family, I watched and learned

in that kitchen.

These days, noodles in every shape imaginable are served flavored with

influences from Asia, Mexico, Europe, the Southwest, and Italy. Using soups

to help you put some great pastas on the table is simple and speedy. With a few additions, condensed soup can become a creamy sauce, and a dried soup can help to punch up the flavors and season the dish.

Rice is a side dish that can jazz up an otherwise plain broiled chicken breast or steak. Seasoned with soup, rice becomes the star on the plate. During the past fifty years, we have witnessed the emergence of rice, with risotto on restaurant menus and jasmine, basmati, and popcorn rice readily available to chase away the idea that rice has to be just plain steamed rice. The next time you prepare rice, cook it with a soup mix for added flavor and pizzazz.

Unless otherwise specified in the following recipes, we will be using raw converted rice, like Uncle Ben's. This rice has been steamed under pressure, it is enriched, and, when it's cooked, its texture is light and fluffy and the grains are separate.

Wild rice is not a rice at all but a tall grass that is harvested in northern regions of the Americas. Hand harvested, it is expensive, but it expands to almost four times its volume when cooked, so you get a lot of bang for the buck.

Eggs, whether used in an omelette or soufflé, are a great way to serve your family protein, and the addition of soup helps to make the meal. Whether it's a quiche flavored with a dried soup mix or a breakfast *strata* or casserole that gets some creamy help from a condensed soup, you'll find that soups can be your passport out of the mealtime doldrums and into a new way of preparing special foods for your family.

Stuffings seem to be served only at holiday time, but you can serve them year-round from your soup pantry. Savory and studded with vegetables and fruits, stuffings can turn ordinary meats and poultry into celebratory foods.

Penne Pasta with Pork Rib Ragu

2 tablespoons olive oil

1 slab baby back ribs, cut into 2-rib sections

1 cup chopped onion

½ cup chopped carrot

2 envelopes Lipton Savory Herb with Garlic Soup Mix

Two 28-ounce cans chopped tomatoes, with their juices

1 teaspoon freshly ground black pepper

¼ cup chopped fresh Italian parsley leaves

1 pound penne pasta, cooked until al dente, drained, tossed
   with 2 tablespoons olive oil, and kept warm

½ cup freshly grated Parmesan cheese

1. In a 5-quart Dutch oven over high heat, heat the oil, add the ribs, and brown them on all sides. Add the onion, carrot, and soup mix and cook the vegetables, stirring, until the onions are softened, 4 to 6 minutes. Add the tomatoes and pepper, reduce the heat to medium-low, and simmer the ragu, covered, for 1 hour, stirring occasionally to prevent sticking.

2. Stir in the parsley and toss the sauce with the hot cooked pasta. Serve the Parmesan on the side.

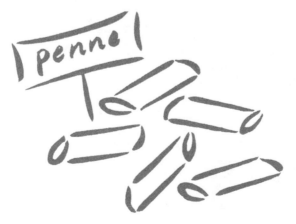

SERVES 6

Tiny baby back ribs simmered in a tomato sauce give you lip-smacking comfort food that would make my grandma proud! The sauce can be made two days ahead of time, since it actually improves with age, or you can freeze it for up to six weeks.

Slow Cooker Savvy

Brown the ribs and vegetables, place them in the slow cooker with the remaining ingredients, and cook the ragu on high for four to five hours.

Pasta with Chicken and Sun-Dried Tomatoes

This one-dish dinner is simple, yet it looks like it has taken you hours to make. The sauce and chicken can be prepared ahead of time; just cook the pasta, heat up the chicken and sauce, and serve.

½ cup (1 stick) butter

1 whole skinless, boneless chicken breast, cut into ½-inch-thick strips

½ cup oil-packed sun-dried tomatoes, drained and cut into matchsticks

2 tablespoons chopped fresh basil leaves

2 tablespoons chopped fresh Italian parsley leaves

1 envelope Knorr Leek Soup Mix

1½ cups heavy cream

½ cup freshly grated Parmesan cheese

1 pound farfalle pasta, cooked until al dente, drained, tossed with 2 tablespoons olive oil, and kept warm

1 teaspoon freshly ground black pepper

1. Melt the butter in a 10-inch sauté pan over medium heat, add the chicken, and cook it, stirring, until it is no longer pink, about 7 minutes. Add the tomatoes, basil, parsley, soup mix, and heavy cream, and stir the sauce until it comes to a boil. Reduce the heat, add ¼ cup of the cheese, and stir until it is melted.

2. Toss the sauce with the hot cooked pasta, seasoning the dish well with pepper, and serve garnished with the remaining ¼ cup cheese.

Linguine with Shellfish

3 tablespoons butter

2 tablespoons olive oil

¼ cup chopped shallots

8 ounces shucked clams, drained, or canned chopped clams, drained

½ pound medium shrimp, peeled and deveined

½ pound bay scallops (if you can find only large scallops, cut them into quarters)

3 tablespoons dry white wine

1 can Campbell's Condensed Cream of Shrimp Soup

½ cup half-and-half

¼ cup plus 2 tablespoons chopped fresh Italian parsley leaves

1 pound fresh linguine, cooked until al dente, drained, tossed with 2 tablespoons olive oil, and kept warm

1. Melt the butter in the olive oil over medium heat in a 10-inch sauté pan. Add the shallots and cook them, stirring, until they are softened, about 2 minutes. Add the clams, shrimp, and scallops and cook them until the shrimp just begin to turn pink. Add the wine, whisk in the soup and half-and-half, and bring the mixture to a boil.

2. Remove the pan from the heat and stir in ¼ cup of the parsley. Toss the sauce with the hot cooked pasta and garnish with the remaining 2 tablespoons parsley.

SERVES 6 TO 8

Bursting with clams, shrimp, and scallops in a creamy sauce, this pasta dish is simple yet elegant enough for a special dinner.

Souper Smart

In Italy, cooks do not garnish seafood pasta dishes with cheese, but you might want to pass a little grated Parmesan just in case your guests like it that way.

Seafood Lasagne

This strikingly beautiful casserole is a takeoff on one that appeared 25 years ago in a *Better Homes and Gardens* recipe contest. Spinach noodles are filled with seafood in a creamy sauce and then covered with tomato sauce and cheese. An easy do-ahead dish, the lasagne can be prepared two days in advance and then popped into the oven while you are serving drinks.

1/4 cup (1/2 stick) butter

2 pounds seafood (use a combination of peeled and deveined shrimp, scallops, crab, and/or firm white-fleshed fish such as halibut, cut into 1-inch chunks)

1/2 cup white wine

1 1/2 cups ricotta cheese

1 cup freshly grated Parmesan cheese

1 large egg

2 tablespoons chopped fresh Italian parsley leaves

1 can Campbell's Condensed Cream of Shrimp Soup

1 1/2 cups heavy cream

1 pound fresh spinach lasagne noodles (if you cannot get fresh lasagne noodles, buy dried, cook for half the time called for on the box, drain, and toss them with olive oil to prevent sticking)

4 to 5 cups Basic Marinara (page 470)

1. Preheat the oven to 350 degrees. Coat a 13-by-9-inch baking dish with nonstick cooking spray.

2. In a 12-inch sauté pan over medium heat, melt the butter, add the seafood, tossing it in the butter, and cook the seafood until the shrimp begin to turn pink and the fish just begins to cook through, about 5 minutes. Add 1/4 cup of the wine and remove the pan from the heat.

3. In a large mixing bowl, blend together the ricotta, 1/4 cup of the Parmesan, the egg, and parsley. Gently fold in the cooked seafood and any liquid that may have accumulated in the pan.

4. In a 2-quart saucepan, heat the soup with the remaining 1/4 cup wine, add the heavy cream, and stir until blended. Remove the pan from the heat and set it aside.

5. Spread 1/2 cup of the marinara on the bottom of the prepared dish. Place lasagne noodles over the marinara, cover the pasta with half of the seafood and ricotta mixture, and spread a thin layer of the cream of shrimp sauce over the seafood and ricotta mixture. Top with another layer of lasagne noodles, spread on some of the marinara, the other half of the seafood and ricotta mixture, some more cream of shrimp sauce, and top with the last layer of lasagne noodles. Spread a thick layer of marinara over the noodles and top that with the remaining cream of shrimp sauce and the remaining $^3/_4$ cup Parmesan.

6. Bake the lasagne, covered with a sheet of aluminum foil, for 45 minutes. Remove the foil and continue baking until the cheese is golden brown and the casserole is bubbling, an additional 15 minutes.

Vegetarian Lasagne

$^1/_4$ cup ($^1/_2$ stick) butter

2 large onions, cut into $^1/_2$-inch-thick rounds

4 medium zucchini, ends trimmed, and cut lengthwise into $^1/_2$-inch-thick slices

2 medium carrots, grated

2 envelopes Knorr Cream of Broccoli Soup Mix

2 cups milk

$^1/_8$ teaspoon freshly grated nutmeg

1 teaspoon freshly ground black pepper

3 sheets fresh lasagne noodles large enough to fit a 13-by-9-inch pan, or $^3/_4$ pound dried no-boil lasagne noodles

1 cup freshly grated Parmesan cheese

$^1/_2$ cup shredded Gruyère cheese

1. Preheat the oven to 350 degrees. Coat a 13-by-9-inch baking dish with nonstick cooking spray.

SERVES 8

Lasagne is a special dish, and this creamy vegetable version will have even the staunchest meat and potatoes person begging for more.

2. In a 12-inch sauté pan over medium heat, melt the butter, add the onion, and cook, stirring, until the onion begins to caramelize and turn a light golden brown, about 10 minutes. Add the zucchini and carrots and cook them, stirring, until they are tender, 4 to 7 minutes. Sprinkle the soup mix over the vegetables, gently stir in the milk, nutmeg, and pepper, and bring the mixture to a boil. Remove the pan from the heat and refrigerate the vegetable cream sauce until you are ready to assemble the lasagne.

3. Spread a thin layer of the vegetable cream sauce over the bottom of the prepared dish. Cover the sauce with a sheet of pasta and then cover that with one third of the remaining sauce. Sprinkle on one third of the two cheeses, and layer on another sheet of pasta. Repeat the layering process, ending with a layer of lasagne, sauce, and cheese.

4. Cover the casserole with a sheet of aluminum foil and bake the lasagne for 45 minutes. Remove the foil and bake the lasagne until the cheese is golden, an additional 15 to 20 minutes.

Red, White, and Green Cannelloni

One 12-ounce box no-boil cannelloni tubes

One 16-ounce bag frozen chopped spinach, defrosted and
squeezed dry

2 cups ricotta cheese

1½ cup freshly grated Parmesan cheese

3 large eggs

¼ pound thinly sliced prosciutto, finely chopped

1 envelope Knorr Cream of Spinach Soup Mix

½ teaspoon freshly ground black pepper

⅛ teaspoon freshly grated nutmeg

6 cups Basic Marinara (page 470) or other tomato sauce,
divided

1. Preheat the oven to 350 degrees. Coat a 13-by-9-inch baking dish with nonstick cooking spray. Soak the cannelloni tubes in a large bowl of cold water until they are softened.

2. Meanwhile, in a large mixing bowl, stir together the spinach, ricotta, 1 cup of the Parmesan, the eggs, prosciutto, soup mix, pepper, and nutmeg until well combined.

3. Spread 1½ cups of the marinara over the bottom of the prepared dish.

4. Drain the cannelloni and stuff them with the spinach and ricotta mixture. Set the cannelloni over the marinara sauce in the baking dish, pour 3 cups of marinara over the cannelloni, and sprinkle on the remaining ½ cup Parmesan.

5. Bake the cannelloni until the cheese on top is golden and the filling is set, 30 to 40 minutes. Let the dish rest for 5 minutes before serving. Heat the remaining marinara and serve it on the side.

SERVES 8

Filled with spinach, ricotta, and prosciutto and looking a bit like the Italian flag, this cannelloni will be on your family's top ten list. The cannelloni noodles don't have to be cooked, saving you a step, and the rest of the ingredients come together in a snap.

Souper Smart

No-cook lasagne and cannelloni noodles absorb a lot of moisture. If your cannelloni begin to look dry, add ½ cup water or stock to the pan.

More Souper Smarts

If you don't have any homemade marinara in your freezer, try using a bottled imported marinara instead.

Pasta Primavera

A jumble of colorful vegetables bound in a light creamy sauce, paired with egg and spinach pasta, this dish is simple and visually appealing. The sauce can be made earlier in the day and then tossed with the pasta just before serving.

½ cup (1 stick) butter

½ cup chopped red onion

2 medium carrots, cut into matchsticks

1 cup broccoli florets

1 cup sugar snap peas, ends trimmed and strings removed

1 cup halved baby yellow pattypan squash

1 envelope Knorr Leek Soup Mix, Cream of Broccoli, or Cream of Spinach Soup Mix

1½ cups half-and-half

½ teaspoon freshly ground black pepper

⅛ teaspoon freshly grated nutmeg

2 tablespoons chopped fresh dill

1 tablespoon chopped fresh chives, plus more for garnish

½ pound fresh egg pasta

½ pound fresh spinach pasta

Sprigs fresh dill for garnish

1. In a 12-inch sauté pan or wok, melt the butter over medium heat, add the onion, and cook, stirring, until it is softened, 2 to 3 minutes. Add the carrots and broccoli and cook, stirring, for another 2 to 3 minutes. Add the sugar snap peas and squash and cook, stirring, for 2 minutes.

2. Sprinkle the soup mix over the vegetables, stir in the half-and-half, and bring the mixture to a boil. Stir in the pepper, nutmeg, dill, and chives and keep the sauce warm over low heat.

3. Cook the pastas in boiling salted water until al dente. Drain thoroughly and toss with the warm sauce. Serve garnished with additional chopped chives and sprigs of dill.

Pasta with Roasted Vegetables

½ cup olive oil

1 envelope Lipton Savory Herb with Garlic Soup Mix

1 teaspoon chopped fresh oregano leaves

1 teaspoon freshly ground black pepper

½ teaspoon salt

4 cloves garlic

6 shallots, halved

4 ripe plum tomatoes, cut into quarters

12 crimini mushrooms, cut into quarters

4 baby eggplants, stems removed, and cut into quarters

1 pound fresh egg pasta, cooked until al dente, drained, tossed with 2 tablespoons olive oil, and kept warm

½ cup freshly grated Parmesan cheese for garnish

1. Preheat the oven to 400 degrees.

2. In a large nonreactive bowl, combine the olive oil, soup mix, oregano, pepper, and salt.

3. Arrange the vegetables in a large roasting pan, big enough to hold them in a single layer. Pour the oil mixture over them and toss to coat them evenly. Bake the vegetables, stirring occasionally, until they are tender and slightly charred on the edges, 30 to 40 minutes.

4. Toss the hot cooked pasta with the vegetables and all the juices from the pan. Serve immediately garnished with the Parmesan.

An irresistible combination with fresh cooked pasta, the vegetables in this recipe are roasted until the sugars in them make them taste like candy. The vegetables can be roasted the day before and reheated in a sauté pan just before tossing them with the pasta.

Pasta with Tomato Basil Salsa

This dish comes together in the time it takes the pasta to cook. The salsa can be made a day ahead and refrigerated until you are ready to serve it with the pasta.

Souper Smart

Olive oil will solidify in the refrigerator, so make sure to take the salsa out at least an hour before you plan to serve it, so that the oil can return to a liquid state.

¼ cup extra virgin olive oil

2 tablespoons olive oil

4 cloves garlic, minced

One 14.5-ounce can chopped tomatoes, drained

1 envelope Knorr Tomato Basil Soup Mix

¼ cup chopped fresh basil leaves

2 tablespoons chopped fresh Italian parsley leaves

1 teaspoon freshly ground black pepper

1 pound fettuccine

1. In a large mixing bowl, combine the oils, garlic, tomatoes, soup mix, basil, parsley, and pepper, stirring to blend. Allow the salsa to stand at room temperature for 2 hours so that the flavors can get to know one another. (The salsa will keep in the refrigerator for up to 3 days.)

2. Cook the fettuccine in boiling water until al dente, drain it, and toss it with the salsa. Serve immediately.

Quickie Farfalle with Mushroom Ragout

1 tablespoon butter

2 tablespoons extra virgin olive oil

1½ pounds crimini mushrooms, sliced ½ inch thick

1 teaspoon dried thyme

One 14.5-ounce can chopped tomatoes, with their juices

½ cup white wine

1 can Campbell's Condensed Cream of Mushroom Soup

½ cup milk

Salt and freshly ground black pepper

1 pound farfalle, cooked al dente, drained, tossed with
    2 tablespoons olive oil, and kept warm

2 tablespoons chopped fresh Italian parsley leaves for garnish

¼ to ½ cup shredded Parmesan cheese for garnish

1. Melt the butter in the olive oil in a 10-inch skillet over medium-high heat. Add the mushrooms and thyme and cook the mushrooms, stirring, until they begin to soften, 4 to 5 minutes. Add the tomatoes, reduce the heat to medium, and simmer them until their juices begin to evaporate, another 5 minutes. Add the wine, bring the mixture to a boil, and let it boil for 2 minutes.

2. In a small mixing bowl, whisk together the soup and milk. Stir the soup mixture into the mushrooms and bring to a boil. Taste the sauce and correct the seasoning with salt and pepper. (At this point, the sauce may be covered with plastic wrap and refrigerated for up to 2 days.)

3. Toss the warm sauce with the hot drained pasta and serve garnished with the parsley and Parmesan.

Everyone needs quick pasta dishes they can serve on a rushed weeknight, and this one is easily put together in the time it takes the pasta to boil. I like crimini mushrooms in this, but you can substitute white mushrooms if crimini are not available.

CAMPBELL'S CONDENSED CREAM OF MUSHROOM SOUP FIRST APPEARED ON GROCERY STORE SHELVES IN 1934.

Souper Baked Four-Cheese Pasta

This hearty dish is comfort food with style and can be served as a side dish with grilled fish, chicken, or meat. Although I liked this combination the best, you can certainly vary the cheeses to your family's tastes.

2 tablespoons butter

3 cloves garlic, minced

1 envelope Knorr Leek Soup Mix

2 cups milk

1/2 cup freshly grated Parmesan cheese

1/2 cup shredded mozzarella cheese

1/2 cup crumbled Gorgonzola or Maytag blue cheese

1/4 cup shredded Fontina cheese

4 shakes Tabasco sauce

1/8 teaspoon freshly grated nutmeg

1/2 teaspoon freshly ground black pepper

1 pound pasta, cooked until al dente, drained, tossed with 2 tablespoons olive oil, and kept warm

2 tablespoons chopped fresh chives for garnish

1. Preheat the oven to 350 degrees. Coat a 13-by-9-inch baking dish with nonstick cooking spray.

2. In a 3-quart saucepan, melt the butter over medium heat and cook the garlic, stirring, for 1 to 2 minutes. Add the soup mix, and then whisk in the milk and bring to a boil. Remove the pan from the heat, add the cheeses, and stir just until they have melted. Stir in the Tabasco, nutmeg, and pepper.

3. Place the pasta in a large mixing bowl and pour all but 1/4 cup of the sauce over the pasta, stirring to combine. Transfer the pasta to the prepared baking dish and spread the reserved sauce over the top. (At this point, the casserole can be refrigerated for up to 12 hours. Remove the casserole from the refrigerator 1 hour before baking.)

4. Bake the casserole until it bubbles and the top is golden brown, 30 to 40 minutes. Garnish with the chives and serve.

Lemon Garlic Orzo

2 tablespoons butter

1 tablespoon olive oil

½ cup chopped shallots

3 cups water

1 envelope Lipton Savory Herb with Garlic Soup Mix

1½ cups orzo

Grated zest of 1 lemon

1. In a 2-quart saucepan, melt the butter in the olive oil over medium heat. Add the shallots and cook them, stirring, until softened, about 3 minutes. Add the water and soup mix and bring the mixture to a boil.

2. Stir in the orzo and lemon zest. Reduce the heat to medium-low and simmer gently until the orzo is tender and most of the liquid is absorbed, about 10 minutes. Drain off any excess liquid and serve.

Lemon seems to perk up most dishes, and this one is no exception. Savory with garlic, herbs, and bits of lemon zest, it's not only pretty to serve; it's just as good to eat. Toss leftovers with a 6.5-ounce can of drained tuna, and 2 to 4 tablespoons lemon juice, for a luncheon salad.

Flavored Orzo

Orzo is a rice-shaped pasta. To flavor orzo, follow the instructions on the package for cooking it and add 1 envelope dry soup mix to the boiling water while the orzo is cooking. Drain the cooked orzo, stir in ¼ cup (½ stick) butter, and serve. (I particularly recommend Lipton Golden Onion Soup Mix, Knorr Cream of Spinach or Cream of Broccoli Soup Mix, Lipton Fiesta Herb with Red Pepper Soup Mix, and Lipton Savory Herb with Garlic Soup Mix.)

Pasta, Rice, Eggs, and Stuffings

Blue Plate Macaroni and Cheese

If I had my way, all macaroni and cheese would be made with Maytag blue cheese! Smooth and tangy, this blue macaroni will warm up any cold winter's menu. I love to serve this comforting side dish with grilled steaks or in place of mashed potatoes with roast beef.

2 tablespoons butter

¼ cup chopped shallots

1 envelope Knorr Leek Soup Mix

1¼ cups milk

6 ounces Maytag or other blue cheese, crumbled

1 teaspoon Worcestershire sauce

4 shakes Tabasco sauce

3 cups cooked elbow macaroni

½ cup fresh breadcrumbs

2 tablespoons butter, melted

1. Preheat the oven to 350 degrees. Coat a 2-quart casserole dish with nonstick cooking spray.

2. Melt the butter over medium heat in a 3-quart saucepan. Add the shallots, and cook, stirring, until they are softened, about 3 minutes. Whisk in the soup mix and milk and bring the mixture to a boil. Remove the pan from the heat. Add the cheese, Worcestershire, and Tabasco and stir until the cheese melts.

3. Add the cooked macaroni to the sauce and pour the mixture into the prepared casserole dish.

4. In a small bowl, toss together the breadcrumbs and melted butter, sprinkle the breadcrumbs over the macaroni, and bake until the breadcrumbs are golden, 35 to 40 minutes.

Breadcrumbs

Baked Macaroni and Cheese

1 tablespoon butter

¼ cup chopped onion

1 can Campbell's Condensed Cheddar Cheese Soup

¼ cup milk

¼ teaspoon Tabasco sauce

2 cups shredded mild cheddar cheese

3 cups cooked macaroni

1. Preheat the oven to 375 degrees. Coat a 9-inch square baking dish with nonstick cooking spray.

2. In a 3-quart saucepan, melt the butter over medium heat, add the onion, and cook it, stirring, until softened, about 3 minutes. Whisk in the soup, milk, Tabasco, and half the cheddar cheese, stirring just until the cheese is melted. Stir the cooked macaroni into the sauce and pour the mixture into the prepared baking dish. Top the macaroni with the remaining cheddar cheese. Bake the macaroni and cheese until the cheese on top is golden and the sauce is bubbling, 35 to 45 minutes.

Baking gives this classic a crunchy cheesy topping.

HAM OR BACON MACARONI BAKE: Before baking, add 1 cup ½-inch dice of ham or 12 strips bacon, cooked until crisp, drained on paper towels, and crumbled, to the macaroni and sauce.

PIZZA MACARONI BAKE: Substitute mozzarella cheese for the cheddar cheese, and top the casserole with 1 cup seeded and chopped ripe tomatoes that have been drained and tossed with 1½ teaspoons dried oregano. Top the tomatoes with the additional mozzarella and bake as directed.

FOUR-CHEESE MACARONI BAKE: Reduce the cheddar to ½ cup and add ¾ cup crumbled blue cheese, ½ cup grated Fontina cheese, and ½ cup freshly grated Parmesan cheese. Mix all the cheeses together and use half in the sauce and half to sprinkle on top.

The introduction of Campbell's Cheddar Cheese Soup helped to put macaroni and cheese onto the culinary map. No longer did mom have to make her own sauce; she could cook the macaroni and toss it with the soup, thereby creating a meal in minutes.

Old-Fashioned Macaroni and Cheese

1 tablespoon butter

1/4 cup chopped onion

1 can Campbell's Condensed Cheddar Cheese Soup

1/2 cup milk

3 cups cooked macaroni

Melt the butter in a large saucepan over medium heat. Cook the onion, stirring, until it is softened. Stir in the soup, and then gradually add the milk and heat the mixture through. Mix in the cooked macaroni and heat it to serving temperature.

Yaki Soba

I lived in Japan for three years, and this quick dish, literally translated, means "fried noodles." It is kind of a "use up all the leftovers" dish. I found it humorous to see this dish, featuring hot dogs or canned Vienna sausage, on menus at tourist restaurants. The recipe is very flexible, so you can substitute your favorite veggies or protein; just make sure to follow the recipe for the sauce.

2 quarts water

2 packages beef, chicken, or oriental flavor ramen noodles

3 tablespoons vegetable oil

2 cloves garlic, minced

1 teaspoon peeled and grated fresh ginger

2 cups leftover cooked chicken, beef, or pork cut into strips or 1/2-inch dice

1 large onion, thinly sliced

2 medium carrots, cut into matchsticks

1 cup fresh spinach, washed well, and tough stems removed

2 tablespoons toasted sesame oil

1 tablespoon sugar

1/4 cup soy sauce

1 teaspoon mirin (rice wine)

2 tablespoons sesame seeds

4 green onions (white parts and some of the green top), chopped, for garnish

1. In a 4-quart saucepan, bring the water to a boil. Add the ramen noodles (setting aside the flavor packets), and bring back to a boil. Drain the noodles and toss them with 1 tablespoon of the vegetable oil. Set the noodles aside.

2. In a wok, heat the remaining 2 tablespoons vegetable oil over high heat, add the garlic and ginger, and stir-fry them for 2 minutes. Add the meat and stir to coat it with the oil. Add the onion and stir-fry it until it is softened, about 3 minutes. Add the carrots and stir-fry them for 2 minutes. Add the spinach and the reserved noodles, stirring until all the ingredients are combined.

3. In a small mixing bowl, combine one of the ramen flavor packets (reserve the other one for another use) with the sesame oil, sugar, soy sauce, mirin, and sesame seeds. Pour this sauce over the noodles in the wok and toss the noodles in the sauce for 2 minutes.

4. Serve the noodles garnished with the green onions.

Vegetable Couscous

Couscous is a small, granular pasta made from semolina. Part of our new global pantry, couscous cooks quickly and can be on the table in about 15 minutes.

VARIATIONS:
Try these flavors in place of the Knorr Spring Vegetable Soup Mix:

- Lipton Golden Onion Soup Mix
- Lipton Savory Herb with Garlic Soup Mix
- Knorr Cream of Spinach Soup Mix
- Knorr Cream of Broccoli Soup Mix
- Knorr or Lipton Vegetable Soup Mix
- Knorr Leek Soup Mix

2 tablespoons butter

¼ cup chopped shallots

1 cup fine couscous

1 envelope Knorr Spring Vegetable Soup Mix

3 cups boiling water

1. In a 3-quart saucepan over medium heat, melt the butter and cook the shallots, stirring, until they are softened, 2 to 3 minutes. Add the couscous to the pan, stir to coat the grains with the butter, and cook for 2 to 3 minutes.

2. Remove the pan from the heat, stir in the soup mix, add 2 cups of the water, and stir. Let the mixture stand in the pan for 7 minutes.

3. Fluff the couscous and add the remaining cup water. Cover the pan and let the couscous stand for 5 more minutes. Stir the couscous before serving.

Basic Souped-Up Risotto

3 tablespoons butter

1 tablespoon olive oil

½ cup finely chopped onion

2 envelopes Lipton Golden Onion Soup Mix

5 cups boiling water

2 cups Arborio rice

½ cup white wine

1 cup freshly grated Parmesan cheese

1. In a 4-quart saucepan over medium heat, melt the butter in the oil, add the onion, and cook, stirring, until it is softened, 3 to 4 minutes.

2. Stir the soup mix into the boiling water and set it aside.

3. Stir the rice into the onion and toss to coat the rice with the butter. Add 3 cups of the onion soup and the wine to the rice. Bring the mixture to a boil, reduce the heat to medium-low, and simmer the rice, stirring it occasionally, until the rice has absorbed most of the liquid, about 10 minutes. Continue to add more soup gradually, ½ to ¾ cup at a time, stirring each time until the liquid is absorbed. Continue this process for 10 to 12 minutes more, adding the soup until the rice is creamy but still a bit firm in the center. Stir in the cheese and serve immediately.

SERVES 6

I like the strong flavor that soup mix gives to the rather bland Arborio rice. The secret to risotto is to stir it and to add more liquid as it is absorbed.

BEEF AND ONION RISOTTO: Substitute Lipton Beefy Onion Soup Mix.

BEEF AND MUSHROOM RISOTTO: Substitute Lipton Beefy Mushroom Soup Mix and stir in 1 cup sautéed mushrooms at the end of the cooking time.

ASPARAGUS AND LEEK RISOTTO: Substitute Knorr Leek Soup Mix and stir in 1 cup sautéed asparagus tips at the end.

CREAMY SPINACH RISOTTO: Substitute Knorr Cream of Spinach Soup Mix and stir in ⅛ teaspoon grated nutmeg.

CREAMY BROCCOLI RISOTTO: Substitute Knorr Cream of Broccoli Soup Mix.

GARLICKY HERBED RISOTTO: Substitute Lipton Savory Herb with Garlic Soup Mix.

Pasta, Rice, Eggs, and Stuffings

Feta Florentine Rice

SERVES 8

Flecked with bright green spinach and flavored with tangy feta cheese, this rice is a great side dish to serve along with grilled meats. For extra zip, try one of the new flavored feta cheeses.

2 tablespoons olive oil

1/4 cup chopped onion

One 16-ounce package frozen chopped spinach, defrosted and squeezed dry

1 cup converted rice

1 envelope Knorr Cream of Spinach Soup Mix

2 1/2 cups water

4 ounces feta cheese, crumbled

1. Heat the oil in a 3-quart saucepan over medium heat, add the onion, and cook, stirring, until it is softened, about 2 minutes. Add the spinach and cook it for 3 to 4 minutes, stirring to blend with the onion. Stir in the rice and soup mix. Add the water, cover the pan, and cook the rice over medium-low heat for 15 minutes.

2. Fold the feta into the rice, cover, and cook until the liquid is absorbed and the rice is tender, about another 5 minutes.

Kaleidoscope Garden Vegetable Rice

SERVES 8

2 tablespoons olive oil

½ cup finely chopped onion

½ cup finely diced carrot

1 cup grated zucchini

1 cup finely diced yellow squash

1 cup converted rice

2½ cups water

1 package Knorr Spring Vegetable Soup Mix

Freshly ground black pepper

1. Heat the oil in a 3-quart saucepan over medium heat, add the onion and carrot, and cook, stirring, until the onion begins to soften, 2 to 3 minutes. Add the zucchini, yellow squash, and rice and stir to blend.

2. Gradually pour in the water, and then stir in the soup mix. Bring the mixture to a boil, reduce the heat to medium-low, and simmer the rice until it is tender and the liquid is absorbed, 16 to 18 minutes.

3. Taste the rice and add pepper to taste.

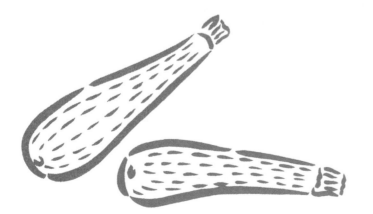

Colorful, with flecks of finely chopped vegetables, and savory, with the flavors of the soup, this easy-to-prepare side dish is ready in 20 minutes. Try stirring in cooked shrimp or chicken to make it into a simple supper.

IN 1884 KNORR OFFERED SOUPS IN A COMPRESSED TABLET FORM, WEIGHING ABOUT THREE OUNCES.

Pasta, Rice, Eggs, and Stuffings

Company Rice

This recipe is an old standby from the 1950s and is still a great way to serve rice to a crowd. The original recipe called for grated cheddar cheese, but I loved it with Maytag blue. Other cheeses that worked well were Swiss, smoked Gouda, and any of the flavored feta cheeses.

½ cup (1 stick) butter

1 cup chopped onion

½ pound mushrooms, sliced

1¾ cups converted rice

2 cans Campbell's Condensed French Onion Soup

1 cup sliced almonds

1½ cups crumbled blue cheese

1. Preheat the oven to 325 degrees. Coat a 13-by-9-inch baking dish with nonstick cooking spray.

2. Melt the butter in a 10-inch sauté pan over medium heat, add the onion, and cook, stirring, until it is softened, about 3 minutes. Add the mushrooms and cook, stirring, until they begin to turn golden, 4 to 5 minutes. Add the rice to the skillet and toss to coat it with the onion and mushroom mixture.

3. Pour the rice mixture into the prepared baking dish and stir in the soup, almonds, and blue cheese. (At this point you can refrigerate the rice for up to 8 hours. Bring it to room temperature before proceeding.)

4. Cover the dish with aluminum foil and bake the rice for 1 hour. Remove the cover and continue to bake until the liquid is absorbed and the rice is tender, about an additional 15 minutes.

BY ELIMINATING THE WATER IN CANNED SOUP, DR. JOHN T. DORRANCE LOWERED THE COSTS FOR PACKAGING, SHIPPING, AND STORAGE, AND MAKING IT POSSIBLE TO OFFER A 10.75-OUNCE CAN OF CAMPBELL'S CONDENSED SOUP FOR A DIME, VERSUS MORE THAN 30 CENTS FOR A TYPICAL 32-OUNCE CAN OF SOUP. THE IDEA BECAME SO HOT WITH AMERICANS THAT IN 1922 THE COMPANY FORMALLY ADOPTED "SOUP" AS ITS MIDDLE NAME.

The Soup Mix Gourmet

Santa Fe Rice

1 can Campbell's Condensed Fiesta Nacho Cheese Soup

1 cup sour cream

One 4-ounce can diced green chiles, drained and rinsed

One 2½-ounce can sliced black olives, drained

4 cups cooked white rice

1 cup grated Monterey Jack cheese

1. Preheat the oven to 350 degrees. Coat a 2-quart casserole dish with nonstick cooking spray.

2. In a large mixing bowl, whisk together the soup, sour cream, chiles, and olives. Add the rice and stir until the ingredients are blended.

3. Turn the mixture into the prepared dish and sprinkle on the cheese. (At this point, the casserole can be refrigerated for up to 2 days. Remove the casserole from the refrigerator 30 minutes before baking.)

4. Bake the casserole until the mixture bubbles and the cheese is melted, 30 to 40 minutes.

Another Santa Fe Rice

2 tablespoons butter

1 cup converted rice

1 envelope Lipton Fiesta Herb with Red Pepper Soup Mix

2½ cups water

Melt the butter in a 3-quart saucepan over medium heat. Add the rice, stirring to coat. Add the soup mix and cook, stirring, for 1 minute. Add the water, bring to a boil, reduce the heat to medium-low, and simmer until the rice is tender, 17 to 20 minutes.

Here are two wonderful ways to prepare spicy Southwestern-flavored rice. Both are simple, have totally different flavors, and will get rave reviews.

VARIATION: For a spicier topping, use pepper Jack cheese.

SERVES 6

Souper Smart

Both of these Santa Fe rice dishes are great with South of the Border Carne Asada (page 398), Fajitas (page 349), or chili.

Side Dish Paella

This colorful dish takes its flavorings from the classic Spanish dish, but without a lot of the fuss. Traditional paella uses short-grain Arborio rice, but for this dish we use converted rice. Saffron is a very expensive spice, but it gives the rice a gorgeous color and flavor.

2 tablespoons olive oil

1/2 cup chopped shallots

2 cloves garlic, minced

1 medium red bell pepper, seeded and cut into 1/2-inch-wide strips

1 cup peeled, seeded, and chopped fresh or canned tomatoes

1 envelope Lipton Savory Herb with Garlic Soup Mix

1 1/2 cups converted rice

3 cups boiling water

1/2 teaspoon ground saffron or saffron threads, crumbled

1/2 cup frozen petite peas, defrosted

1. In a 10-inch sauté pan over medium heat, heat the oil, add the shallots and garlic, and cook, stirring, until they are softened, 2 to 3 minutes. Add the bell pepper, tomatoes, and soup mix and let the mixture simmer for 3 to 4 minutes. Stir in the rice, water, and saffron and bring the mixture to a boil. Cover, reduce the heat to medium-low, and simmer the rice and vegetables for 15 minutes.

2. Stir in the peas, cover, and cook until the rice is tender and the liquid is absorbed, about another 5 minutes.

Herbed Wild Cranberry Rice

1 cup wild rice

11 cups water

¼ cup (½ stick) butter

½ cup chopped onion

1½ teaspoons dried thyme

2 envelopes Lipton Golden Onion Soup Mix

1 cup dried cranberries

¼ cup chopped fresh Italian parsley leaves

1. Wash the wild rice under cold running water until the water runs clear. Place the rice in a 4-quart saucepan with 6 cups of water. Bring to a boil, reduce the heat to medium-low, and simmer the rice for 15 minutes. Remove the rice from the pan and drain it.

2. While the rice is cooking, melt the butter in a 4-quart saucepan over medium heat and cook the onion and thyme, stirring, until the onion is softened, 3 to 4 minutes. Add the soup mix, 5 cups of water, and the cranberries. Bring the mixture to a boil.

3. Add the drained rice to the soup mixture. Simmer the rice, covered, until it is tender and the liquid is absorbed, 20 to 25 minutes.

4. Stir in the parsley and serve.

SERVES 6 TO 8

This side dish combines crunchy wild rice with piquant red cranberries. Delicious with poultry and pork, it can be stuffed into pounded chicken breasts or pork loins for a dynamite entrée. The leftover rice can be refrigerated for two days or frozen for up to a month.

Easy Flavored Rice

For an out-of-the-ordinary rice dish, bring 2½ cups water to a boil, add 1 cup rice and 1 envelope dry soup of your choice, reduce the heat to low, and simmer the rice until it is tender and the water is absorbed, about 20 minutes.

Fruited Rice

Studded with dried apricots and cranberries, this colorful rice has the added crunch of almonds and a touch of citrus. Serve this dish alongside chicken, turkey, or pork, or use it as a stuffing for Cornish game hens. It's easily put together and can be made ahead of time and then reheated just before serving.

In the fourth century B.C., primitive man had the basic ingredients for soup—cultivated wheat and barley, plus sheep and goats. As he began to make pottery, he was able to boil foods, thus releasing the starches from the cereals into the liquid, creating the all important "soupy" texture.

2 tablespoons butter

1/4 cup finely chopped onion

2 teaspoons fresh thyme leaves or 1 teaspoon dried

1/2 cup finely chopped dried apricots

1/4 cup dried cranberries

1 cup long-grain rice

1 envelope Lipton Golden Onion Soup Mix

2 cups water

1/4 cup orange juice

1/4 cup slivered almonds

2 tablespoons chopped fresh Italian parsley leaves

2 tablespoons thin strips orange zest for garnish

1. In a 3-quart saucepan, melt the butter over medium heat, add the onion and thyme, and cook, stirring, until the onion begins to soften, 2 to 3 minutes. Add the apricots, cranberries, and rice and toss to coat them with the butter.

2. Add the soup mix, water, and orange juice, bring the mixture to a boil, reduce the heat to medium-low, and simmer for 17 minutes. (At this point, you can cool the rice, and refrigerate it. Before proceeding, reheat the rice, covered, in the microwave or in a covered saucepan with 1/4 cup water, until it is heated through.)

3. Add the almonds and cook until the rice is tender, about another 3 minutes. Just before serving, stir in the parsley and garnish with the orange zest.

Triple Mushroom Oven-Baked Rice

2 tablespoons butter

2 tablespoons olive oil

½ cup chopped shallots

½ pound white mushrooms, sliced

½ pound shiitake mushrooms, stems removed and caps sliced

½ pound crimini mushrooms, sliced

1 envelope Lipton Garlic Mushroom, Onion, Golden Onion, or Beefy Onion Soup Mix

1 cup converted rice

¼ cup chopped fresh Italian parsley leaves

2 tablespoons chopped fresh chives

1. Preheat the oven to 350 degrees.

2. In a 5-quart Dutch oven, melt the butter in the olive oil over medium heat and cook the shallots, stirring, until they have softened, about 3 minutes. Add the mushrooms and cook, stirring, until they are golden.

3. Stir in the soup mix, rice, and 2¼ cups of water.

4. Bake, covered, for 20 minutes. Remove the cover and continue baking until the rice is tender and the liquid is absorbed, an additional 10 to 15 minutes. Stir in the parsley and chives and serve.

SERVES 8

This simple rice dish is a star when served alongside a roast. You can prepare the mushrooms and soup two days ahead of time and then just toss them together and bake.

Quick Rice Pilaf

This speedy dish benefits from the flavor punch of dry soup mix and the bright yellow coloring of turmeric. Orzo, a rice-shaped pasta, and long-grain rice are used here. If you don't have orzo, break spaghetti noodles into tiny pieces to get the same effect. Try adding grated carrot or chopped rehydrated dried porcini mushrooms to this dish for a different taste, or toss any leftover pilaf with tuna and a vinaigrette for a main course salad.

2 tablespoons butter

¼ cup finely chopped onion

¼ cup orzo pasta

1 cup long-grain rice

1 envelope Lipton Golden Onion Soup Mix

2½ cups water

¼ teaspoon turmeric

1. Melt the butter in a 3-quart saucepan over medium heat, add the onion, and cook, stirring, until it is softened, about 2 minutes. Add the orzo and rice and toss to coat them with the butter.

2. Add the soup mix, water, and turmeric. Bring the mixture to a boil, reduce the heat to medium-low, and simmer until the rice is tender, about 20 minutes.

Souper Smart

A great way to jazz up rice is to cook it in broth instead of water. Add sautéed vegetables and you have a wonderful side dish.

Wild Rice Casserole

2 tablespoons butter

$\frac{1}{2}$ cup finely chopped onion

$\frac{1}{2}$ cup finely chopped celery

$\frac{1}{2}$ cup grated carrot

4 cups cooked wild rice

1 can Campbell's Condensed Cream of Chicken, Cream of Mushroom, or Cream of Celery Soup

1 cup sour cream

3 tablespoons cream sherry

$\frac{1}{2}$ teaspoon freshly ground black pepper

2 tablespoons chopped fresh Italian parsley leaves

1. Preheat the oven to 350 degrees. Coat a 2-quart casserole dish with nonstick cooking spray.

2. In a 10-inch sauté pan over medium heat, melt the butter. Add the onion, celery, and carrot, and cook, stirring, until the vegetables have softened, about 3 minutes.

3. Transfer the vegetables to a large mixing bowl and stir in the wild rice.

4. In a medium mixing bowl, stir together the soup, sour cream, sherry, and pepper. Pour the soup mixture over the wild rice and stir to blend.

5. Transfer the rice mixture to the prepared dish and bake the casserole until bubbling, about 30 minutes.

This bit of Midwest Americana is a staple in many homes across the country. The basic ingredients are wild rice, "cream of" soup, and bits of onion, celery, and carrot. The entire casserole can be made up ahead of time and refrigerated for up to two days before baking.

Creamy Seafood Rice

In this recipe a creamy sauce filled with bay scallops and shrimp and flavored with white wine combines with rice to create a quick and easy side dish that will make your guests think they are eating at a four-star restaurant.

3 tablespoons butter

2 cloves garlic, minced

¼ pound bay scallops (if using large sea scallops, cut them into small dice)

¼ pound bay shrimp

2 teaspoons Old Bay seasoning

1 tablespoon fresh lemon juice

1 can Campbell's Condensed Cream of Shrimp Soup

1½ cups milk

3 tablespoons white wine, such as Sauvignon Blanc

1 cup converted rice

2 tablespoons chopped fresh parsley leaves

1. Melt the butter in a 3-quart saucepan over medium heat, add the garlic, and cook, stirring, until it is softened, about 2 minutes. Add the scallops, shrimp, Old Bay seasoning, and lemon juice and cook, stirring, for 3 minutes. Whisk in the soup, milk, and wine. Stir in the rice, cover, reduce the heat to medium-low, and simmer the mixture until the rice is tender and the liquid is absorbed, 17 to 20 minutes, stirring occasionally.

2. Stir in the parsley and serve.

Kitchen Sink Fried Rice

This is the kind of recipe I love, because it uses up all those little bits of things in the refrigerator. Be sure to use *cold* cooked rice; otherwise it will clump when you fry it.

¼ cup soy sauce

Flavor packet from 1 package chicken, beef, or oriental flavor ramen noodles (reserve the noodles for another use)

2 tablespoons mirin (rice wine)

2 teaspoons toasted sesame oil

2 tablespoons vegetable oil

2 large eggs, beaten

2 cloves garlic, minced

2 teaspoons peeled and minced fresh ginger

1½ cups ½-inch cubes cooked chicken, pork, beef, or shrimp

½ cup chopped green onions

¼ pound snow peas, strings removed

2 medium carrots, cut into matchsticks (about ½ cup)

4 cups cold cooked rice

1. In a small mixing bowl, combine the soy sauce, ramen flavor packet, mirin, water, and sesame oil. Set aside.

2. Heat 1 tablespoon of the vegetable oil in a wok over high heat, add the eggs, and stir-fry them until the eggs are scrambled. Remove from the wok.

3. Heat the remaining 1 tablespoon vegetable oil in the wok over high heat, add the garlic and ginger, and stir-fry for 2 minutes. Add the meat, green onions, snow peas, and carrots and stir-fry them for 2 to 3 minutes. Add the rice and scrambled eggs and stir-fry the mixture until the rice is warmed through and is thoroughly mixed with the vegetables and meat. Add the soy mixture and stir-fry until it is heated through and incorporated, another 2 to 3 minutes. Serve immediately.

Souper Smart

This recipe is a bare outline of what you can do with this dish. Substitute any leftover vegetables or meats for those called for here.

Yin and Yang Foods

In China, soup, as a cure for what ails you, is designed to balance the yin (cooling) and yang (heating) forces that affect the body. Yin ingredients are meant to reduce inflammation and help lower fevers. Yang ingredients promote blood formation and circulation and improve vitality.

A Chinese grandmother might ask to look into the eyes of her grandchild to see if they are "wet and cold" (then she'd create a yang soup, such as chrysanthemum flowers and sugar to soothe and warm) or "hot," in which case she'd prepare a yin soup such as winter melon or a sweet dessert soup of poached pears, honey, and lemon balm to cool and cleanse.

Cajun Crawfish Rice Stuffing

SERVES 8

I know that stuffing is supposed to be a side dish, but I loved eating this right out of the pan! It is savory with vegetables, succulent crawfish, and a little kick of cayenne. You'll be finding ways to stuff this into all manner of food! Served as a side dish or stuffed into poultry (it is especially good in Cornish hens), pork, and seafood, this is a dish you'll make often. If you cannot find crawfish, I recommend using medium shrimp, coarsely chopped.

Souper Smart

In Cajun and Creole kitchens, what is known as the "trinity"—onion, bell pepper, and celery sautéed together in equal amounts—is the flavor foundation of many dishes.

¼ cup (½ stick) butter

½ cup chopped onion

½ cup seeded and chopped green bell pepper

½ cup chopped celery

1 clove garlic, minced

1 envelope Lipton Golden Onion Soup Mix

½ teaspoon sweet paprika

⅛ teaspoon cayenne pepper

1 cup converted rice

2½ cups water

1½ cups cooked crawfish tails (about 1 pound peeled)

4 green onions, white parts and some of the green tops, chopped

1. Melt the butter in a 3-quart saucepan over medium heat, add the onion, bell pepper, celery, and garlic, and cook, stirring, until the vegetables start to soften, 5 to 7 minutes. Add the soup mix, paprika, and cayenne and cook, stirring, for another 1 to 2 minutes. Add the rice and toss it with the vegetables. Add the water, cover the pot, reduce the heat to medium-low, and simmer the mixture for 15 minutes.

2. Stir in the crawfish, cover, and cook until the rice is tender and the liquid is absorbed, about another 5 minutes.

3. Stir in the green onions and serve, or let the mixture cool and use it as a stuffing for poultry, pork, or seafood.

Kiss My Grits Casserole

3 cups water

2 cups milk

1 envelope Knorr Leek Soup Mix

1¼ cups quick-cooking grits

½ cup (1 stick) butter

¼ cup finely chopped onion

1 clove garlic, minced

2 large eggs, lightly beaten

1 cup shredded sharp cheddar cheese

1. Preheat the oven to 350 degrees. Coat a 1½-quart casserole dish with nonstick cooking spray.

2. In a 4-quart saucepan, bring the water and milk to a boil. Add the soup mix and stir until the soup is blended in.

3. Slowly stir in the grits, beating with a wooden spoon, until the consistency is smooth. Cook the grits, always stirring, until they are thick and creamy, about 5 minutes. Remove the pan from the heat.

4. Melt the butter in a small saucepan over medium heat and cook the onion and garlic, stirring, until they are softened, 3 to 5 minutes. Stir them into the grits. Stir the eggs and cheese into the grits and transfer the grits mixture to the prepared casserole.

5. Bake the casserole until it is set, about 1 hour.

A traditional Southern dish gets an update with the addition of leek soup mix and some cheese. Serve with pork, poultry, or shellfish.

Pasta, Rice, Eggs, and Stuffings

Huevos Rancheros Casserole

SERVES 8

This easy south of the border egg dish will have everyone out of bed early. Try adding chorizo, a spicy Portuguese sausage, or chicken to create a dinner entrée. When guests are over, serve the casserole with fruit on the side and plenty of frosty margaritas.

8 large eggs

1 can Campbell's Condensed Cream of Chicken Soup

½ cup chopped green onions

1½ cups shredded mild cheddar cheese

½ cup chunky salsa (medium-hot works best)

½ cup sour cream, plus extra for garnish

One 4-ounce can roasted green chiles, drained, rinsed, and chopped

Twelve 6-inch corn tortillas, torn into 1-inch-wide strips

1 cup shredded Monterey Jack cheese

Salsa for garnish

1. Coat a 13-by-9-inch baking dish with nonstick cooking spray.

2. Beat the eggs together in a large mixing bowl. Add the soup and whisk until the mixture is smooth. Add the green onions, cheddar cheese, salsa, sour cream, chiles, and tortillas and stir until blended.

3. Pour the egg mixture into the prepared dish and sprinkle the top with the Monterey Jack cheese. Refrigerate the casserole, covered, for at least 4 hours and for up to 24 hours.

4. Preheat the oven to 350 degrees. Bring the casserole to room temperature, and then bake it until the top is browned and the eggs are set, about 45 minutes. Let the dish rest for 5 to 10 minutes before cutting. Pass additional sour cream and salsa.

DR. JOHN T. DORRANCE DISCOVERED THE PROCESS FOR MAKING CONDENSED SOUPS IN 1897, HELPING TO MAKE SOUP ONE OF THE FIRST CONVENIENCE FOODS.

Country Hash Browns and Egg Casserole

1 pound bulk pork sausage

1 cup chopped onion

2 cups frozen hash brown potatoes, defrosted

8 large eggs, beaten

1 envelope Knorr Leek Soup Mix

$\frac{1}{2}$ cup mayonnaise

$\frac{3}{4}$ cup milk

3 tablespoons all-purpose flour

1 cup grated sharp cheddar cheese

1. Preheat the oven to 325 degrees. Coat a 13-by-9-inch baking dish with nonstick cooking spray.

2. In a 10-inch skillet over high heat, cook the sausage, breaking it into smaller pieces, until it loses its pink color. Drain off the fat, add the onion, and cook, stirring, until it is softened, 4 to 5 minutes. Remove the pan from the heat and transfer the mixture to a large mixing bowl. Add the hash browns.

3. In another large mixing bowl, beat together the eggs, soup mix, mayonnaise, milk, and flour. Fold the egg mixture into the sausage mixture and pour into the prepared dish.

4. Sprinkle the top of the casserole with the cheese and bake the casserole until it is set, about 25 minutes. Let it sit for 5 minutes before serving. Serve with country ham and fruit.

SERVES 8

Hungry-man hearty and yet simple to make, this casserole is one of our favorites on Sunday mornings. It's delicious served with sautéed apples or fresh fruit.

SOUTH OF THE BORDER SAUSAGE AND EGG CASSEROLE: Substitute chopped chorizo for the pork sausage and pepper Jack cheese for the cheddar.

ITALIAN SAUSAGE AND EGG CASSEROLE: Substitute sweet Italian sausage, removed from its casing, for the pork sausage and mozzarella cheese for the cheddar.

THE KNORR BRAND WAS OFFICIALLY INTRODUCED INTO THE UNITED STATES IN 1928.

Del Mar Soufflé

This is a simple egg dish, named for the beach near my house. We love to eat this while sitting on the patio watching the waves. Filled with Canadian bacon, green chiles, mushrooms, and potatoes, this casserole will become a favorite brunch dish.

2 tablespoons butter

½ cup chopped onion

One 4-ounce can chopped green chiles, drained and rinsed

1 cup sliced mushrooms

1 cup diced Canadian bacon

1 envelope Knorr Leek Soup Mix

6 large eggs

2 cups milk

3 cups frozen hash browns, defrosted

1 cup grated mild cheddar cheese

1 cup grated Monterey Jack cheese

1. Preheat the oven to 350 degrees. Coat a 13-by-9-inch baking dish with nonstick cooking spray.

2. Melt the butter over medium heat in a 12-inch sauté pan, add the onion and chiles, and cook, stirring, until the onion is softened, 4 to 6 minutes. Add the mushrooms and Canadian bacon and cook, stirring, for 4 minutes.

3. In a large mixing bowl, whisk together the soup mix, eggs, and milk. Add the vegetables and bacon to the eggs and stir in the hash browns.

4. Pour the mixture into the prepared dish, sprinkle with the cheeses, and bake the soufflé until it is set and the cheese is golden, 35 to 40 minutes.

Chile Relleno Soufflé

Two 7-ounce cans roasted whole green chile peppers, drained and rinsed

12 ounces Monterey Jack cheese, cut into 3-inch-long ½-inch-diameter logs

2 tablespoons butter

½ cup chopped onion

½ cup seeded and chopped red bell pepper

1 cup corn kernels, either cut fresh from the cob or frozen (and defrosted)

½ teaspoon ground cumin

Pinch of cayenne pepper

1 can Campbell's Condensed Cream of Celery Soup

6 large eggs

½ cup yellow cornmeal

1 cup grated mild cheddar cheese

¼ cup chopped fresh cilantro leaves for garnish

1. Preheat the oven to 350 degrees. Coat a 13-by-9-inch baking dish with nonstick cooking spray.

2. Slit the chiles and stuff each one with a piece of Monterey Jack cheese. Place the chiles in the prepared dish.

3. In a 10-inch sauté pan over medium heat, melt the butter, add the onion, red bell pepper, and corn, and cook, stirring, until the onion and pepper are softened, 3 to 4 minutes. Add the cumin and cayenne and cook, stirring, for another 2 minutes. Remove the pan from the heat and set it aside.

4. In a large mixing bowl, whisk together the soup, eggs, and cornmeal until well blended. Stir in the vegetable mixture.

5. Gently pour the egg and vegetable mixture over the chiles, sprinkle on the cheddar cheese, and bake the soufflé until it is set, 30 to 40 minutes. Serve garnished with the cilantro.

SERVES 6 TO 8

Another great Southwestern egg dish, this one stuffs roasted chiles with Monterey Jack cheese, and then covers the chiles with a creamy egg sauce flavored with sweet corn and cornmeal.

ON AVERAGE, AMERICANS PURCHASE 80 CANS OF CAMPBELL'S SOUPS EVERY SECOND OF EVERY DAY OF THE YEAR.

Spinach and Artichoke Quiche

This colorful quiche is so simple to put together and makes a savory and satisfying lunch or light supper entrée. I am pretty lazy, so I love the convenience of not having to make a pie crust for my quiches. Not only does it save me time, but it also puts dinner on the table sooner. The baked quiche keeps, refrigerated, for two to three days or frozen for one month.

2 tablespoons butter

1/2 cup chopped onion

One 16-ounce package frozen chopped spinach, defrosted and squeezed dry

1 teaspoon salt

1/2 teaspoon freshly ground black pepper

1/4 teaspoon freshly grated nutmeg

6 large eggs

1 envelope Knorr Cream of Spinach Soup Mix

1 cup heavy cream

One 14-ounce can artichoke hearts, drained and cut into quarters

2 cups shredded Swiss cheese

1. Preheat the oven to 350 degrees and coat a 10-inch round pie plate that is at least 2 1/2 inches deep with nonstick cooking spray.

2. Melt the butter in a sauté pan over medium heat, add the onion, and cook, stirring, until it is softened, 2 to 3 minutes. Add the spinach, salt, pepper, and nutmeg, and cook, stirring, until the spinach is tender, 3 to 4 minutes. Remove the pan from the heat.

3. In a large bowl, stir together the eggs, soup mix, heavy cream, spinach mixture, and artichoke hearts. Add 1 cup of the cheese to the egg mixture and then pour the mixture into the prepared pie plate. Sprinkle on the remaining 1 cup cheese.

4. Bake the quiche until it is set, 35 to 45 minutes. Let the dish rest for at least 5 minutes before cutting it. Serve the quiche warm or at room temperature.

Chicken and Broccoli Quiche

6 large eggs

1 envelope Knorr Cream of Broccoli Soup Mix

1 cup milk

1½ cups ½-inch cubes cooked chicken

1 cup broccoli florets, steamed until crisp-tender

2 cups shredded sharp white cheddar cheese

1. Preheat the oven to 350 degrees. Coat a 10-inch round pie plate that is at least 2½ inches deep with nonstick cooking spray.

2. In a large mixing bowl, whisk together the eggs, soup mix, and milk until they are well combined. Stir in the chicken, broccoli, and 1 cup of the cheese.

3. Pour the egg mixture into the prepared pie plate and sprinkle on the remaining 1 cup cheese.

4. Bake the quiche until it is golden brown and set, 30 to 40 minutes. Let it rest at least 5 minutes before cutting it. Serve the quiche hot or at room temperature.

SERVES 6

This is a good way to use up leftover chicken and broccoli from another dinner, combining them with sharp white cheddar cheese for a great lunch or light supper. I like to serve this with a sliced tomato salad on the side.

Green Chile Frittata

SERVES 6 TO 8

This brunch or luncheon dish is simple to put together, and then you can refrigerate it until you're ready to bake it. Full of green chiles and smooth Monterey Jack cheese, it's a great side dish served with South of the Border Carne Asada (page 398) as well.

2 tablespoons butter

½ cup chopped onion

One 4-ounce can chopped green chiles, drained and rinsed

1 can Campbell's Condensed Cream of Celery Soup

6 large eggs

2 cups shredded Monterey Jack cheese

1. Preheat the oven to 350 degrees. Coat a 10-inch round pie plate that is at least 2½ inches deep with nonstick cooking spray.

2. In a small sauté pan over medium heat, melt the butter, add the onion and chiles, and cook, stirring, until the onion is softened, 3 to 5 minutes.

3. In a large mixing bowl, whisk together the soup, eggs, and 1 cup of the cheese. Add the chiles and onion.

4. Pour the egg mixture into the prepared pie plate, sprinkle on the remaining 1 cup cheese, and bake the frittata until it is puffed and golden, about 30 minutes. Let it rest for 10 minutes before serving.

Asparagus Frittata

2 tablespoons butter

2 cloves garlic, minced

1 pound fresh asparagus, bottoms trimmed, and cut into
4½-inch lengths

1 can Campbell's Condensed Cream of Celery Soup

6 large eggs

1 cup shredded Gruyère cheese

½ cup freshly grated Parmesan cheese

1. Preheat the oven to 350 degrees. Coat a 10-inch pie pan that is at least 2½ inches deep with nonstick cooking spray.

2. Melt the butter in a 12-inch sauté pan over medium heat and cook the garlic, stirring, until it begins to soften, about 2 minutes. Add the asparagus and turn it in the garlic butter for 2 minutes. Remove the pan from the heat.

3. Reserving the garlic butter in the sauté pan, remove the asparagus and arrange in the pie plate in a spoke pattern, with the tips pointed toward the center.

4. In a large mixing bowl, whisk together the soup and eggs. Scrape the garlic butter from the sauté pan into the bowl and whisk it in together with the Gruyère and ¼ cup of the Parmesan.

5. Pour the egg mixture over the asparagus in the pie pan and sprinkle on the remaining ¼ cup Parmesan.

6. Bake the frittata until a knife inserted into the center comes out clean, about 45 minutes. Let the frittata rest for 5 minutes before cutting it.

SERVES 6 TO 8

A sure sign of spring in colder climates is the appearance of asparagus in the grocery stores. This pie is a great way to use up any leftovers, but it is also a wonderful vehicle to showcase fresh asparagus.

Souper Smart

Sprinkle ¼ pound smoked salmon over the asparagus for a real taste treat.

RESIDUES OF SOUPS MADE DURING THE IRON AGE HAVE BEEN FOUND CLINGING TO POTS FOUND IN A LAKE VILLAGE IN SWITZERLAND. THE FAIRLY APPETIZING STEW CONTAINED RASPBERRIES, STRAWBERRIES, ELDERBERRIES, WHEAT, NUTS, AND FISH.

In New Orleans, bread pudding is generally a sweet served with a warm sauce over it, but here we are using leftover bread to make a comforting side dish to serve alongside roasted poultry, pork, or beef. The pudding should be refrigerated for at least 12 hours before baking, so that the egg mixture soaks into the bread and saturates it.

SERVES 8

Mushroom and Onion Bread Pudding

¼ cup (½ stick) butter

2 cups thinly sliced onion

1 pound mushrooms, sliced

5 large eggs

1 envelope Lipton Golden Onion Soup Mix

2 cups heavy cream

1 teaspoon Worcestershire sauce

6 cups ½-inch cubes French bread, crusts removed

1 cup freshly grated Parmesan cheese

1. Coat a 13-by-9-inch baking dish with nonstick cooking spray.

2. In a 10-inch sauté pan over medium heat, melt the butter, add the onion, and cook, stirring, until they begin to turn a golden color, about 10 minutes. Add the mushrooms and cook them until they are golden brown, another 6 to 8 minutes. Remove the pan from the heat.

3. In a large mixing bowl, whisk together the eggs, soup mix, heavy cream, and Worcestershire. Stir in the bread cubes until they are well coated. Stir in the onions and mushrooms.

4. Pour the mixture into the prepared dish and sprinkle on the cheese. Refrigerate for at least 12 hours before baking.

5. Preheat the oven to 350 degrees. Bring the pudding to room temperature, and then bake it until it is golden brown, 35 to 45 minutes. Let the pudding rest for 10 minutes before serving.

Bacon and Leek Bread Pudding

SERVES 8

¼ cup (½ stick) butter

2 cups thinly sliced leeks, white and pale green parts only, washed well and patted dry

5 large eggs

1 envelope Knorr Leek Soup Mix

2 cups milk

1 teaspoon Worcestershire sauce

½ pound bacon, cooked until crisp, drained on paper towels, and crumbled

2 teaspoons chopped fresh tarragon leaves or 1 teaspoon dried

6 cups ½-inch cubes French bread, crusts removed

1 cup shredded Gruyère cheese

1. Coat a 13-by-9-inch baking dish with nonstick cooking spray.

2. In a 10-inch sauté pan over medium heat, melt the butter, add the leeks, and cook, stirring, until they are softened, about 5 minutes.

3. In a large mixing bowl, whisk together the eggs, soup mix, milk, Worcestershire, bacon, and tarragon. Stir in the bread cubes until they are well coated. Blend in the leeks.

4. Pour the mixture into the prepared dish and sprinkle on the cheese. Refrigerate for at least 12 hours before baking.

5. Preheat the oven to 350 degrees. Bring the bread pudding to room temperature, and then bake it until it is golden brown, 35 to 45 minutes. Let the pudding rest for 10 minutes before serving.

Spinach and Canadian Bacon Bread Pudding

1/4 cup (1/2 stick) butter

1 cup 1/2-inch cubes Canadian bacon

1/2 cup chopped shallots

One 16-ounce package frozen chopped spinach, defrosted and squeezed dry

1/4 teaspoon freshly grated nutmeg

5 large eggs

1 envelope Knorr Cream of Spinach Soup Mix

2 cups milk

1 teaspoon Worcestershire sauce

6 cups 1/2-inch cubes French bread, crusts removed

1 cup shredded sharp white cheddar cheese

1. Coat a 13-by-9-inch baking dish with nonstick cooking spray.

2. In a 10-inch sauté pan over medium heat, melt the butter, add the Canadian bacon, and cook, stirring, for 5 minutes. Add the shallots and cook, stirring, until they are softened, 3 to 4 minutes. Stir in the spinach and nutmeg and cook the spinach until it is heated through.

3. In a large mixing bowl, whisk together the eggs, soup mix, milk, and Worcestershire. Stir in the bread cubes until they are well coated. Stir in the spinach mixture.

4. Pour the mixture into the prepared dish and sprinkle on the cheese. Refrigerate the pudding for at least 12 hours before baking.

5. Preheat the oven to 350 degrees. Bring the bread pudding to room temperature, and then bake it until it is golden brown, 35 to 45 minutes. Let the pudding rest for 10 minutes before serving.

IN A YEAR, MORE THAN A BILLION KNORR BOUILLON CUBES ARE MANUFACTURED IN NORTH AMERICA.

Zucchini Strata

2 tablespoons olive oil

1 cup chopped onion

2 cloves garlic, minced

3 medium zucchini, ends trimmed, and cut into $\frac{1}{2}$-inch-thick rounds

One 14.5-ounce can chopped tomatoes, drained

1 envelope Knorr Tomato with Basil Soup Mix

One 8-ounce loaf Italian or French bread, cut into slices

6 large eggs

2 cups milk

$\frac{3}{4}$ cup freshly grated Parmesan cheese

1. Coat a 13-by-9-inch baking dish with nonstick cooking spray.

2. In a 10-inch sauté pan, heat the oil, add the onion and garlic, and cook, stirring, until they are softened, 2 to 4 minutes. Add the zucchini slices and cook, stirring, until they begin to turn golden, 4 to 5 minutes. Add the tomatoes and soup mix, and cook for 4 minutes, stirring frequently. Remove the pan from the heat.

3. Lay some slices of bread in the prepared dish, cutting the slices where necessary to make them fit in a single layer. Spread all of the zucchini mixture over the bread, and then top that with another layer of bread.

4. In a large mixing bowl, whisk together the eggs and milk. Carefully pour the egg mixture over the bread in the dish, tilting the dish to make sure that the bottom slices absorb some of the liquid. Sprinkle the casserole with the cheese and refrigerate it for at least 12 hours before baking.

5. Preheat the oven to 350 degrees. Bring the casserole to room temperature, and then bake it until the eggs are set, 40 to 45 minutes. Let the casserole rest for 5 minutes and serve.

You'll love this simple dish to serve for brunch or as a side dish. It's a great way to use up those zucchini in the garden or from the farmers' market, as well as left-over Italian or French bread.

Absolutely the Best Corn Bread Stuffing

Everyone has his or her favorite stuffing recipe, and I think this one is mighty tasty. Studded with sweet nuggets of dried apricots and prosciutto, this simple dish goes well with poultry and pork.

¼ cup (½ stick) butter

½ cup chopped onion

½ cup chopped celery

¼ pound thinly sliced prosciutto, cut into matchsticks

½ cup dried apricots, chopped

1 envelope Lipton Golden Onion Soup Mix

2 cups water

6 cups crumbled corn bread

1 large egg, beaten

1. Preheat the oven to 350 degrees. Coat a 4-quart casserole dish with nonstick cooking spray.

2. Melt the butter over medium heat in a 12-inch sauté pan, add the onion and celery, and cook, stirring, until they are softened, 4 to 6 minutes. Stir in the prosciutto, apricots, soup mix, and water and bring the mixture to a boil.

3. Place the corn bread in a large mixing bowl. Add the contents of the sauté pan and the egg to the corn bread and stir to blend.

4. (If you would like to use the stuffing for poultry, stuff and bake the bird at this point.) Turn the corn bread mixture into the prepared dish, and bake it, covered with aluminum foil, for 35 to 45 minutes. Remove the foil and cook the stuffing until the top is golden brown, about another 10 minutes. Serve immediately.

Old-Fashioned Bread Stuffing

1 cup (2 sticks) butter or margarine

2 cups chopped celery

2 cups chopped onion

4 quarts dry or stale bread cubes

1 tablespoon salt

½ teaspoon freshly ground black pepper

1½ teaspoons dried sage, crushed

1¼ teaspoon dried thyme, crushed

1½ to 2 cups chicken broth, as needed

1 or 2 large eggs

1. Preheat the oven to 350 degrees. Coat a 13-by-9-inch baking dish with nonstick cooking spray.

2. In a 10-inch sauté pan over low heat, melt the butter and cook the celery and onion, stirring, until they are golden, about 5 minutes.

3. In a large mixing bowl, combine the bread cubes and seasonings. Stir the celery and onion into the bread cubes, tossing lightly to combine. Pour 1 cup of the broth over the bread and stir to blend. Stir in 1 egg and ½ cup more broth, stirring until the liquid is blended in. If the stuffing seems dry, add more broth and the other egg.

4. (If you would like to use the stuffing for poultry, stuff and bake the bird at this point.) Place the stuffing in the prepared dish and bake, covered with a sheet of aluminum foil, for 35 minutes. Remove the foil and bake the stuffing until the top is golden brown and crisp, about an additional 15 minutes.

SERVES 8; ENOUGH TO
STUFF A 10- TO 12-POUND TURKEY

This is a basic recipe, and there are lots of variations to try as well.

VARIATIONS:

Here are a few of the additions that can be thrown in while sautéing the onion and celery:

- 1 pound mushrooms, sliced
- ½ cup chopped dried apricots
- ½ cup dried cranberries
- 1 dozen oysters, chopped
- 1 cup pecan halves

Souper Smart

If you are having a crowd for dinner, stuff the mixture into greased loaf pans and, when cooked, turn it out, cut into slices with a serrated knife, and serve.

Pasta, Rice, Eggs, and Stuffings

Poultry

WHEN THE CAMPBELL'S SOUP COMPANY INTRODUCED its Condensed Cream of Chicken Soup, I'm sure they never imagined that it would become the fourth most widely used ingredient for preparing dinner in the United States.

Poultry and soup have been mixing it up for a long time. Campbell's debuted its recipe for Glori-Fried Chicken (page 335) in the 1940s, and dinner tables haven't been the same since. Dry soup mixes have been coating versions of oven-fried chicken and seasoning all manner of poultry since they were introduced in the 1950s. In this chapter we'll update the classics and explore new ways to use soups in cooking poultry.

Chicken Divan

1½ pounds broccoli florets, steamed for 3 minutes

1 tablespoon vegetable oil

2 tablespoons butter

6 boneless, skinless chicken breast halves

1 teaspoon salt

½ teaspoon freshly ground black pepper

2 cans Campbell's Condensed Cream of Chicken Soup

1 cup mayonnaise

1 teaspoon curry powder

1 cup shredded mild cheddar cheese

½ cup soft breadcrumbs

3 tablespoons butter, melted

1. Preheat the oven to 350 degrees.

2. Arrange the broccoli in the bottom of a 13-by-9-inch baking dish. Heat the oil and butter together in a 10-inch sauté pan over medium-high heat. Sprinkle the chicken halves with the salt and pepper. Sauté in the hot butter and oil until the chicken is browned on both sides but not cooked through. Place the chicken over the broccoli in the casserole.

3. In a medium mixing bowl, whisk together the soup, mayonnaise, and curry powder. Pour the soup mixture evenly over the chicken.

4. In a small mixing bowl, combine the cheese, breadcrumbs, and melted butter, tossing to distribute the butter. Sprinkle the mixture over the top of the casserole. Bake until the sauce is bubbling and the crumbs are golden, 25 to 30 minutes.

This dish pairs broccoli and chicken and covers them with a curry-flavored sauce. It's simple and was considered a bit exotic in the 1950s. It is a staple in many modern kitchens. This recipe is from the Nixon White House, where it was said to be a favorite of both the President and the First Lady.

VARIATIONS:
Slices of cooked turkey may be substituted for the chicken breasts.

One Campbell's cookbook suggests using cooked asparagus spears in place of the broccoli; if you decide to do this, do not steam the asparagus first, or they will be too limp after baking. Place the raw asparagus in the bottom of the dish and proceed as directed in the recipe.

Chicken Tetrazzini

¼ cup (½ stick) butter

¼ cup chopped shallots

½ pound mushrooms, sliced

½ teaspoon salt

½ teaspoon freshly ground black pepper

One 14-ounce can artichoke hearts, drained and chopped

1 can Campbell's Condensed Cream of Chicken Soup

1¼ cups heavy cream

2 tablespoons cream sherry

1 cup freshly grated Parmesan cheese

3 cups diced cooked chicken

½ pound spaghetti, linguine, or fettuccine, cooked until
   al dente, drained, and tossed with 1 tablespoon olive oil

linguine

SERVES 8

This old standby is a recipe that I can always count on. Chicken is cooked in a luxurious cheesy mushroom sauce studded with artichokes and is then tossed with pasta and baked. The dish can be prepared up to two days ahead of time and then baked just before serving.

1. Preheat the oven to 375 degrees. Coat a 13-by-9-inch baking dish with nonstick cooking spray.

2. In a 3-quart saucepan, melt the butter over medium heat, add the shallots, and cook, stirring, until they are soft, about 2 minutes. Add the mushrooms, season with the salt and pepper, and cook, stirring, until the mushrooms begin to soften, 3 to 4 minutes. Add the artichoke hearts, soup, heavy cream, and sherry and stir to blend. Bring the mixture to a simmer, add ½ cup of the Parmesan, and stir the sauce until the cheese is melted.

3. Stir the chicken into the sauce and then toss the chicken and sauce with the pasta in the baking dish. Sprinkle the remaining ½ cup Parmesan on top. Bake the casserole until it is bubbling and the cheese is golden, 20 to 25 minutes.

Campbell's deserves the credit for making Chicken Tetrazzini a household name. This is their recipe.

The Original Campbell's Chicken Tetrazzini

1 can Campbell's Condensed Cream of Mushroom Soup

¹⁄₂ cup milk

1 small onion, finely chopped

¹⁄₄ cup grated Parmesan cheese

¹⁄₄ cup sour cream

1¹⁄₂ cups cubed cooked chicken or turkey

1 small zucchini, cut in half lengthwise, and thinly sliced

1¹⁄₂ cups hot, cooked very thin spaghetti

Mix soup, milk, onion, cheese, and sour cream. Add chicken, zucchini, and spaghetti. Toss to coat. Spoon into 1¹⁄₂-qt. casserole.

Bake at 375°F. for 30 minutes or until hot. Serve with additional cheese, if desired.

Mexican Tetrazzini

2 tablespoons butter

¼ cup chopped onion

¼ cup canned chopped green chiles, rinsed and drained

1 teaspoon ground cumin

1 can Campbell's Condensed Cheddar Cheese Soup

½ cup milk

2 cups ½-inch cubes cooked chicken

5 shakes Tabasco sauce

3 cups cooked pasta (linguine, spaghetti, or fettuccine)

¼ cup chopped fresh cilantro leaves

1 cup shredded Monterey Jack cheese

1. Preheat the oven to 350 degrees. Coat a 2-quart casserole dish with nonstick cooking spray.

2. Melt the butter over medium heat in a 10-inch sauté pan. Add the onion and cook, stirring, until it is softened, about 3 minutes. Add the chiles and cumin and cook the vegetables, stirring, for 2 more minutes. Stir in the soup, milk, chicken, and Tabasco and bring to a boil.

3. Place the pasta and cilantro in a large mixing bowl and blend in all but ¼ cup of the sauce.

4. Spoon the pasta mixture into the prepared dish, top with the remaining sauce, and sprinkle with the cheese. Bake the casserole until the sauce is bubbling and the cheese is golden brown, about 30 minutes.

Although it's almost too simple, I had to include this because I love it so much. Almost like a Southwestern macaroni and cheese, but a little more sophisticated, this dish can transform left-over pasta into a comforting dish for dinner.

"FURTHER TO THE RIGHT THAN A SOUP SPOON," SAID JAMES THURBER, MEANING VERY CONSERVATIVE, INDEED.

Artichoke Herbed Chicken

This elegant entrée never fails to please my guests, and the secret ingredients are cream of chicken soup and marinated artichoke hearts. The dish can be prepared one day ahead of time and then popped into the oven just before serving.

2 tablespoons olive oil

6 boneless, skinless chicken breast halves

1 teaspoon salt

½ teaspoon freshly ground black pepper

One 6-ounce jar marinated artichoke hearts, drained (marinade reserved) and sliced in half

1 can Campbell's Condensed Cream of Chicken Soup

½ cup sour cream

¼ cup Dijon mustard

1 cup grated Swiss cheese

1. Preheat the oven to 350 degrees.

2. Heat the oil in a 12-inch sauté pan over medium-high heat, sprinkle the chicken with the salt and pepper, brown the chicken on both sides, about 3 minutes per side, and then place it in a 13-by-9-inch baking dish. Cover the chicken with the artichoke hearts.

3. In a medium mixing bowl, whisk together the soup, sour cream, mustard, and reserved artichoke marinade. Pour the sauce over the chicken and cover with the grated cheese. (At this point, the dish can be refrigerated overnight. Bring the casserole to room temperature before baking it.)

4. Bake the casserole until the sauce is bubbling and the cheese is melted, about 30 minutes.

Nonnie's Company Chicken

1 cup Armour dried beef, cut into thin strips

3 tablespoons butter

8 boneless, skinless chicken breast halves

1 can Campbell's Condensed Cream of Mushroom Soup

One 8-ounce container sour cream

½ pound mushrooms, sliced

2 cups grated Swiss cheese

1. Preheat the oven to 325 degrees. Coat a 13-by-9-inch baking dish with nonstick cooking spray. Sprinkle the dried beef evenly over the bottom of the casserole dish.

2. Melt 1 tablespoon of the butter in a large sauté pan over medium heat and cook the chicken until it is white on both sides. Transfer the chicken to the casserole.

3. Stir the soup and sour cream together until smooth and spread the mixture over the chicken.

4. Melt the remaining 2 tablespoons butter in the same sauté pan over medium-high heat and cook the mushrooms, stirring, until they begin to turn golden. Spread them over the casserole, top with the cheese, and bake the casserole until the sauce is bubbling and the cheese is golden, 45 minutes to 1 hour. Serve immediately.

This recipe does not appear in any of the early Campbell's cookbooks, but it does show up in a lot of cookbooks put together by organizations. There are several different versions, but this one is from my friend Nonnie, who first introduced me to it.

Dried beef is a staple from the 1950s, when it was used to make creamed beef on toast. It is sold in the same section of the grocery store as tuna and deviled ham. You can also cut it into julienne and stir it into scrambled eggs, hash browns, or cream of chicken soup and serve it over toast.

Chicken Tarragon

This one-dish meal is a real crowd pleaser, and you won't spend all your time in the kitchen getting it ready. The sauce, rice, and chicken can be prepared ahead of time, and then you can simply bake the casserole in the oven.

4 cups cooked wild rice

2 tablespoons olive oil

3 tablespoons butter

8 boneless, skinless chicken breast halves

1 teaspoon salt

½ teaspoons freshly ground black pepper

2 cups sliced mushrooms

2 cans Campbell's Condensed Cream of Chicken Soup

½ cup milk

1 tablespoon fresh chopped tarragon leaves or 1½ teaspoons dried

½ cup sliced almonds

1. Preheat the oven to 350 degrees. Coat a 13-by-9-inch baking dish with nonstick cooking spray. Spread the cooked wild rice over the bottom of the dish.

2. Heat the oil and 1 tablespoon of the butter together in a 10-inch sauté pan over medium-high heat. Sprinkle the chicken breasts with the salt and pepper and add them to the pan. Cook until they are white on each side but not cooked through. Remove the chicken from the pan and place it atop the rice in the baking dish.

3. In the same pan, melt the remaining 2 tablespoons butter over medium heat and cook the mushrooms, stirring, until they are softened, about 4 minutes. Add the soup, milk, and tarragon and whisk until smooth. Taste the sauce and adjust the seasoning by adding more salt and pepper.

4. Pour the sauce over the chicken in the dish and sprinkle the top evenly with the almonds. At this point, the casserole may be refrigerated overnight.

5. When you are ready to bake the casserole, remove it from the refrigerator and let it stand at room temperature for 15 minutes. Bake the casserole until the sauce is bubbling and the chicken is cooked through, 30 to 40 minutes.

Aunt Ele's Baked Chicken Salad

2 cans Campbell's Condensed Cream of Chicken Soup

¾ cup mayonnaise

2 tablespoons fresh lemon juice

6 cups 1-inch cubes cooked chicken breasts

2 cups finely chopped celery

¼ cup finely chopped onion

6 hard-boiled eggs, peeled and chopped

1 teaspoon salt

½ teaspoon freshly ground black pepper

½ cup slivered almonds

2 cups crushed potato chips

1. Preheat the oven to 350 degrees. Coat a 3-quart casserole dish with nonstick cooking spray.

2. In a medium mixing bowl, combine the soup, mayonnaise, and lemon juice.

3. In a large mixing bowl, toss together the cooked chicken, celery, onion, eggs, salt, and pepper. Gently stir the soup mixture into the chicken and pour the mixture into the prepared casserole. (At this point, the casserole can be refrigerated overnight.)

4. Top the casserole with the almonds and potato chips and bake it until it is golden brown, 35 to 45 minutes.

SERVES 6

Some of my fondest memories are the times I have spent with my Aunt Eleonore. A gracious hostess and a championship bridge player, she serves this chicken salad to her guests, who love every morsel. I like to serve this with fruit salad.

Updated Baked Chicken Salad

SERVES 8

This update of my aunt's recipe adds one of my favorite flavorings for chicken: curry. Golden raisins, toasted coconut, chopped peanuts, and a touch of chutney round out this tasty dish. Serve this with curry condiments: chutney, raisins, coconut, finely chopped peanuts, chopped green onions, and chopped bananas that have been sprinkled with lemon juice.

Souper Smart

To toast coconut, preheat the oven to 400 degrees, spread the coconut on a baking sheet, and bake, stirring occasionally, until it is golden, five to seven minutes. Remove the coconut from the oven and let it cool.

2 cans Campbell's Condensed Cream of Chicken Soup

$\frac{1}{2}$ cup mayonnaise

1 tablespoon fresh lemon juice

2 teaspoons curry powder

2 tablespoons finely chopped Major Grey chutney

6 cups 1-inch cubes skinless, boneless cooked chicken breasts

2 cups finely chopped celery

$\frac{1}{4}$ cup finely chopped onion

$\frac{1}{2}$ cup peeled, cored, and chopped apple

6 hard-boiled eggs, peeled and chopped

1 cup golden raisins

$\frac{1}{2}$ teaspoon salt

$\frac{1}{8}$ teaspoon freshly ground black pepper

1 cup sweetened flaked coconut, toasted (see Souper Smart)

$1\frac{1}{2}$ cups finely chopped peanuts

1. Preheat the oven to 350 degrees. Coat a 3-quart casserole dish with nonstick cooking spray.

2. In a medium mixing bowl, combine the soup, mayonnaise, lemon juice, curry powder, and chutney.

3. In a large mixing bowl, toss together the chicken, celery, onion, apple, eggs, raisins, salt, and pepper. Gently stir in the soup mixture, and then pour the contents into the prepared casserole. (At this point, the casserole can be refrigerated overnight.)

4. Top the casserole with the coconut and peanuts and bake the casserole until it is golden brown, 35 to 40 minutes.

King Ranch Casserole

Twelve 6-inch corn tortillas, torn into strips, divided

1/4 cup (1/2 stick) butter

1 cup chopped onion

2 cloves garlic, minced

Two 4-ounce cans chopped green chiles, drained and rinsed

One 14.5-ounce can diced tomatoes, drained

1/4 cup chopped fresh cilantro leaves

1 teaspoon salt

1/2 teaspoon freshly ground black pepper

6 cups bite-size pieces cooked chicken

2 cans Campbell's Condensed Cream of Chicken or Cream of Mushroom Soup

1 cup sour cream

2 cups grated mild cheddar cheese

2 cups grated Monterey Jack cheese

2 cups chicken broth

Flavored with chiles and cheese, this great party dish originated in Texas, and it's one of my favorites for entertaining a crowd. The tortillas melt into the casserole, giving it wonderful flavor and texture. I like to serve it with guacamole, salsa, and sour cream on the side.

1. Coat a 13-by-9-inch baking dish with nonstick cooking spray and spread half of the tortillas over the bottom.

2. In a large sauté pan over medium heat, melt the butter and cook the onion, garlic, and chiles together, stirring, until they are softened, 3 to 4 minutes. Add the tomatoes and cook them until the liquid in the pan evaporates. Stir in the cilantro, salt, pepper, and cooked chicken, and then spread half of this mixture over the tortillas.

3. In a medium mixing bowl, combine the soup and sour cream. Spread half of the soup mixture over the chicken and tomatoes. Sprinkle on half of each of the cheeses, and top with the remaining tortillas. Create more layers using the remaining chicken, soup mixture, and cheese. Pour the chicken broth over the entire casserole and refrigerate it, covered with plastic wrap, overnight.

4. When you are ready to serve the casserole, preheat the oven to 325 degrees. Take the casserole out of the refrigerator and let it sit for 15 minutes. Bake it until the cheese is golden brown and the casserole is bubbling, about 1 hour and 10 minutes.

Crabby Chicken Breasts

SERVES 6

This elegant dinner pairs chicken, wild rice, and crabmeat with a delectable sauce, all with the help of cream of chicken soup and a few other additions. The entire dish can be made the day before and refrigerated, or frozen for up to one month.

8 boneless, skinless chicken breast halves, pounded thin

1 teaspoon salt

1/2 teaspoon freshly ground black pepper

10 tablespoons (1 1/4 sticks) butter

1 shallot, minced

1/4 cup chopped celery

1 medium carrot, grated

1/2 cup cooked wild rice

8 ounces lump crabmeat, picked over for cartilage and shells

1 can Campbell's Condensed Cream of Chicken Soup, plus extra for serving

2 cups dry breadcrumbs

1 cup freshly grated Parmesan cheese

1/4 cup chicken broth

1/2 cup heavy cream

1/2 cup grated Swiss cheese

Pinch of freshly grated nutmeg

1 teaspoon cream sherry

1. Season the chicken breasts with salt and pepper and refrigerate them while you make the filling.

2. Melt 2 tablespoons of the butter in a 10-inch sauté pan over medium heat, add the shallot, celery, and carrot, and cook, stirring, until the vegetables are softened, 3 to 4 minutes. Add the cooked wild rice and crabmeat, turn the mixture into a medium mixing bowl, and stir in 1/2 cup of the soup.

3. Lay the chicken breasts on a flat surface. Place 2 tablespoons of filling in the center of each chicken breast. Fold the top portion of the breast over the filling, fold in the sides, and roll up the chicken breast. Secure it with a toothpick, if necessary. Cover and refrigerate the stuffed chicken breasts for an hour or for up to 8 hours.

4. Preheat the oven to 350 degrees. Coat a 13-by-9-inch baking dish with nonstick cooking spray.

5. Melt the remaining 1/2 cup (1 stick) butter in a small saucepan and combine the breadcrumbs with the Parmesan in a shallow plate. Dip the chicken rolls in the melted butter, and then roll them in the crumb mixture to coat them evenly. Place the chicken rolls seam side down in the prepared dish. Drizzle any remaining melted butter over the stuffed chicken breasts. (At this point you may refrigerate the dish overnight or up to 24 hours.) Bake until the chicken is golden brown, 30 to 40 minutes.

6. Meanwhile, prepare the sauce. Place the remaining soup in a 2-quart saucepan. Whisk in the broth and heavy cream and bring the sauce to a simmer. Add the cheese, nutmeg, and sherry, stirring until the cheese is melted. Serve the sauce with the chicken.

Chicken Florentine

Chicken and spinach are a match made in culinary heaven. The bright green spinach and the creamy chicken sauce make a beautiful presentation. The entire dish can be made the day before, and then baked just before serving.

8 boneless, skinless chicken breast halves

1 teaspoon salt

$1/2$ teaspoon freshly ground black pepper

3 tablespoons butter

2 tablespoons olive oil

Two 10-ounce bags fresh spinach, washed well, dried, heavy stems discarded, and chopped, or two 10-ounce packages frozen chopped spinach, defrosted and squeezed dry

$1/8$ teaspoon freshly grated nutmeg

1 envelope Knorr Cream of Spinach Soup

$1^1/_2$ cups milk

2 cans Campbell's Condensed Cream of Chicken Soup

$1/2$ cup freshly grated Parmesan cheese

1. Preheat the oven to 350 degrees.

2. Sprinkle the chicken with the salt and pepper. Melt the butter in the oil in a 12-inch sauté pan over medium-high heat and, when the foam subsides, add the chicken and brown it on both sides, 3 to 4 minutes per side.

3. Remove the chicken from the pan and add the spinach. Cook it until it wilts, about 2 minutes. Season the spinach with the nutmeg, and then stir in the soup mix and $3/4$ cup of the milk. Bring the sauce to a boil and pour the spinach mixture into a 13-by-9-inch baking dish. Lay the chicken on top.

4. In a small mixing bowl, combine the Cream of Chicken soup with the remaining $3/4$ cup milk, whisking until smooth. Pour this mixture over the chicken. Sprinkle the top with the Parmesan cheese. (At this point, the dish may be refrigerated for up to 24 hours before baking. Remove the dish from the refrigerator 30 minutes before baking it.)

5. Bake the casserole until the cheese is golden brown and the sauce is bubbling, 35 to 45 minutes.

Old-Fashioned Chicken Pot Pie

1 can Campbell's Condensed Cream of Chicken Soup

1 can Campbell's Condensed Cream of Potato Soup

1 cup chicken broth

1 teaspoon dried thyme

$^1/_2$ teaspoon freshly ground black pepper

4 cups bite-size pieces cooked chicken or turkey

1 cup frozen mixed peas and carrots, defrosted

1 sheet Pepperidge Farm Puff Pastry, defrosted

1. Preheat the oven to 400 degrees.

2. In a large mixing bowl, whisk together the soups, broth, thyme, and pepper. Add the cooked chicken, peas, and carrots and fold to blend. Pour the mixture into a 3-quart casserole dish.

3. On a floured board, roll out the puff pastry to fit the casserole and cover the dish with the pastry, fluting the edges or crimping them with the tines of a fork. Slash the crust in 2 or 3 places so steam can escape. Bake the pot pie until the crust is golden, about 20 minutes.

SERVES 6

Soothing, satisfying, and oh so nostalgic, this chicken pot pie will take you back to grandma's house, and all in less than 30 minutes!

VARIATION: If you would like to have a bottom crust, coat the inside of the casserole dish with nonstick cooking spray and roll out a second sheet of puff pastry to fit into the casserole dish. Place the pastry in the dish, prick it with a fork all over, and bake it for ten minutes in a preheated 400 degree oven. Proceed with the pie as directed in the recipe.

AMERICANS USE MORE THAN 440 MILLION CANS OF SOUP EACH YEAR.

Enchiladas Suissa

These enchiladas are my favorite entrée at a popular local restaurant in San Diego. They feature chicken in a creamy sauce, topped with Swiss cheese and a stripe of tomatillo sauce. Tomatillos are small green tomato-like fruits that are covered with a papery skin that needs to be removed. Served with guacamole and sour cream, these enchiladas are a great brunch or dinner dish.

Souper Smart

I normally include the cilantro in the chicken filling, but some people are terribly allergic to cilantro, so if you are not sure of your guests, leave it out of the filling and just garnish the finished dish with it.

2 tablespoons butter

1 cup chopped onion

1/2 cup chopped canned roasted green chiles

1 cup corn kernels, either cut fresh from the cob or frozen (and defrosted)

1 teaspoon ground cumin

1 teaspoon salt

1/8 teaspoon cayenne pepper

4 cups 1/2-inch cubes cooked chicken

2 cans Campbell's Condensed Cream of Chicken Soup

1 cup sour cream

Twelve 6-inch corn tortillas

2 cups Tomatillo Sauce (recipe follows)

2 cups grated Swiss cheese

1 cup chopped fresh cilantro leaves for garnish

1. Preheat the oven to 350 degrees. Coat a 13-by-9-inch baking dish with nonstick cooking spray.

2. In a 10-inch sauté pan over medium heat, melt the butter, add the onion, and cook, stirring, until it is softened, 3 to 4 minutes. Add the chiles, corn, cumin, salt, and cayenne and cook, stirring, for another 2 minutes. Remove the vegetables from the heat and stir in the cooked chicken.

3. In a small mixing bowl, whisk together the soup and sour cream and stir 1 cup of it into the chicken and vegetable mixture. Spread a thin layer of the soup mixture over the bottom of the prepared baking dish.

4. Place 2 tablespoons of the chicken mixture down the center of each tortilla, and then roll up the tortilla and place it seam side down in the baking dish. Repeat with the remaining tortillas and filling. Cover the enchiladas with the remaining soup mixture, then apply the tomatillo sauce in stripes across the top. Cover the casserole with the Swiss cheese and bake until the sauce is bubbling and the cheese is golden brown, 35 to 45 minutes. Garnish with the cilantro and serve.

TOMATILLO SAUCE

1 tablespoon vegetable oil

1 large onion, cut in half and sliced

½ cup canned roasted green chiles, peeled and cut into half-moons

2 cloves garlic, minced

1 envelope Lipton Savory Herb with Garlic Soup Mix

One 13-ounce can tomatillos, drained

1. In a 2-quart saucepan, heat the oil over medium heat, add the onion, and cook, stirring, until it is softened, 3 to 4 minutes. Add the chiles and garlic and cook, stirring, until they are softened but not browned, about 3 minutes. Add the soup mix and tomatillos and simmer the sauce for 10 minutes.

2. Remove the pan from the heat, let the sauce cool, and then purée it in a food processor or blender. The sauce can be refrigerated for up to 5 days.

Fresh tomatillos are seasonal; if you can get them and have the time, use 1 pound of fresh tomatillos for this sauce.

Friday Night Bistro Chicken

Friday nights seem to be the worst when you want something comforting for dinner but are too tired to cook. This chicken dish has just three principal ingredients that are surely in your pantry. The result is a delicious and soothing home-cooked dinner. Be sure to serve lots of crusty bread to dip in the sauce.

Slow Cooker Savvy

This recipe is divine prepared in a slow cooker. Sauté the chicken breasts, place them in the slow cooker, add the sauce ingredients, and cook on high for four to six hours. Garnish with Swiss cheese before serving.

2 tablespoons butter

1 tablespoon olive oil

6 boneless, skinless chicken breast halves

1 teaspoon salt

$1/2$ teaspoon freshly ground black pepper

$1/2$ cup chopped shallots

One 14.5-ounce can diced tomatoes, with their juices

$1^{1}/2$ teaspoons dried thyme

1 can Campbell's Condensed French Onion Soup

1 cup grated Swiss cheese (optional)

1. Preheat the oven to 375 degrees.

2. In a 12-inch ovenproof skillet, melt the butter in the olive oil over medium-high heat. Sprinkle the chicken breasts with half the salt and pepper, reserving the rest for the sauce. Pan-fry the chicken until both sides are golden but the chicken is not cooked through. Remove the chicken from the skillet, add the shallots, and cook, stirring, until they are softened, 3 to 4 minutes. Add the tomatoes and thyme and cook until the sauce has reduced a bit, 4 to 5 minutes. Add the soup and cook another 4 minutes, seasoning with the remaining salt and pepper.

3. Return the chicken to the skillet, cover with the cheese, and bake until the cheese is melted and the chicken is cooked through, about 20 minutes.

Chicken Ragout

¼ cup (½ stick) butter

2 cups sliced onion

1 pound crimini mushrooms, sliced

4 boneless, skinless chicken breast halves

4 boneless, skinless chicken thighs

1 teaspoon salt

½ teaspoon freshly ground black pepper

2 tablespoons vegetable oil

1 cup red wine

1 envelope Knorr Leek Soup Mix

1 teaspoon dried fines herbes (see page 3)

2 cups chicken broth

1 bay leaf

1. Melt the butter in a 10-inch skillet over medium heat, add the onion, and cook, stirring, until golden, 9 to 10 minutes. Add the mushrooms and cook, stirring, another 4 minutes. Set the mixture aside.

2. Sprinkle the chicken with the salt and pepper. Heat the oil in a 5-quart Dutch oven over medium-high heat. Add the chicken and brown it on each side. Deglaze the pan with the wine, scraping up any of the browned bits on the bottom. Add the soup mix, dried fines herbes, broth, bay leaf, and reserved onions and mushrooms. Cover the pan and simmer the chicken in the sauce for 45 minutes, turning the chicken several times during the cooking time. Remove the bay leaf from the sauce and serve.

Ragout is a French term for stew, and this chicken stew is elegant yet hearty with wine, herbs, and vegetables. It is especially grand when served with Garlic Herb Mashed Potatoes (page 233).

Slow Cooker Savvy

Brown the vegetables and chicken. Place in a slow cooker, add remaining ingredients and cook on high for four to six hours.

A dish that is put togeth-er in minutes, with the help of Minute Rice, this classic has graced more tables than I can count. It seems to be a staple in the Midwest, where I teach, as my students have given me every vari-ation they could possibly think of. I offer you this classic and my own varia-tion, which uses wild rice.

CHICKEN AND WILD RICE BAKE: Substitute 2 cups cooked wild rice for the Minute Rice and add 2 cups cooked baby carrots to the mixture. Cook as directed.

Old-Fashioned Chicken and Rice Skillet

1 tablespoon vegetable oil

4 boneless, skinless chicken breast halves

1 cup Campbell's Condensed Cream of Chicken Soup

$1\frac{1}{2}$ cups water

$\frac{1}{4}$ teaspoon sweet paprika

$\frac{1}{4}$ teaspoon freshly ground black pepper

$1\frac{1}{2}$ cups Minute Rice

2 cups broccoli florets

1. In a medium skillet over medium-high heat, heat the oil. Add the chicken breast halves and cook until they are browned on each side. Set the chicken aside and pour off any fat in the skillet.

2. Add the soup, water, paprika, and pepper to the skillet and heat to a boil. Stir in the rice and broccoli and place the chicken on top of the rice mixture. Reduce the heat to low, cover, and cook until the chicken is no longer pink, 10 minutes.

S picy and comforting, this easy dish comes together in no time, and your family will love the flavor. Leftovers are great tossed with a sher-ry vinaigrette for a cold entrée later in the week.

Spanish Chicken and Rice Bake

2 tablespoons olive oil

6 boneless, skinless chicken breast halves

1 large onion, thinly sliced

1 medium red bell pepper, seeded and cut into $\frac{1}{2}$-inch-wide strips

1 clove garlic, minced

One 14.5-ounce can diced tomatoes, with their juices

1 envelope Lipton Golden Onion Soup Mix

2 cups water

1 cup converted rice

1 cup frozen petite peas

1. Preheat the oven to 400 degrees.

2. Heat the oil in a 5-quart Dutch oven over medium-high heat and brown the chicken breasts on each side, about 3 minutes per side. Remove to a plate.

3. Add the onion, bell pepper, and garlic to the pan. Cook, stirring, until the vegetables are softened, about 4 minutes. Add the tomatoes, soup mix, and water and stir up any browned bits that may have stuck to the bottom of the pan.

4. Stir in the rice, return the chicken to the pan, and bake for 20 minutes. Add the peas and continue to bake until the rice is tender, an additional 10 minutes.

Glori-Fried Chicken

2 pounds chicken parts

2 tablespoons shortening

1 can Campbell's Condensed Cream of Mushroom, Cream of Celery, or Cream of Chicken Soup

In skillet, brown chicken in shortening. Pour off fat. Stir in soup. Cover; cook over low heat 45 minutes or until tender. Stir now and then. Uncover; cook until desired consistency.

SERVES 4

This recipe comes from the Campbell's home economists, who were trying to simplify dinner for their customers. I am sure this dish was served with mashed potatoes and green vegetables at many a table in the 1950s and 1960s.

Poultry

Glorious Chicken

With the availability of boneless chicken breasts, this dish becomes a dressed-up version of its cousin, and cooks in half the time.

GLORIOUS ITALIAN CHICKEN: Sauté ¹/₂ cup red bell pepper strips and ¹/₂ green bell pepper strips with the shallots. Add 1 teaspoon chopped fresh or ¹/₂ teaspoon dried oregano instead of the thyme to the soup, and ¹/₄ cup freshly grated Parmesan cheese to the sauce with the soup and wine.

1 tablespoons vegetable oil

2 tablespoons butter

6 boneless, skinless chicken breast halves

1 teaspoon salt

¹/₂ teaspoon freshly ground black pepper

¹/₄ cup chopped shallots

1 cup sliced mushrooms

1 can Campbell's Condensed Cream of Chicken Soup

¹/₂ cup white wine

1 teaspoon chopped fresh thyme leaves or ¹/₂ teaspoon dried

1. In a 10- or 12-inch skillet, heat the oil and butter together until the butter begins to bubble. Season the chicken with the salt and pepper, and then cook it in the hot butter and oil until the halves are white on each side. Remove the chicken to a plate.

2. Add the shallots to the skillet and cook, stirring, for 2 minutes. Add the mushrooms and cook, stirring, until they are softened, 2 to 3 minutes. Stir in the soup and wine, stirring up any browned bits on the bottom of the skillet. Add the thyme and return the chicken to the skillet. Simmer, covered, for 10 minutes. Serve immediately.

Chicken in Tarragon and Tomato Cream Sauce

2 tablespoons olive oil

2 tablespoons butter

8 boneless, skinless chicken breast halves, pounded thin

1 teaspoon salt

$\frac{1}{2}$ teaspoon freshly ground black pepper

$\frac{1}{2}$ cup chopped shallots

1 pound mushrooms, sliced

$\frac{1}{2}$ cup white wine

One 14.5-ounce can diced tomatoes, drained

1 teaspoon dried tarragon

1 can Campbell's Condensed Cream of Chicken Soup

$\frac{1}{2}$ cup heavy cream

1. Melt the butter in the oil in a 10- to 12-inch sauté pan over medium-high heat. Sprinkle the chicken with the salt and pepper and brown it on both sides, about 4 minutes per side.

2. Remove the chicken from the pan, add the shallots, and cook, stirring, until they are softened. Add the mushrooms and cook, stirring, until the mushrooms begin to turn golden, 4 to 5 minutes. Add the wine and bring the sauce to a boil. Add the tomatoes and tarragon and cook until the mixture begins to reduce, about 4 minutes. Stir in the soup and heavy cream, bring to a simmer, and return the chicken to the pan. Heat until the chicken is cooked through, about another 5 minutes.

SERVES 6

This elegant chicken dish is an easy do-ahead dish to serve at a special dinner, or you can have it on the table in less than 45 minutes from start to finish. The entire dish can be made the day before, with just a brief warming up before serving.

Chicken Cacciatore

SERVES 6

This easy dinner is terrific served with pasta to soak up the delicious sauce that the chicken cooks in. I like to use boneless, skinless chicken thighs in this recipe because they absorb the flavors of the sauce so well and benefit from the longer cooking time.

IF YOU MADE ONE LIPTON RECIPE SECRETS RECIPE PER DAY, IT WOULD TAKE YOU ALMOST 11 YEARS TO MAKE ALL THE DISHES—THAT'S BECAUSE THERE ARE MORE THAN 4,000 LIPTON RECIPE SECRETS RECIPES!

1/4 cup olive oil

8 boneless, skinless chicken thighs

1 teaspoon salt

1/2 teaspoon freshly ground black pepper

2 large onions, thinly sliced

2 cloves garlic, minced

Two 14.5-ounce cans crushed tomatoes

1 envelope Lipton Savory Herb with Garlic Soup Mix

2 tablespoons balsamic vinegar

1 tablespoon crumbled dried rosemary

Hot cooked pasta or rice of your choice

1. Heat 2 tablespoons of the oil in a 10- to 12-inch sauté pan over medium-high heat. Season the chicken with the salt and pepper and brown the chicken on both sides in the hot oil.

2. Remove the chicken from the skillet, add the remaining 2 tablespoons oil and the onions, and cook, stirring, until the onions are softened, 3 to 4 minutes. Add the garlic and cook, stirring, for another 3 minutes. Add the tomatoes, soup mix, vinegar, and rosemary and bring the sauce to a boil.

3. Return the chicken to the pan, reduce the heat to medium-low, and simmer, covered, for 30 minutes. (The chicken can be refrigerated overnight. Bring the dish to room temperature, and then reheat it over medium heat.) Serve with pasta or rice.

penne

Chicken Piccata

8 boneless, skinless chicken breast halves, pounded thin

1 teaspoon salt

½ teaspoon freshly ground black pepper

2 tablespoons butter

1 tablespoon olive oil

¼ cup fresh lemon juice

1 can Campbell's Condensed Cream of Chicken Soup

⅓ cup capers, drained

1. Sprinkle each chicken breast with some of the salt and pepper.

2. In a 10-inch sauté pan, melt the butter in the olive oil over high heat. Add the chicken breasts and pan-fry them until they are browned on both sides. Remove the chicken to a heated platter and keep it warm.

3. Add the lemon juice to the pan, stirring up any browned bits on the bottom. Add the soup and whisk until the sauce is smooth. Add the capers, bring the sauce to a boil, taste for seasoning, and adjust.

4. To serve, place a chicken breast on each plate and cover it with some of the sauce.

SERVES 8

This savory dish is the perfect spur-of-the-moment company meal. With the help of a can of Cream of Chicken Soup, the sauce and chicken can be on the table in under 20 minutes, giving you just enough time to simmer the orzo or rice and toss a salad.

Flattening Chicken Breasts

To pound chicken breasts, place them between two pieces of waxed paper on a cutting board and pound them with a meat tenderizer or the flat bottom of a wine bottle until they are ¼ inch thick. Store in the refrigerator until you are ready to use them.

SOUP IS THE FOURTH MOST WIDELY USED INGREDIENT FOR PREPARING DINNER IN THE UNITED STATES.

This elegant dish is special enough for company, and you can have it ready in the freezer for that unexpected guest who might show up. The chicken rolls are stuffed with an herbed cream cheese blend, and a sauce is made from the same mixture.

Zucchini Herb Stuffed Chicken Breasts

6 boneless, skinless chicken breast halves, pounded thin

1 teaspoon salt

1/2 teaspoon freshly ground black pepper

Two 8-ounce packages cream cheese, softened

1 envelope Knorr Leek Soup Mix

1 teaspoon dried fines herbes (see page 3)

2 medium zucchini, ends trimmed, grated, and patted dry

1/2 cup freshly grated Parmesan cheese

2 tablespoons butter

2 tablespoons olive oil

1/2 cup white wine

1 cup chicken broth

1. Sprinkle the chicken breasts with the salt and pepper and set them aside while you make the filling.

2. In a large mixing bowl, using an electric mixer, or in a food processor, cream together the cream cheese, soup mix, zucchini, and Parmesan. Place 2 tablespoons of this mixture in the center of each chicken breast and roll up the chicken, tucking in the sides, to form a small package. Refrigerate the chicken and the remaining herbed cream cheese mixture covered tightly in plastic wrap, for at least an hour before cooking, or freeze the chicken and cream cheese mixture in resealable plastic bags for up to 1 month.

3. Melt the butter in the oil in a large sauté pan over medium-high heat, add the stuffed chicken, and brown on all sides. Remove the chicken to a warm platter and cover it with aluminum foil while you make the sauce.

4. Deglaze the pan with the wine, scraping any browned bits off the bottom, and reduce the wine to almost a glaze (this should take about 4 minutes). Add the chicken broth and $1/4$ cup of the remaining cream cheese mixture, stirring with a whisk until smooth. You will have some leftover herbed cream cheese.

5. Return the chicken to the pan and turn the chicken in the sauce to rewarm it thoroughly before serving.

Rotisserie-Style Broiled Chicken

Two 2$1/2$-pound frying chickens, cut into serving pieces, washed, and dried with paper towels

$1/2$ cup olive oil

$1/2$ cup fresh lemon juice (from 2 lemons)

Chopped zest of 2 lemons

1 envelope Lipton Savory Herb with Garlic Soup Mix

1. Place the chicken pieces in a resealable plastic bag or 13-by-9-inch baking dish.

2. In a small mixing bowl, whisk together the oil, lemon juice and zest, and soup mix until blended. Pour the marinade over the chicken and turn the chicken to coat it. Refrigerate the chicken in the marinade for at least 2 hours and for up to 6 hours. Turn the chicken several times while marinating.

3. Preheat the broiler. Remove the chicken from the marinade, saving any marinade in a small bowl. Place the chicken on the rack of a broiler pan, skin side down, and broil the chicken until it begins to brown, 5 to 7 minutes. Turn the chicken and broil it until the skin is crispy, another 5 to 7 minutes. Turn off the broiler and set the oven temperature at 400 degrees. Bake the chicken for 5 minutes, baste with the remaining marinade, and bake until the chicken is golden brown, about an additional 10 minutes.

My local Greek café serves a rotisserie chicken that I love. It's lemony, flavored with garlic and herbs, the skin glistening and crispy, and the meat is tender and juicy. I've become a pest asking the owner for his secret recipe. This simple dish is every bit as good as the one served at the café, and you can make it at home! Great picnic food, this chicken can be made ahead of time. It's great hot, at room temperature, and cold at seven in the morning!

ROTISSERIE-STYLE BROILED CORNISH HENS: This recipe is also delicious with Cornish game hens; split the hens in half, and then marinate, broil, and bake them as directed.

Poultry

Mom's Sunday Roast Chicken with Vegetables

There is nothing more beautiful that a roasted chicken surrounded by vegetables and served with its pan juices. This chicken is simplicity at its best, and the aromas in your kitchen will perfume the entire house. Don't wait for Sunday to try this!

VARIATIONS:

Try substituting one of the following:

- **Lipton Onion Soup Mix**
- **Lipton Savory Herb with Garlic Soup Mix**
- **Knorr Tomato with Basil Soup Mix**
- **Knorr Leek Soup Mix and 1 teaspoon dried fines herbes**

One 4-pound roasting chicken

1 teaspoon salt

½ cup olive oil

¼ cup fresh lemon juice

2 envelopes Lipton Golden Onion Soup Mix

1 teaspoon freshly ground black pepper

6 medium red potatoes, quartered

6 medium carrots, cut into 2-inch lengths

4 stalks celery, cut into 2-inch lengths

4 large yellow onions, quartered

1. Preheat the oven to 425 degrees.

2. Wash the chicken and pat it dry with paper towels inside and out. Salt the inside of the chicken and refrigerate in plastic wrap, until you are ready to proceed.

2. In a small mixing bowl, blend together the oil, lemon juice, soup mix, and pepper. Place the vegetables in the bottom of the pan, and drizzle them with some of the oil mixture. Place the chicken on a wire rack in a roasting pan and rub the outside of the chicken with some of the flavored oil mixture. Reserve ¼ cup of the oil mixture for basting the chicken during cooking.

3. Roast the chicken for 25 minutes. Reduce the oven temperature to 350 degrees, baste the chicken with some of the oil mixture, drizzle the vegetables with the remaining oil mixture, and bake until the chicken registers 175 degrees on a meat thermometer, about an additional 35 minutes.

4. Remove the chicken from the rack and let it rest for 20 minutes before carving.

Barbecue Chicken

1 frying chicken (about 3 pounds), cut into serving pieces, washed, and patted dry

1 teaspoon salt

$1/2$ teaspoon freshly ground black pepper

1 can Campbell's Condensed Tomato Soup

1 clove garlic, minced

$1/2$ cup chopped onion

$1/3$ cup rice vinegar

$1/4$ cup firmly packed light brown sugar

2 tablespoons Worcestershire sauce

1 teaspoon dry mustard

1. Preheat the broiler. Season the chicken with the salt and pepper.

2. In a 2-quart saucepan combine the soup, garlic, onion, vinegar, sugar, Worcestershire, and dry mustard and bring to a boil. Let it cool to room temperature.

3. Place the chicken skin side down on a wire rack in a roasting pan and brush it with the sauce. Broil the chicken for 3 minutes, turn, baste it again with more barbecue sauce, and broil it for another 5 minutes. Turn the broiler off and set the oven at 375 degrees. Bake the chicken for another 30 minutes, basting it every 10 minutes with more sauce.

SERVES 6

When I lived in a cold climate, we only barbecued chicken when it was warm and sunny and we could use the grill. Now, with this recipe, you can barbecue chicken in the oven anytime you want. The barbecue sauce can be made a day ahead, and the chicken is great hot or at room temperature. Serve this with Creamy Garlic Potato Salad (page 79).

MORE THAN 1 MILLION CANS OF CAMPBELL'S SOUP ARE USED EACH DAY AS AN INGREDIENT FOR PREPARING DINNER.

Poultry

Sesame Chicken Breasts

SERVES 6

Golden sesame seeds and herbs crust these chicken breasts, and the resulting dish is elegant yet so easy for the hostess to prepare. I usually make this recipe the day before serving, and then just pop the chicken in the oven to reheat. I like to serve this dish with Creamy Mushroom Sauce (page 475).

2 cups buttermilk

6 shakes Tabasco sauce

8 boneless, skinless chicken breast halves

2 cups dry breadcrumbs

1 cup sesame seeds

1 envelope Knorr Leek Soup Mix

1 teaspoon dried fines herbes (see page 3)

½ cup (1 stick) butter, melted

1. In a large mixing bowl, combine the buttermilk and Tabasco. Add the chicken, turning to coat, and let it marinate, covered with plastic wrap, in the refrigerator for at least 2 hours and for up to 12 hours.

2. In a shallow dish, combine the breadcrumbs, sesame seeds, soup mix, and dried fines herbes.

3. Remove the chicken from the marinade, draining off the excess. Roll the chicken in the crumb mixture to coat evenly, and place the chicken in a 13-by-9-inch baking dish. Drizzle the butter over the top of the chicken. Refrigerate for 1 hour before baking.

4. Preheat the oven to 350 degrees. While the oven is preheating, remove the chicken from the refrigerator.

5. Bake until it is golden brown, 30 to 35 minutes.

CRISPY OVEN-FRIED CHICKEN (FOUR WAYS)

Although each of these recipes has its own distinctive character, they all rely on powdered soup mix for that extra pizzazz. I love crispy chicken skin, but if you do not wish to eat the skin, stuff some of the coating under the skin, bake as directed, and then remove the skin after baking. The skin will help to keep the chicken moist during the baking process.

Golden Brown Fried Chicken

1 cup dry breadcrumbs

1 envelope Lipton Golden Onion Soup Mix

1 frying chicken (about 2 1/2 pounds), cut into serving pieces, washed, and patted dry

2 large eggs, beaten

1/4 cup (1/2 stick) butter, melted

1. Preheat the oven to 350 degrees.

2. Combine the breadcrumbs and soup mix in a shallow dish.

3. Dip the chicken pieces into the beaten eggs, and then roll them in the breadcrumb mixture to coat evenly.

4. Place the chicken in a 13-by-9-inch baking dish, drizzle with the melted butter, and bake until the chicken is golden brown, 35 to 45 minutes. Serve hot or at room temperature.

SERVES 4 TO 6

Golden Onion Soup mix gives this chicken a beautiful color as well as a nice flavor. If you would like to substitute regular onion soup, I recommend that you add 1 tablespoon dried parsley and 1/2 teaspoon more black pepper to the breadcrumb mixture.

Spicy Oven-Fried Chicken

SERVES 8 TO 10

Marinating the chicken in buttermilk and spices not only flavors it, it also helps to ensure that the chicken remains tender.

2 cups buttermilk

3 tablespoons Tabasco sauce

3 tablespoons Dijon mustard

1 envelope Lipton Savory Herb with Garlic Soup Mix

10 to 12 chicken pieces (breasts, drumsticks, and thighs), washed and patted dry

2½ cups dry breadcrumbs

½ cup freshly grated Parmesan cheese

1 envelope Knorr Leek Soup Mix

1 teaspoon freshly ground black pepper

3 tablespoons olive oil

1. In a large mixing bowl, combine the buttermilk, Tabasco, mustard, and garlic herb soup mix. Add the chicken, turning to coat all the pieces. Cover the bowl with plastic wrap and refrigerate the chicken in the marinade for at least 6 hours and for up to 24 hours.

2. Preheat the oven to 425 degrees. Line a jelly roll pan or rimmed baking sheet with aluminum foil. Place a wire rack on the pan.

3. In a large mixing bowl, blend together the breadcrumbs, cheese, leek soup mix, pepper, and oil.

4. Remove the chicken from the marinade, letting the excess drain off. Coat the chicken in the crumb mixture evenly and place the chicken on the rack. Bake the chicken until it is golden brown, 50 to 60 minutes. Serve hot, at room temperature, or cold.

Fried Chicken Italiano

½ cup olive oil

1 envelope Knorr Tomato with Basil Soup Mix

1 frying chicken (about 2½ pounds), cut into serving pieces, washed, and patted dry

1 cup dry breadcrumbs

1 cup freshly grated Parmesan cheese

1. Preheat the oven to 350 degrees.

2. Combine the oil and soup mix in a shallow dish. Place the chicken in the oil mixture and turn to coat the pieces evenly.

3. In another shallow dish, combine the breadcrumbs and cheese. Dip the chicken into the crumbs to coat evenly and place the chicken in a 13-by-9-inch baking dish.

4. Drizzle any remaining flavored oil over the top of the chicken and bake until the chicken is golden brown, about 40 minutes.

This delicious chicken dish can be the centerpiece for an alfresco picnic or a tailgate party. The chicken can be served warm or cold, and it pairs well with pasta salads.

Herbed Fried Chicken

The taste of Provence flavors this chicken, and you will be amazed at the nice crispy texture that the mayonnaise lends to the coating.

VARIATION: Boneless breasts and thighs can also be prepared this way, using the same breading technique. Cook boneless breasts for 20 minutes and thighs for 30 minutes.

2 envelopes Knorr Leek Soup Mix

2 teaspoons dried fines herbes (see page 3)

1½ cups mayonnaise

2 cups dry breadcrumbs

1 frying chicken (about 2½ pounds), cut into serving pieces, washed, and patted dry

1. Preheat the oven to 375 degrees.

2. Combine 1 envelope of the soup mix and 1 teaspoon of the dried fines herbes with the mayonnaise in a large mixing bowl, stirring to blend.

3. In a large shallow dish, combine the remaining envelope of soup mix and the remaining teaspoon of dried fines herbes with the breadcrumbs.

4. Dip the chicken pieces into the mayonnaise mixture to coat evenly, and then turn them in the breadcrumbs to coat.

5. Place the chicken in a 13-by-9-inch baking dish and bake the chicken until it is golden brown, about 40 minutes. Serve it hot or at room temperature.

Chicken Fajitas

¼ cup vegetable oil

2 large onions, thinly sliced

2 medium green bell peppers, seeded and cut into ½-inch-wide strips

1 medium red bell pepper, seeded and cut into ½-inch-wide strips

1 envelope Lipton Savory Herb with Garlic Soup Mix

One 4-ounce can tomato sauce

2 pounds chicken tenders, tendons removed

1 teaspoon salt

½ teaspoon freshly ground black pepper

Twelve 6-inch flour or corn tortillas

1. Heat 2 tablespoons of the oil in a 12-inch sauté pan over medium heat. Add the onions and bell peppers and cook, stirring until the vegetables are softened, 5 to 7 minutes. Stir in the soup mix and tomato sauce and cook until the mixture begins to thicken, about another 5 minutes. Keep it warm.

2. Season the chicken with the salt and pepper. In another large skillet, heat the remaining 2 tablespoons oil over medium-high heat and brown the chicken on each side. When the chicken is browned and cooked through, transfer it to the onion and pepper mixture and keep it warm until you are ready to serve the fajitas.

3. Spoon the chicken and vegetables into corn or flour tortillas and pass the condiments.

Fajitas are great to serve when you want your guests or family to be involved in the construction of their dinner. The chicken can be prepared early in the day, and then reheated just before serving or kept warm in a slow cooker. Make sure to serve lots of condiments: guacamole, grated cheese, sour cream, pickled jalapeños, salsa, and chopped fresh cilantro.

Lettuce Entertain You Asian Chicken Wraps

Souper Smart

You may keep the chicken mixture warm in a slow cooker, and then your guests can roll their own.

5 tablespoons vegetable oil

1 tablespoon plus 1 teaspoon toasted sesame oil

1 clove garlic, minced

1 teaspoon peeled and grated fresh ginger

2 boneless, skinless chicken breast halves, finely diced

1/2 cup grated carrot

1/2 cup finely chopped ham

1/2 cup finely chopped water chestnuts

6 green onions, chopped

1 tablespoon soy sauce

1 package chicken flavor ramen noodles (break up the noodles into small pieces and reserve them for use as a garnish)

1 tablespoon hoisin sauce

1 tablespoon cornstarch

1/3 cup water

1/4 cup sesame seeds

12 whole leaves iceberg or Bibb lettuce, washed and dried

1. In a wok or large sauté pan, heat 1 tablespoon of the vegetable oil and 1 tablespoon of the sesame oil together over high heat. Add the garlic and ginger and stir-fry them for 2 minutes. Add the chicken and stir-fry it until it turns white on all sides.

2. Remove the chicken from the pan with a slotted spoon. Add the carrot, ham, water chestnuts, and green onions, and stir-fry them for 2 minutes. Return the chicken to the pan and add the soy sauce, ramen flavor packet, and hoisin sauce.

3. In a small bowl, dissolve the cornstarch in the water, and add that mixture to the pan, blending until the sauce is thickened. Sprinkle on the remaining 1 teaspoon sesame oil and the sesame seeds.

4. Heat the remaining 1/4 cup vegetable oil in a small skillet over medium-high heat and fry the reserved noodles until they are golden.

5. To serve, place 2 to 3 tablespoons of the chicken mixture in the center of each lettuce leaf. Top the chicken with the noodles, roll up the lettuce into a packet, and eat.

Lemon Herb Chicken

1/2 cup fresh lemon juice (about 2 lemons)

2 tablespoons olive oil

2 tablespoons chopped lemon zest

1 package Lipton Savory Herb with Garlic Soup Mix, or Knorr Leek Soup Mix mixed with 1 teaspoon dried fines herbes (see page 3)

1 teaspoon freshly ground black pepper

8 boneless, skinless chicken breast halves

1. In a large mixing bowl, combine the lemon juice, oil, lemon zest, soup mix, and pepper. Add the chicken breasts, turning them to coat, and marinate them, covered with plastic wrap, in the refrigerator for at least 30 minutes and for up to 4 hours.

2. Preheat the broiler or grill, remove the chicken from the marinade, and place the chicken on a rack (if using the broiler) or on the grill.

3. Cook the chicken until it is no longer pink in the middle when slashed at the thickest point with a knife, 4 to 5 minutes on each side. Serve hot or at room temperature.

Boneless chicken breasts are a great time-saver for dinner, because they cook quickly and absorb flavors readily. Fragrant with lemon zest and garlic, this simple dish is terrific grilled or broiled for a patio supper or picnic.

Poultry

Cashew Chicken Stir-Fry

My family loves this simple dish, and I usually have all the ingredients in the pantry. Crunchy cashews, spicy chicken, and bright green onions combine to make this a great weeknight meal. It takes longer to cook the rice than it does to put this spicy dish together.

Souper Smart

No time for rice? Boil water and add the noodles from the ramen package. Cook for two minutes, drain, and place on a serving plate. Top with the chicken mixture and serve family-style.

Flavor packet from 1 package chicken flavor ramen noodles (reserve the noodles for another use)

$1/4$ cup water

2 tablespoons soy sauce

1 tablespoon hoisin sauce

1 teaspoon cornstarch

2 tablespoons vegetable oil

1 tablespoon toasted sesame oil

2 cloves garlic, chopped

1 teaspoon peeled and grated fresh ginger

$1/8$ teaspoon red pepper flakes

3 cups chicken breast strips (about 2 whole boneless, skinless breasts cut into $1/2$-inch strips)

4 green onions, cut into 1-inch lengths

1 cup cashews (roasted salted peanuts work well, too)

Cooked rice

1. In a small mixing bowl, combine the ramen flavor packet, water, soy sauce, hoisin, and cornstarch.

2. In a wok or 12-inch sauté pan, heat the oils together over high heat, add the garlic and ginger, and stir-fry them for 2 minutes. Add the red pepper flakes and chicken and stir-fry the chicken until it is white on all sides. Stir in the soy sauce and cornstarch mixture, bringing the sauce to a boil. Add the green onions and cashews and stir to coat them with the sauce. Serve immediately over rice.

Teriyaki Chicken

1 cup soy sauce

3 cloves garlic, minced

2 teaspoons peeled and grated fresh ginger

¼ cup mirin (rice wine)

¼ cup firmly packed light brown sugar

Flavor packet from 1 package oriental flavor ramen noodles (reserve the noodles for another use)

8 boneless, skinless chicken breast halves

1. In a large mixing bowl, combine the soy sauce, garlic, ginger, mirin, brown sugar, and ramen flavor packet, whisking until the brown sugar and seasonings dissolve. Add the chicken, turning to coat, and marinate it, covered with plastic wrap, in the refrigerator for at least 2 hours and for up to 12 hours.

2. Preheat the broiler or grill.

3. Broil or grill the chicken until it is no longer pink in the middle when slashed with a knife at the thickest point, about 5 minutes on each side.

SERVES 6

I can never seem to make enough of this delicious mahogany-colored chicken flavored with soy, ginger, garlic, and sweet rice wine. If you have any leftovers, they are great tossed with noodles for a quick stir-fry or served in Chinese chicken salad.

Chicken Satays with Spicy Peanut Sauce

Satays are marinated skewers of chicken, beef, or shrimp that work well as appetizers and for dinner. The spicy peanut sauce is wonderful for dipping the chicken. If you are using bamboo skewers to grill, be sure to soak them in water for 30 minutes to keep them from burning.

1/2 cup soy sauce

Flavor packets from 2 packages chicken flavor ramen noodles (reserve the noodles for another use)

4 cloves garlic, minced

2 tablespoons fresh lime juice

1 teaspoon peeled and grated fresh ginger

3 tablespoons firmly packed light brown sugar

1 pound chicken tenders, cut in half lengthwise and tendons removed

Spicy Peanut Dipping Sauce (recipe follows)

1. In a large mixing bowl, combine the soy sauce, ramen flavor packets, garlic, lime juice, ginger, and brown sugar, stirring until the mixture is well combined. Add the chicken tenders and marinate them, covered with plastic wrap, in the refrigerator for at least 2 hours, and for up to 6 hours.

2. Preheat the broiler or barbecue grill.

3. Thread the chicken onto skewers and broil or grill them until they are cooked through, about 3 minutes on each side. Remove the skewers from the heat and serve 2 skewers per person with the dipping sauce on the side.

SPICY PEANUT DIPPING SAUCE

1 1/2 cups chicken broth

1 cup smooth peanut butter

1/4 cup firmly packed light brown sugar

3 tablespoons soy sauce

HOT AND SPICY PEANUT DIPPING SAUCE: Like more heat? Add up to 1/2 teaspoon more red pepper flakes.

The Soup Mix Gourmet

2 tablespoons peeled and grated fresh ginger

¹/₄ teaspoon red pepper flakes

1. In a 3-quart saucepan, whisk the chicken broth into the peanut butter. Add the brown sugar, soy sauce, ginger, and red pepper and cook over medium heat until the sauce is smooth and thick, 6 to 10 minutes. The sauce can be refrigerated for up to 3 days.

2. To serve, reheat the sauce, thinning it with additional chicken broth as necessary.

Chicken Kabobs

1 cup olive oil

¹/₂ cup fresh lemon juice (about 2 lemons)

1 envelope Knorr Leek Soup Mix

1 teaspoon dried fines herbes (see page 3)

1 teaspoon freshly ground black pepper

6 boneless, skinless chicken breast halves, cut into 1-inch chunks

1. Combine the oil, lemon juice, soup mix, dried fines herbes, and pepper in a resealable plastic bag or large mixing bowl, stirring to blend. Add the chicken to the marinade, stirring it to coat evenly, and marinate it in the refrigerator, covered with plastic wrap, for at least 2 hours.

2. Preheat the grill or broiler. Thread 4 to 5 pieces of chicken on each skewer and place the skewers on the grill or under the broiler. Cook the chicken until it is no longer pink in the middle when slashed with a knife at the thickest point, 4 to 5 minutes on each side.

SPICY COCONUT PEANUT DIPPING SAUCE: For a more exotic taste, substitute unsweetened coconut milk for the chicken broth and add 2 tablespoons chopped fresh cilantro leaves to the finished sauce just before serving.

SERVES 6

Skewers of chicken, fragrant with herbs and glistening with lemon juice, will be the stars of your summer dinner. Marinate the chicken for up to 12 hours before cooking, and make separate skewers using your favorite vegetables to serve alongside. Since the vegetables will cook faster than the chicken, cook them first and keep them warm or serve at room temperature. If using bamboo skewers, be sure to soak them in water for 30 minutes before grilling to keep them from burning.

Poultry

Souped-Up Turkey Cutlets

My son, Ryan, loves these easy cutlets, and I can never seem to make enough of them, because they are just as good when they are cold! Make sure to let the turkey rest for at least an hour in the refrigerator after breading; otherwise the breading will come off in the pan.

2 large eggs

1 teaspoon salt

½ teaspoon freshly ground black pepper

3 cups dry breadcrumbs

1 envelope Knorr Leek Soup Mix mixed with 1 teaspoon dried fines herbes (see page 3), Lipton Savory Herb with Garlic Soup Mix, or Lipton Golden Onion Soup Mix

½ cup freshly grated Parmesan cheese

8 turkey cutlets, pounded thin

¼ cup (½ stick) butter

¼ cup olive oil

Basic Marinara Sauce (page 470) or Quick Creamy Chicken Sauce (recipe follows)

1. In a large, shallow bowl, beat the eggs and season them with the salt and pepper.

2. On a large flat plate, mix together the breadcrumbs, soup mix, and cheese.

3. Dip each turkey cutlet into the egg mixture, letting the excess drip off, and then dredge in the crumb mixture, making sure each cutlet is completely coated. Place the cutlets on a plate and refrigerate them, covered with plastic wrap, for at least 1 hour before you cook them.

4. In a 10- to 12-inch skillet, melt the butter in the oil over medium-high heat. When the foam subsides, add the turkey cutlets, being careful not to crowd them. Brown the cutlets on each side and remove them to paper towels to drain. Keep the turkey cutlets warm in a low oven until all the cutlets are cooked.

5. Serve the turkey cutlets with the sauce of your choice.

QUICK CREAMY CHICKEN SAUCE

1 can Campbell's Condensed Cream of Chicken Soup

2 teaspoons dry sherry

½ cup milk

¼ cup chopped fresh chives

½ cup freshly grated Parmesan cheese

Heat the soup, sherry, milk, chives, and Parmesan together in a medium saucepan, stirring, until the cheese melts. Keeps refrigerated for 3 to 4 days.

We like our cutlets with a green salad, but if you want to serve them with a sauce, this one makes an easy and elegant accompaniment. This sauce is great served over rice, pasta, vegetables, fried chicken, or sautéed chicken breasts.

Hot Browns

This very old recipe is actually an open-faced sandwich of sliced turkey, tomato, and bacon covered with a delectable sauce and then run under the broiler. It makes a great luncheon dish or a light supper to serve with soup or salad.

8 English muffin halves or 8 slices good-quality white bread, toasted

$1/2$ pound thinly sliced turkey breast

8 slices ripe tomato

12 strips bacon, cooked until crisp and drained on paper towels

2 tablespoons butter

$1/4$ cup chopped onion

1 can Campbell's Condensed Cream of Chicken Soup

1 tablespoon cream sherry

Pinch of cayenne pepper

Pinch of freshly grated nutmeg

1 cup grated sharp cheddar cheese

$1/4$ cup freshly grated Parmesan cheese

1. Preheat the broiler.

2. Place the muffin halves on a baking sheet. Lay slices of turkey breast over each English muffin or slice of bread, and then top with a tomato slice and strip of bacon.

3. In a 2-quart saucepan, melt the butter over medium heat and cook the onion, stirring, until it is softened, 3 to 4 minutes. Add the soup, sherry, cayenne, nutmeg, and cheddar and bring the sauce to a boil. Remove the sauce from the heat and spoon some of it over each sandwich.

4. Sprinkle each sandwich with some of the Parmesan and run the pan of sandwiches under the broiler until the tops are golden brown.

Southwestern Turkey Meat Loaf

SERVES 6 TO 8

2 pounds ground turkey

1 envelope Lipton Golden Onion Soup Mix

2 cups crushed tortilla chips (not flavored)

1 cup corn kernels, either cut fresh from the cob or frozen (and defrosted)

1½ cups medium-hot salsa

1 large egg

½ cup sour cream, plus more for garnish

2 tablespoons chopped fresh cilantro leaves

1 medium ripe Hass avocado, peeled, pitted, and sliced, for garnish

This meat loaf is made with ground turkey and Southwestern flavors. It's terrific with a side of Spanish rice or Gazpacho Salad (page 70).

1. Preheat the oven to 350 degrees. Coat a 9-inch baking dish with nonstick cooking spray.

2. In a large mixing bowl, combine the turkey, soup mix, tortilla chips, corn, ½ cup of the salsa, the egg, sour cream, and cilantro, stirring until the mixture is well combined. Shape the turkey mixture into an 8-by-4-inch loaf.

3. Transfer the loaf to the prepared dish. Cover the dish with the remaining 1 cup salsa and bake the meat loaf until the internal temperature registers 180 on an instant-read thermometer, 45 minutes to 1 hour.

4. Let the loaf rest for 10 minutes, and then drain the excess fat from the pan before slicing. Turn the meat loaf out of the pan, slice, and serve the meat loaf garnished with the sliced avocado and sour cream.

Turkey Meat Loaf with Spicy Cranberry Sauce

This meat loaf tastes almost like Thanksgiving dinner, with herbed stuffing as one of the ingredients, and a sweet and spicy cranberry sauce to glaze it. Leftover meat loaf makes great sandwiches the next day.

2 tablespoons butter

1/2 cup chopped onion

1/2 cup chopped celery

2 pounds ground turkey

2 large eggs

2 cups herbed stuffing cubes or crumbs

1 envelope Lipton Golden Onion Soup Mix

1/2 cup Spicy Cranberry Sauce (recipe follows)

1. Preheat the oven to 350 degrees. Coat a 9-by-5-inch loaf pan with nonstick cooking spray.

2. In a small sauté pan over medium heat, melt the butter, add the onion and celery, and cook, stirring, until the vegetables are softened, 4 to 5 minutes. Let the vegetables cool and set them aside.

3. In a large mixing bowl, combine the turkey, eggs, stuffing cubes or crumbs, soup mix, and onion and celery mixture.

4. Pack the mixture into the prepared loaf pan. Pour 1/2 cup Spicy Cranberry Sauce over the meat loaf and bake the meat loaf until it is browned, 50 to 60 minutes. Spoon some of the cranberry sauce over the meat loaf every 15 minutes.

5. Remove the meat loaf from the oven, let it rest for 5 minutes, and drain off excess fat from the pan. Turn the loaf out of the pan, and slice. Serve with additional cranberry sauce.

SPICY CRANBERRY SAUCE

One 10-ounce bag fresh cranberries, rinsed and picked over
    for stems

1½ cups sugar

1 cup chopped onion

1 cup apple juice

1 envelope Lipton Savory Herb with Garlic Soup Mix

In a medium saucepan, combine the cranberries, sugar, onion,
apple juice, and soup mix and bring to a boil. Reduce the heat to a
simmer and cook the sauce until it is thickened, about 10 minutes.

Pesto Turkey Rolls

These dinner rolls are filled with basil and garlic–flavored cheese, and then covered with a sun-dried tomato cream sauce.

8 turkey cutlets, pounded thin

1 teaspoon salt

$1/2$ teaspoon freshly ground black pepper

One 8-ounce package cream cheese, softened

1 envelope Lipton Savory Herb with Garlic Soup Mix

$1/2$ cup packed fresh basil leaves, chopped

$1/4$ cup pine nuts

$1/2$ cup freshly grated Parmesan cheese

3 tablespoons butter

2 tablespoons olive oil

$1/2$ cup oil-packed sun-dried tomatoes, drained and finely chopped

2 tablespoons chopped fresh basil leaves

$1^{1/2}$ cups heavy cream

1. Sprinkle the turkey cutlets with the salt and pepper.

2. In a medium mixing bowl, cream together the cream cheese, soup mix, $1/4$ cup of the basil, the pine nuts, and $1/4$ cup of the Parmesan. Place 2 tablespoons of the cheese mixture down the center of each cutlet, from end to end, and roll up the cutlet, tucking in the sides, to form a neat roll. (At this point you can refrigerate the cutlets, covered, until you are ready to proceed.)

3. Melt the butter in the oil in a 12-inch sauté pan over medium-high heat, add the turkey rolls, and cook until the turkey is white on all sides, about 3 minutes on each side. Remove the turkey from the pan.

4. Add the tomatoes, 2 tablespoons basil, and the heavy cream to the pan and bring the sauce to a boil, stirring up any browned bits that are on the bottom. Add the remaining $1/4$ cup

Parmesan, reduce the heat to medium-low, and return the turkey rolls to the pan. Turn the rolls in the sauce, simmering them for 5 minutes before serving.

Turkey Stuffing Bake

¼ cup (½ stick) butter

1 cup chopped onion

1 cup chopped celery

1 teaspoon dried thyme

½ teaspoon dried sage

5 cups herb-seasoned stuffing (regular or cornbread)

2 cups 1-inch cubes cooked turkey or chicken

2 cans Campbell's Condensed Cream of Chicken Soup

1 cup chicken broth

Do-Ahead Gravy (page 477)

1. Preheat the oven to 350 degrees. Coat a 3-quart casserole dish with nonstick cooking spray.

2. In a 10-inch skillet over medium heat, melt the butter and cook the onion, celery, thyme, and sage, stirring, until the vegetables are softened, 4 to 5 minutes.

3. Place the stuffing and turkey or chicken in a large mixing bowl. Add the chicken soup and broth to the vegetables in the skillet and stir until blended. Pour the vegetable mixture over the stuffing and turkey and stir until blended.

4. Transfer the stuffing to the prepared dish and bake it until it is golden brown, 35 to 45 minutes. Serve with gravy.

A great way to use up leftovers, this stuffing bake has been around for a very long time. You can substitute cooked chicken for the turkey if you would like.

FRUITED TURKEY STUFFING BAKE:
Add 1 cup chopped dried apricots and ½ cup dried cranberries to the stuffing mixture and proceed as directed.

Turkey Cassoulet

Slow Cooker Savvy

Brown the turkey and sausage, and add to the slow cooker with the remaining ingredients. Cook on high for six hours.

1/4 cup olive oil

3 pounds turkey tenderloins, tendons removed and cut into 1-inch chunks

1 teaspoon salt

1 1/2 teaspoons freshly ground black pepper

1 1/2 pounds smoked sausage (kielbasa or andouille), sliced into 1/2-inch-thick rounds

2 large onions, chopped

6 cloves garlic, minced

1 cup red wine

One 14.5-ounce can diced tomatoes, with their juices

1 envelope Knorr Tomato Beef Soup Mix

1 envelope Knorr Leek Soup Mix

1 teaspoon dried fines herbes (see page 3)

4 cups water

4 cups cooked small white beans (either fresh or canned, drained and rinsed)

2 bay leaves

2 cups dry breadcrumbs

1/2 cup chopped fresh Italian parsley leaves

1/4 cup freshly grated Parmesan cheese

2 cloves garlic, minced

1. Heat 2 tablespoons of the oil in a 6-quart Dutch oven over medium-high heat and add the turkey, sprinkling it with the salt and 1/2 teaspoon of the pepper. Brown the turkey on both sides, 5 to 7 minutes, and then add the sausage and cook, stirring, until it begins to brown, an additional 5 minutes. Add the onions and 2/3 of the garlic and cook until they begin to soften, about 5 minutes. Add the wine and stir up any browned bits that have stuck to the bottom of the pan. Add the tomatoes, both soup mixes, and fines herbes and bring to a boil. Add the water, beans, bay leaves, and remaining 1 teaspoon black pepper, reduce the heat to low, and simmer for 1 hour.

2. Remove the bay leaves, taste the cassoulet, and adjust the seasoning. (At this point, you may refrigerate the cassoulet for up to 3 days or freeze it for 1 month. Bring the dish back to room temperature before proceeding.)

3. Preheat the broiler.

4. In a small mixing bowl, combine the breadcrumbs, parsley, Parmesan, the remaining garlic, and the remaining 2 tablespoons oil. Spread the crumb mixture over the top of the cassoulet and broil the cassoulet until the topping is golden brown.

Sombrero Tortilla Pie

Beefy Macaroni Bake

That's Italian Macaroni Bake

Beefy Macaroni Bake Olé

Onion Burgers

Garlic Herb Burgers

Red, White, and Blue Burgers

California Burgers

Stuffed Burgers Olé

Old-Fashioned Meat Loaf

Italian Meat Loaf

Lipton's Old-Fashioned Meat Loaf

Bistecca alla Nona

Seoul Food Beef Kabobs

Christmas Standing Prime Rib Roast

Boris Badinov Stroganoff

Campbell's Original Beef Stroganoff

Better Than Dinty Moore's Beef Stew

Beef Burgundy

Shepherd's Pie with Garlic Mashed Potatoes

Beef and Wild Mushroom Ragout

Vintner's Stew

Old-Fashioned Pot Roast of Beef with Roasted Root Vegetables

Mamma Mia's Pot Roast

Pepper Steak

Amazing Flank Steak

Mom's Barbecue Beef Brisket

South of the Border Carne Asada

Alpine Veal Stew with Mushrooms

Butterflied Grilled Leg of Lamb

When Irish Eyes Are Smiling Stew

Slow Cooker Lamb

Gyros

Lamb and Eggplant Lasagne

Wokking on the Wild Side Pork Noodles

Pork and Peanut Stir-Fry

Wild Cranberry Stuffed Pork Loin

Smothered Pork Chops

Lip-Smacking Golden Onion Pork Ribs

Ragin' Cajun Red Beans and Rice

Ballpark Sausage and Peppers

Meat

FOR YEARS, MY MOTHER WOULD MAKE us a delicious pot roast that had the most magnificent gravy I had ever tasted. As a child growing up, I never paid attention to the preparation, but when I wanted to impress my husband-to-be, I wanted to make the pot roast. When she showed me that she used Lipton Onion Soup Mix as the key ingredient for the gravy, I was stunned. This was a woman who wouldn't buy us store-bought bread, because she made her own, who wouldn't let us eat a canned soup—she would make it herself—but when it came to the pot roast, she used a mix and a lot of love!

Soup can mean the difference between a comforting dinner at home or fast food drive-through. Just a few ingredients and you can have dinner on the table in under one hour. With no complicated sauces to make, and no lengthy instructions to follow, these recipes will become your family's favorites for years to come.

Sombrero Tortilla Pie

SERVES 6 TO 8

This south of the border pie has something for everyone, with crunchy tortilla chips layered with meat and beans, then covered with cheese and baked. When it comes out of the oven, cold salad ingredients are layered on top to create a fiesta any night of the week.

Slow Cooker Savvy

Many of my students love their slow cookers, and your soup pantry and slow cooker are a match made in heaven. Long, slow simmering brings out the best in dry soup mixes and condensed soups. If you decide to prepare any of these recipes in a slow cooker, take the time to brown the meat first; it will give the sauce a rich flavor and eliminate the scum that forms on the sides of the slow cooker if you just throw things in.

1 pound lean ground beef

1 cup chopped onion

1 can Campbell's Condensed Fiesta Chili Beef Soup

One 15-ounce can refried beans

One 10-ounce bag tortilla chips (not flavored), crushed

2 cups shredded cheddar cheese (or ½ cheddar and ½ Monterey Jack)

2 cups sour cream

2 cups shredded lettuce

1 cup chopped fresh tomatoes

¼ cup chopped red onion

¼ cup sliced pickled jalapeños, drained

1 large ripe Hass avocado, peeled, pitted, diced, and tossed with 1 teaspoon fresh lemon juice

½ cup chopped fresh cilantro leaves

1. Preheat the oven to 350 degrees. Coat a 13-by-9-inch baking dish with nonstick cooking spray.

2. In a 10- to 12-inch skillet over high heat, brown the ground beef, draining off the fat as it accumulates in the pan. Add the onion and cook, stirring, until softened, about 3 to 4 minutes. Add the soup, stirring to combine. Set the mixture aside.

3. Spread the refried beans in the bottom of the prepared baking dish. Sprinkle with half of the crushed tortilla chips. Top with the beef mixture, layer with the remaining tortilla chips, and sprinkle with the grated cheese.

4. Bake the casserole until the cheese is bubbling, 20 to 30 minutes.

5. Remove the casserole from the oven and layer over the top, in order, the sour cream, lettuce, tomato, red onion, jalapeños, avocado, and cilantro, tucking more tortilla chips in around the sides of the casserole dish.

VARIATION: If you have non-bean eaters in your house, sauté the beef and onion, omit the Fiesta Chili Beef Soup, and substitute ½ can Fiesta Nacho Cheese Sauce. Layer the meat mixture in the pan, omitting the refried beans, and pour the remaining sauce over the top of the casserole, cutting the amount of grated cheese to 1 cup.

Beefy Macaroni Bake

1 pound lean ground beef

1 cup chopped onion

1 can Campbell's Condensed Tomato Soup

¼ cup water

1 tablespoons Worcestershire sauce

½ cup shredded mild cheddar cheese

2 cups cooked macaroni (rotelle or elbows work well)

SERVES 6

This dish is the older cousin to what is now called Hamburger Helper. Warm and filling, the dish comes together in an instant, and there is only one pot to wash. Make sure to try the variations that follow.

1. In a medium skillet over high heat, cook the beef until it no longer has any pink color. Pour off any fat, add the onion, and cook, stirring, until it is softened, 3 to 4 minutes.

2. Add the soup, water, Worcestershire, cheese, and macaroni, stir well to combine, reduce the heat to medium-low, and cook just until the cheese is melted.

Meat

That's Italian Macaroni Bake

1 pound lean ground beef

1 cup chopped onion

One 14.5-ounce can diced tomatoes, drained

1 envelope Knorr Tomato with Basil Soup Mix

1/2 cup water

1 teaspoon chopped fresh oregano leaves or 1/2 teaspoon dried

3 cups cooked macaroni (rotelle or elbows work well)

2 cups shredded mozzarella cheese

1. Preheat the broiler for 10 minutes.

2. In an ovenproof sauté pan over high heat, cook the ground beef until it is no longer pink in color. Drain off any fat, add the onion, and cook, stirring, until it is softened, 3 to 4 minutes.

3. Stir in the tomatoes, soup mix, water, and oregano, reduce the heat to medium-low, and simmer for 5 minutes. Add the macaroni and stir until blended.

4. Sprinkle the mozzarella over the top and run the pan under the broiler until the cheese melts, 4 to 5 minutes.

Beefy Macaroni Bake Olé

1 pound lean ground beef

1 cup chopped onion

½ cup canned roasted green chiles, drained, seeded, and chopped

½ teaspoon ground cumin

One 14.5-ounce can diced tomatoes, drained

1 can Campbell's Condensed cheddar Cheese Soup

¼ cup milk

4 shakes Tabasco sauce

2 cups cooked macaroni (rotelle or elbows work well)

1 cup grated mild cheddar or Monterey Jack cheese

1 cup sour cream for garnish

¼ cup chopped fresh cilantro leaves for garnish

1. In a 10- or 12-inch skillet over high heat, cook the ground beef until it is no longer pink. Drain off any fat, add the onion, chiles, and cumin and cook, stirring, until the onion softens, 3 to 4 minutes.

2. Add the tomatoes and cook for another 2 minutes. Add the soup, milk, and Tabasco, and stir until the mixture is well blended. Add the macaroni, then the cheese, and heat until the cheese is melted.

3. Serve immediately, garnished with the sour cream and cilantro.

TURKEY MACARONI SKILLET OLÉ: Substitute ground turkey for the ground beef and proceed as directed.

BEEFY SKILLET DIP OLÉ: For a great party dip, omit the macaroni and serve the mixture as a dip with tortilla chips.

Meat

Onion Burgers

What dish defines the summer grilling season better than succulent hamburgers right off the grill served with potato salad and iced cold lemonade? This recipe comes straight from the back of the Lipton Onion Soup Mix box, but I've included some great variations.

GOLDEN ONION BURGERS: Substitute Lipton Golden Onion Soup Mix.

ONION MUSHROOM BURGERS: Substitute Lipton Onion-Mushroom Soup Mix.

GARLIC HERB BURGERS: Substitute Lipton Savory Herb with Garlic Soup Mix.

FULL OF VEGGIE FLAVOR BURGERS: Substitute Knorr Vegetable Soup Mix.

2 pounds ground chuck

1 envelope Lipton Onion Soup Mix

½ cup water

1. Preheat the grill or broiler for 10 minutes.

2. Combine the chuck, soup mix, and water in a large mixing bowl. Shape the hamburger into 8 patties.

3. Grill or broil the patties for 4 to 5 minutes on each side, until they reach the desired degree of doneness. Serve immediately on buns.

The Fixings

Burgers may seem a little too simple for some gatherings, but they can be dressed up by offering a condiment bar featuring ingredients such as

- Sun-dried Tomato Mayonnaise (page 468)
- sliced avocado sprinkled with lemon to prevent discoloration
- slices of vine-ripened tomato
- thinly sliced red onion or caramelized sautéed onions
- grilled eggplant slices
- pickles, olives, and/or Caponata (page 46)
- ketchup, mustard, and fresh pickle relish
- sliced pickled jalapeños
- roasted red peppers
- crumbled blue cheese and assorted sliced cheeses
- sautéed mushrooms

STUFFED BURGERS (FOUR WAYS)

A little surprise will greet you when you bite into these succulent burgers hot off the grill. You can make each recipe ahead of time and refrigerate the burgers for 24 hours or freeze them, tightly wrapped, for up to one month.

Garlic Herb Burgers

2 pounds lean ground beef

1 envelope Lipton Savory Herb with Garlic Soup Mix

One 8-ounce package cream cheese, softened

¼ cup chopped green onion

1. Place the ground beef in a large mixing bowl, add 1 tablespoon of the soup mix, and mix it in well. Shape the hamburger into twelve ½-inch-thick patties.

2. In a medium mixing bowl, beat together the cream cheese, remaining soup mix, and the green onions.

3. Place 1 tablespoon of the cream cheese filling on a patty, and then cover with another patty, sealing the edges together. Refrigerate the hamburgers for at least 1 hour before cooking.

SERVES 6

Meat

Red, White, and Blue Burgers

2 pounds lean ground beef

1 envelope Lipton Savory Herb with Garlic Soup Mix

1/4 cup chopped red onion

1/2 cup crumbled blue cheese

One 3-ounce package cream cheese, softened

1. Place the ground beef in a large mixing bowl, add 1 tablespoon of the soup mix, and mix it in well. Shape the hamburger into twelve 1/2-inch-thick patties. Set the patties aside while you make the filling.

2. In a medium mixing bowl, beat together the remaining soup mix, the onion, blue cheese, and cream cheese.

3. Place 1 tablespoon of the filling on a patty, and then cover with another patty, sealing the edges together. Refrigerate the hamburger patties for at least 1 hour before cooking.

California Burgers

2 pounds lean ground beef

One 8-ounce package cream cheese, softened

1 envelope Lipton Onion Soup Mix

1. Shape the ground beef into twelve ½-inch-thick patties.

2. In a medium mixing bowl, cream the cream cheese and soup mix together until smooth.

3. Place 1 tablespoon of the cream cheese mixture on top of a patty and cover the patty with a second one, sealing the edges together. Refrigerate the hamburger patties for at least 1 hour before cooking.

Stuffed Burgers Olé

2 pounds lean ground beef

1 envelope Lipton Fiesta Herb with Red Pepper Soup Mix

One 8-ounce package cream cheese, softened

1. Shape the ground beef into twelve ½-inch-thick patties.

2. In a medium mixing bowl, beat together the soup mix and cream cheese until smooth.

3. Place 1 tablespoon of the cream cheese mixture on a patty and top that patty with another patty, sealing the edges together. Refrigerate the hamburger patties for at least 1 hour before cooking.

Grilling Burgers

Preheat a gas grill for ten minutes or a charcoal grill until the briquets form a white ash. Grill the burgers for three to four minutes on each side if you like your burgers medium.

Pan-Frying Burgers

Preheat a nonstick skillet over high heat and pan-fry the burgers for three to four minutes on each side, or until they reach the desired degree of doneness. If the stuffed burgers are sealed properly, you shouldn't get any leakage, but if the burgers do leak, just pour the filling over the burger when it's served.

Meat

SERVES 6 TO 8

This meat loaf comes from the Campbell's company with a little addition of my own. The dry onion soup mix and condensed tomato soup make a great combination.

MOM'S MEAT LOAF (THREE WAYS)

Meat loaf is one of those foods from childhood that makes your mouth water and your tummy smile. Being raised in an Italian-Irish household, my mom made a meat loaf that tasted like meatballs and my dad (the Irishman) would cover it with ketchup! After living this childhood drama, it's no wonder I can't make up my mind which meat loaf is my favorite. What I do know is that all of these recipes are stellar meals for your family, and you can put them together and forget about them once they are in the oven.

In all these recipes, you may substitute ground turkey for beef or pork if desired.

Old-Fashioned Meat Loaf

1 can Campbell's Condensed Tomato Soup

2 pounds lean ground beef

1 envelope Lipton Onion Soup Mix

1/2 cup dry breadcrumbs

1 large egg

1/4 cup chopped fresh Italian parsley leaves

2 teaspoons fresh thyme leaves or 1 teaspoon dried

1/4 cup water

1 small onion, thinly sliced and separated into rings

3 strips bacon

1. Preheat the oven to 350 degrees. Coat a 9-inch baking dish with nonstick cooking spray.

2. In a large mixing bowl, combine 1/2 cup of the tomato soup, the ground beef, soup mix, breadcrumbs, egg, parsley, and thyme. Stir the mixture together and form it into an 8-by-4-inch loaf. Transfer the meat loaf to the prepared dish.

3. Combine the remaining tomato soup with the water and pour the mixture over the top of the meat loaf. Arrange the onion rings over the loaf and the bacon strips on top of the onions. Bake the meat loaf until the internal temperature on a instant-read thermometer reaches 180 degrees, about 1 hour and 10 minutes, basting with the sauce as the meat loaf cooks.

4. Let the meat loaf rest for 10 minutes, drain the excess fat from the pan, and slice.

Italian Meat Loaf

3 slices good Italian or French bread, crusts removed and bread torn into pieces (should measure 1½ cups)

½ cup milk

2 pounds lean ground beef

2 large eggs

½ cup freshly grated Parmesan cheese

1 envelope Lipton Savory Herb with Garlic Soup Mix

4 cups Basic Marinara (page 470)

1. Preheat the oven to 350 degrees. Coat a 9-inch baking dish with nonstick cooking spray.

2. Place the bread in a small mixing bowl and pour the milk over it, pressing down to moisten the bread. Set the bread and milk aside.

3. In a large mixing bowl, combine the ground beef, eggs, Parmesan, and soup mix.

4. Squeeze moisture out of the bread and add it to the beef mixture. Shape the ground beef mixture into an 8-by-4-inch loaf. Transfer the meat loaf to the prepared dish.

SERVES 6 TO 8

Reminiscent of my mom's spicy meatball meat loaf, this one is a lot easier to make, and the results are terrific.

Meat

5. Cover the loaf with 1 cup of the marinara and bake it until the internal temperature registers 180 degrees on an instant-read thermometer, about 1 hour and 10 minutes, basting the meat loaf with the sauce occasionally.

6. Let the meat loaf rest for 10 minutes, drain the excess fat from the pan, and slice. Serve with additional marinara.

SERVES 6 TO 8

This delicious loaf is a combination of recipes, but the constant is the onion soup mix, which gives it a robust flavor.

Lipton's Old-Fashioned Meat Loaf

2 pounds lean ground beef

1 envelope Lipton Onion Soup Mix

2 large eggs

1½ cups fresh breadcrumbs

¾ cup water

1 cup ketchup

1. Preheat the oven to 350 degrees. Coat a 9-by-5-inch loaf pan with nonstick cooking spray.

2. Place the ground beef in a large mixing bowl. Add the soup mix, eggs, breadcrumbs, ½ cup of the water, and ½ cup of the ketchup. Blend the mixture well and pack it into the prepared loaf pan.

3. Combine ¼ cup water and the remaining ½ cup ketchup, spreading the mixture over the top of the loaf. Bake the meat loaf until the internal temperature registers 180 on an instant-read thermometer, 45 minutes to 1 hour.

4. Let the meat loaf rest for 10 minutes, drain off the excess fat from the pan, and slice.

Bistecca alla Nona

½ cup olive oil

1 envelope Lipton Savory Herb with Garlic Soup Mix

One 2-pound top sirloin steak, about 1 inch thick

1. Preheat the grill or broiler for 10 minutes.

2. In a dish large enough to hold the steak, combine the oil and soup mix. Turn the steak in the mixture so that it is well coated. Marinate the steak at room temperature for 10 to 15 minutes.

3. Grill the steak for about 5 minutes on each side (for rare), or cook it to the desired degree of doneness.

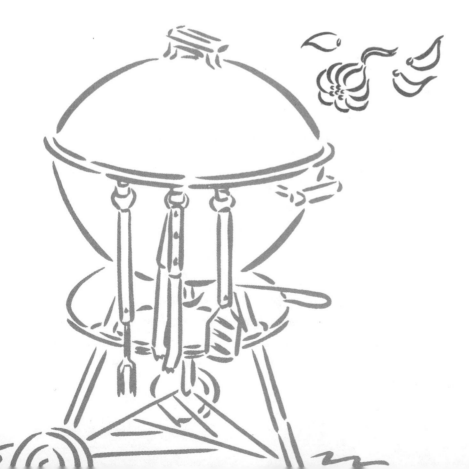

SERVES 6

Most of the time, the simple things in life are the best, and this grilled sirloin is no exception. Reminiscent of steaks that my grandmother would cook when we went on picnics with other Italian families, this steak is coated with olive oil and seasonings, and then grilled rare over hot coals. This recipe is a great example of how your soup pantry can help to make a four-star entrée in no time, with fewer than four ingredients.

Souper Smart

If you have trouble telling whether your steak is cooked to the desired degree of doneness, cut a small slit into the thickest part of the meat, and that will tell you if you are on target. Most chefs can tell by touching the meat, but home cooks may have a harder time determining doneness, so feel free to slash and peek!

Meat

Seoul Food Beef Kabobs

The national dish of Korea, *bul goki*, is thinly sliced marinated beef cooked on a grill. These kabobs use the same marinade, but the beef is threaded on skewers with vegetables for a great party dish. If you are using bamboo skewers, soak them in water for 30 minutes.

MARINADE

2 tablespoons vegetable oil

¼ cup toasted sesame oil

⅔ cup soy sauce

Flavor packet from 1 package beef flavor ramen noodles (reserve the noodles for another use)

4 cloves garlic, minced

4 green onions, chopped

¼ cup firmly packed light brown sugar

¼ cup mirin (rice wine)

¼ cup sesame seeds

KABOBS

2 pounds beef sirloin, trimmed of fat and cut into 1-inch cubes

1 pound mushrooms

1 large red onion, cut into quarters

2 medium zucchini, ends trimmed, and cut into 1-inch chunks

12 cherry tomatoes, stemmed

Vegetable oil for brushing

1. In a medium glass mixing bowl, whisk together the marinade ingredients.

2. Pour the marinade into a large resealable plastic bag and add the beef, tossing to coat it well. Marinate the meat in the refrigerator, covered, for at least 4 hours and for up to 12 hours, turning it occasionally.

3. Preheat the grill or broiler for 10 minutes.

4. Brush the vegetables with vegetable oil. Remove the beef from the marinade and thread it onto the skewers, alternating the beef with the vegetables. Grill or broil the kabobs for 3 to 4 minutes on each side, to the desired degree of doneness. Serve immediately.

Christmas Standing Prime Rib Roast

4 cloves garlic, minced

¼ cup olive oil

1 envelope Lipton Savory Herb with Garlic Soup Mix

1 teaspoon freshly ground black pepper

One 6-pound 2- or 3-rib roast, small end, bones cut and the roast tied

1. Preheat the oven to 425 degrees.

2. In a small mixing bowl, combine the garlic, oil, soup mix, and pepper. Rub the flavored oil all over the roast and pour a little of the flavored oil between the ribs and the meat.

3. Place the roast, fat side up, in a roasting pan and roast it for 15 minutes.

4. Reduce the oven temperature to 325 degrees. Roast the meat until a meat thermometer registers 125 to 130 degrees for medium rare, about 1 hour.

5. Remove the roast from the oven, allow it to rest for 10 minutes, covered with a sheet of aluminum foil. Drain any fat from the roasting pan. Carve the roast into slices and serve them with the pan juices.

SERVES 8

There is nothing more beautiful than a standing rib roast served on a special occasion. Have your butcher remove the roast from the ribs and then tie the whole thing together—the ribs will come right off and you will be left with a solid piece of meat to carve.

VARIATIONS: Try substituting Lipton Beefy Onion, Golden Onion, or Garlic Mushroom Soup Mix.

QUICK AU JUS FOR ROAST BEEF: Open a can of Campbell's Condensed Beef Broth, pour it into a saucepan, adding ½ cup water and 1 teaspoon dried thyme, and bring to a boil. If there are any pan juices, stir them in and serve.

Roasting Times for Prime Rib

For a 6-pound roast, 13 minutes per pound for rare; 16 minutes per pound for medium rare; 18 to 20 minutes per pound for medium.

Meat

Boris Badinov Stroganoff

This dish was all the rage in the 1950s during the cold war, when home cooks thought that sour cream, fresh mushrooms, and Russian foods were pretty exotic. Good and bad versions of this classic abound, but this one is our favorite. I've also included the original version from the *Campbell's Soup Cookbook* for you to try; it's great prepared in a slow cooker.

Souper Smart

Stroganoff can also be made with meatballs if you are looking to stretch your food dollar. Use the meat mixture for Old-Fashioned Meat Loaf (page 376), shape the meat into 1-inch balls, brown them in oil, add the meatballs to the stroganoff sauce without the sour cream, and cook them in the sauce for 45 minutes to one hour. Stir in the sour cream at the end of the cooking time.

1 envelope Lipton Beefy Onion Soup Mix

1 cup boiling water

1/4 cup (1/2 stick) butter

1/2 cup finely chopped shallots

1 pound mushrooms, sliced

1 tablespoon Worcestershire sauce

1 pound filet mignon, cut into 2-inch-long strips 1/2 inch wide

1/2 teaspoon salt

1/4 teaspoon freshly ground black pepper

3/4 cup sour cream

1 tablespoon chopped fresh dill

Hot cooked egg noodles

1. Place the soup mix in a 4-cup measure and pour the boiling water over it. Let the soup stand for 5 minutes, stirring occasionally.

2. In a 10- to 12-inch skillet, melt 2 tablespoons of the butter over medium-high heat, add the shallots, and cook, stirring, until they are softened, about 2 minutes. Add the mushrooms and cook, stirring, until they are golden, about 6 minutes. Stir in the Worcestershire, remove the vegetables from the skillet, and keep them covered. Wipe out the skillet.

3. Sprinkle the meat with the salt and pepper, and then melt the remaining 2 tablespoons butter in the skillet. Add the meat a few pieces at a time and cook it until it is browned on all sides.

4. Deglaze the pan with the dissolved soup mixture, add the mushrooms and shallots, and bring to a boil.

5. Remove the pan from the heat and whisk in the sour cream. Keep the stroganoff warm over low heat and stir in the chopped dill. Serve over egg noodles.

Campbell's Original Beef Stroganoff

1 pound round steak, cut into thin strips

$\frac{1}{2}$ cup chopped onion

2 tablespoons butter or margarine

1 can Campbell's Condensed Cream of Mushroom Soup

$\frac{1}{4}$ cup water

$\frac{1}{2}$ cup sour cream

$\frac{1}{2}$ teaspoon paprika

2 cups cooked noodles

Brown steak and onion in butter. Stir in soup, water, sour cream, and paprika. Cover; cook over low heat 45 minutes or until meat is tender. Stir often. Serve over noodles.

SERVES 4

Filet mignon can be very expensive, so the Campbell's folks had a great idea for a cheaper version of this classic dish using round steak. This is the original recipe, but we liked browning the meat and onion and then putting everything in the slow cooker pot and cooking the stroganoff on low for four hours.

SERVES 6 TO 8

Better Than Dinty Moore's Beef Stew

Growing up in New England, there was something about coming home on a cold afternoon and smelling this hearty, homey beef stew on the stove. The vegetables would absorb the flavors of the meat and sauce, so that when the stew was served, everything had a rich, beefy flavor. Even though there were potatoes in the stew, my mom would serve this with buttered noodles—just one more carbohydrate to fill us up!

ONION BEEF STEW:
Substitute Lipton Onion Soup Mix.

MUSHROOM BEEF STEW:
Substitute Lipton Beefy Mushroom Soup Mix.

GARLIC BEEF STEW:
Substitute Lipton Savory Herb with Garlic Soup Mix.

1/2 cup all-purpose flour

1 teaspoon salt

1/2 teaspoon freshly ground black pepper

2 1/2 pounds beef stew meat, trimmed of fat and cut into 1-inch chunks

2 tablespoons vegetable oil

2 envelopes Lipton Beefy Onion Soup Mix

One 14.5-ounce can chopped tomatoes, with their juices

1 teaspoon dried thyme

1 bay leaf

6 medium red potatoes (about 2 pounds), quartered

6 medium carrots, cut into 1-inch pieces

6 ounces pearl onions (about 12), peeled (page 387)

2 tablespoons butter (optional)

2 tablespoons all-purpose flour (optional)

2 cups green beans cut into 1-inch pieces

1 cup frozen corn kernels, defrosted

1. In a resealable plastic bag or shallow dish, mix together the flour, salt, and pepper. Toss the beef in the mixture until it is coated, tapping off any excess.

2. Heat the oil in a 5-quart Dutch oven over high heat and add the beef a few cubes at a time, browning the beef on all sides.

3. Add the soup mix, tomatoes, thyme, bay leaf, and 3 cups water and bring the stew to a boil, scraping the bottom of the pan to pick up any browned bits.

The Soup Mix Gourmet

384

4. Add the potatoes, carrots, and onions, reduce the heat to low, and simmer the stew until the meat is tender, 2 to 3 hours. Skim off any fat that may have accumulated on the surface of the stew.

5. If the stew is not thick enough, make a paste of the butter and flour and whisk that into the stew, stirring until the stew thickens.

6. Add the green beans and corn and simmer the stew for another 15 minutes. Serve immediately.

Slow Cooker Savvy

Brown the meat, transfer it to the slow cooker along with the remaining ingredients, and cook the stew on high for six hours.

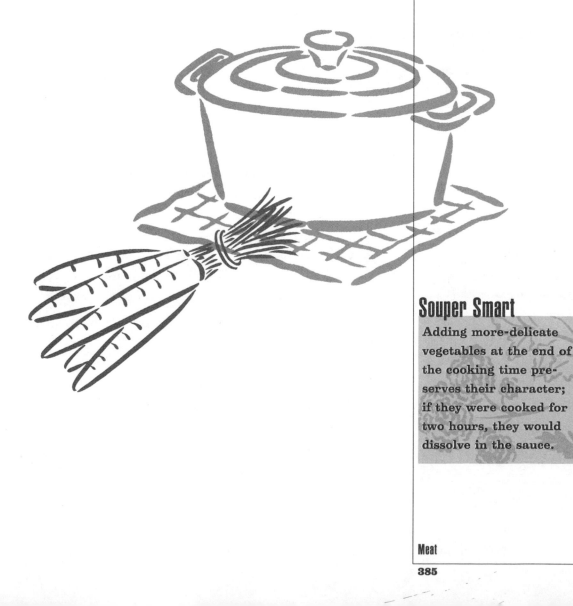

Souper Smart

Adding more-delicate vegetables at the end of the cooking time preserves their character; if they were cooked for two hours, they would dissolve in the sauce.

Beef Burgundy

This French comfort food features chunks of meat that are slowly simmered with wine and beef broth. Then the stew is finished with bacon, caramelized onions, and mushrooms. A perfect do-ahead entrée, the stew can be made two days ahead of time and refrigerated, or frozen for up to one month. I like to serve this dish with mashed potatoes flavored with Boursin cheese.

Souper Smart

To prepare this dish ahead of time, sauté the onions and mushrooms up to two days ahead of time, make the stew two days ahead of time, or freeze the cooked stew. I don't recommend freezing the onion-mushroom mixture because the mushrooms lose some of their character in the freezing process.

4 strips bacon, cut into 1-inch pieces

2 tablespoons olive oil

3 pounds beef chuck, trimmed of fat and cut into 1-inch pieces

1 teaspoon salt

1½ teaspoons freshly ground black pepper

1 large onion, chopped

One 14.5-ounce can chopped tomatoes, with their juices

2 envelopes Lipton Beefy Onion Soup Mix

2 cups Burgundy wine

1 bay leaf

1 teaspoon dried thyme

½ cup (1 stick) butter

24 small pearl onions, peeled (see page 387)

1 tablespoon sugar

1½ pounds mushrooms, cut in half

3 tablespoons butter, softened and creamed with 3 tablespoons all-purpose flour

1. Fry the bacon in a 5-quart Dutch oven over medium-high heat, stirring, until it is crisp. Remove the bacon from the pan with a slotted spoon and let it drain on paper towels.

2. Add the oil to the pan and brown the beef on all sides, seasoning it with the salt and pepper. Add the chopped onions and cook, stirring, for 3 minutes. Add the tomatoes, soup mix, wine, bay leaf, thyme, and 1 cup water and bring to a boil. Cover, reduce the heat to low, and simmer the stew until the meat is tender, 2 to 3 hours.

3. While the stew is cooking, melt half the stick of butter over medium heat in a large sauté pan. Add the pearl onions, sprinkle them with the sugar, and cook them until they begin to turn a caramel color, about 20 minutes.

4. In another large sauté pan, melt the remaining half stick of butter over medium-high heat, add the mushrooms, and cook, stirring, until they are golden brown. Add the mushrooms to the onions and set aside until the stew is done.

5. At the end of the cooking time, remove any fat that may have accumulated on the surface of the stew. Taste the stew for seasoning, correct the seasoning, and remove the bay leaf. Whisk the butter and flour paste into the stew, bringing it to a boil. Stir the reserved bacon, onions, and mushrooms into the stew and serve.

Peeling Pearls

To peel pearl onions, place them in boiling water for one minute, drain off the water, allow the onions to cool, and cut off the root end of each onion; the onion should slip right out of its skin.

Slow Cooker Savvy

Brown the beef, transfer it to a slow cooker along with the chopped onions, tomatoes, soup mix, wine, bay leaf, thyme, and water, and cook on high for six hours. Pick up with steps 4 and 5 to finish the dish.

Shepherd's Pie with Garlic Mashed Potatoes

When I wrote my book *Pot Pies: Comfort Food Under Cover*, I tested more versions of this dish than I care to remember. I finally decided that I liked a savory beef stew made with chunks of beef, rather than ground beef, and that garlic mashed potatoes were far superior to plain mashed potatoes.

Souper Smart

If you would like to prepare the shepherd's pie in individual ramekins, pour ³/₄ cup stew into each ramekin and cover the meat with mashed potatoes. Bake for 12 to 17 minutes.

BEEF STEW

¹/₂ cup all-purpose flour

1 teaspoon salt

¹/₂ teaspoon freshly ground black pepper

2¹/₂ pounds beef stew meat, trimmed of fat and cut into 1-inch chunks

2 tablespoons olive oil

1 large onion, chopped

1 can Campbell's Condensed French Onion Soup

1 envelope Lipton Beefy Onion Soup Mix

1 cup water

1 teaspoon dried thyme

1 bay leaf

SLURRY (OPTIONAL)

2 tablespoons all-purpose flour

GARLIC MASHED POTATOES

6 medium russet potatoes peeled and cut into 2-inch chunks

3 cloves garlic, peeled

¹/₄ cup (¹/₂ stick) butter, plus 2 tablespoons butter, cut into bits

¹/₄ cup milk, as needed

1 teaspoon salt

¹/₂ teaspoon freshly ground black pepper

1. Combine the flour, salt, and pepper in a resealable plastic bag or shallow dish. Toss the beef in the flour, shaking off the excess.

2. Heat the oil in a 5-quart Dutch oven over high heat and brown the beef on all sides. Add the onion and cook, stirring, until it is softened, 3 to 4 minutes. Add the condensed soup, soup mix, and the water, scraping up any browned bits that may have stuck to the bottom of the pan. Add the thyme and bay leaf and simmer until the beef is tender, 1½ to 2 hours.

3. If you would like a thicker gravy, make a slurry of the flour and ¼ cup water and whisk the mixture into the stew, bringing it to a boil. (At this point, the stew can be refrigerated for up to 2 days or frozen for up to 6 weeks.)

4. Place the potatoes and garlic in a 4-quart saucepan with water to cover. Bring the pot to a boil, and let the water continue to boil until the potatoes are fork tender, 15 to 20 minutes. Drain the potatoes and garlic and return them both to the pan over low heat, allowing the potatoes to dry a bit. Mash the potatoes with the butter. If the potatoes are very stiff, thin them with some of the milk. (They should be pretty stiff so that they don't sink into the stew.) Season the potatoes with the salt and pepper.

5. Preheat the oven to 350 degrees.

6. Using two flat spatulas, flatten some of the potatoes to ½-inch thickness and slide them onto the top of the stew, starting on the sides. Fill in around the sides, then toward the middle. Once the stew is covered with mashed potatoes, dot the potatoes with the remaining 2 tablespoons butter and bake the casserole until the stew is bubbling and the potatoes begin to turn golden, 20 to 30 minutes.

Slow Cooker Savvy

Brown the beef, and add it to the slow cooker with the rest of the stew ingredients. Cook on high for six hours. Proceed from step 3.

More Souper Smarts

To prepare the mashed potatoes as a side dish rather than as a crust, use ½ cup milk when mashing them.

Beef and Wild Mushroom Ragout

This flavorful, hearty beef stew shows off the benefits of using dried soups in a long-simmering sauce. The soups help to flavor as well as thicken the sauce, and the flavor intensifies as the stew cooks. Try serving this over Garlic Herb Mashed Potatoes (page 233).

2 tablespoons olive oil

3 pounds beef round, trimmed of fat and cut into 1-inch chunks

1 teaspoon salt

$\frac{1}{2}$ teaspoon freshly ground black pepper

2 large onions, thinly sliced and separated into rings

1 pound crimini mushrooms, sliced

1 envelope Knorr Tomato Beef Soup Mix

1 envelope Lipton Beefy Onion Soup Mix

1 cup red wine (Merlot, Cabernet, or Chianti)

One 14.5-ounce can chopped tomatoes, with their juices

2 cups water

$1\frac{1}{2}$ teaspoons dried thyme

1 bay leaf

1. Heat the oil in a 5-quart Dutch oven. Dry the beef with paper towels and sprinkle it with salt and pepper. Add the beef to the pan, browning it on all sides.

2. Stir in the onions and cook, stirring, until they are softened, 3 to 4 minutes. Add the mushrooms and cook for another 3 minutes, stirring often. Add the soup mixes and stir to blend. Add the wine, stirring up any browned bits on the bottom of the pan, and cook for 2 to 3 minutes. Add the tomatoes, water, thyme, and bay leaf, and bring the ragout to a boil. Reduce the heat to low and simmer the stew, covered, stirring occasionally, until the meat is tender, 2 to 3 hours.

3. Taste the sauce adding additional salt and pepper if needed. Remove the bay leaf before serving. The stew can be made 2 days ahead of time and refrigerated, or it can also be frozen for up to 2 months.

Slow Cooker Savvy

This is an easy slow cooker meal, but I do recommend that you take the time to brown the meat and sauté the vegetables before transferring them to the slow cooker. Cook the stew on low for six to eight hours.

Vintner's Stew

2 tablespoons olive oil

2 pounds beef chuck, trimmed of fat and cut into 1-inch pieces

1 teaspoon salt

1/2 teaspoon freshly ground black pepper

6 ounces pearl onions (about 12), peeled (page 387)

1 cup red wine, preferably Merlot

1 envelope Lipton Onion Soup Mix

1 can Campbell's Condensed Golden Mushroom Soup

1 cup water

1 pound small new potatoes, cut in half

2 teaspoons dried rosemary

1 tablespoon butter

1 pound mushrooms

1. In a 5-quart Dutch oven or casserole dish, heat the oil over medium-high heat. Sprinkle the beef with the salt and pepper and brown the beef on all sides. Add the onions and cook, stirring, with the beef for another 3 minutes.

2. Deglaze the pan with the wine, scraping up any browned bits that may have stuck to the bottom of the pan. Add the soup mix, mushroom soup, water, potatoes, and rosemary. Bring the stew to a simmer, reduce the heat to low, cover, and simmer until the meat is tender, 2 to 3 hours.

3. Melt the butter in a large sauté pan over high heat, add the mushrooms, and cook, stirring, until they are golden brown. Add the mushrooms to the stew, simmer for another 15 minutes, and serve.

Meat

This is my mother's pot roast. Simple, straight-forward, with a gravy that is delicious, it is my definition of home cook-ing at its best. My hus-band proposed to me after I made this for him.

Old-Fashioned Pot Roast of Beef with Roasted Root Vegetables

2 tablespoons olive oil

One 4-pound top or bottom round roast, tied

2 cloves garlic, minced

1 envelope Lipton Beefy Onion Soup Mix

1 envelope Lipton Onion Soup Mix

2½ cups water

1 pound medium new red or white potatoes, cut in half

4 medium carrots, cut into ½-inch-thick rounds

6 ounces pearl onions (about 12), peeled (see page 387)

¼ cup all-purpose flour

Salt and freshly ground black pepper

1. Preheat the oven to 325 degrees.

2. Heat the oil in a 6- to 8-quart Dutch oven or roasting pan over medium-high heat. Add the beef and brown it on all sides. Add the garlic and cook, stirring, until it is softened, about 2 minutes. Add the soup mixes and 2 cups water and stir until the mixture comes to a boil. Cover the Dutch oven or roasting pan, transfer the pot roast and its cooking liquid to the oven, and cook for 1 hour, basting with the pan juices several times.

3. Add the potatoes, carrots, and onions and cook the roast for another hour.

4. Remove the meat and vegetables to a serving platter and keep them warm.

5. Place the Dutch oven over medium-high heat, whisk together ½ cup water and the flour in a small bowl, and slowly whisk this mixture into the pan juices, bringing the mixture to a boil. Taste for seasoning, adding additional water if the gravy is too salty or adjusting the seasoning with additional salt and pepper, if necessary.

6. Cut the pot roast into thin slices, and transfer it to the platter with the vegetables, and serve with the gravy on the side.

Mamma Mia's Pot Roast

3 cloves garlic, mashed

1 teaspoon salt

1/2 teaspoon freshly ground black pepper

One 3-pound eye of the round roast

2 tablespoons olive oil

1 large onion, chopped

3 medium carrots, coarsely chopped

3 stalks celery, coarsely chopped

One 14.5-ounce can chopped tomatoes, with their juices

2 cans Campbell's Condensed French Onion Soup

1/2 cup red wine

2 teaspoons dried rosemary

2 tablespoons chopped fresh Italian parsley leaves

1. Preheat the oven to 325 degrees.

2. Make a paste with the garlic, salt, and pepper by mashing it together with a mortar and pestle or the butt end of a knife. Spread the paste over the roast.

3. Heat the oil in a 5-quart Dutch oven over medium-high heat and brown the roast on all sides.

SERVES 6 TO 8

This delectable roast simmers slowly in the oven, and the result is a tender piece of beef, accompanied by a delicious tomato and vegetable sauce. Serve the roast with a side of **Garlic Herb Mashed Potatoes (page 233)**, and your significant other will be putty in your hands! I like to use eye of the round because there isn't much waste, but if you would like to substitute another cut, try a rump roast or sirloin tip.

This dish can also be made in the slow cooker. Brown the meat before placing it in the slow cooker, and then add the remaining ingredients. Cook the roast on high for six to eight hours.

4. Add the onion, carrots, and celery and cook, stirring, until they are softened, 3 to 4 minutes. Add the tomatoes and bring to a boil, stirring up any browned bits that may be stuck to the bottom of the pan. Add the onion soup, wine, and rosemary, stirring to blend. Cover the Dutch oven, place it in the oven, and bake the roast until the meat is fork tender, 2 to 3 hours.

5. When the meat is done, remove it to a serving platter and keep it warm. Spoon off any excess fat that may have accumulated on top of the sauce in the pan. Stir in the parsley and season the sauce with salt and pepper.

6. Cut the meat into thin slices and serve it with the sauce on the side.

SERVES 6

Pepper Steak

Reminiscent of a Philly cheese steak, with lots of peppers and onions in a tomato sauce, this recipe takes a lean London broil and simmers it to create a tender, juicy, and comforting dinner. Great side dishes to go with this would be pasta or mashed potatoes to soak up the delicious sauce.

2 tablespoons olive oil

2 large onions, thinly sliced

2 medium red bell peppers, seeded and thinly sliced

2 medium green bell peppers, seeded and thinly sliced

One 2-pound top round steak, about 1 inch thick, trimmed of fat

2 cloves garlic, minced

1 envelope Knorr Tomato with Basil Soup Mix

One 8-ounce can tomato sauce

1½ cups water

½ teaspoon freshly ground black pepper

1. In a 12-inch sauté pan, heat the oil over medium-high heat, add the onions and bell peppers, and cook, stirring, until the peppers are limp and the onions begin to caramelize.

2. Rub the steak with the garlic, and brown the steak on all sides in a 5-quart Dutch oven over high heat. Add the soup mix, tomato sauce, and water and stir to blend. Add the sautéed vegetables and black pepper and simmer over low heat, covered, until the meat is fork tender, 1½ to 2 hours.

3. Remove the meat from the sauce, skim any fat off the top of the sauce. Cut the steak into thin slices, serving it with some of the sauce poured over the top.

Amazing Flank Steak

One 2-pound flank steak (see Souper Smart)

1 teaspoon salt

½ teaspoon freshly ground black pepper

2 tablespoons olive oil

¼ cup chopped onion

2 cloves garlic, chopped

½ cup pine nuts

One 16-ounce bag frozen chopped spinach, defrosted and squeezed dry

⅛ teaspoon freshly grated nutmeg

½ cup freshly grated Parmesan cheese

1 envelope Knorr Cream of Spinach Soup Mix

1 large egg

2 tablespoons extra virgin olive oil

Two 28-ounce cans crushed tomatoes

1 envelope Lipton Savory Herb with Garlic Soup Mix

1 cup Chianti or other red wine

¼ cup chopped fresh Italian parsley leaves

SERVES 6

The reason this flank steak is amazing is that it takes a tough cut of meat, fills it with a spinach and pine nuts, simmers it in a red wine tomato sauce, and produces a tender and beautiful dinner entrée. This dish is great with Garlic Herb Mashed Potatoes (page 233) or Basic Souped-Up Risotto (page 285).

1. Preheat the oven to 350 degrees.

2. Using a meat tenderizer, pound the meat until it is of uniform thickness. Season it with the salt and pepper.

3. In a 10-inch sauté pan, heat the olive oil over medium heat, add the onion and garlic, and cook, stirring, until they are softened, 3 to 4 minutes. Add the pine nuts and brown them in the oil for 2 minutes. Add the spinach and nutmeg, stirring the mixture over high heat for 3 minutes. Remove the spinach mixture to a medium mixing bowl. Add the Parmesan, spinach soup mix, and egg, stirring to blend.

4. Spread the spinach mixture over the meat and roll up the meat from the long side, like a jelly roll. Secure the roll with large toothpicks or skewers or tie it up with kitchen string.

5. Heat the extra virgin olive oil in a 5-quart Dutch oven over medium-high heat and brown the meat on all sides. Add the tomatoes, herb soup mix, and wine and bring to a boil.

6. Cover the Dutch oven and bake the steak in the oven until the meat is fork tender, about 2 hours, basting occasionally. Remove the meat from the sauce to a platter, skim any fat from the top of the sauce, and stir in the parsley.

7. Remove the string, toothpicks, or skewers from the meat, cut the roll into 1-inch-thick slices, and serve with the sauce.

Mom's Barbecue Beef Brisket

1 package Lipton Onion Soup Mix

3 large onions, thinly sliced

One 12-ounce jar chili sauce

One 12-ounce bottle beer

One 4- to 5-pound piece beef brisket or chuck

Salt and freshly ground black pepper

Beef broth (optional)

Kaiser rolls

1. Preheat the oven to 350 degrees.

2. Combine the soup mix, onions, chili sauce, and beer together in a 5-quart Dutch oven or casserole. Add the meat and spoon some of the sauce over it. Cover with foil and bake the brisket for 3 hours, turning the meat over once during the cooking time, basting the meat with the sauce every half hour.

3. After 3 hours, the meat should be fork tender. Remove the meat from the sauce and allow it to rest for 15 minutes before cutting it into thin slices on the diagonal.

4. Simmer the sauce on top of the stove and correct the seasoning with salt and pepper. If the sauce is too thick, thin it with some beef broth. Skim off any fat that may have accumulated on the surface of the sauce. Transfer the sliced meat into the sauce and serve it on Kaiser rolls.

This dish has been around a long time, but it is still a crowd pleaser. All the ingredients can be found in your pantry. Just add the beef, and you're all set for a patio supper that makes itself. Great sides for this dinner are Crunchy Cabbage Salad with Cashews (page 71) and Mom's Picnic Potato Salad (page 81). A chuck roast or short ribs also work well with this recipe, but make sure to trim the meat of all its fat.

BEFORE POTS WERE DEVELOPED TO WITHSTAND DIRECT HEAT FROM A FIRE, SOUP WAS COOKED BY PLACING HEATED STONES INTO THE BOWL OF LIQUID.

Meat

South of the Border Carne Asada

This is a bit of Mexican home cooking. Tender, falling-apart meat, seasoned with Southwestern flavors, this dish is a great meal to serve on a Sunday afternoon while watching your favorite teams on TV. Easily put together, either in the slow cooker or the oven, it goes well with tortillas, salsa, guacamole, and sour cream.

Slow Cooker Savvy

Follow the instructions through step 3, transfer everything to the slow cooker, and cook on medium until the beef is fork tender, six to eight hours.

2 tablespoons vegetable oil

2 cloves garlic, minced

1 large onion, thinly sliced

One 3-pound beef brisket

1 teaspoon salt

$\frac{1}{2}$ teaspoon freshly ground black pepper

One 8-ounce jar medium-hot salsa

1 envelope Lipton Onion Soup Mix

One 12-ounce bottle beer (try a Mexican beer such as Corona or Dos Equis)

1. Preheat the oven to 350 degrees.

2. Heat the oil in a 5-quart Dutch oven over medium-high heat. Add the garlic and onion, stirring, until they are softened, 3 to 4 minutes.

3. Add the beef, sprinkle it with the salt and pepper, and brown it on all sides, about 5 minutes. Stir in the salsa, soup mix, and beer, scraping up any browned bits from the bottom of the pan.

4. Cover the Dutch oven and bake the beef in the oven until the meat is fork tender, about 2 hours.

5. Remove the beef from the sauce and skim off any fat that may have accumulated on the top of the sauce. Let the meat rest, covered with a sheet of aluminum foil, for 15 minutes. Cut the meat across the grain into thin slices. Return the beef to the sauce and serve immediately.

Alpine Veal Stew with Mushrooms

¼ cup (½ stick) butter

1 pound boneless veal loin, trimmed of fat and cut into 1-inch chunks

½ pound mushrooms, sliced

½ cup beef broth

1 envelope Knorr Leek Soup Mix

1¼ cups milk

½ teaspoon dried thyme

¼ cup chopped fresh Italian parsley leaves

Hot cooked egg noodles or rice

1. In a 10- to 12-inch skillet, melt 2 tablespoons of the butter over medium-high heat and brown the veal on all sides.

2. Add the remaining 2 tablespoons butter and the mushrooms to the skillet and cook, stirring, for 3 to 5 minutes. Add the broth and scrape up any browned bits that may have stuck to the bottom of the skillet. Stir in the soup mix, milk, and thyme and bring to a simmer. Cover, reduce the heat to low, and simmer the stew until the veal is fork tender, about 45 minutes.

3. Stir in the parsley and serve the stew over egg noodles or rice.

This delectable dish is reminiscent of one that I had in Lucerne, Switzerland, where veal in cream sauce is a specialty. To be truly authentic, serve this with rösti, a Swiss hash brown potato dish.

Meat

Butterflied Grilled Leg of Lamb

There is something magical about a grilled leg of lamb. The crispy bits that form on the outside, the succulent, tender meat, and the scent of garlic and rosemary all contribute to make this a memorable meal for family and friends. A butterflied leg of lamb has had the bone removed and is then either tied or rolled; you can ask your butcher to do this for you.

1 cup olive oil

1/2 cup fresh lemon juice

Grated zest of 2 lemons

1/4 cup Dijon mustard

2 envelopes Lipton Savory Herb with Garlic Soup Mix

1 tablespoon dried rosemary

1 teaspoon freshly ground black pepper

One 4- to 6-pound leg of lamb, trimmed of fat and butterflied

1. In a small glass mixing bowl, whisk together the oil, lemon juice, zest, mustard, soup mix, rosemary, and pepper, until combined.

2. Place the lamb in a jumbo resealable plastic bag and pour in the marinade. Refrigerate the lamb for 24 hours, turning it occasionally.

3. Preheat the grill for 10 minutes.

4. Drain the marinade from the lamb, discard it, and grill the lamb, turning it once, until it reaches the desired degree of doneness as measured on an instant-read thermometer: 130 degrees for medium rare, 140 degrees for medium, and 150 degrees for well done. If you would like to use more marinade for brushing the lamb during the cooking time, make up a fresh batch.

5. Remove the lamb from the grill, let it rest for 5 to 10 minutes, and then carve it.

When Irish Eyes Are Smiling Stew

2 tablespoons butter

2 pounds lamb stew meat, trimmed of fat and cut into 1-inch chunks

1 teaspoon salt

$\frac{1}{2}$ teaspoon freshly ground black pepper

1 envelope Lipton Golden Onion Soup Mix

1 can Campbell's Condensed French Onion Soup

1 cup water

6 ounces pearl onions (about 12), peeled (page 387)

1 pound small new potatoes, scrubbed

2 cups baby carrots

1 cup frozen petite peas, defrosted

1. Melt the butter in a 5-quart Dutch oven over medium-high heat, season the lamb with the salt and pepper, and brown the meat on all sides.

2. Stir in the soup mix, condensed soup, water, onions, potatoes, and carrots, cover the pan, reduce the heat to low, and simmer the stew for 2 hours, stirring occasionally.

3. At the end of 2 hours, add the peas to the stew and cook it for another 10 minutes. Skim off any fat from the sauce and serve immediately.

When I was a child, I would visit my Irish grandmother, who was a cook for an aristocratic Boston family, and she would serve a version of this dish to me in the kitchen. It smelled so good, mixed with the smells of homemade bread and tea cakes. When I asked her if she served this "upstairs," she said no, that it was special for me, just as it had been for her when her grandmother had made it.

Slow Cooker Savvy

Brown the meat and add it to the slow cooker with the rest of the ingredients. Cook on high for four to six hours.

Meat

Slow Cooker Lamb

One of my students told me she was never without Lipton Savory Herb with Garlic Soup Mix and that this was her favorite recipe. I'm indebted to her for the idea and hope that those who don't have slow cookers will also try this recipe in the oven. The lamb is melt-in-your-mouth tender, with a rich rosemary-infused sauce.

Souper Smart

If you are cooking this dish in the oven, preheat the oven to 325 degrees and, using a 5-quart Dutch oven, follow step 1. Add the leeks to the pan and cook, stirring, until they are softened, about five minutes. Add the soup mixes, water, wine, rosemary, and beans, bring to a boil, partially cover the Dutch oven, and transfer it to the oven. Bake the lamb until it is tender, two to two and a half hours. Skim the fat from the sauce, stir in the parsley, and serve immediately.

The Soup Mix Gourmet

3½ pounds lamb stew meat, trimmed of fat and cut into 1-inch chunks

1 teaspoon salt

½ teaspoon freshly ground black pepper

2 tablespoons olive oil

4 leeks, white parts, washed well and cut into 1-inch lengths

1 envelope Lipton Savory Herb with Garlic Soup Mix

1 envelope Knorr Leek Soup Mix

2 cups water

1 cup white wine

2 teaspoons dried rosemary, crumbled

One 15-ounce can small white beans, drained and rinsed

¼ cup chopped fresh Italian parsley leaves

1. Sprinkle the lamb with the salt and pepper. Heat the oil in a large sauté pan over medium-high heat, add the lamb, and brown it well on all sides.

2. Place the leeks in the bottom of the slow cooker and place the lamb over the leeks. Add the soup mixes, water, wine, and rosemary and stir the mixture a bit until the soups begin to dissolve. Add the beans.

3. Cook the lamb and vegetables on medium until the lamb is tender, 6 to 8 hours, stirring occasionally. Skim the fat from the top of the sauce, stir in the parsley, and serve.

Gyros

½ cup torn French bread with crusts removed

¼ cup milk

1 pound ground lamb

½ pound lean ground beef

2 large eggs

½ cup finely chopped onion

¼ teaspoon dried rosemary, crumbled

¼ teaspoon dried basil

½ teaspoon dried oregano

1 envelope Lipton Savory Herb with Garlic Soup Mix

¼ cup olive oil

Pita bread

Cucumber Yogurt Dip (page 32) for garnish

Chopped lettuce for garnish

Chopped tomatoes for garnish

1. In a small mixing bowl, soak the pieces of bread in the milk for 15 minutes and then squeeze the bread dry.

2. In a large mixing bowl, combine the bread, ground meat, eggs, onion, rosemary, basil, oregano, and soup mix. Form the mixture into 2-by-½-inch patties or 1-inch meatballs. (You can cover the patties or meatballs with plastic wrap and refrigerate them for up to 8 hours or freeze them for up to 6 weeks.)

3. Heat the oil in a 10- to 12-inch sauté pan over medium-high heat and brown the patties or meatballs until they are cooked through, 3 to 4 minutes on each side.

4. Stuff two patties or meatballs into split pita bread, top with 2 tablespoons of the Cucumber Yogurt Dip, chopped lettuce and tomato, and serve.

A spicy lamb meatball, this Middle Eastern treat is grilled or sautéed, stuffed into pita bread, then topped with a garlic yogurt sauce, lettuce, and fresh tomato. The meatballs can be prepared ahead of time and frozen to give you a quick weeknight dinner, or you can make mini-meatballs to serve as part of an hors d'oeuvres tray.

Meat

Lamb and Eggplant Lasagne

In this spicy lasagne, grilled eggplant is used in place of noodles, and tangy feta cheese lends a lovely flavor. Simple to put together, this dish can be made two days ahead or frozen for up to one month.

1 large purple eggplant (about 1¼ pounds)

½ cup olive oil

1 envelope Lipton Savory Herb with Garlic Soup Mix

1 pound ground lamb

1 cup chopped onion

1 cup red wine

1 envelope Knorr Tomato with Basil Soup Mix

One 14.5-ounce can chopped tomatoes, with their juices

½ cup water

½ cup chopped fresh Italian parsley leaves

2 tablespoons butter

2 tablespoons all-purpose flour

2½ cups milk

6 ounces feta cheese, crumbled

¼ teaspoon freshly ground black pepper

1. Preheat the broiler for 10 minutes.

2. Line 1 or 2 baking sheets with aluminum foil.

3. Cut the stem off the top of the eggplant. Cut the eggplant lengthwise into ½-inch-thick slices and lay the slices on the baking sheet(s).

4. Combine the oil with the soup mix in a small bowl, and brush the flavored oil over the eggplant slices. Broil the eggplant until it is golden, turn the slices, brush them with the remaining flavored oil, and broil the eggplant until it is golden. Let the eggplant cool.

5. Reduce the oven temperature to 350 degrees and coat a 9-inch square baking dish with nonstick cooking spray.

6. In a 10-inch skillet over high heat, brown the lamb, add the onion, and cook, stirring, until it is softened.

7. Deglaze the skillet with the wine, scraping up any browned bits from the bottom, and stir in the soup mix, tomatoes, and water. Reduce the heat to medium-low and simmer the lamb and onion for 20 minutes, stirring occasionally. Stir in the parsley and set aside.

8. In a 3-quart saucepan, melt the butter over medium heat and whisk in the flour. When the flour begins to form white bubbles, continue whisking for 2 minutes. Gradually add the milk, bringing the sauce to a boil. Remove the saucepan from the heat. Add 4 ounces of the feta to the sauce, stirring until the feta is melted. Season the sauce with the pepper.

9. Spread a thin layer of the lamb mixture over the bottom of the prepared baking dish. Top with a layer of eggplant, then a thin layer of cheese sauce, and then more of the lamb mixture. Continue to layer, ending with the cheese sauce. Sprinkle the remaining feta over the top of the casserole and bake until the top is golden brown, 30 to 45 minutes. Let the casserole rest for 10 minutes before serving.

Even Quicker Feta Cream Sauce!

For a quick feta cream sauce, heat 1 can Campbell's Condensed Cream of Celery Soup and ½ cup milk together, remove from the heat, stir in the feta, and use this mixture as the cheese sauce. Try this cream sauce over leftover lamb slices, chicken breasts, scalloped potatoes, or vegetables. Try using one of the flavored feta cheeses in the sauce for added kick!

Wokking on the Wild Side Pork Noodles

An old favorite of mine is a recipe called **Peking Meat Sauce Noodles** from chef and restaurateur Joyce Chen. When I was a teenager, it was exotic, and, at the same time, it was a kind of comfort food. This recipe is a little bit of a twist on that theme, using ramen noodles, eggplant, and ground pork for a quick dinner.

4 quarts water

2 packages oriental or chicken flavor ramen noodles

2 tablespoons vegetable oil

2 tablespoons toasted sesame oil

3 cloves garlic, minced

1 teaspoon peeled and grated fresh ginger

1/2 cup chopped green onions

1 pound ground pork

1 medium eggplant, peeled and cut into cubes (about 4 cups)

2 tablespoons soy sauce

Salt (optional)

1. In a large saucepan, heat the water to boiling, add the ramen noodles, and bring the water back to a boil. Drain the noodles immediately. Toss them with 1 teaspoon of the vegetable oil and keep them warm.

2. In a wok or a 12-inch skillet, heat the remaining 1²/₃ tablespoons vegetable oil and 1 tablespoon of the sesame oil over high heat. Add the garlic and ginger and stir-fry them until the garlic begins to soften, but do not let it get brown. Add the green onions and the 2 ramen flavor packets and stir-fry the mixture for another minute. Add the pork and stir-fry it until it loses its pink color.

3. Drain any water from the bottom of the wok or skillet. Add the eggplant and stir-fry it until it is soft, about 4 minutes. Add the soy sauce and the remaining 1 tablespoon sesame oil. Taste for seasonings and add salt if desired.

4. Stir in the noodles and serve immediately.

Pork and Peanut Stir-Fry

2 cups water

1 package chicken flavor ramen noodles

1 teaspoon plus 1 tablespoon sesame oil

2 tablespoons rice vinegar

2 tablespoons smooth peanut butter

2 tablespoons soy sauce

2 tablespoons firmly packed light brown sugar

1 teaspoon peeled and grated fresh ginger

1 clove garlic, minced

4 shakes Tabasco sauce

1/4 cup vegetable oil

2 cups 1-by-1/2-inch strips boneless pork loin

6 green onions, cut on the diagonal into 1/2-inch-wide slices

1/3 cup honey-roasted peanuts

1. Heat the water to boiling in a medium saucepan and add the ramen noodles. Let the water come back to a boil, drain the noodles, toss them with 1 teaspoon of the sesame oil, and set them aside.

2. In a blender or food processor, combine the ramen flavor packet with the vinegar, peanut butter, soy sauce, brown sugar, ginger, garlic, Tabasco, 2 tablespoons of the vegetable oil and process until smooth. Set the sauce aside or refrigerate it until you are ready to use it.

3. In a wok, heat the remaining 2 tablespoons vegetable oil and 1 tablespoon sesame oil over high heat until almost smoking. Add the pork and stir-fry it until it is cooked through. Add the green onions, toss them with the pork, and then stir in the drained ramen noodles. Pour the peanut sauce over the pork mixture, continue to stir-fry the pork and onions for another minute to heat the sauce through. Sprinkle on the peanuts, and serve immediately.

This spicy, crunchy dish can be on the table in less than 15 minutes. The pork cooks quickly, and the peanut sauce is a great addition to anyone's kitchen repertoire. Serve this dish with Asian Slaw (page 73) and steamed rice for a great weeknight dinner.

Wild Cranberry Stuffed Pork Loin

2 pork tenderloins, about 1 pound each

2 cups cooked wild rice

2 tablespoons butter

$\frac{1}{2}$ cup chopped onion

$\frac{1}{2}$ cup chopped celery

$\frac{1}{2}$ cup dried cranberries

$\frac{1}{2}$ teaspoon dried thyme

$\frac{1}{2}$ teaspoon dried sage

1 envelope Lipton Golden Onion Soup Mix

2 tablespoons vegetable oil

$\frac{3}{4}$ cup chicken broth

$\frac{1}{4}$ cup bourbon

$\frac{1}{4}$ cup heavy cream

$\frac{1}{4}$ cup chopped fresh Italian parsley leaves

1. Preheat the oven to 375 degrees.

2. Trim the pork tenderloins of all fat and silver skin and slit each one lengthwise down the center to within $\frac{1}{2}$ inch of the bottom. Place each tenderloin between sheets of plastic or waxed paper and pound it to $\frac{1}{2}$-inch thickness.

3. Place the wild rice in a medium mixing bowl.

4. In a small sauté pan, melt the butter over medium-high heat, add the onion, celery, cranberries, thyme, sage, and 2 table-spoons of the soup mix, and cook, stirring, until the onion is softened, 3 to 4 minutes. Add the vegetable and cranberry mix-ture to the wild rice and blend well.

5. Use half of the rice stuffing to stuff the center of each tenderloin. Roll up each stuffed tenderloin, tying it with kitchen string to secure it.

6. Heat the oil in an ovenproof 12-inch sauté pan over high heat, add the tenderloins to the pan, and brown them on all sides. Transfer the pan to the oven and bake the tenderloins until the center of the pork reaches an internal temperature of 160 degrees on a meat thermometer, 20 to 25 minutes. Remove the tenderloins from the oven, place them on a warm serving platter, and cover with aluminum foil.

7. Place the same sauté pan on the stove, add the remaining soup mix, the chicken broth, and bourbon, scraping up any browned bits from the bottom of the pan. Bring the sauce to a boil, and simmer it for 5 minutes. Stir in the cream and parsley and heat the sauce through.

8. Cut the pork into 1-inch-thick slices and serve it topped with the sauce.

Smothered Pork Chops

Pork smothered with apples and onions is a dinner your family will love. I like to use Golden Delicious apples, because they hold their shape well when cooked, but you can use any apple that you have on hand.

2 strips bacon, cut into 1-inch pieces

6 boneless pork chops, 1 inch thick

1 large onion, sliced 1/2 inch thick

4 large Golden Delicious apples, cored, peeled, and cut into 1/2-inch-thick slices

1 envelope Lipton Golden Onion Soup Mix

1 cup apple juice

1. Preheat the oven to 350 degrees.

2. Fry the bacon in a 5-quart Dutch oven over medium-high heat until it is crisp. Remove the bacon with a slotted spoon to drain on paper towels, and remove all but 2 tablespoons of fat from the pan.

3. Brown the pork chops on both sides in the hot fat.

4. Remove the chops from the pan, add the onion, and cook, stirring, until golden, 4 to 6 minutes. Add the apples and cook them, stirring, for 3 minutes. Add the soup mix and apple juice and stir until the mixture comes to a boil. Return the pork chops to the pan, covering them with the apple mixture.

5. Cover the pan and transfer it to the oven. Bake the pork chops in the oven until they are tender, about 45 minutes. Serve the pork chops garnished with the reserved bacon.

Lip-Smacking Golden Onion Pork Ribs

1 tablespoon vegetable oil

$\frac{1}{2}$ cup chopped onion

2 cloves garlic, minced

2 envelopes Lipton Golden Onion Soup Mix

2 cans Campbell's Condensed Tomato Soup

$\frac{1}{4}$ cup firmly packed light brown sugar

2 tablespoons Worcestershire sauce

5 shakes Tabasco sauce

1 slab baby back ribs

1. Preheat the oven to 300 degrees.

2. In a 2-quart saucepan, heat the oil over medium-high heat, add the onion, and cook, stirring, until softened, 3 to 4 minutes. Add the garlic and soup mix, stirring, another 2 to 3 minutes. Stir in the tomato soup, brown sugar, Worcestershire, and Tabasco and bring to a boil. Reduce the heat to medium-low and simmer the sauce for 15 minutes.

3. Remove 1 cup of the sauce from the saucepan and set it aside.

4. Place the ribs on a rack in a roasting pan and brush them with some of the remaining sauce. Bake the ribs for 1 hour, basting them every 10 minutes with the sauce.

5. When the ribs are done, baste them again with more sauce, and serve with the reserved sauce on the side.

SERVES 6

These tender, slow-cooked ribs are cooked in a savory onion and tomato sauce. The sauce can be served alongside the finished dish as well. Make sure to offer lots of napkins to clean up sticky faces!

LIP-SMACKIN' COUNTRY-STYLE PORK AND BEEF RIBS: This recipe works well with meatier country-style ribs, but they will take two hours to cook. If you would like to do this with beef ribs, substitute Lipton Beefy Onion Soup Mix and bake the ribs for two hours.

Meat

Ragin' Cajun Red Beans and Rice

This Cajun treat is stick-to-your-ribs comfort food from the bayou. Originally made on wash day in the South, so that it could cook while the wash was being done, this dish comes together in no time and makes enough for a small army of hungry folks. I like to serve it with an assortment of hot sauces on the side.

1 tablespoon vegetable oil

2 pounds andouille or smoked sausage, cut into ½-inch-thick rounds

1 cup chopped red onion

1 cup chopped celery

3 cloves garlic, minced

1 envelope Lipton Savory Herb with Garlic Soup Mix

1 envelope Lipton Golden Onion Soup Mix

1 tablespoon Worcestershire sauce

½ teaspoon cayenne pepper

1 teaspoon dried thyme

2 bay leaves

3 cups water

Two 16-ounce cans red kidney beans, drained and rinsed

4 cups hot cooked long-grain rice

Chopped fresh Italian parsley leaves and green onions for garnish

1. Heat the oil in a 5-quart Dutch oven over high heat, add the sausage, and cook it until it begins to brown.

2. Add the onion, celery, and garlic, and cook, stirring, until they are softened, 5 to 7 minutes. Add the soup mixes, Worcestershire, cayenne, and thyme and cook, stirring, for another 3 minutes. Add the bay leaves, water, and kidney beans, bring the mixture to a boil, reduce the heat to low, and simmer for 1 hour, stirring occasionally so that the beans don't stick. Remove the bay leaves.

3. Serve the red beans over the rice, garnished with parsley and green onions.

Slow Cooker Savvy

Combine all the ingredients in the slow cooker and cook on medium for four to six hours.

Ballpark Sausage and Peppers

1 cup water

2 pounds sweet Italian sausage

2 large onions, thinly sliced and separated into rings

2 medium green bell peppers, seeded and thinly sliced into rings

2 medium red bell peppers, seeded and thinly sliced into rings

1 envelope Lipton Savory Herb with Garlic Soup Mix

One 14.5-ounce can crushed tomatoes, with their juices

$1/2$ teaspoon freshly ground black pepper

1 teaspoon dried basil

1. Pour $1/2$ cup water into a 10- to 12-inch skillet and bring to a boil. Add the sausage, pricking each one with the sharp tip of a knife in several places, and steam, covered, for about 5 minutes. Remove the cover from the pan and cook the sausage over medium heat until it is cooked through and browned on all sides, 10 to 15 minutes.

2. Remove the sausage from the pan, leaving 2 tablespoons of fat in the pan. Add the onions and bell peppers and cook, stirring, over medium-high heat until softened, 5 to 7 minutes. Add the soup mix, tomatoes, $1/2$ cup water, the black pepper, and basil and simmer the mixture for 10 minutes. Return the sausage to the skillet and simmer for another 20 minutes before serving.

I love Italian sausage, and when it's paired with peppers, onions, and tomatoes, I'm in heaven. This dish is great served in Italian rolls for a tailgate party, or served over pasta or polenta as a main course.

HOT BALLPARK SAUSAGE AND PEPPERS: Like your sausages hot? Substitute hot sausages for the sweet in this recipe.

Souper Smart

The sausage and peppers can be made up to two days ahead and refrigerated.

Slow Cooker Savvy

Instead of steaming the sausages, brown them with the peppers and onions, transfer the mixture to a slow cooker along with the remaining ingredients (including the full cup of water), and cook on high for four hours.

Tuna Noodle Casserole

Millennium Tuna Noodle Bake

Miso-Glazed Salmon

Bill's Barbecued Stuffed Salmon

Cajun Salmon

Ten-Minute Baked Halibut

Crabmeat-Stuffed Sole with Creamy Lobster Sauce

Lemon Caper Fillets of Sole

Snapper Florentine

Snapper Vera Cruz

Tomato Basil Sea Bass

Herb-Crusted Fish Fillets

Baja Fish Tacos

Shrimp Quesadillas

Jerk Shrimp

Peel-and-Eat Shrimp Boil

Baked Stuffed Shrimp

Shrimp Imperial with Pasta and Broccoli

Garlic Prawns with Linguine

Creole Jambalaya

Shrimp Creole

The Original Campbell's Shrimp Creole

Mediterranean Shrimp and Rice

Scallops in Herbed Butter Sauce

Mussels Marinara

Christmas Eve Clams

Clam Pie

Stuffed Garlic Oysters

Stuffed Spinach Oysters

Lobster Stuffed Potatoes

Maryland-Style Crab Cakes

Mixed Seafood Kabobs

Streamlined Paella

Souper Fish

FOR MANY YEARS, THE ONLY SEAFOOD that the home cook would have for dinner was the tuna in tuna noodle casserole. Today, with better shipping and storage, your local supermarket can be a gold mine of delicious seafood. Seafood and soup go back a long way, from tuna noodle casserole to shrimp wiggle (don't ask) and salmon croquettes. Today soup pairs beautifully with fish to bake in the oven, as part of the sauce or in a stuffing, or as an ingredient in the preparation of crab cakes, or peel-and-eat shrimp. Both condensed soups and soup mixes can turn ordinary fish fillets into gourmet delights in under 30 minutes. Fish suppers are some of the easiest and quickest meals you can make because fish cooks quickly and doesn't need too much to make it into a five-star entrée. Leftover fish from the grill can be made into some delectable dishes as well, with just a little soup and some imagination.

Tuna Noodle Casserole

As a child, I would beg to go to my friends' homes on Fridays and eat tuna noodle casserole. You can jazz this up with the variations listed below.

CHEESY TUNA NOODLE CASSEROLE: Top the casserole with ½ cup shredded mild cheddar cheese mixed with the breadcrumb mixture.

CHICKEN OR TURKEY NOODLE CASSEROLE: Substitute Campbell's Condensed Cream of Chicken Soup and 3 cups bite-size pieces of cooked chicken or turkey for the tuna.

SOUTHWESTERN TUNA NOODLE CASSEROLE: Substitute ¼ cup canned chopped green chiles, drained and rinsed, for the pimiento and peas and top the casserole with ⅓ cup grated Monterey Jack cheese combined with ½ cup crushed tortilla chips instead of the buttered breadcrumbs.

The Soup Mix Gourmet

416

1 can Campbell's Condensed Cream of Celery Soup

¾ cup milk

2 tablespoons chopped pimiento (optional)

2 cups hot cooked medium egg noodles

1 cup cooked peas, drained

Two 6-ounce cans tuna, drained and flaked

2 tablespoons dry breadcrumbs

1 tablespoon butter, melted

1. Preheat the oven to 400 degrees. Coat a 1½-quart casserole dish with nonstick cooking spray.

2. Mix the soup, milk, and pimiento together in the casserole dish. Stir in the noodles, peas, and tuna.

3. In a small mixing bowl, toss the breadcrumbs with the melted butter and sprinkle them over the top of the casserole. Bake the casserole until it is bubbling and the crumbs are browned, about 20 minutes.

Millennium Tuna Noodle Bake

SERVES 6

2 tablespoons butter

½ cup finely chopped onion

½ cup finely chopped celery

1 cup sliced mushrooms

2 tablespoons dry sherry

1 can Campbell's Condensed Cream of Mushroom Soup

½ cup milk

Salt and freshly ground black pepper

2 cups hot cooked medium egg noodles

Two 6-ounce cans oil-packed solid white albacore tuna, drained and flaked

2 tablespoons butter, melted

¼ cup dry breadcrumbs

2 tablespoons freshly grated Parmesan cheese

1 tablespoon chopped fresh Italian parsley leaves

The basic tuna noodle bake is warm and filling, but it could be so much better. This is my version of this comforting classic.

1. Preheat the oven to 400 degrees. Coat a 1½-quart casserole dish with nonstick cooking spray.

2. In a 3-quart saucepan, melt the butter over medium heat, add the onion and celery, and cook, stirring, until they are softened, 3 to 4 minutes. Add the mushrooms and cook, stirring, until they begin to soften, about 4 minutes. Add the sherry, and then stir in the soup and milk. Taste the sauce and adjust the seasoning with salt and pepper.

3. Stir the sauce into the noodles, add the tuna, and stir to blend. Pour the mixture into the prepared dish.

4. In a small mixing bowl, toss together the melted butter, breadcrumbs, cheese, and parsley and sprinkle the mixture evenly over the top of the casserole. (At this point, you may refrigerate the casserole for up to 24 hours.) Bake the casserole until it is bubbling and the crumbs are golden, 20 to 25 minutes.

Souper Fish

Miso-Glazed Salmon

SERVES 6

My daughter Carrie's favorite dish is the miso-glazed cod at the restaurant Nobu in New York City. We tried this home-style variation, and all agreed that it was very close to the original. If salmon is not available, try using sea bass, halibut, or cod. This dish is just as good grilled as it is broiled.

2 pounds salmon fillets, skin left on

1 box Kikkoman Shiro Miso Soup Mix (containing 3 envelopes)

⅓ cup mirin (rice wine)

¼ cup sugar

¼ cup vegetable oil

2 tablespoon soy sauce

6 shakes Tabasco sauce

2 tablespoons chopped green onions for garnish

1 tablespoon sesame seeds for garnish

1. Place the salmon in a resealable plastic bag or a 13-by-9-inch baking dish.

2. Empty the soup mix into a small mixing bowl and whisk in the mirin, sugar, oil, soy sauce, and Tabasco. Pour this mixture over the fish fillets, turning them to coat. Seal the bag or cover the baking dish with plastic wrap and marinate the fish in the refrigerator for at least 1 hour.

3. Preheat the broiler for 10 minutes. Line a rimmed baking sheet with aluminum foil.

4. Remove the fish from the marinade and place it on the baking sheet. Broil the salmon 6 inches from the heat until it is opaque in the center, 6 to 10 minutes.

5. Remove the salmon to a serving platter and garnish it with green onions and sesame seeds.

Bill's Barbecued Stuffed Salmon

¼ cup (½ stick) butter

¼ cup chopped shallots

½ cup chopped mushrooms

2 tablespoons seeded and chopped red bell pepper

2 tablespoons seeded and chopped green bell pepper

1 envelope Lipton Savory Herb with Garlic Soup Mix

2 cups fresh French breadcrumbs

One 4-pound salmon, cleaned

5 strips bacon

1. In a small sauté pan, melt the butter over medium heat, add the shallots, and cook, stirring, until they are softened, about 2 minutes. Add the mushrooms and bell peppers and cook, stirring, until they are softened, another 2 to 3 minutes. Add the soup mix, reserving 2 tablespoons for seasoning the salmon. Cook the vegetables and soup mix for another minute, stirring. Remove the pan from the heat, allow the vegetables to cool, and then mix in the breadcrumbs, blending well. (At this point, you may refrigerate the stuffing for up to 8 hours.)

2. Preheat the grill for 10 minutes.

3. Wash the salmon with cold water and pat it dry. Season the inside cavity with the reserved soup mix. Stuff the salmon with the breadcrumb mixture and place the stuffed fish on a sheet of heavy-duty aluminum foil. Lay the bacon strips across the top.

4. Transfer the salmon to the grill and cook the fish until it is cooked through, about 30 minutes. The fish will feel firm, and when a knife is inserted at the backbone the flesh should appear light pink.

5. Remove the fish from the grill, allow it to rest for 5 minutes, and then remove the bacon strips. Cut the fish into individual portions. Leftovers make wonderful salmon burgers.

My cousin Bill is the barbecue master; he is also an all-around good guy. He served this salmon on a beautiful summer night in Washington, D.C., along with fresh corn on the cob and a tossed salad. Life doesn't get much better than this.

Cajun Salmon

When Chef Paul Prudhomme introduced the world to Cajun cuisine, he changed the face of seafood restaurant menus nationwide. Today Cajun or blackened seafood is standard fare on menus through the country. This salmon dish can be prepared with any firm white-fleshed fish, and it is best when grilled over hot coals, but you can do it in a broiler. Spicy, but not overly hot, the salmon benefits from being marinated in the spices for several hours.

IN 1952 LIPTON INTRODUCED ITS DRY ONION SOUP MIX.

CAJUN SEASONING

1 envelope Lipton Savory Herb with Garlic Soup Mix

1 teaspoon cayenne pepper

$1/4$ teaspoon freshly ground black pepper

1 teaspoon sweet paprika

CAJUN SALMON

$1/3$ cup olive oil

2 pounds salmon fillets

1 lemon, cut into wedges

1. Combine the Cajun Seasoning ingredients in a small mixing bowl.

2. In a shallow dish, combine the oil and Cajun seasoning. Dip the salmon fillets in the flavored oil and turn to coat them well. Cover the fish fillets with plastic wrap and marinate them in the refrigerator for up to 4 hours.

3. Preheat the broiler or grill.

4. Broil or grill the salmon until it is cooked through, about 4 minutes on each side. Squeeze the lemon wedges over the salmon before serving.

Ten-Minute Baked Halibut

½ cup (1 stick) butter, melted

½ cup olive oil

1 package Lipton Savory Herb with Garlic Soup Mix

2½ pounds halibut fillets (or other firm white-fleshed fish, such as sea bass)

1 cup dry breadcrumbs

½ cup freshly grated Parmesan cheese

1. Preheat the oven to 425 degrees.

2. In a small mixing bowl, combine the melted butter, oil, and 2 tablespoons of the soup mix. Pour 2 tablespoons of the flavored butter into a 13-by-9 inch baking dish. Place the halibut in the baking dish and pour all but 2 tablespoons of the flavored butter over the fish.

3. In another small mixing bowl, combine the rest of the soup mix with the breadcrumbs and cheese. Toss the breadcrumb mixture with the remaining 2 tablespoons of the flavored butter. Spread the breadcrumb mixture over the fish fillets. Bake the fish for 10 minutes. To check for doneness, slash the fish at the thickest part; if it is still translucent, cook for an additional 2 to 3 minutes, until the flesh is white all the way through.

SERVES 8

Soup in your pantry helps to make elegant yet easy dishes like this one a reality in your kitchen. Since this recipe requires only a few ingredients and takes only 10 minutes to bake, you can have a five star meal for your family or friends in a jiffy. Round out the meal with rice or pasta and Gazpacho Salad (page 70) and you'll get rave reviews. You can substitute large sea scallops for the fish in this recipe.

NAPOLEON BONAPARTE ONCE SAID, "AN ARMY TRAVELS ON ITS STOMACH. SOUP MAKES THE SOLDIER."

Souper Fish

Crabmeat-Stuffed Sole with Creamy Lobster Sauce

SERVES 8

This is a deceptively easy entrée that can be on the table in less than 45 minutes, or you can make it ahead of time. Fillet of sole is stuffed with a delicate crabmeat stuffing and then covered with a luscious lobster sauce.

2 tablespoons butter

2 tablespoons chopped shallots

1 teaspoon Old Bay seasoning

1 cup fresh lump crabmeat, picked over for cartilage and shells

1 cup soft breadcrumbs

2 tablespoons mayonnaise

8 fillets of sole

2 cans Pepperidge Farm Condensed Lobster Bisque

2 tablespoons brandy

¼ cup heavy cream

1. Preheat the oven to 350 degrees. Coat a 10-inch round baking dish with nonstick cooking spray.

2. Melt the butter in a small sauté pan over medium heat, add the shallots, swirl them in the butter for 1 minute, add the Old Bay seasoning, and cook for another minute. Add the crabmeat and toss it in the butter mixture. Transfer to a medium mixing bowl and stir in the breadcrumbs and mayonnaise.

3. Place the sole fillets on a flat surface. Center 1 tablespoon of the crab stuffing on each fillet. Roll up the fillet and transfer it, seam side down, to the prepared baking dish. Any additional stuffing can be formed into small ovals.

4. In another medium mixing bowl, combine the bisque, brandy, and heavy cream. Pour the sauce over the fillets and top each fillet with an oval of stuffing, if you have any remaining. (Some fillets are small and don't take as much filling as others; if you would like to top each fillet with stuffing, double the stuffing recipe.) Bake the sole until it is cooked through, about 10 minutes.

Lemon Caper Fillets of Sole

½ cup (1 stick) butter

2 tablespoons olive oil

1 envelope Knorr Leek Soup Mix

1 teaspoon dried fines herbes (see page 3)

¼ cup fresh lemon juice

¼ cup chopped fresh Italian parsley leaves

¼ cup capers, drained

½ teaspoon freshly ground black pepper

8 fillets of sole

1. In a 12-inch sauté pan, melt the butter in the oil over medium heat. Add the soup mix and cook the sauce, stirring, for 2 minutes. Add the lemon juice, parsley, capers, and pepper and cook, stirring, for 2 minutes more.

2. Add the fillets to the sauce and simmer the fish until it is cooked through, 4 to 5 minutes.

Fillet of sole cooked in this simple lemon butter sauce is just minutes away from the dinner table. Serve the fillets with orzo or rice to soak up the sauce.

Souper Smart

Make the sauce ahead of time and refrigerate it for up to two days. Melt the sauce in the sauté pan and proceed as directed.

Snapper Florentine

SERVES 6

This versatile dish can be made with any firm-fleshed fish, or it can be made with crab, shrimp, scallops, or lobster. The fish sits atop a bed of spinach and is finished with a creamy spinach and cheese sauce.

6 tablespoons ($^3/_4$ stick) butter

Two 10-ounce bags fresh spinach, chopped, or two 10-ounce packages frozen chopped spinach, defrosted and squeezed dry

1 teaspoon salt

$^1/_2$ teaspoon freshly ground black pepper

$^1/_4$ teaspoon freshly grated nutmeg

2 pounds red snapper fillets

2 tablespoons finely chopped shallots

1 envelope Knorr Spinach Soup Mix

2 cups milk

1 tablespoon cream sherry

2 cups grated Swiss cheese

1. Preheat the oven to 350 degrees. Coat a 13-by-9-inch baking dish with nonstick cooking spray.

2. Melt 2 tablespoons of the butter in a 10- to 12-inch sauté pan over medium heat. Add the spinach and cook, stirring, until it is wilted and heated through. Season the spinach with the salt, pepper, and $^1/_8$ teaspoon of the nutmeg. Spoon the spinach into the prepared baking dish and spread it over the bottom. Place the fish fillets over the spinach.

3. In a 2-quart saucepan, melt the remaining 4 tablespoons butter over medium heat and add the shallots, swirling them in the butter. Add the soup mix and cook for 1 minute. Whisk in the milk and bring the mixture to a boil. Reduce the heat to medium-low, add the sherry, the remaining $^1/_8$ teaspoon nutmeg, and the cheese, and stir the sauce until the cheese melts. Spoon the sauce over the fish and spinach.

4. Bake the casserole until the sauce is bubbling and the fish is cooked through, about 20 minutes.

Snapper Vera Cruz

2 tablespoons vegetable oil

1 cup chopped onion

2 Anaheim chiles, seeded and finely chopped

1 envelope Lipton Savory Herb with Garlic Soup Mix

1 teaspoon ground cumin

Two 14.5-ounce cans diced tomatoes, drained

2 teaspoons fresh lime juice

2 pounds red snapper fillets

1. Preheat the oven to 400 degrees.

2. In a 3-quart saucepan, heat the oil over medium heat, add the onion and chiles, and cook, stirring, until they are softened, about 3 minutes. Add the soup mix and cumin and stir for 2 more minutes. Add the tomatoes and lime juice and bring the sauce to a boil. Reduce the heat to medium-low and simmer the sauce for 15 minutes.

3. Place the snapper fillets in a 13-by-9-inch baking dish and cover them with the sauce. Bake the fish until it is cooked through, 12 to 15 minutes.

This south of the border dish is a favorite with its spicy sauce of chiles and tomatoes. The sauce can be made up to three days ahead of time and refrigerated, and then baked with the fish. It is also delicious with shrimp. Serve this dish with tortillas, rice, and beans.

CHEESY SNAPPER VERA CRUZ: Grated pepper Jack cheese is delicious melted on top of this dish. Use 1 cup and sprinkle it evenly over the sauce.

Tomato Basil Sea Bass

This recipe proves the theory that less is more. When I was testing different recipes, I thought, what if I just spread the soup mix over fish and baked it? Voilà, a delicious, savory, and satisfying meal with just three ingredients.

This easy salsa makes a great companion to the fish.

¹/₂ cup olive oil

1 envelope Knorr Tomato with Basil Soup Mix

2 pounds sea bass fillets

1. Preheat the oven to 400 degrees.

2. In a 13-by-9-inch baking dish, combine the oil and soup mix. Dip the fillets in the flavored oil, coating both sides. Cover the dish with plastic wrap and marinate in the refrigerator for up to 2 hours, until you are ready to proceed.

3. Bake the fish until it is cooked through, 10 to 12 minutes, spooning some of the flavored oil over the top while it cooks.

FRESH TOMATO SALSA

2 cloves garlic, mashed to a paste

4 medium ripe tomatoes, chopped

1 cup packed fresh basil leaves, chopped

1 teaspoon salt

¹/₂ teaspoon freshly ground black pepper

3 tablespoons balsamic vinegar

In a medium glass mixing bowl, combine the garlic, tomatoes, basil, salt, pepper, and balsamic vinegar. Refrigerate the salsa for at least 3 hours before serving.

Herb-Crusted Fish Fillets

2 cups dry breadcrumbs

1 envelope Knorr Leek Soup Mix

1 teaspoon dried fines herbes (see page 3)

2 pounds fish fillets

1/2 cup (1 stick) butter, melted and cooled

1. Preheat the oven to 400 degrees.

2. In a shallow dish, combine the breadcrumbs and soup mix.

3. Dip each fillet into the melted butter and then into the crumb mixture, coating the fillets thoroughly on both sides. Place the fillets in a 13-by-9-inch baking dish in a single layer and bake the fish until it is cooked through, about 10 minutes.

SERVES 6

Baked fish is simple, yet so many of my students will not try to prepare it at home. This elegant entrée with its herbed breadcrumb coating can be on the table in less than 15 minutes. Use firm white-fleshed fish such as sea bass, salmon, or halibut with this recipe.

Baja Fish Tacos

1/2 cup plus 1/3 cup vegetable oil

1/4 cup fresh lime juice

1 envelope Lipton Savory Herb with Garlic Soup Mix

2 pounds firm white-fleshed fish fillets, such as sea bass, halibut, or mako shark

2 cups cored and shredded green cabbage

1/2 head red cabbage, cored and shredded

1 teaspoon sugar

2 teaspoons chopped fresh cilantro leaves

1/4 cup Fresh Tomato Salsa (see page 426)

2 cups sour cream

Twelve 6-inch corn tortillas

2 cups guacamole (optional)

1 1/2 cups grated Monterey Jack cheese (optional)

SERVES 6

Fish tacos originated in San Felipe, a sleepy little fishing village in Baja California. Street vendors load deep-fried fish into soft corn tortillas and then top them with sour cream, red salsa, and cabbage salad. The result is my idea of heaven. These fish tacos are broiled, and then topped with salsa, cabbage, guacamole, and grated Monterey Jack cheese.

Souper Fish

1. In a shallow dish, combine ½ cup of the oil, 2 tablespoons of the lime juice, and 2 tablespoons of the soup mix. Add the fish and turn it to coat in the marinade. Cover the dish with plastic wrap, and marinate the fish in the refrigerator for 30 minutes, but for no longer than 2 hours.

2. In a large mixing bowl, combine the cabbages. In a small mixing bowl, whisk together the remaining ⅓ cup oil and 2 tablespoons lime juice, the sugar, cilantro, and remaining soup mix. Pour the mixture over the cabbage and toss. Refrigerate the cabbage until you are ready to serve the tacos.

3. In a medium mixing bowl, stir the salsa into the sour cream, cover the bowl with plastic wrap, and refrigerate it.

4. Preheat the grill or broiler.

5. Remove the fish from the marinade and grill or broil the fish until it is cooked through, about 4 minutes per side.

6. For each taco, place a piece of fish in the center of each tortilla, top it with cabbage salad and sour cream salsa, adding guacamole and cheese, if desired. Roll up the tacos and place 2 on each plate.

Shrimp Quesadillas

2 tablespoons vegetable oil

1 large onion, thinly sliced

1 medium red bell pepper, seeded and thinly sliced into rings

1 medium green bell pepper, seeded and thinly sliced into rings

2 teaspoons ground cumin

½ teaspoon chili powder

1 envelope Lipton Golden Onion Soup Mix

Three 14.5-ounce cans diced tomatoes, drained

Twelve 12-inch flour tortillas

3 cups grated Monterey Jack cheese

1 pound medium cooked shrimp, peeled and deveined

1. Preheat the oven to 400 degrees.

2. In a 12-inch sauté pan, heat the oil over medium heat, add the onion, and cook it, stirring, for 2 minutes. Add the bell peppers and cook them, stirring, for 3 minutes. Add the cumin, chili powder, and soup mix and cook, stirring, for 2 minutes. Add the tomatoes and bring the sauce to a boil. Simmer the sauce until it has thickened, about 20 minutes. Keep it warm.

3. Lay 6 of the tortillas on baking sheets, distribute the cheese and shrimp evenly over them, and then cover them with the remaining 6 tortillas. Bake until the cheese is melted, about 10 minutes. Remove the quesadillas to dinner plates.

4. Taste the sauce for final seasoning, and then spread it over each quesadilla and serve.

SERVES 6

Large flour tortillas are filled with cheese and shrimp, and then covered with a delicious ranchera sauce, making these quesadillas something special. For spicy quesadillas, substitute pepper Jack cheese for the Monterey Jack cheese.

Jerk Shrimp

SERVES 6

These spicy shrimp on skewers have a tropical taste of the islands. Whether you serve these fragrant shrimp as the main course or an appetizer, they are sure to be a hit with your guests. If you are using bamboo skewers, be sure to soak them in water for 30 minutes to keep them from burning.

½ cup olive oil

3 tablespoons fresh lime juice

2 tablespoons sugar

1 envelope Lipton Savory Herb with Garlic Soup Mix

¼ teaspoon ground allspice

⅛ teaspoon ground cinnamon

Pinch of freshly grated nutmeg

Pinch of cayenne pepper

1½ pounds large shrimp, peeled and deveined

1. In a medium glass mixing bowl, combine the oil, lime juice, sugar, soup mix, allspice, cinnamon, nutmeg, and cayenne. Add the shrimp, stirring to coat them well, cover the bowl with plastic wrap, and marinate the shrimp in the refrigerator for 1 hour.

2. Preheat the broiler or grill.

3. Thread the shrimp onto skewers and broil or grill them until they are pink, about 3 minutes on each side.

Peel-and-Eat Shrimp Boil

Four 12-ounce bottles beer

2 envelopes Lipton Savory Herb with Garlic Soup Mix

2 teaspoons cayenne pepper

2 cups water

2 lemons, cut into quarters

1 bay leaf

3 pounds medium or large shrimp

1. In an 8-quart stockpot, combine the beer, soup mix, cayenne, and water. Squeeze the juice from the lemons, and add the juice and lemons to the pot along with the bay leaf. Bring the mixture to a boil, stirring with a whisk if the consistency appears lumpy.

2. When the liquid comes to a boil, add the shrimp. When the liquid comes back to a boil, remove the pot from the heat and allow it to sit, covered, for 10 minutes. Drain the shrimp well and serve.

Hot and spicy, this dinner should be served on butcher paper—without table settings, just side dishes and lots of sauces. Depending on your preference, you can serve these shrimp hot or cold; I prefer to serve them hot, but you might want to make the shrimp earlier in the day and serve them cold at supper.

Souper Fish

Baked Stuffed Shrimp

SERVES 6

Buttery and savory, these shrimp can be made ahead of time, and then popped into a hot oven to bake for just a few minutes. The same stuffing can be used with scallops or red snapper fillets.

3 tablespoons olive oil

24 jumbo shrimp, butterflied

2 cups crushed Ritz crackers

1 envelope Knorr Leek Soup Mix

1 cup peeled, deveined, and chopped bay shrimp or small shrimp

1 cup mayonnaise

1 teaspoon Worcestershire sauce

1 teaspoon sweet paprika

$\frac{1}{8}$ teaspoon cayenne pepper

$\frac{1}{2}$ cup (1 stick) butter, melted

1. Preheat the oven to 400 degrees.

2. Pour the oil in a 13-by-9-inch baking dish. Place the jumbo shrimp in the baking dish, cut side up.

3. In a medium mixing bowl, combine the crackers, soup mix, chopped shrimp, mayonnaise, Worcestershire, paprika, cayenne, and half the melted butter. Mound 1 tablespoon of the stuffing onto each shrimp.

4. Pour the remaining melted butter over the shrimp and bake until they are pink and the stuffing is golden brown, 10 to 15 minutes.

Shrimp Imperial with Pasta and Broccoli

2 tablespoons butter

¼ cup chopped shallots

1 teaspoon Old Bay seasoning

½ pound medium shrimp, peeled and deveined

1 can Campbell's Condensed Cream of Shrimp Soup

½ cup milk

½ cup mayonnaise

1 tablespoon cream sherry

1½ teaspoons Worcestershire sauce

½ teaspoon prepared horseradish

½ cup grated sharp white cheddar cheese

2 cups cooked fettuccine

1 cup broccoli florets, cooked in water to cover until tender and drained

1. Preheat the oven to 350 degrees. Coat a 2-quart casserole dish with nonstick cooking spray.

2. In a 3-quart saucepan, melt the butter over medium heat, add the shallots and Old Bay seasoning, and cook, stirring, until the shallots are softened, about 2 minutes. Add the shrimp and cook it until it begins to turn pink, about 2 minutes. Stir in the soup, milk, mayonnaise, sherry, Worcestershire, horseradish, and ¼ cup of the cheese. Cook just until the cheese melts.

3. Add the pasta and broccoli, stir to combine well, and turn the mixture into the prepared dish. Top the casserole with the remaining ¼ cup cheese. (At this point, the casserole may be refrigerated overnight.)

4. Bake the casserole until it bubbles and the cheese is golden, 30 to 45 minutes.

Reminiscent of crab imperial, that wonderful Chesapeake Bay treat, this dish came about when I had leftover pasta and broccoli and some shrimp. Having my pantry stocked with Cream of Shrimp Soup helped me create this delicious casserole.

Souper Smart

Substitute 1½ cups leftover crab, fish, or chicken for the shrimp.

Garlic Prawns with Linguine

SERVES 6

This dish is the type of dinner that I love; the sauce can be made while the pasta is boiling, and everything comes together in an elegant but easy meal. Garlicky shrimp and buttery sauce bathe the linguine, and there is lots of sauce for dipping crusty bread.

1/2 cup (1 stick) butter

3 tablespoons olive oil

3 cloves garlic, minced

1 envelope Lipton Savory Herb with Garlic Soup Mix

2 tablespoons dry sherry

2 tablespoons brandy

1/4 cup chopped fresh Italian parsley leaves

1 1/2 pounds large shrimp, peeled and deveined

1 pound linguine, cooked until al dente, drained and kept warm

1. In a large sauté pan, melt the butter in the oil over medium heat. When the butter begins to foam, add the garlic and cook, stirring, until it is softened, about 3 minutes. Add the soup mix and cook, stirring, for another minute. Add the sherry, brandy, and parsley and bring the sauce to a boil. Add the shrimp and toss them in the garlic sauce until they begin to turn pink.

2. Remove the pan from the stove, toss the shrimp and sauce with the cooked pasta, and serve immediately.

Creole Jambalaya

SERVES 8 TO 10

Don't let the list of ingredients scare you away from making this dish; it can be on the table in 45 minutes, and it serves an army of hungry people. I like to serve an assortment of

2 tablespoons canola oil

1 1/2 pounds andouille or kielbasa sausage, cut into 1/2-inch-thick rounds

1 cup chopped celery

1 cup seeded and chopped green bell pepper

1 cup chopped onion

3 cloves garlic, minced

½ teaspoon dried thyme

1 bay leaf

½ teaspoon dried oregano

¼ teaspoon cayenne pepper

½ teaspoon dried basil

½ teaspoon freshly ground black pepper

One 14.5-ounce can diced tomatoes, with their juices

2 envelopes Lipton Golden Onion Soup Mix

7 cups water

1½ cups converted rice

2 pounds medium shrimp, peeled and deveined

1 cup chopped green onions for garnish

1. In an 8-quart stock pot or casserole, heat the oil over medium-high, add the sausages, and cook them until they begin to brown, about 5 minutes. Add the celery, bell pepper, onion, garlic, thyme, bay leaf, oregano, cayenne, basil, and black pepper and cook for 5 minutes, stirring frequently so the spices do not burn. Add the tomatoes and continue to cook for another 3 minutes, until some of the juice is absorbed.

2. Add the soup mix and water and bring to a boil. (At this point, you may cool the mixture and refrigerate it for up to 2 days. When you are ready to serve the jambalaya, bring the sauce to a simmer and continue with the recipe.)

3. Stir in the rice and cook it for 17 minutes. Add the shrimp and cook them until they have turned pink, another 3 to 4 minutes. Serve the dish garnished with the green onions.

hot sauces on the side, as well as lots of cold beer. Any leftovers are great cold, tossed with sherry vinaigrette from the Gazpacho Salad (page 70).

Souper Fish

Shrimp Creole

Based on an old standby in the Campbell's cookbook, this updated version is bursting with succulent shrimp in a spicy sauce. If you have leftover cooked chicken, you can substitute it for the shrimp in the recipe to create a spicy leftover dinner.

MOLDED SHRIMP CREOLE:
To make a ring of rice, pack a ring mold with cooked rice, cover the mold with aluminum foil, and keep it warm in a low oven. Unmold the rice onto a serving platter and spoon the shrimp mixture into the center and around the outside. Garnish with the green onions and additional parsley.

1/4 cup vegetable oil

1 cup chopped onion

1 cup seeded and chopped green bell pepper

1 cup chopped celery

2 cloves garlic, chopped

1 envelope Lipton Savory Herb with Garlic Soup Mix

1 bay leaf

1/8 teaspoon cayenne pepper

2 teaspoons Worcestershire sauce

Two 28-ounce cans crushed tomatoes

2 pounds medium shrimp, peeled and deveined

1/4 cup chopped fresh Italian parsley leaves

4 cups cooked rice

4 green onions, chopped, for garnish

1. In a 5-quart Dutch oven, heat the oil over medium heat, add the onion, bell pepper, and celery, and cook, stirring, until they are softened, 4 to 5 minutes. Add the garlic, soup mix, bay leaf, and cayenne and cook, stirring, for another 2 minutes. Stir in the Worcestershire and tomatoes, bring the sauce to a boil, reduce the heat to medium-low, and simmer until it begins to thicken, about 20 minutes. (At this point, you may refrigerate the sauce for up to 2 days. When you are ready to serve the shrimp, bring the sauce back to a simmer and proceed.)

2. Add the shrimp to the sauce and simmer until they turn pink. Remove the pot from the stove, discard the bay leaf, and stir in the parsley. Serve the shrimp and sauce over the rice, and garnish each serving with the green onions.

The Original Campbell's Shrimp Creole

1 large green bell pepper, sliced

1 large onion, sliced

1 small clove garlic, minced

2 tablespoons shortening

$\frac{1}{3}$ cup water

1 can Campbell's Condensed Tomato Soup

2 teaspoons lemon juice

$\frac{1}{4}$ teaspoon salt

Dash pepper

Dash Tabasco sauce

1 pound medium shrimp, cooked and cleaned (or two 6-ounce cans, drained)

3 cups cooked rice

Cook green pepper, onion, and garlic in shortening in covered skillet over low heat until tender. Stir in soup, water, lemon juice, seasonings, and shrimp. Cook about 10 minutes; stir often. Serve over rice.

Souper Fish

Mediterranean Shrimp and Rice

SERVES 6

This is one of those beat-the-clock recipes, where you use five main ingredients and everything is ready in under 30 minutes. Succulent shrimp are cooked in an herbed sauce with flavors of the Mediterranean, and then served over rice.

½ cup olive oil

2 tablespoons butter

1 envelope Knorr Leek Soup Mix mixed with 1 teaspoon dried fines herbes (see page 3) or Lipton Savory Herb with Garlic Soup Mix

1 cup white wine

1½ pounds large shrimp, peeled and deveined

½ teaspoon freshly ground black pepper

1 teaspoon chopped fresh oregano leaves

4 cups cooked converted rice

1. In a large sauté pan, heat the oil and butter together over medium-high heat. When the butter is melted, add the soup mix and cook, stirring, for 2 minutes. Add the wine, bring it to a boil, and let it boil until it has reduced a bit, 4 to 5 minutes. Add the shrimp and cook them until they turn pink. Season with the pepper and oregano.

2. Place the rice on a serving platter, cover it with the shrimp and sauce, and serve.

Scallops in Herbed Butter Sauce

3/4 cup (1 1/2 sticks) butter

3 tablespoons olive oil

2 tablespoons finely chopped shallots

2 cloves garlic, minced

1/4 cup white wine

1/2 cup seeded and chopped fresh tomato

1 envelope Knorr Leek Soup Mix

1 teaspoon dried fines herbes (see page 3)

1 pound sea scallops

1. Preheat the oven to 400 degrees.

2. In a medium sauté pan, melt the butter in the oil over medium heat. Add the shallots and cook, stirring, until they are softened, about 3 minutes. Add the garlic and cook, stirring, for another minute. Add the wine, and then stir in the tomato. Allow the mixture to come to a boil and add the soup mix and the dried fines herbes. Simmer the sauce until it has thickened, about 5 minutes.

3. Place the scallops in a single layer in a 13-by-9-inch baking dish. Spoon the sauce over the top of the scallops, bake for 10 minutes, and serve immediately.

This super simple entrée is a takeoff on an appetizer at Jimmy's Harborside Restaurant in Boston. Since scallops are delicate and cook rapidly, I had better luck using large sea scallops for this dish. If you can get only bay scallops, make sure not to overcook them.

Souper Fish

Mussels Marinara

Gorgeous black mussels peek out from a brilliant red and green sauce to produce a feast for the eyes as well as the stomach. The sauce can be prepared ahead of time, and the mussels take no time at all to cook. Make sure to serve lots of crusty bread to dip in the sauce.

MUSSELS PROVENÇALE: Substitute Knorr Leek Soup Mix and 1 teaspoon dried fines herbes (see page 3) for the Savory Herb with Garlic Soup Mix.

2 tablespoons olive oil

3 cloves garlic, minced

1 cup chopped onion

1 envelope Lipton Savory Herb with Garlic Soup Mix

½ cup dry white wine

One 28-ounce can chopped tomatoes

½ teaspoon freshly ground black pepper

1 teaspoon chopped fresh oregano leaves or ½ teaspoon dried

2½ pounds mussels, scrubbed and debearded

¼ cup packed fresh basil leaves, chopped

½ cup packed fresh Italian parsley leaves, chopped

1. Heat the oil in a 5-quart Dutch oven over medium heat. Add the garlic and onion and cook, stirring, until they are softened, about 3 to 4 minutes. Add the soup mix, stir for 1 minute, and add the wine, tomatoes, pepper, and oregano. Simmer the sauce for 20 minutes. (At this point, you may refrigerate the sauce for up to 3 days, or freeze it for up to 6 weeks.)

2. Bring the sauce to a boil and add the mussels, turning to coat them in the sauce. Cover the Dutch oven, reduce the heat to medium-low, and simmer the mussels until they open, about 5 minutes. Discard any mussels that do not open. Stir in the basil and parsley and serve immediately.

Christmas Eve Clams

SERVES 6

¼ cup olive oil

4 cloves garlic, minced

1 envelope Lipton Savory Herb with Garlic Soup Mix

1 cup white wine

Grated zest and juice of 2 lemons

½ teaspoon freshly ground black pepper

Salt

2 pounds littleneck clams, scrubbed

Every Christmas Eve at my friend Carolyn's house, the family steams hundreds of clams for their celebration. Fragrant with garlic, lemon, and herbs, these clams are delicious served any day of the year.

1. Heat the oil in a 5-quart Dutch oven over medium heat. Add the garlic and soup mix and cook, stirring, until the garlic is softened, 2 minutes. Add the wine and bring to a boil. Add the lemon zest, juice, and pepper. Taste the sauce and adjust the seasoning by adding salt or more pepper.

2. Add the clams, cover, and simmer them until they have all opened, about 5 minutes. Discard any clams that have not opened and serve immediately.

Souper Fish

Clam Pie

I first served this dish to my husband over 30 years ago, and we are still eating it today. Chock full of clams in a smoky, creamy sauce, with a crispy topping, it's a great Saturday night supper. If fresh clams are not readily available, use canned clams.

6 strips bacon, cut into ½-inch pieces

½ cup chopped onion

1 cup corn kernels, either cut fresh from the cob or frozen (and defrosted)

2 cans Campbell's Condensed New England Clam Chowder

2 cups minced fresh clams or two 8-ounce cans chopped clams, drained

1 teaspoon dried thyme

4 shakes Tabasco sauce

2 cups soft breadcrumbs

½ cup (1 stick) butter, melted

¼ cup chopped fresh Italian parsley leaves

1. Preheat the oven to 350 degrees. Coat a 9-inch round pie plate or individual ramekins with nonstick cooking spray.

2. In a 3-quart saucepan, fry the bacon over medium-high heat until it is crisp. Add the onion and cook, stirring, until softened, 3 to 4 minutes. Stir in the corn, chowder, clams, thyme, and Tabasco and bring to a boil. Transfer the mixture to the prepared pie plate or ramekins.

3. In a small mixing bowl, toss together the breadcrumbs, melted butter, and parsley. Sprinkle the crumbs evenly over the clam mixture and bake until the crumbs are golden brown, about 30 minutes.

STUFFED OYSTERS (TWO WAYS)

These gems of the sea are filled with a garlicky bread stuffing or a spinach cheese stuffing that is reminiscent of oysters Rockefeller. These oysters are delicious served as a first course or as a main course. You can use the same treatment with large clams as well.

Stuffed Garlic Oysters

SERVES 6

¼ cup (½ stick) butter

¼ cup finely chopped shallots

¼ cup finely chopped celery

1 envelope Lipton Savory Herb with Garlic Soup Mix

1½ cups soft breadcrumbs

Tabasco sauce

16 oysters on the half shell

1. Preheat the broiler for 10 minutes. Line a rimmed baking sheet with aluminum foil.

2. In a small sauté pan, melt the butter over medium heat, add the shallots and celery, and cook, stirring, until the vegetables are softened, 2 minutes. Add the soup mix and cook for another 2 minutes. Transfer the mixture to a bowl, add the breadcrumbs, and stir to combine.

3. Place the oysters on the baking sheet. Loosen them from their shells with a small knife. Sprinkle a dash of Tabasco over each oyster, and then top each oyster with 2 to 3 teaspoons of stuffing.

4. Broil the oysters until the topping is browned, about 4 minutes. Serve immediately.

Stuffed Spinach Oysters

SERVES 6

1 cup mayonnaise

1 package Knorr Cream of Spinach Soup Mix

$\frac{1}{2}$ cup grated Swiss cheese

$\frac{1}{2}$ cup freshly grated Parmesan cheese

Tabasco sauce

16 oysters on the half shell

1. Preheat the broiler for 10 minutes. Line a rimmed baking sheet with aluminum foil.

2. In a small mixing bowl, combine the mayonnaise, soup mix, and cheeses until they are well blended.

3. Place the oysters on the baking sheet. Loosen them from their shells with a small knife. Sprinkle a dash of Tabasco over each oyster and top the oyster with a tablespoon of the cheese mixture.

4. Broil the oysters until the cheese is golden brown, about 4 minutes. Serve immediately.

Lobster Stuffed Potatoes

8 baking potatoes

2 tablespoons olive oil

$^{1}/_{2}$ cup (1 stick) butter, as needed

$1^{1}/_{2}$ cups lobster meat cut into $^{1}/_{2}$-inch dice

2 cans Pepperidge Farm Condensed Lobster Bisque

2 tablespoons brandy

$^{1}/_{4}$ cup chopped fresh chives

$^{1}/_{2}$ cup freshly grated Parmesan cheese

1. Preheat the oven to 425 degrees.

2. Rub the potatoes with the oil and pierce them with a knife in several places. Bake the potatoes until they are soft when squeezed with a pot holder, about 60 minutes. Remove them from the oven. When they are cool enough to handle, cut the tops off the potatoes and scoop the insides out, leaving a $^{1}/_{2}$-inch-thick shell all the way around. Reduce the oven temperature to 375 degrees. Place the potato pulp in a large mixing bowl.

3. Melt $^{1}/_{4}$ cup ($^{1}/_{2}$ stick) of the butter in a medium sauté pan over medium heat and add the lobster meat. Toss the lobster in the butter, and then stir in the bisque, brandy, and chives. Add the soup mixture to the potatoes and mash the potatoes together with the lobster mixture, adding more butter as necessary.

4. Refill the potato skins with the mixture and top each potato with some of the grated cheese. Place the potatoes in a baking dish and bake them until the tops of the potatoes are golden brown, 15 to 20 minutes.

Succulent pieces of lobster in a creamy lobster bisque combine to make elegant comfort food fit for the boss. The potatoes can be made the day before you plan to serve them.

Souper Fish

Maryland-Style Crab Cakes

1 pound lump crabmeat, picked over for cartilage and shells

¼ cup dry breadcrumbs

½ cup (1 stick) butter, melted

1 large egg

1 tablespoon chopped fresh Italian parsley leaves

⅛ teaspoon cayenne pepper

¼ cup mayonnaise

2 teaspoon Worcestershire sauce

1 envelope Knorr Leek Soup Mix

½ cup vegetable oil

There are lots of crab houses in Maryland, and each one serves its own style of crab cake. These are simple to put together, and the crab flavor comes through because there isn't a lot of bread in the mixture. I like to serve these crab cakes with dilled tartar sauce.

1. In a medium mixing bowl, combine the crabmeat, breadcrumbs, ¼ cup (½ stick) of the butter, the egg, parsley, cayenne, mayonnaise, Worcestershire, and soup mix until they are well mixed. Form the mixture into 2-inch cakes.

2. Melt the remaining ¼ cup (½ stick) butter in the oil over medium heat and cook the crab cakes until they are golden brown on each side. Drain them on paper towels and serve immediately.

Mixed Seafood Kabobs

1 cup olive oil

½ cup fresh lemon juice

1 envelope Knorr Leek Soup Mix

1 teaspoon dried fines herbes (see page 3)

2 pounds firm-fleshed fish fillets, such as sea bass, halibut, swordfish, or salmon cut into 1-inch chunks

½ pound large shrimp

8 large sea scallops

1. In a large glass mixing bowl, combine the oil, lemon juice, soup mix, and fines herbes. Add the fish and shellfish, stirring to coat, and let marinate, covered, in the refrigerator for 2 hours.

2. Preheat the broiler or grill for 10 minutes.

3. Thread the fish and shellfish onto skewers, alternating fish with shrimp and scallops. Broil or grill the skewers until the shrimp are pink and the fish is cooked through, 4 to 5 minutes on each side.

These tasty morsels on skewers marinate for two hours. Then they are grilled over hot coals to produce an easy yet elegant entrée. Use your favorite firm-fleshed fish or shellfish for this dinner. If you are using bamboo skewers, be sure to soak them in water for 30 minutes before using them to keep them from burning.

Souper Smart

Whole fish fillets, shrimp, and scallops can be marinated in the same manner, and then grilled on the barbecue without the skewers.

Souper Fish

Streamlined Paella

This is a one-pot meal that makes an elegant presentation.

NOTE: If you are able to get Portuguese chorizo sausage, use that for a spicy flavor; otherwise, use Polish sausage or andouille.

3 tablespoons olive oil

1 pound smoked sausage (see note), cut into ½-inch-thick rounds

2 large onions, thinly sliced

1 medium red bell pepper, seeded and cut into thin strips

1 medium green bell pepper, seeded and cut into thin strips

3 cloves garlic, minced

One 14.5-ounce can diced tomatoes, with their juices

1 envelope Lipton Golden Onion Soup Mix

⅛ teaspoon saffron threads

2½ cups water

1 cup converted rice

1 pound large shrimp, peeled and deveined

2 lobster tails, shelled and cut into pieces

16 little neck clams, discarding any with broken shells, scrubbed

1 cups petite peas, fresh or frozen (and defrosted)

1. Heat the oil in a 12-inch sauté pan that is at least 3 inches deep over medium-high heat. Add the sausage and cook, stirring, until it begins to brown, about 4 minutes. Add the onion, bell peppers, and garlic and cook, stirring, until softened, 3 to 4 minutes. Add the tomatoes and soup mix and bring to a boil. Add the saffron to the water to dissolve, then add the saffron water to the pan. Stir in the rice, cover, and cook for 10 minutes.

2. Add the shrimp, lobster tails, and clams and cook for another 10 minutes. Discard any of the clams that have not opened. Stir in the peas, cover, and cook the paella for another 5 minutes. Serve immediately.

Rubs, Marinades, Sauces, and More

DRY RUBS AND MARINADES FLAVOR MEAT, fish, and poultry before cooking. Helping to tenderize as well as flavor the meat, they give it that little something extra that makes the meal memorable.

Dry rubs are combinations of dried herbs and spices that are rubbed or sprinkled onto meats before they are cooked. They often contain salt, as well as granulated garlic and onion powders for added punch. These flavorings are present in most dry soup mixes, so by adding a few more spices to a dry soup mix, you've got a rub that's good to go.

Marinades generally consist of oil, spices, and some type of acid, such as vinegar or fruit juice. Marinades tenderize and flavor dishes, but be careful not to marinate meat for too long, or it will actually start to "cook" in the marinade and become mushy.

Sauces and gravies are simple to make with soups. Sauces can be prepared ahead of time and stored in the refrigerator or freezer. You will also be able to make Thanksgiving gravy way ahead of time and keep it in the freezer. When you are ready to serve the gravy, skim the fat off the turkey drippings and add it to the gravy. No more last-minute fuss with lumps and timing issues. You can have perfect gravy, or sauce, every time.

RUBS AND DRY SEASONING MIXES

Spice rubs help create a deep brown crust on the outside of grilled foods. Consisting of a combination of spices, they can be used on chicken, fish, or meats. Rubs should be stored in airtight jars and kept on your spice shelf. Make sure to label them, because they tend to look alike even though each has a different flavor combination.

Most barbecue aficionados recommend that you not "rub" a dry rub into the meat, but rather sprinkle it over the meat. Others recommend the "massage" technique, gently rubbing the spices into the meat. For me, I find that the "less is more" adage works with these rubs, as they are pretty potent; a nice sprinkling on both sides is adequate. If you like a more concentrated flavor, massage your way to barbecue heaven.

THE ENGLISH WORD "SOUP" DERIVES FROM THE MIDDLE AGES WORD "SOP," WHICH REFERRED TO A PIECE OF BREAD OVER WHICH ROAST DRIPPINGS WERE POURED.

All-Purpose Barbecue Rub

½ cup firmly packed dark brown sugar

¼ cup sweet paprika

1 envelope Lipton Onion Soup Mix

1 teaspoon cayenne pepper

1 teaspoon ground allspice

2 tablespoons salt

1 tablespoon ground cumin

1. Combine all the ingredients in a small airtight jar, and shake to blend.

2. Label and store the rub in a cool, dry place. Sprinkle or rub the mixture over the meat before grilling or roasting.

MAKES ABOUT 1 CUP

This rub is sweet and spicy, with a kick of cayenne for good measure. Sprinkle this on beef, pork, or chicken for a down-home barbecue taste. The mixture will keep well in an airtight jar for three to four months.

Red Hot Chile Pepper Rub

1 envelope Lipton Fiesta Herb with Red Pepper Soup Mix

2 tablespoons ancho or New Mexican red chile powder

2 teaspoons ground cumin

2 teaspoons dried oregano

2 tablespoons firmly packed dark brown sugar

1. Combine all the ingredients in a small airtight jar, and shake to mix well.

2. Label and store in a cool, dry place for up to 4 months.

MAKES ½ CUP

This rub is not for the faint of heart, so be forewarned. Ancho chiles are a little less potent than their cousins the jalapeños, so you'll feel the heat, but be able to stay in the kitchen!

Souper Smart

Chiles seem to lose their potency sooner rather than later, so don't let this one stay on the shelf for too long.

Rubs, Marinades, Sauces, and More

Texas Dry Rub

2 tablespoons coriander seeds

1 tablespoon cumin seeds

2 teaspoons chili powder

2 teaspoons mustard seeds

2 teaspoons sweet paprika

1 tablespoon firmly packed light brown sugar

1 envelope Lipton Savory Herb with Garlic Soup Mix

In Texas, beef is king, and this rub is for crusting prime rib or any other roast beef. Toasting the spices brings out their flavors; just be careful not to burn them.

1. Heat a 10-inch nonstick skillet over medium-high heat. Add the coriander seeds, cumin seeds, chili powder, mustard seeds, and paprika, stirring constantly and shaking the pan for 2 to 3 minutes. Remove the pan from the heat and let the spices cool.

2. In a small airtight jar, combine the spice mixture with the sugar and soup mix, and shake to mix well.

3. Label the rub and store it in the refrigerator for up to 1 month.

Cajun Rub

1 envelope Lipton Savory Herb with Garlic Soup Mix

1 envelope Lipton Golden Onion Soup Mix

2 tablespoons celery salt

2 tablespoons firmly packed light brown sugar

½ teaspoon cayenne pepper

2 teaspoons dried thyme

1 teaspoon freshly ground black pepper

1. Combine all the ingredients in a small airtight jar and shake to blend.

2. Label the rub and store it in a cool, dry place for up to 6 months.

Moroccan-Style Rub

1 tablespoon sweet paprika

2 teaspoons ground cumin

1 teaspoon ground coriander

1 teaspoon dried mint

1 teaspoon turmeric

1 envelope Lipton Golden Onion Soup Mix

1. Combine all the ingredients in a small airtight jar and shake to blend.

2. Label and store the rub in a cool, dry place for up to 6 months.

Herb and Garlic Rub

This savory rub combines the best of dry soup mixes with fresh ingredients to make a combination that can't be beat on beef, chicken, or lamb. Try this the next time you grill steaks or slow-roast beef or chicken; you'll love the garlic herb combination.

6 cloves garlic, crushed

1 envelope Lipton Savory Herb with Garlic Soup Mix

1 tablespoon chopped fresh rosemary leaves or 1½ teaspoons dried, crumbled

1 teaspoon freshly ground black pepper

1. In a small mixing bowl, stir all the ingredients together. Refrigerate the rub, tightly covered, for up to 1 week until ready to use.

2. Spread the mixture over the roast, steak, or chicken and refrigerate the meat for up to 2 hours before cooking.

COMPOUND BUTTERS

- Lipton Onion Soup Mix
- Lipton Beefy Onion Soup Mix
- Lipton Golden Onion Soup Mix
- Lipton Fiesta Herb with Red Pepper Soup Mix
- Knorr Spinach Soup Mix
- Knorr Vegetable Soup Mix
- Knorr Leek Soup Mix
- Knorr Tomato with Basil Soup Mix

Another throwback to the days when waiters would serve you tableside, a maitre d'hotel butter was a butter that was mixed with various herbs and spices and then served on steak or vegetables. Versatile, compound butters store well frozen. You can have a little stash of these in no time using your food processor and some soup mixes. I like to stir a pat of compound butter into steamed vegetables or use it to top baked potatoes or grilled steak, chicken, or fish; and it's great melted and poured over popcorn!

The following soup mixes (1 envelope), see left, can be mixed with 1 cup (2 sticks) softened butter. Once the ingredients are mixed, roll the flavored butter into plastic wrap and shape it into a 1-inch-diameter log. Freeze it for up to 6 months until you are ready to use it. Slice off 1-tablespoon portions.

Asian Five-Spice Onion Rub

1 envelope Lipton Onion Soup Mix

1 tablespoon five-spice powder

Flavor packet from 1 package chicken flavor ramen noodles (reserve the noodles for another use)

1. Combine all the ingredients in a small airtight jar and shake to blend.

2. Label and store the rub in a cool, dry place for up to 6 months.

MAKES ABOUT ⅓ CUP

This rub from the east takes a little bit from the American heartland by combining Lipton Onion Soup Mix with five-spice powder. Sold in the spice section or the Asian foods section of your grocery store, fragrant and spicy five-spice powder consists of ground star anise, cinnamon, Szechuan peppercorns, fennel seeds, and cloves. It is great on pork ribs or chicken. You'll love the smoky flavor of this rub.

Confetti Pepper Rub

2 tablespoons coarsely ground black pepper

2 tablespoons coarsely ground green peppercorns

1 teaspoon cayenne pepper

1 envelope Lipton Savory Herb with Garlic Soup Mix

1. Combine all the ingredients in a small airtight jar and shake to blend well.

2. Label and store the rub in a cool, dry place for up to 6 months.

MAKES ½ CUP

Those of you who just can't get enough pepper will love this rub. A multicolor jumble of red, black, and green pepper tossed together with garlic and herbs, it is great on beef and lamb.

Caribbean Jerk Rub

This taste of the islands is great on grilled pork or chicken. Serve the grilled meat with a cooling slaw or fruit to balance the heat in the rub.

1 envelope Lipton Golden Onion Soup Mix

1 envelope Lipton Savory Herb with Garlic Soup Mix

3 tablespoons ground allspice

3 tablespoons firmly packed dark brown sugar

2 teaspoons ground cinnamon

$\frac{1}{2}$ teaspoon freshly grated nutmeg

$\frac{1}{8}$ teaspoon cayenne pepper

$\frac{1}{4}$ teaspoon freshly ground black pepper

1. Combine all the ingredients in a small airtight jar and shake to blend.

2. Label and store the rub in a cool, dry place for up to 6 months.

Creole Seasoning

Chef Paul Prudhomme made us all aware of Creole seasonings when he published his first cookbook. I keep a jar of Creole Seasoning in my cupboard for flavoring just about any dish that strikes my fancy. Some people shy away from using this seasoning because they think that it is overly hot, but I find it to be a balanced blend that enhances the flavor of many dishes, especially seafood.

$\frac{1}{4}$ cup sweet paprika

1 teaspoon salt

1 tablespoon freshly ground black pepper

$\frac{1}{2}$ teaspoon cayenne pepper

2 tablespoons dried oregano

2 tablespoons dried thyme

1 envelope Lipton Savory Herb with Garlic Soup Mix

1 envelope Lipton Golden Onion Soup Mix

1. Combine all the ingredients in a small airtight jar and shake to blend.

2. Label and store the seasoning in a cool, dry place for up to 3 months.

Since marinades usually contain an acid of some sort, mix a marinade in a nonreactive container. I like to use glass bowls or jars to store marinades; all-purpose resealable plastic bags work really well if storage space is a problem. You can refrigerate these marinades for up to a week unless otherwise noted. After marinating meat or poultry, discard the marinade, as it will contain bacteria. Some cooks boil the marinade to kill the bacteria, which is acceptable, but I like to make up a new batch of marinade for brushing on the meat during the cooking time.

Margaritaville Citrus Rum Marinade

½ cup fresh orange juice

¼ cup fresh lime juice

2 tablespoons fresh lemon juice

¼ cup sugar

¼ cup vegetable oil

¼ cup Meyer's dark rum

2 envelopes Lipton Golden Onion Soup Mix

1. In a medium glass mixing bowl, whisk together all the ingredients.

2. Use the marinade immediately or pour it into an airtight jar, cover it tightly, and keep it refrigerated for up to 2 weeks.

MAKES 2 CUPS

A combination of citrus juices and rum, this marinade is a great way to bring a taste of the tropics into your summer grilling. This recipe is awesome for marinating chicken and pork, but it is also delicious brushed on grilled fruits and vegetables. Marinate chicken for one to two hours, and pork for up to four hours.

Apple Cranberry Marinade

MAKES 1¹/₂ CUPS

This pretty pink combination flavors pork and chicken for grilling or sautéing. Marinate chicken for one hour; pork can be marinated for up to six hours.

ACCORDING TO LEGEND, LOUIS XIV ORDERED HIS CHEFS TO CREATE A CONSOMMÉ THAT WAS SO CLEAR IT WOULD REFLECT HIS ROYAL IMAGE.

¹/₂ cup vegetable oil

¹/₄ cup cider vinegar

¹/₂ cup cranberry juice (make sure to use full-strength cranberry juice and not Cranapple)

¹/₄ cup firmly packed dark brown sugar

2 envelopes Lipton Onion or Golden Onion Soup Mix

1. Combine all the ingredients in a medium glass bowl until well blended.

2. Use the marinade immediately or pour it into an airtight jar, cover it tightly, and keep it refrigerated for up to 2 weeks.

Citrus Herb Marinade

MAKES 1 CUP

Fragrant lemon and tarragon combine in this marinade for chicken or lamb. Marinate chicken for one to two hours and meat for two to six hours. Serve the meat or poultry with Feta Florentine Rice (page 286) on the side.

¹/₂ cup fresh lemon juice

¹/₄ cup vegetable oil

¹/₄ cup olive oil

2 cloves garlic, minced

1 tablespoon dried tarragon

1 envelope Lipton Savory Herb with Garlic Soup Mix

1. In a small glass mixing bowl, whisk together the ingredients until they are well blended.

2. Use the marinade immediately or pour it into an airtight jar, cover it tightly, and keep it refrigerated for up to 5 days.

Awesome Flank Steak Marinade

1 cup soy sauce

¼ cup canola oil

1 envelope Lipton Onion or Beefy Onion Soup Mix

¼ cup balsamic vinegar

1 teaspoon dried oregano

1. In a medium glass mixing bowl, combine all the ingredients with ½ cup water until they are well blended.

2. Use the marinade immediately or pour it into an airtight jar, cover it tightly, and keep it refrigerated for up to 2 weeks.

Dijon Rosemary Marinade

½ cup Dijon mustard

½ cup olive oil

¼ cup red wine vinegar

1 envelope Lipton Savory Herb with Garlic Soup Mix

3 tablespoons chopped fresh rosemary leaves or 1 tablespoon dried, crumbled

1 teaspoon freshly ground black pepper

1. In a small glass mixing bowl, whisk together the ingredients until they are well blended.

2. Use the marinade immediately or pour it into an airtight jar, cover it tightly, and keep it refrigerated for up to 1 week.

This simple marinade takes a tough cut of beef and transforms it into a tender steak you can grill over hot coals. Marinate the flank steak for at least four hours or overnight.

IF ALL THE CANS OF SOUP SOLD IN A YEAR WERE LAID END TO END, THEY WOULD ENCIRCLE THE EQUATOR SIX TIMES.

MAKES ABOUT 1¼ CUPS

Scented with rosemary, luxuriously smooth with Dijon mustard and olive oil, this marinade is delicious with poultry, lamb, or pork. Marinate chicken for one to two hours and meat for two to six hours.

Sweet and Spicy Marinade

MAKES ABOUT 2 CUPS

A mouthwatering marinade for chicken or pork, this will be one of your favorites for summertime grilling. Marinate the meat for at least two and up to six hours.

1 cup apricot preserves

1/2 cup vegetable oil

1/4 cup sugar

1/2 cup red wine vinegar

1 envelope Lipton Golden Onion Soup Mix

1. In a food processor or blender, process the ingredients together until the marinade is smooth.

2. Use the marinade immediately or pour it into an airtight jar, cover it tightly, and keep it refrigerated for up to 2 weeks.

Wiki Wiki Teriyaki Sauce

MAKES 1 CUP

This all-purpose Asian sauce is great for marinating chicken, fish, beef, or pork, or served as a dipping sauce on the side. I usually have some in the fridge to throw into stir-fries. Marinate chicken for two to four hours and beef and pork for four to six hours.

1/2 cup soy sauce

2 tablespoons vegetable oil

1/4 cup mirin (rice wine)

3 tablespoons firmly packed light brown sugar

1 teaspoon peeled and grated fresh ginger

2 cloves garlic, minced

Flavor packet from 1 package oriental flavor ramen noodles (reserve the noodles for another use)

2 teaspoons toasted sesame oil

2 green onions (whites and part of green tops), chopped

1. In a 2-quart saucepan, stir together all the ingredients. Bring the sauce to a boil and remove the pan from the heat.

2. Use the sauce immediately or pour it into an airtight jar, let it cool completely, cover it tightly, and keep it refrigerated for up to 2 weeks.

Greek Marinade

½ cup fresh lemon juice

Grated zest of 1 lemon

¼ cup vegetable oil

¼ cup olive oil

1 tablespoon chopped fresh rosemary leaves or 1½ teaspoons dried, crumbled

2 teaspoons chopped fresh oregano leaves or 1 teaspoon dried

1 teaspoon chopped fresh mint leaves or ½ teaspoon dried

1 envelope Lipton Savory Herb with Garlic Soup Mix

1. In a medium glass mixing bowl, whisk together all the ingredients until they are well blended.

2. Use the marinade immediately or pour it into an airtight jar, cover it tightly, and keep it refrigerated for up to 2 weeks.

Ginger Hoisin Marinade

1 tablespoon peeled and grated fresh ginger

3 cloves garlic, crushed

¼ cup water

1 cup soy sauce

⅓ cup mirin (rice wine)

¼ cup hoisin sauce

Flavor packet from 1 package chicken flavor ramen noodles (reserve the noodles for another use)

1. In a medium glass mixing bowl, combine all the ingredients, whisking them together until the marinade is smooth.

2. Use the marinade immediately or pour it into an airtight jar, cover it tightly, and keep it refrigerated for up to 7 days.

MAKES 1¼ CUPS

The flavors of sunny Greece shine through in this lemony herb marinade. It's terrific for lamb, chicken, and fish. It's best to marinate chicken and fish for only one hour; lamb can marinate for up to eight hours.

MAKES 1½ CUPS

An Asian-inspired marinade, this is very good on poultry or pork. Try splitting pork tenderloins, marinating, then grilling them. Also try marinating chicken quarters and grilling or roasting them at 400 degrees for 25 minutes. Hoisin sauce is sold in the Asian section of your supermarket—I like the imported brands better.

Bastes, glazes, and sauces enhance grilled food, and soups help to give these sauces an intense flavor. Barbecue sauces for basting are easy to put together with condensed soups to provide extra punch. Dry soups can be combined with just a few ingredients to create a baste or glaze for foods cooked on the grill. Most of the sauces here can be refrigerated for up to two weeks and can also be served on the side for dipping, if you'd like. A creative way to liven up your next dinner, these sauces can mean the difference between a good meal and a great meal.

Honey Lime Barbecue Baste

MAKES 1½ CUPS

This Southwestern sweet and pungent basting sauce is great brushed on grilled chicken, shrimp, fish, or pork.

½ cup fresh lime juice

Grated zest of 2 limes

½ cup vegetable oil

¼ cup honey

1 envelope Lipton Fiesta Herb with Red Pepper Soup Mix

1. In a medium glass mixing bowl, whisk together all the ingredients.

2. Use the baste immediately or cover it tightly and keep it refrigerated for up to 2 weeks.

Miso Sesame Glaze

1 box Kikkoman Shiro Miso Soup Mix (containing 3 envelopes)

⅓ cup mirin (rice wine)

2 tablespoons sugar

¼ cup vegetable oil

2 tablespoons soy sauce

6 shakes Tabasco sauce

1½ teaspoons toasted sesame oil

2 tablespoons chopped green onions

1 tablespoon sesame seeds

1. In a 2-quart saucepan, whisk together all the ingredients. Stir the glaze over medium heat for 5 minutes, but do not let it come to a boil.

2. Remove the pan from the heat and let the glaze cool.

3. Use the glaze immediately or pour it into an airtight jar, cover it tightly, and keep it refrigerated for up to 2 weeks.

This light glaze is delicious on broiled or grilled fish, scallops, shrimp, or chicken. Brush the glaze on before grilling, and then serve a little on the side for dipping.

Miso Every Day

Miso, a paste that is derived from soybeans, is the basis for the Kikkoman Shiro Miso Soup Mix. In Japan the making of miso soup is a part of everyday life, and if you eat in a Japanese restaurant, chances are you will begin the meal with a bowl of miso, garnished with cubes of tofu, seaweed, and finely chopped green onion.

Old-Fashioned Barbecue Sauce

MAKES ABOUT 3 CUPS

This sauce is our favorite for chicken, pork, and to serve on the side with barbecued beef sandwiches.

2 tablespoons vegetable oil

½ cup chopped onion

2 cloves garlic, minced

Three 8-ounce cans tomato sauce

1 envelope Lipton Onion, Beefy Onion, or Golden Onion Soup Mix

½ cup firmly packed light brown sugar

2 tablespoons Worcestershire sauce

5 shakes Tabasco sauce

½ teaspoon dry mustard

1. In a 3-quart saucepan, heat the oil over medium heat and cook the onion and garlic, stirring, until they are softened, 2 to 3 minutes. Add the tomato sauce and soup mix and bring to a boil. Stir in the brown sugar, Worcestershire, Tabasco, and mustard, reduce the heat to medium-low, and let the sauce simmer until it is thickened, 30 to 45 minutes.

2. Use the sauce immediately or let it cool and pour it into a container for storage. Cover it tightly and keep refrigerated for up to 3 days or freeze it for up to 3 months.

Another Old-Fashioned Barbecue Sauce

2 tablespoons vegetable oil

1/2 cup chopped red onion

2 cans Campbell's Condensed Tomato Soup

2 envelopes Lipton Golden Onion, Onion, or Beefy Onion Soup Mix

1/2 cup water

1 tablespoon Worcestershire sauce

1 teaspoon dry mustard

1. Heat the oil in a 2-quart saucepan over medium heat, add the onion, and cook, stirring, until it is softened, 2 to 3 minutes. Stir in the condensed soup, soup mix, water, Worcestershire, and mustard and bring to a boil. Reduce the heat to medium-low and let the sauce simmer until it is thickened, about 20 minutes.

2. Use the sauce immediately or cover it tightly and keep it refrigerated for up to 2 weeks or freeze it for up to 3 months.

This recipe is an adaptation of the Campbell's barbecue sauce recipe, using Campbell's Condensed Tomato Soup and dried onion soup mix. The sweetness of the tomato soup is balanced by the hearty flavor of the onions. This is a great substitute for your favorite bottled barbecue sauce.

ELVIS PRESLEY WAS NOT MUCH OF A SOUP EATER, ACCORDING TO PETER GURALNICK IN THE BOOK Careless Love; THE KING ALMOST DROWNED IN A BOWL OF CHICKEN SOUP.

Rubs, Marinades, Sauces, and More

Mayonnaise combined with dry soup mixes become spreads for sandwiches, sauces for fish or chicken, or salad dressings.

Southwestern Mayonnaise

MAKES ABOUT 2 CUPS

This spicy number can be used to coat a fish steak for grilling, turn an ordinary club sandwich into a fiesta, and transform good old romaine lettuce into a delectable south of the border salad.

2 cups mayonnaise

1 envelope Lipton Fiesta Herb and Red Pepper Soup Mix

2 tablespoons chopped canned roasted green chiles

2 tablespoons fresh lime juice

1/2 teaspoon ground cumin

2 tablespoons chopped fresh cilantro leaves

1. In a medium glass bowl, whisk everything together.

2. Use immediately or store, covered and refrigerated, up to 2 weeks.

Sun-Dried Tomato Mayonnaise

MAKES 2 1/3 CUPS

This pink mayonnaise is great on focaccia sandwiches or tossed with romaine lettuce and slivers of Parmesan cheese. Try spreading it on bread rounds and broiling it for a great appetizer.

2 cups mayonnaise

1 envelope Lipton Savory Herb with Garlic Soup Mix

1/4 cup oil-packed sun-dried tomatoes, drained

2 tablespoons chopped fresh basil leaves

2 tablespoons chopped fresh Italian parsley leaves

2 teaspoons balsamic vinegar

2 tablespoons capers, drained

1. Combine all the ingredients in a food processor and pulse on and off 5 to 6 times. (I like chunky bits in my mayonnaise, but you can process the mayonnaise until it is smooth, if you prefer.)

2. Use immediately or store, covered and refrigerated, up to 2 weeks.

Kicked-Up Creole Mayonnaise

2 cups mayonnaise

2 tablespoons whole-grain or Creole mustard

1 envelope Lipton Savory Herb with Garlic Soup Mix

$\frac{1}{4}$ teaspoon cayenne pepper

1 teaspoon sweet paprika

2 teaspoon dried thyme

1 teaspoon dried oregano

2 cloves garlic, minced

2 green onions (whites and part of the green tops), chopped

1 teaspoon freshly ground black pepper

1. In a medium glass mixing bowl, whisk together all the ingredients.

2. Use the mayonnaise immediately or store it, tightly covered, in the refrigerator for up to 2 weeks.

MAKES 2¼ CUPS

This spicy sauce is great on sandwiches, spread on chicken or fish before grilling or baking, or served as a dipping sauce for crudités.

Dilled Tartar Sauce

2 cups mayonnaise

2 tablespoons chopped red onion

$\frac{1}{4}$ cup pimiento-stuffed green olives, drained

$\frac{1}{4}$ cup capers, drained

$\frac{1}{4}$ cup chopped dill pickle

1 envelope Knorr Leek Soup Mix

1 tablespoon dillweed

1. Place all the ingredients in the work bowl of a food processor. Pulse 5 to 7 times, until the ingredients are combined. Scrape down the bowl and pulse 2 more times.

2. Use the sauce immediately or store in a tightly covered container and keep it refrigerated for up to 7 days.

MAKES ABOUT 3 CUPS

Studded with capers, olives, and dill pickle, this sauce is great served with Maryland crab cakes or crispy fish filets. I like my sauce a little crunchy, so I don't process it till it's smooth, but for a smoother sauce, process the sauce just a bit longer.

Rubs, Marinades, Sauces, and More

A quick little sauce is just the thing to perk up plain grilled meat, poultry, or seafood. Condensed soup needs only the addition of milk and a few herbs to become a creamy counterpart to a leftover rotisserie chicken. Dry cream soups are ready made to become the perfect saucing partners, and they are available in all kinds of flavors, spanning the global pantry. Mom's pasta sauce can be re-created just by adding an envelope of soup mix to tomatoes and a few other ingredients. Thanksgiving gravy can be made way ahead, with the help of canned broth.

Basic Marinara

MAKES 4 TO 5 CUPS; USE 1½ TO 2 CUPS TO SAUCE 1 POUND PASTA

This simple sauce is a staple in my freezer. With just a few ingredients you can have a great sauce for pasta, or to serve over meats, chicken, and fish. I make up batches and freeze them in 2-cup portions.

2 tablespoons olive oil

1 cup chopped onion

1 envelope Lipton Savory Herb with Garlic Soup Mix

Three 14.5-ounce cans crushed tomatoes

1 teaspoon dried basil

2 teaspoons sugar

½ teaspoon freshly ground black pepper

2 tablespoons chopped fresh Italian parsley leaves

1. In a 3-quart saucepan, heat the olive oil over medium heat, add the onion, and cook stirring, until it is softened, 3 to 4 minutes. Add the soup mix and cook, stirring, for 1 minute. Add the tomatoes, basil, sugar, and pepper, reduce the heat to medium-low, and simmer the sauce for 30 minutes.

2. Stir in the parsley and simmer the sauce for an additional 10 minutes.

3. Use the sauce immediately or store it, covered tightly, in the refrigerator for up to 3 days or in the freezer for up to 2 months.

Herb and Garlic Alfredo Sauce

½ cup (1 stick) butter

1 tablespoon olive oil

1 envelope Lipton Savory Herb with Garlic Soup Mix

1 cup heavy cream

¾ cup freshly grated Parmesan cheese

1 teaspoon freshly ground black pepper

1. Melt the butter in the oil over medium heat in a 3-quart saucepan. Add the soup mix and heavy cream and barely bring the mixture to a boil.

2. Remove the pan from the heat, add ½ cup of the cheese and the pepper, and stir the sauce until the cheese melts.

3. Serve the sauce immediately over cooked pasta, garnished with the remaining ¼ cup cheese.

This simple sauce is great served over pasta, then garnished with slivers of Parmigiano-Reggiano cheese. Try it as a sauce for chicken or pork cutlets as well.

Apollo **11** ASTRONAUTS BUZZ ALDRIN AND NEIL ARMSTRONG, THE FIRST TO LAND ON THE MOON, WERE FOND OF THE NEW IMPROVED FREEZE-DRIED POTATO SOUP THAT BECAME A PART OF THE NEW CUISINE ON BOARD APOLLO MISSION FLIGHTS. IT REPLACED THE "GOO" THAT WAS SERVED ON THE GEMINI FLIGHTS.

Rubs, Marinades, Sauces, and More

Mom's Ragu

1½ pounds ground pork

1½ cups chopped onion

½ cup finely chopped carrot

2 cloves garlic, minced

1 envelope Lipton Savory Herb with Garlic Soup Mix

Two 28-ounce cans crushed tomatoes or tomato purée

½ teaspoon freshly ground black pepper

1½ teaspoons dried basil

¼ cup chopped fresh Italian parsley leaves

Mom's kitchen was the home of so many wonderful smells, but this sauce and her baking bread were two of my all-time favorites. Mom said that the best sauce was made with pork; I think that was a throwback to her Tuscan roots. It's still my favorite, and using the soup mix makes it simple.

1. Heat a 5-quart Dutch oven over high heat, add the pork, breaking it up, and cook the pork until it is no longer pink.

2. Spoon off any accumulated fat or water in the bottom of the pan and add the onion, carrot, and garlic. Cook the vegetables with the pork until the onion is softened, about 5 minutes. Add the soup mix and cook for another 3 minutes. Add the tomatoes, pepper, and basil, reduce the heat to medium-low, and simmer, uncovered, until the sauce is thickened, about 45 minutes.

3. Stir in the parsley and cook the sauce for another 10 minutes.

4. Use the sauce immediately or store it, covered tightly, in the refrigerator for up to 3 days or in the freezer for up to 3 months.

Tomato Basil Caper Sauce

1 tablespoon extra virgin olive oil

½ cup minced shallots

1 clove garlic, minced

Two 14.5 ounce cans chopped tomatoes, with their juices

2 tablespoons white wine

1 envelope Knorr Tomato with Basil Soup Mix

¼ cup capers, drained

¼ cup minced fresh Italian parsley leaves

¼ teaspoon freshly ground black pepper

1. In a 10-inch sauté pan, heat the oil over medium heat, add the shallots and garlic, and cook, stirring, until they are softened, 2 to 3 minutes. Stir in the tomatoes, wine, and soup mix and simmer until some of the juice from the tomatoes has evaporated, about 10 minutes.

2. Stir in the capers, parsley, and pepper and simmer the sauce for another 5 minutes. Remove the pan from the heat.

3. Use the sauce immediately or store it, covered tightly, in the refrigerator for up to 2 weeks.

This is a simple sauce for chicken or fish. You'll love the Mediterranean flavors and the ease of preparation. This sauce will keep in the refrigerator for up to two weeks. I have even used it as a spread for crackers.

Shiitake Merlot Sauce

This elegant sauce is simple to make with a packet of soup mix and some red wine. I like to serve this with grilled beef fillets or a roast.

3 tablespoons butter

½ cup finely chopped onion

2 cloves garlic, minced

½ pound shiitake mushrooms, stems removed and caps sliced ½ inch thick

1 teaspoon dried thyme

1 envelope Lipton Beefy Mushroom Soup Mix

1½ cups water

½ cup Merlot or other red wine

1. Melt the butter in a 4-quart saucepan over medium heat. Add the onion and garlic and cook, stirring, until they are softened, 2 to 3 minutes. Add the mushrooms and thyme and cook, stirring, for another 2 to 3 minutes. Stir in the soup mix, water, and wine and bring the mixture to a boil. Reduce the heat to medium-low and simmer the sauce until it is reduced by one quarter and has begun to thicken, about 20 minutes.

2. Use the sauce immediately or store it, covered tightly, in the refrigerator for up to 3 days.

Creamy Mushroom Sauce

2 tablespoons butter

¼ cup chopped shallots

½ pound mushrooms, sliced

1 can Campbell's Condensed Cream of Mushroom Soup

1 cup milk

2 tablespoons cream sherry

2 tablespoons chopped fresh Italian parsley leaves

1. Melt the butter in a 2-quart saucepan over medium heat. Add the shallots and cook, stirring, until they are softened, 2 to 3 minutes. Add the mushrooms and cook, stirring, until they are golden. Stir in the soup, milk, and sherry and bring the sauce to a boil.

2. Remove the pan from the heat and stir in the parsley.

3. Use the sauce immediately or store it, covered tightly, in the refrigerator for up to 3 days.

MAKES ABOUT 3 CUPS

This sauce showcases the ease of preparation that comes with having soup in your pantry. This elegant sauce is jazzed up with sherry, fresh mushrooms, and parsley. Serve it over sautéed chicken breasts or rice.

Rubs, Marinades, Sauces, and More

Lemon Caper Sauce

MAKES 1½ CUPS

This delectable sauce is wonderful served over sautéed veal, chicken, or fish.

½ cup (1 stick) butter

½ cup fresh lemon juice

1 envelope Knorr Leek Soup Mix

½ cup capers, drained

1. Melt the butter in a 10-inch skillet over medium heat. Add the lemon juice and soup mix, whisking until the mixture is well combined. Stir in the capers and keep the sauce warm until you are ready to serve it.

2. Use the sauce immediately or store it, covered tightly, in the refrigerator for up to a week.

ALL-PURPOSE "CREAM OF" SAUCES

Campbell's Condensed Cream of Mushroom, Chicken, and Celery Soups make delicious creamy sauces to pour over rice, pasta, chicken, or seafood. To make a "cream of" sauce, dilute one can of "cream of" soup with 1¼ cups milk (2 percent milk is okay, but not 1 percent or skim), stirring with a whisk. You can add a few tablespoons of white wine or sherry or chopped chives, parsley, or other fresh herbs to these "cream of" sauces.

Knorr Cream of Broccoli, Leek, and Cream of Spinach Soup Mixes all make cream sauces as well. Just add 1¼ cups milk to the soup mix and bring to a boil. You can make the same additions as suggested above.

Do-Ahead Gravy

6 tablespoons (³⁄₄ stick) butter

6 tablespoons all-purpose flour

4 cups stock (chicken, beef, or vegetable)

Salt and freshly ground black pepper

1. In a 4-quart saucepan, melt the butter over medium-high heat, and whisk in the flour. Cook, whisking, until white bubbles form on the top of the flour mixture.

2. Continue whisking and gradually pour in the stock. Bring the mixture to a boil, whisking constantly. Remove the pan from the heat and season the gravy with salt and pepper.

3. At this point, you can refrigerate the gravy, covered tightly, for up to 2 days or freeze it for 2 months. When you are ready to serve the gravy, defrost it, if necessary, and heat it up. Pour the drippings off your roasting pan and separate the fat from the meat juices. Pour the meat juices into the hot gravy and whisk until smooth. Serve immediately.

MAKES 4¹⁄₂ CUPS

Many of my cooking students are what I term "gravy challenged," meaning that they are convinced they can't make gravy. This recipe comes from a class that I teach called "Do-Ahead Cele-brations," where we take a holiday celebration and break it down into man-ageable pieces by doing most of it ahead of time. Gravy is something that you can make two days ahead and refrigerate or freeze for two months. If you have a family of gravy lovers, you'll want to double or triple this recipe.

THOUSANDS OF AMERICANS TAKE "STOCK" IN SOUP AS A FOLK REMEDY——A WAY TO RESTORE OUR FLUIDS AND OUR SPIRITS WHEN WE'RE FEELING DOWN AND UNDER THE WEATHER.

Rubs, Marinades, Sauces, and More

Salsa Fresca

This salsa, chunky with tomatoes, jalapeños, and onions, is about a six on the 10-point heat meter, but you can fire it up even more by adding extra chiles to it. You can smooth out this salsa by pulsing it in a food processor or blender. Serve this salsa on the side with meat, over grilled chicken or fish, as a dip for tortillas, or stir it into 2 cups of sour cream to create a fiesta dip.

> ANDY WARHOL BESTOWED THE ULTIMATE STATUS OF AMERICAN CULTURAL ICON ON CAMPBELL'S SOUPS BY PAINTING THEM MORE OFTEN THAN HE DID MARILYN MONROE. WARHOL IMMORTALIZED THE FOLLOWING CAMPBELL'S SOUPS: TOMATO, VEGETABLE WITH BEEF STOCK, BEEF NOODLE, BLACK BEAN, NEW ENGLAND CLAM CHOWDER, CREAM OF CHICKEN, AND HOT DOG BEAN.

The Soup Mix Gourmet

4 cups peeled, seeded, and chopped fresh tomatoes

1/3 cup canned tomato purée

1/2 cup finely chopped onion

2 cloves garlic, minced

2 jalapeño chiles, seeded and minced

3 tablespoons chopped fresh cilantro leaves

1 envelope Lipton Fiesta Herb with Red Pepper Soup Mix

2 tablespoons fresh lime juice

1. In a large glass mixing bowl, stir together all the ingredients.

2. Cover the bowl tightly and refrigerate the salsa for at least 8 hours to let the flavors develop, and for up to 1 week before serving.

Cranberry Chutney

1 cup sugar

1 envelope Lipton Golden Onion Soup Mix

One 12-ounce bag fresh cranberries

2 cups coarsely chopped peaches, either frozen (and defrosted) or canned (and drained)

1 cup pecan halves

1 teaspoon ground cinnamon

½ teaspoon ground ginger

1. Place 1 cup water, sugar, soup mix, and cranberries in a 2-quart saucepan and cook over medium-high heat until the cranberries begin to "pop"; this may take 10 minutes.

2. Add the peaches, pecans, cinnamon, and ginger, reduce the heat to medium-low, and simmer the chutney for 10 minutes.

3. Remove the pan from the heat, bring the chutney to room temperature, and serve or refrigerate.

This unusual combination of onions, peaches, cranberries, and pecans is a welcome change of pace from the ordinary cranberry sauce that we generally serve during the holidays. It keeps for about three weeks in the refrigerator.

Sunset Onion Apricot Sauce

This brilliant red-orange sauce looks just like a California sunset. It's delicious with fried or grilled chicken, and it also makes a great dipping sauce for egg rolls.

PRESIDENT ABRAHAM LINCOLN ORDERED MOCK TURTLE SOUP TO BE SERVED ON MARCH 4, 1861, AT A LUNCHEON AT THE WILLARD HOTEL TO CELEBRATE HIS INAUGURATION AS THE SIXTEENTH PRESIDENT.

12 dried apricots

One 12-ounce can apricot nectar

$2/3$ cup sugar

$1/2$ cup rice vinegar or $1/3$ cup white wine vinegar

1 envelope Lipton Onion or Golden Onion Soup Mix

1 tablespoon peeled and finely minced fresh ginger

1 clove garlic, minced

5 shakes Tabasco sauce

1. In a 2-quart saucepan, combine all the ingredients with $2/3$ cup water and bring the sauce to a boil. Reduce the heat to medium-low, cover the pan, and simmer for 30 minutes. Remove the pan from the heat and let the sauce cool.

2. Using an immersion blender, food processor, or blender, process the sauce until it is smooth.

3. If you are using the sauce immediately, reheat it. Otherwise store the sauce in a tightly covered container and refrigerate it for up to 2 weeks.

Source Guide

THIS IS A LISTING OF MY favorite sources for sometimes hard-to-find items, as well as addresses and phone numbers for the different soup manufacturers.

Campbell's Soup Company
1 Campbell Place
Camden, NJ 08103-1799
(800) 257-8443
www.campbellsoup.com

King Arthur Flour
P.O. Box 876
Norwich, VT 05055
(800) 777-4434
www.kingarthurflour.com
Baking equipment, exceptional flours, grains, spices, oils, and unusual ingredients.

Knorr Products
700 Sylvan Avenue
Englewood Cliffs, NJ 07632
(800) 338-8831
www.knorr.com

Lipton Products by Mail
P.O. Box 3000
Grand Rapids, MN 55745-3000

Lipton Soup Company
800 Sylvan Avenue
Englewood Cliffs, NJ 07632
(800) 697-7897
www.lipton.com

Williams-Sonoma
P.O. Box 7456
San Francisco, CA 94120
(800) 541-2233
www.williams-sonoma.com
Catalogue and stores with just about anything you could need to make anything edible.

Index